PROFESSION, VOCATION AND CULTURE IN LATER MEDIEVAL ENGLAND

A. R. MYERS
Photograph taken in 1978

Profession Vocation, and Culture in Later Medieval England

ESSAYS DEDICATED TO
THE MEMORY OF A. R. MYERS
EDITED BY
CECIL H. CLOUGH
University of Liverpool

LIVERPOOL UNIVERSITY PRESS

Published by
LIVERPOOL UNIVERSITY PRESS
Press Building, Grove Street, Liverpool L7 7 AF

Copyright © 1982 by
Liverpool University Press

First published in 1982

British Library Cataloguing in Publication Data
Profession, vocation, and culture in later medieval
  England
  1. Myers, A. R.   2. Middle classes – Great
  Britain   3. Great Britain – Civilization –
  Medieval period, 1066–1485
  I. Clough, Cecil H.   II. Myers, A. R.
  942.03′7   DA185

ISBN 0-85323-324-1

Designed by Bernard Crossland
Text set in monophoto Melior by
Santype Ltd, Salisbury, Wilts
Printed and bound in Great Britain by
Camelot Press Ltd, Southampton

THIS VOLUME
IS DEDICATED IN
HOMAGE AND AFFECTION
TO THE MEMORY OF
A. R. MYERS

PREFACE

These studies were written with the object of providing a unified volume on a theme which it was believed would much interest Alec Myers. The volume, first conceived in 1976, was to be presented to him to mark his retirement in September 1980. Alec Myers died in July 1980, and the publication of the volume was delayed for reasons in no way related to his illness. It is, though, some consolation that Alec Myers read the essays in typescript in the summer of 1980, and that he was as delighted with them as the contributors could have wished; he much appreciated the motives, too, that had inspired the collection.

The collection has been a long time in gestation, and personally I wish to express my sincere thanks to the contributors who have loyally and steadfastly supported the volume. Increasingly over the past few years research in the areas covered by this collection has appeared in print. While this marks the significance of the volume, it has presented contributors with problems. There has been the need continually to up-date references, and in a few instances some material in these essays has been anticipated by other scholars.

I wish to acknowledge the help of Liverpool University Press in ensuring not only that the collection has been published, but that it has so attractive a format. I am particularly indebted to Mr. John O'Kane, former Secretary of the Press, to Mrs. Rosalind Campbell, the Secretary, and to Mr. Bernard Crossland, who has had the responsibility for the layout. I am grateful to the Faculty of Arts for a grant to enable the portrait photograph of Alec Myers to appear on fine art paper as a frontispiece.

I rightly conclude with a tribute to my wife, who has sustained me at the various times of frustration that I have suffered as editor. Moreover, she has found time to compile the index.

C. H. C.

CONTENTS

ABBREVIATIONS

Add. Ch.	Additional Charter
Add. MS.	Additional Manuscript
B.L.	British Library (formerly British Museum)
C.C.R.	*Calendar of Close Rolls*
C.P.R.	*Calendar of Patent Rolls*
C.S.	Camden Series
D.N.B.	*Dictionary of National Biography*
E.H.R.	*English Historical Review*
Emden, *Cambridge*	A.B. Emden, *A biographical register of the University of Cambridge to 1500*, Cambridge, 1963
Emden, *Oxford*	A. B. Emden, *A biographical register of the University of Oxford*, Oxford, 3 vols., 1957–9
Fasti	J. Le Neve, *Fasti Ecclesiae Anglicanae 1300–1541*, London, 12 vols., 1962–7
O.E.D.	*Oxford English Dictionary*
P.R.O.	Public Record Office
Rot. Parl.	*Rotuli Parliamentorum ...*, 1278–1503
R.S.	Rolls Series
T.R.Hist.S.	*Transactions of the Royal Historical Society*
V.C.H.	*The Victoria History of the Counties of England*

1

Introduction: Culture and society

CECIL H. CLOUGH

The year 1976 marked the quincentenary of the introduction of printing into England. In commemoration several scholarly bio-graphies of William Caxton were published, as were many articles on related aspects of printing and literature. This is perhaps the most outstanding example of an area in which monographs and articles of importance for the cultural historian of England in the later middle ages have been appearing in recent decades at an ever-increasing rate. Seminal was Roberto Weiss's *Humanism in England during the fifteenth century*, published in 1941; a third revised edition appeared in 1967. This study was inspired by Burckhardt's approach to the cult of Antiquity in Renaissance Italy. However, so far there has been no attempt to provide an analysis of culture as seen against the broad backcloth of English society. This in some measure only—the upper and lower strata of society are essentially excluded—is what is attempted in this collection of studies. The venture is a pioneer undertaking in what for English history is largely *terra incognita*.

Culture in this volume is defined broadly as relating to the creativity of the 'finer things of the mind', which are deemed to be civilizing influences. Emphasis is on the visual arts, but included are literature and education, as well as the Christian religion. The collection attempts an original methodological approach whereby culture is investigated in terms of cohesive groups within society. A fundamental difficulty is that in the course of a career some individuals moved from one group to another, or were actually for a time a member of two or more groups: an administrator might be a canon lawyer and become a bishop; a merchant might be a part-time local government official. It must be appreciated that it is impossible to define any group so as to exclude such overlapping, and to try to do so, indeed, would distort the fabric of society as it existed in the later middle ages, when some groups did merge into

each other. The result is that the same individual may, and in these
essays on occasion does, appear in at least two groups. It should
also be remarked that the examples provided in any one group
may not adequately illustrate its cultural interests, for obviously
all the evidence is the result of chance survival—a point that is
strikingly illustrated in the study on merchants. It should be remembered that there is no certainty as to how typical of a group the
culture that is presented by the examples really was. In the final
analysis one can only judge that the probability is high that it is a
representative sample. Certainly, too, the probability is high that
only a minority of any group comprised what can be called the
'creative elite'. Moreover the reader of this collection of studies
should be alert to the danger of seeking to make definitive comparisons between groups on the evidence that is provided. Much
more information on the subject needs to be available before such
comparisons can be made with confidence. This volume is a conscious attempt to stimulate interest in a generally neglected area,
and it is not the definitive synthesis that may one day be attempted.

The groups that have been selected for examination are not just
picked at random, but before examining them in greater detail it is
as well to repeat that two strata of society are virtually excluded. If
one considers society as a whole in the later middle ages it was the
sovereign, with the nobles and the upper ranks of the clerics who
had control of a large proportion of the country's wealth. This
remains true even in the fifteenth century, though then merchants
significantly increased their share. A priori the upper stratum of
society had potentially the greatest opportunity for patronage of a
civilizing kind. At its heart was the Court, which undoubtedly
made the prime contribution to culture. One thinks of Richard II's
commission of the lovely painting now known as the Wilton dip-
tych; of Humphrey, duke of Gloucester, and his gifts to the University of Oxford; of Margaret Beaufort, countess of Richmond and
Derby, who generously endowed St. John's College, Cambridge.
Studies focused upon the Court and its nucleus, comprising some
of the nobility and upper ranks of the clergy, would be most rewarding, but such is the wealth of material that an adequate
survey would require a volume in itself. Besides this area is the
most familiar, being the subject of more published work than any
other. The lowest stratum of society consisted of the peasants, and
is not considered in this volume. The peasant's position in society
has been examined in depth particularly by Professor R. H. Hilton.

In terms of a peasant's contribution to the finer things of the mind, however, there appears to be nothing to say. Little is known, even, of individual peasants beyond their being the parents or the grand-parents of a person who had advanced from the status of peasant up the social ladder. These latter, of course, had moved into what can be called the professional and vocational groups of the kind considered in this volume.

The focus of this collection of studies is on the stratum of society between the nobility and the peasantry, though it does take in the bishops (who might be deemed of the nobility) for reasons that will be explained. The approach is to define each group, such as 'bishops' and 'civil lawyers', and to furnish precise information concerning individuals of each group to serve as illustrative exam-ples. The information provided about the individuals that com-prised a group throws also a new light on the professions and on the religious vocation in the period, at the same time as illumi-nating the group's contribution to culture. It is a truism that be-coming a cleric was a common means of social advancement. Some members of the clergy, though, on the evidence available, could claim to have a vocational calling. In this collection the essay on the episcopate examines that group in detail over the whole period, and some of the bishops stand out as being more than mere career-ists. Some bishops were of the Court circle and noble by birth, but others clearly were neither. Many who became bishops were pro-fessional administrators. In the words of Dr. Davies 'as the period went on, more and more bishops were appointed who had entered ecclesiastical, and even especially diocesan, service' (p. 63). It is clear that the episcopate straddled both the upper and the profes-sional classes, and became increasingly vocational. It is because of this fact, so ably demonstrated in Dr. Davies's essay, that the group has its place in this volume. It follows, too, that because of the nature of the groups selected for consideration the collection has been entitled with justification: *Profession, vocation, and culture in later medieval England.*

As indicated the core of this collection of studies is what can be termed the professions, which by the later middle ages were com-posed of distinct and cohesive groups, which hitherto have been little studied as professional groupings. For instance little has previously been known of the gentleman-bureaucrats and of the lesser lay personnel of the central administration; indeed it has not yet always been appreciated the extent to which ordained clergy were losing their dominance of bureaucratic functions. The lesser lay personnel were to be found over the length and breadth of the Kingdom of England and Wales, and hence coverage in depth would have presented problems. Dr. Jewell's study is concerned with Yorkshire, though on occasion, and for obvious reasons, contiguous counties are brought in. It is not suggested that this particular region was in any way typical, for such a concept would be very much out of historical context. The north was generally opposed to the interests of the midlands and south, as the lining-up at the Battle of Bosworth underlines. Rather, therefore, Yorkshire might be said to be representative of the regionalism that was such an influential factor in the period. Because the lesser lay personnel drew largely on local talent the local government itself gave emphasis to regionalism. Yorkshire has been chosen, too, because it links neatly with the merchant class of the same area so carefully examined by Mrs. Kermode's study. The composite result is that for the first time one can see something of the character of that shire's city government and local administration.

It is a generality that in the fifteenth century a new class, that of merchants, was steadily accruing wealth and taking an ever-increasing part in local government as well as in cultural patronage. Some thirty years ago Professor Sylvia Thrupp's volume, *The Merchant Class of Medieval London, 1300–1500*, indicated the broad outlines of the cultural proclivities of that group. In this present volume for broad comparative purposes the cultural role of the merchant class of three northern boroughs, York, Beverley, and Hull, is examined for the narrower period of *c*.1390 to 1500. This study by Mrs. Kermode shows the piety of the merchant class of Yorkshire, and so indicates the deep roots of Roman Catholicism in the North.

In recent years Dr. Orme has furnished a wealth of new information on education in England in the later middle ages. He draws on this for his study in this collection, which considers schoolmasters as a group. With remarkable sharpness and clarity one learns of this group's cultural interests. The common lawyers and the civil lawyers were important professional bodies, which have attracted increasing interest in recent years, as numerous related articles testify. In comparison with the essays on the Yorkshire merchants and on the schoolmasters, the two concerned with lawyers are broader surveys. Given the present state of knowledge in the various fields of interest such unevenness in presentation is inevitable.

Increasingly throughout the period the universities appear to have provided a link between the various professional groups. Thereby these groups received something in the nature of a common cultural stamp and their cultural aspirations seem similar, with emphasis on learning and on preserving knowledge. Gentleman-bureaucrats, lay personnel and merchants were almost exclusively non-graduates and their attitude to culture is less sophisticated, with more concern on display and on personal piety. The episcopate was made up of graduates, and in large measure its cultural aspirations conformed to the professional graduate groupings. However the vocational nature of the clerical career appears to have made for some diversity, and there is evidence of pietistic benefactions by some bishops.

It is worth remarking that it is men who exclusively comprised the episcopate and the professions. It would be a serious mistake to suppose that women had no part to play in culture. For instance, a few women were merchants, and Mrs. Kermode's essay indicates something of the cultural influence of women of the merchant class above all in their capacity as wives and mothers. A study concerned with women and culture in the period is a *lacuna* that ought to be filled.

On the basis of the collection one sees something of the mechanics of social change as far as advancement is concerned, though no example is provided of the reverse process, which certainly did take place. There are examples of a family in three generations advancing from peasantry to gentry. The Church, the universities and the professions were the means by which such advancement was possible. One can also discern that culture was linked to social status. In other words there is evidence that the acquisition of a certain social position brought with it responsibilities in terms of culture which were understood and accepted by those of the same social standing. That such should have been the case was an inevitable consequence of the organizations that moulded the groups—the universities, the Church and the inns of court. Viewed in yet another way it would also appear that investment in culture enabled one to advance one's social status. A merchant, say, endowed a school and the intelligent son of a peasant received his instruction at the school free of charge. That boy became a priest or an administrator and was enabled by this process to advance to even higher office. The merchant had made his endowment because it was seen as a way of securing entry into Heaven; the peasant father, too, had invested in culture, since he was willing to forego his son's work; the boy himself had to invest in it also, as he had to be willing to leave his family and study hard. It happened because it was advantageous to all the parties involved. It was, of course, a slow process, not least because a priest could not marry and have legitimate children, and this blocked the direct line. The family could advance none-the-less, and did, since the priest was able to pay in his turn for training in one of the professions a promising nephew, and so use his influence to enable that nephew to obtain a post. Investment in culture as a way of social advance appears to be a new factor in the later middle ages. It was inspired by piety, essentially for the remission of sins in the world to come, but its social consequences on this earth were of considerable importance. It resulted, too, in the works of art, some of which have been handed down to us, and which remain as testimony of the finer things of the mind.

2

The merchants of three northern English towns

JENNIFER I. KERMODE

Merchants were at the apex of urban society in the later middle ages.[1] Differentiated by their mode of dress, life style, economic and political expectations, they constituted a powerful class.[2] Collectively and individually they exercised what can be described as a civilizing influence within their communities through their attitude to religion, their desire for social survival, their cultural and literary interests, their attempts to improve their environment, and their concern for good government.[3]

York, Beverley, and Hull, the three towns which are the subject of this study, are boroughs in east Yorkshire. During the period c.1390–1500 they shared commercial interests which drew their merchants together into an economic community that transcended town boundaries. In addition, the bonds shared by those merchants as a consequence of their status within their own communities, must often have meant that they had more in common with each other than they did with their fellow townsmen.[4]

The three towns were very different from each other. York was the largest, with a population of c.13,000 in 1377. In 1396 it became a county of a city, the ultimate in terms of local autonomy and a fitting status for the second city in the kingdom. It had enjoyed prominence for several centuries, as an administrative and religious centre, and as a major textile producer.[5] Beverley was also a long-established community with an earlier reputation as a textile centre and a continuing popularity as a place of pilgrimage. Smaller than York, with a population of c.4,000 in 1377, it was a seignorial borough with limited self government under the supervision of its lord, the archbishop of York.[6] Hull, in contrast to the other two, was a new town founded by Edward I in 1293 as a port on the Humber estuary. Six years later it was created a free royal borough and in 1440 Hull acquired corporate county status. It had no major industries and it served the traders of the north-east. In 1377 its population was c.2,500.[7]

During the fourteenth century Yorkshire was closely involved in the export of wool and the region prospered as a consequence. The number of merchants actively engaged in overseas trade increased, and at the same time York's textile producers briefly enjoyed the benefits of England's expanding overseas trade in cloth. During the first decades of the fifteenth century, this momentum was lost. The shift in the now predominant cloth trade from the east coast ports to London, meant that Yorkshire merchants faced a period of accelerating contraction. Their share in exports declined and they had to compete with southern merchants for the carrying trade in rural textiles, as well as in other commodities such as corn and lead.[8] In spite of these economic difficulties, some merchants from York, Beverley, and Hull, prospered, and in each of the three towns merchants survived as the dominant group in local government.[9]

Merchants were men[10] who were engaged in wholesale trade, usually in overseas as well as in regional markets, and those living in a borough were virtually always burgesses, freemen, of that borough because burgess-ship was compulsory for anyone who wanted to set up as a master in his occupation.[11] A burgess had considerable legal and commercial privileges[12] as well as responsibilities and, as the Hull burgess-oath stated, a man had to work and act for the common good and not for his own profit. If he paid his borough taxes he could enjoy the borough's liberties, if not then he would be treated like any other foreigner.[13]

By the late fourteenth century there were usually three methods of admission to the freedom of a borough: by purchase, patrimony, or the completion of an apprenticeship coupled with a reduced fine. Admission by purchase was apparently the most common in York, Beverley, and Hull but this impression must be qualified by the inconsistency with which admissions were recorded.[14] There were few disqualifications to entry: Scots and other aliens were not welcome, and bastards could not become freemen by patrimony of Beverley or of York.[15]

It is difficult to estimate the proportion of a borough's population that was of burgess status, but if the example of York in the late fourteenth century is a reliable guide, it may have been somewhere between 25 per cent and 50 per cent.[16] A figure of one in four adult males has been suggested for fourteenth-century

London.[17] In this respect records are usually unhelpful in that they rarely refer specifically to burgesses: more often the term 'commonalty' is used to describe a variety of groups of inhabitants on different occasions.

It is equally difficult to estimate what proportion of the burgesses were merchants, although it is known that of 4,283 men registered as entering the freedom of York between 1350 and 1399, 12 per cent were merchants and mercers, and of the 4,357 entering between 1400 and 1449, 7 per cent were merchants and mercers.[18] Perhaps a more accurate impression of the structure of urban society can be derived from the 1524–5 subsidies and estimates based on them that the wealthiest comprised some 2 to 3 per cent of the total assessed. The merchant class extended beyond the most successful traders and officials, and probably comprised 6 to 7 per cent of those.[19] Taken together, however, the Freemen's Rolls and 1524–5 subsidies confirm that, although influential and politically powerful, the merchant class was indeed small.

It is possible to study the merchants of these three towns in some detail because of the survival of some of their borough records:[20] primarily, memoranda books, compilations of important council decisions and regulations, guild ordinances, and deeds. More useful as personal statements are the wills preserved in the excellent collection in the York Diocesan Probate Registers, which begin in 1389. They contain the copies of wills which were proved before the Diocesan Exchequer Court,[21] in which the archbishop had jurisdiction over testamentary matters. The grant of probate was also recorded, together with the will, and a note of the granting of administration acts. Wills were also enrolled in the general registers of the archbishop (possibly when probate had been administered by him in person) and several of the Beverley and Hull wills are of this kind. The other probate court, the peculiar court of the Dean and Chapter of York Minster, kept a separate register.[22]

It has been said recently that wills constitute a class of record where casualties have been heavy, and the relationship between the number which has survived and the number which was originally written poses a problem. Incomplete registration, exceptional manuscript losses, and wholesale damage may account for the small numbers of wills which have survived in some dioceses for the period before 1500,[23] but where there has been a good survival rate, as in York,[24] there is a steady increase in the number of wills proved each year between 1389 and 1500.

Various explanations of this phenomenon have been suggested.

Many wills which dealt with small estates perhaps never were proved because the beneficiaries were in agreement and the executors thought that it would be a waste of money to pay the probate fees.[25] It might be that there were fewer sizeable estates in the fourteenth century and thus fewer wills, but this would be difficult to prove or disprove,[26] since many wills disposed of small sums of money and property but left the size of the residue unspecified.[27]

Will-making seems to have been a habit acquired by the newly wealthy, merchants and craftsmen in particular, towards the end of the fourteenth century and once adopted by them became fashionable. A person accumulating more possessions became more concerned about their eventual disposal. A similar concern emerged with regard to real estate, and the desire to exercise more control over that hastened the development of the enfiefment to use in the early fifteenth century.[28]

It must also be remembered that York, Beverley, and Hull, as elsewhere, experienced a renewed interest in spiritual benevolence in the early fifteenth century.[29] Even if a testator did not reflect the impact of Lollard teaching in the phraseology of the religious preamble to his will,[30] he may have been encouraged to involve himself more immediately in choosing how to invest his portion in his spiritual future, as well as in his family's future.[31]

From the legal point of view, the position vis-à-vis intestacy did not change from the late fourteenth century to the fifteenth century. In the Northern Province of the Church, wills were subject to the custom of legitim, whereby personal property was divided into three parts. This system of legitim recognized the rights of the wife and children to two thirds of the testator's estate, one third to the wife, the other third equally divided between the children. If either children or the wife were sole survivors, then the estate was divided into two parts.[32]

In the event of intestacy, the same divisions were made, but the administrator appointed by the court had the disposal of the dead's part at his own discretion and it may have been, as Blackstone believed, that the administrator had the use of the dead's part for himself.[33] From the late fourteenth century, it seems that more people were prepared to act positively to ensure that that eventuality would not arise.

The majority (90 per cent) of the 320 wills consulted for this study, all copies, were proved before the Diocesan Exchequer Court in which the archbishop had jurisdiction over testamentary affairs. The remaining 10 per cent were proved before the archbishop in person, or before the peculiar court of the Dean and Chapter of York Minster. Each was drawn up to a standard format: religious preamble, distribution of real estate and moveables, and the appointment of executors and naming of the residuary beneficiaries.

By the late fourteenth century, wills normally dealt with real estate as well as with moveable property.[34] Burgage property was freely devised in York, Beverley, and Hull, and was treated as though it were a piece of moveable property.[35] Inventories of goods are rare before 1500, although the detail in some wills suggests that they may have been compiled with some form of list in mind. The standardized format suggests that clerks were responsible for drawing up most wills,[36] and idiosyncratic comments, or even conditions of inheritance, are rare.[37]

Wills are endlessly fascinating to read, if it is remembered that they were as much a personal statement of the most general kind, as they were instruments for the disposal of estates. Their interpretation, however, poses problems. Older children might have been omitted from a will because they had already received a settlement[38] and could legally claim no more from the estate.[39] Other property might not be included in a will;[40] property acquired after the will was drawn up would have to be dealt with in a codicil. The majority of the wills read, however, were proved within four months of being written and almost all within one year.[41] For this reason the year of probate has been used as the year of death. Debtors were supposed to have the first claim on an estate but testators usually relegated consideration of debts to the end of their wills, before they disposed of any residue. It is therefore not possible to know whether or not an estate could fulfill the bequests made. Occasionally a merchant anticipated such difficulties. John Barden of York made arrangements in his will in 1396 to the effect that if property had to be sold, then it should be his manor of Kydall.[42]

The custom of legitim raises problems of interpretation.[43] Should it be assumed that the married male testator was disposing of only his third, the 'dead's part', in his will? There is some evidence to suggest that such indeed was the case. For example Thomas Graa of York left his wife Alice £10 out of his part, as well as 'the ascertained portion belonging to her by right'.[44] On the other hand, Robert Flinton of Hull (d.1491) asked that all his property (with the exception of 2s. 2d. and some clothing), should be divided into two portions, one each for his wife and his son,[45] and no mention is made of the 'dead's part' at all. Finally, a will was only a statement of intention, and in some instances a testator's ambitions may have exceeded his resources. Nonetheless, wills are one of the best sources available and if it is accepted that wills were, at the very least, an assessment by the testator of his priorities,[46] then testamentary evidence can be used to explore something of the testator's perception of himself, his attitude towards his family, his fellow burgesses, the church and society at large.

Provision for family, friends, and servants, as one might expect, accounted for the bulk of most bequests. John Aldwick of Hull (d.1444) was an exception in that he left all his property in the care of the city to maintain his chantry, while his son Geoffrey received only a life pension. Generally a merchant's concern was to ensure that all his children and his wife would be materially comfortable after his death, as far as the custom of division would allow.

It is difficult to draw any conclusions about the size of households; most merchants mentioned three or less children in wills and there is no evidence as to whether or not a household included parents, aunts, uncles, brothers, or sisters. Thomas Cliff of York, whose parents were still alive at his death in 1438, simply recorded his bequests to them. The majority of merchants' parents predeceased them.[47]

Although merchants as a class had a reasonable life-expectancy—the average[48] age at death being between fifty and sixty—many anticipated leaving minor heirs, and appointed friends as guardian of their children. Thomas Kirkham of York (d.1437) left his children in the care of John Warde, a fellow merchant, and John Gyllyot jnr. left each of his three children to the protection of three separate merchant friends.[49]

As women tended to marry earlier than men, many were widowed and might be expected to remarry. Just as some merchants arranged for guardians for their children, so others left their wives in the care of friends. John Haynson of Hull (d.1458) asked his friends to ensure that his wife should be 'helped in necessities and negotiations' after his death. John Gill, also of Hull (d.1506), asked a friend to help his wife after his death, and to ensure that 'no man do her wrong'.[50] Remarriage was common,[51] but created inheritance problems. Richard Bille of Hull (d.1441) made provision that if his wife remarried, Richard Anson, Nicholas Stubbs, John Green and three other Hull merchants were to have the safekeeping of his sons' portions until they came of age. William Tailor (d.1509), also of Hull, wanted his curate and the mayor to receive 'good and sufficient surety in the town' from any proposed husband of his widow, that he could 'well and truly' pay Tailor's daughter 100 marks when she came of age or married. He even wanted her to receive any interest that accrued in the meantime.[52] Marriages between widows and widowers could produce further complications as often both parties already had children. When John Bedford of Hull married Agnes, widow of John Dalton of Hull, her son John became co-heir together with Bedford's children by his first wife. In 1450, however, Bedford made John Dalton's inheritance conditional upon him not 'molesting' his mother Agnes. Disputes between heirs were anticipated. Elizabeth, widow of Robert Garner of Hull, stipulated in her will in 1513, that if her son Peter tried to defraud his two brothers, he was to be removed from the position of executor.

Daughters constituted a particular problem. William Goodknapp of Hull (d.1504) left his daughter £30 on condition that her father-in-law made satisfactory property settlement upon her and her husband. If Goodknapp's widow thought that the property was inadequate, then the £30 was not to be paid.[53] If daughters were not married at a merchant's death, the best provision he could hope to make was a sum of money *ad maritagium*,[54] in addition to any other share in the estate. The sums varied according to parental wealth. Thomas Brounfleet of York (d.1458) left his daughter Alice 10 marks for her marriage portion in addition to a silver bowl. John Gyllyot jnr. of York, left his two daughters £20 each in 1509,[55] and Stephen Coppendale of Beverley left his two daughters £100 each in 1485. Marriage portions were not always equal in the same family. Margaret, the daughter of Thomas Frost of Beverley (d.1421) was bequeathed £40, of which £30 had to be collected in debts, and her sister Joan was left £30 and their stepsister £20. Occasionally a merchant would leave cash toward the marriage portion of a friend's daughter. John Gyllyot jnr. (d.1509) left £2 to Kate Anlaghby in this way.[56] If an unmarried daughter was not safely lodged in a convent, her merchant father sometimes provided her with accommodation. John Gregg of Hull (d.1437) installed his daughter Agnes in a house in Marketgate, at a fixed rent for 48 years, presumably the expected duration of her life.[57]

Although women could dispose of real estate, most of their bequests were small gifts of cash or personal belongings, *res paraphenales*. Precise care was taken to differentiate the best from the second-best gown or belt, and presumably best from second-best friends! Although widows could make their own wills freely, wives needed the consent of their husbands if they wished to dispose of dowry possessions.[58] Margaret, wife of Adam Baker of Beverley, made her will in 1401 'through the assent and license of her husband'. Husbands were usually the main beneficiary and executor, and had to be trusted to fulfil their wives' wishes. Joan, wife of Peter Steller of Hull, left £10 in 1383 to her son Thomas White when he came of age. When Steller made his will in 1395 he had remarried, but he remembered his stepson's legacy of £10.[59]

It is quite clear from testamentary evidence that most merchants regarded their servants as an extension of their family, and servants were regularly remembered in wills with small gifts of cash, clothing, and bedding. Sometimes a merchant left money towards the marriage portion of his female servants, as he did for his daughters.[60] Servants who married and moved away were not forgotten either and the phrase 'once my servant' frequently appears in wills. Some members of the household had an ambiguous position and although they were clearly not members of the immediate family, they were either distant relatives or particularly favoured. *Cognati* and *famuli* were frequently mentioned as recipients of specific gifts. John Russell of York (d.1443) left 13s. 4d. and clothes and his best horse to his *famulus* John Turner; £2. 13s. 4d. to his famula Joan Chester for her marriage, and 3s. 4d. to all his other servants. He also left £1 to John Brandesby *famulus* of John Bolton, a contemporary merchant, which suggests a degree of familiarity with Bolton's household. Gifts to servants of fellow merchants were uncommon but such as existed were generally to individuals, as if in remembrance of some specific act of goodwill. Apprentices, on the other hand, were rarely mentioned in wills and John Whitfield of Hull (d.1479) was exceptional in leaving 6s. 8d. to each of his apprentices.

The fate of apprentices and servants after their master's death is unclear. Edmund Portington of Beverley who was apparently unmarried, left two of his servants a house each in Beverley for life, and allowed his other servants to remain in his own house for four months after his death in 1463. If he had been leaving his property to a wife or family some of his servants would no doubt have stayed on in their service in any case, but his forethought reveals the degree of dependence of servant upon master. Richard Chase of York (d.1402) wished his apprentice to serve out his indenture with his wife after his own death. Most crafts accepted widows as successors to their husbands' business, although some demanded heavy fines should a non-guildsman take up an occupation by marrying a widow. John Gregg of Hull specifically asked his executors to treat his servants well after his death.[61] Might he have expected the contrary?

This unmistakable concern for their dependents seems to have become barely concealed fear in some cases, when merchants were drawing up their wills. All of a merchant's last pious hopes, his plans for the future of his children, and his generosity to society, would not have been possible without reliable executors.[62] The parish priest[63] was named as an executor in at least three-quarters of the wills read, and in 90 per cent another merchant was named as one of the executors. The more prominent, such as merchant aldermen, would be named as a supervisor, perhaps as an added precaution, but probably for the associated kudos gained by the testator. The dependence of the individual upon the merchant class was thus highlighted as death approached. Wives, sons, and sons-in-law were almost automatically named as executors. William Neleson of York (d.1525), however, was insistent that his sons-in-law should not inherit the money he was leaving to his grandsons, and stated simply that 'their fathers shall not have it'.[64] Long-standing family friendships were occasionally reflected in a merchant's choice of executor. Roger Bushel of Hull (d.1483) appointed Richard Doughty snr. of Hull (d.1488) as one of his executors; Doughty's son Richard (d.1521) in his turn made Bushel's son Roger (d.1538) one of his executors.[65] Sometimes a merchant's choice implied a confidence based on previous business dealings. In 1470 John Day of Hull named as one of his executors John Middleton of Beverley, with whom he had had property dealings in Beverley.[66]

The execution of a will could be extremely time-consuming and onerous. Although provision was usually made to pay executors, such payments rarely exceeded £2 so perhaps the cavalier attitude of some executors was not surprising. Complaints about heirs dispossessed of their inheritance and about dishonest executors were taken to royal Chancery[67] or to the Diocesan court. John Dalton of Hull (d.1496), doubtless with such possibilities in mind, exhorted his executors 'to do their duty as they will answer at the dreadful day of Doom . . . and to do for me as they would I did for them'. Richard Wartre of York (d. 1465) expressed similar doubts by requiring all his bonds, deeds, and silver to be locked up in a strong chest after his death, and to be kept in the Minster until *all* his executors were present.[68]

If the custom of dividing estates was always observed, and we have no evidence to suggest otherwise, then each generation witnessed the destruction of all but the most thriving businesses. Unless an estate was sufficient to allow substantial cash bequests or the creation of several smaller concerns, then a merchant could not anticipate his own commercial achievements surviving intact for several generations of his own family. In addition, the survival of male heirs was not to be taken for granted and few merchant families survived into more than one or two generations in the male line.[69] Allowing for the possibility of wills excluding eldest sons, it is less remarkable that there were few male heirs than how few fathers seem to have had grandsons. Of course it is difficult to be certain that all male descendants have been traced, but if a merchant's grandson was active in trade or local government, or had moved out of town within the see of York, it would be surprising if his name did not occur in any of the relevant sources.

Seemingly several families like the Coppendales, Tirwhits, Ryses, and Holmes of Beverley, and the Holmes of York, survived into four or more generations, but the assumption is based on the continuing appearance of men of wealth and status with those names. The numbers of sons a merchant had ought to have had a direct bearing on the numbers of generations his family survived, but Robert Louth of York (d.1407) had six sons, one of whom married twice, and no grandson has been traced to the family. In contrast William Bowes of York (d.1439) had only one son but four grandsons, and Thomas Neleson of York (d.1484) with two sons and two daughters had eight grandsons through his eldest son William.[70]

Although many merchants acknowledged the existence of a bastard son or daughter, for example John Stockdale of York (d.1506) had one of each, such children were normally excluded from any inheritance except for a small cash bequest. The case of Robert Holme snr. of York was exceptional, and his bastard son Robert inherited because the father had no surviving legitimate son.[71] With unusual generosity, William Girlington of York left £4 in 1444, to the two bastard sons of his uncle John. It was not unusual to give two sons the same name, anticipating that one would die young, and ensuring that a traditional family Christian name survived. Robert Fisher of Beverley (d.1477) and Robert Fisher of Hull (d.1476), were brothers, as were John Carleton snr. (d.1391) and jnr. (d.1401), of Beverley.[72] This anticipation of the death of heirs runs through several wills. John Aldestonemore of

York, who died in 1434, just before York's worst plague years, prefaced almost every bequest in his will with the phrase 'if he/she should live'; this was unusual phraseology. Many merchants had grandsons through their female heirs, but in these cases their families were absorbed into another, and did not continue the family name.

A nephew could, and often did, become an uncle's heir. Henry Pollington of Beverley (d.1479) left the bulk of his estate to his nephew Robert since he had no son of his own to inherit. Similarly Thomas Holme of York made his nephew, Thomas, his heir in 1406.[73] Several families did not survive for reasons other than infertility. Entry into holy orders could also leave a merchant heirless after one generation. Thomas, the only son of Stephen Tilson of Beverley (d.1469), became a clerk. Two sons of Thomas Bracebridge of York (d.1437) became clerks: one predeceased him, and the other migrated to London.[74]

The failure of male heirs had a major effect on the merchant group in each town. It prevented the formation of a dynastic oligarchy based on inherited wealth. Instead there was a steady flow of newcomers into the merchant group and thence into the governing elite. Even in Beverley the handful of long-established families provided only a tiny minority of the governing elite in any generation. The average mercantile business survived two generations at the most, and the wealth of individuals was continually redistributed amongst other members of the merchant group in bequests and through marriage. The merchant group could not and did not depend upon the survival of individual families, but upon the collective strength of each generation. The inter-marriage of merchant families was more than the natural consequence of business association. It was the means whereby capital, investments, real estate, and the goodwill of a business were retained within the group, whereby newcomers were accepted and assisted in their careers, and whereby the recruitment vital to the group's survival was most easily effected.

It is difficult to convey the extensive and complex nature of the network of marriages which linked contemporary merchant families. It was a feature of thirteenth-century London,[75] and in York, Beverley, and Hull could involve two or three families. Thus Adam Baker of Beverley, a merchant active in the council in the early fifteenth century married Elene, the sister-in-law of another merchant keeper, William Rolleston, and their daughter married a third merchant keeper, John Brompton. William Bowes, snr. of

York arranged the marriage of his two daughters Katherine and Joan to two other York merchants, Robert Louth and John Blackburn respectively. His son William married the daughter of a third merchant, Robert de Kirkeby. Hugh Clitheroe of Hull married Joan, the daughter of Robert Holme, another Hull merchant, and his sister Mary married two Hull merchants, John Thwayt and then John Scales.[76] Thomas Beverley snr. of York (d.1480) married Alice, daughter of a fellow merchant Henry Markett (d.1443), and their son John married Anne, daughter of John Ferriby also a merchant of York. Anne's sister Ellen married John Metcalfe of York,[77] thus linking together four of York's mercantile families through the marriage of three merchant mayors and two merchant sheriffs.

The appended genealogies[78] indicate the even more complex pattern of relationships which sometimes existed. Through the marriage of their children, six contemporary and prominent York merchants were inter-connected and through the marriage of their grandchildren, three more merchant families entered the relationship. Thus two generations of the Aldestonemore, Blackburn, Bolton, Bowes, Gascoigne, Holbeck, Kirkeby, Louth, and Ormeshead families were united in a wide family circle. Even more extensive were the connections between Richard Thornton and two other York contemporaries, which extended to include three more mercantile families through the marriage of their grandchildren. When Richard Thornton's great-grand-daughter Catherine married Bartholomew York, Thornton's group of relationships was added to those of the Yorks. The York family connections were not so extensive, but were with a number of lesser gentry families. The extent of intermarriage could bring families within unacceptable degrees of consanguinity. John Beverley of York had to obtain a papal dispensation to marry John Ferriby's daughter Ann, to whom he was related in the third degree, although no marriage between the two families had recently taken place.[79] Intermarriage also united families of the three towns. For example Ralph Langton of Hull married his daughter Ellen to John Middleton of Beverley (d.1475); Ellen, daughter of John Bedford (d.1451) of Hull, was married to Thomas Gare of York.[80]

The pattern of remarriage of merchant widowers and widows again reflected the cohesive nature of the merchant group. Ellen the wife of John Stockdale of York (d.1506), had previously been married to William Hancock and Robert Johnson (d.1497), both York merchants. Isabella, wife of Robert Gaunt of York, had four husbands, three of them merchants. Katherine Stellar of Hull, widow of Peter Stellar, a merchant mayor, married one of her husband's former associates, John Tutbury, who was also a merchant mayor.[81] These marriages ensured that some of the working capital and assets of a merchant's business were retained for the merchant group,[82] since a wife traditionally inherited at least one third of her husband's estate.

One of the most interesting illustrations of this phenomenon was the series of marriages of one woman, Joan, to three established merchants. She first married John Dalton (d.1458) a merchant mayor of Hull, and their son John's marriage united the families of Alcock and Dalton. After Dalton's death she married another Hull merchant mayor, John Whitfield, and their daughter married Henry Mindram, another wealthy merchant mayor of Hull. Joan's two groups of children, three by her marriage with John Dalton, and four by her marriage with John Whitfield, were united into one family of step-brothers and sisters. Finally, she became the third wife of Sir Richard York, a merchant mayor of York, whose grandson Bartholomew married into the Thornton group of families.[83] Some sense of family unity survived so many new additions. John Dalton, the son of Joan's first marriage, made bequests to the York and Alcock families, and John Whitfield, her second husband, made the same John Dalton and his brother Thomas Dalton, his residuary heirs.[84]

It is clear that as a group, the merchant class needed a continual flow of recruits, either of new immigrants or of men from other trades. In York it is possible to trace the emergence of several merchant families from other occupations. William Brereton became a freeman as a cook in 1396; one of his sons, Robert, remained in the same craft, but another, John, became a burgess as a merchant in 1430. John's son, Thomas, became a burgess in his turn as a clerk. In 1433 William Lancaster became a freeman as a clerk, his son John became a merchant, and his two sons, Nicholas and Richard, became a lawyer and clerk respectively in the 1470s. Richard had remained in his father's occupation but Nicholas had definitely moved upward. The Jameson family, which also moved into the merchant group from another craft, remained in that group. William Jameson had become a burgess as a yeoman in 1456 and his son, Thomas, and grandsons, John, Thomas and Michael, all became merchants.[85]

The problems of setting up in business as a newcomer must have been daunting. Apart from the initial capital,[86] the goodwill and respect of the established merchants had to be acquired and contacts with suppliers created. Migrants like Robert Holme of York, who came from the Wolds, had an immediate advantage in their local knowledge of wool producers. Others became apprenticed to established merchants and although apprentices were not allowed to trade for their own profit while indentured,[87] they were introduced to valuable contacts as well as being taught the rudiments of the trade. The custom was noticeably successful in Hull, where merchants who later rose to authority were apprenticed to prominent merchants. Nicholas Ellis and John Liversage, later mayors of Hull, were apprenticed to Robert Shakles a former mayor. Ralph Forne, later mayor, and Stephen Gildhouse, later sheriff, were both apprenticed to John Gregg, one of Hull's most wealthy early fifteenth-century merchants. Roger Bushel and Ralph Langton were typical of successful merchants who attracted, and doubtless needed, apprentices. They and John Gregg each had at least four apprentices during their active lives.

Although not explicitly stated, the help given by an established merchant to a newcomer from his home town or village, must often have been invaluable. Edmund Coppendale, a migrant from Beverley to Hull, took on a fellow townsman from Beverley, Thomas Brackenburgh, as his apprentice.[88] The opportunities of apprenticeship to a prominent merchant were probably the same in Beverley and York but the records of apprenticeships in both towns are sparse. The few recorded instances in York reflect the Hull pattern. For example John Northeby (d.1432) was a 'servant' of William Vescy (d.1407), who was a big wool merchant. John Lincoln, sheriff in 1502 and Master of the Mercers' and Merchant Adventurers' Company in 1507, entered his freedom as an apprentice to John Ferriby, a former mayor. John Beesby jnr., sheriff in 1506, was an apprentice of Thomas Beverley, a former mayor.[89]

References to benefactors appear regularly in merchants' wills and reflect the importance of good early contacts and patronage. William Frost, mayor of York from 1400 to 1404, and in 1406, remembered two established merchants as his benefactors, Roger de Moreton and Roger Hovingham, and endowed a joint chantry in his own and their memory. Such was the great affection of Robert Hancock (d.1495) of York for his master Thomas Barton that he wanted to be buried next to him in St. Michael's, Spurriergate.[90] The advancement of an apprentice through marriage to his master's daughter, or even to his widow, was a possibility. Only one example of such a marriage has been discovered. Robert Harrison of Hull was an apprentice of John Dalton, and after Dalton's death in 1496 he married Dalton's widow, Katherine. Harrison had also enjoyed encouragement and help from Ralph Langton, a successful merchant mayor, and wanted to be buried at Langton's feet in Holy Trinity, Hull.[91] A similar relationship may have existed between Thomas Aldestonemore and another York merchant, John Gare, because Aldestonemore asked to be buried next to Gare if he died while in Calais.[92]

The implications of short-lived merchant families, and of the greater importance of class as opposed to individual family survival, were especially marked in local government. In each of the three boroughs, merchants were the politically dominant occupational group. In the absence of a dynastic pattern of office-holding, continuity of government was sustained by systems of self-perpetuating oligarchies, and by a shared belief in what constituted good government. Not all merchants subscribed to that belief or chose actively to propagate it,[93] but those who did, have left evidence of it in borough records. What has survived are those items which councillors and their successors regarded as important.

At the most basic level of political survival, councillors had to demonstrate an ability to govern, that is they had to maintain law and order. The oaths[94] which each borough official took, emphasized their responsibility for preserving the liberties and customs of their communities. Suspension of borough liberties was a real possibility, an afront to civic pride, which York suffered in 1405–6 when the council was apparently held responsible for the involvement of the city in the Scrope rebellion.[95]

The basis of council authority which had no effective police resources, was tenuous and could be undermined severely when challenged by political discontents, who rallied wide support, probably from non-burgesses and burgesses alike. In October 1484 and again in February, 1494–5, the York council was under pressure from riots, and it was made clear that the city's autonomy was at the king's pleasure. In 1494–5 Henry VII actually threatened to replace the council with men who could 'rule and govern the city according to my laws'.[96]

York was strategically important, and perhaps as a consequence, in spite of its proud county status, it was more vulnerable to royal supervision than other boroughs. The problem of political survival was not unique though, and the solution most often resorted to was a public relations exercise to counter complaints of incompetence and corruption. Suitable candidates for office were described as 'sad and discreet' men. Councils stressed the 'dignity and worship' of civic office. Councillors and officials were exhorted to conduct themselves in a proper manner, particularly with regard to dress,[97] because the myth of a government composed of superior persons was essential to the survival of the council and to its ability to govern.

Attention has been drawn to the importance of civic ritual in Coventry;[98] and in York too the council and officials paraded whenever possible. They were expected to proceed to service in the Minster on Sundays when summoned; aldermen were to be attended by a servant bearing a torch at the Corpus Christi parade.[99] Royal visits were the occasion for decisions about the colour of robes to be worn; usually scarlet for the aldermen and crimson or murrey for the outer council of twenty-four.[100] As symbols of the power and prestige of borough government, the mace and sword, which preceded the mayor, were held in high esteem and the mace- and sword-bearers were salaried, liveried officials. In 1440, the council of Hull even went to the length of buying a second charter, to ensure that the City had a right to a sword which had been omitted in the main charter of incorporation.[101]

Such awareness of appearances could be understood merely as self-importance, and no doubt there was an element of vanity involved, as can be seen in long-drawn out squabbles about the order of precedence of individuals[102] and of craft guilds. The cordwainers and weavers of York argued for at least three years about their relative positions in the Corpus Christi parade, and their dispute was finally settled in 1493 by the formal arbitration of the abbot of St. Mary's and Thomas Lovell.[103] Men could be jealously status conscious but most of the ordinances about behaviour and dress were explicitly directed towards particular senior officials. Correspondingly, the behaviour of the rest of the community towards officials was also subject to council regulation. Burgesses in Beverley, and all the inhabitants of York, were expected to obey all council orders on pain of a fine.[104] Verbal abuse, especially towards or about the mayor of York and Hull was not unusual, and incurred a fine or even disenfranchisement.[105]

Some occupations were considered incompatible with the dignity of civic office above the level of chamberlain, and inn-keeping and the retailing of ale were especially disliked. Councillors in York and Hull were forbidden to retail beer or wine in their homes and one elected mayor of York, John Petty, was asked to take down his inn sign as a condition of taking office in 1504.[106] Similar prejudice existed in other towns.[107]

Ultimately though, the strength of government depended on the aspirations of the community matching those of its ruler. So long as both shared the same values, and the council's conduct of day-to-day affairs was satisfactory, then government had credibility. It is striking that the petitions of the commonalty in York in October 1484 included precise criticism of the conduct of government in areas directly touching the man in the street. The belief that the council mismanaged the city's finances had been long-standing, but in this instance that complaint was coupled with demands that the streets be properly cleaned.[108] As we shall see, such demands accorded with the ambitions of councillors themselves to improve the city environment.[109]

The overwhelming impression left by the majority of late medieval wills is one of insecurity only mitigated by religious benevolence. Spiritual uncertainty was to be expected and was encouraged by the Church, which could not have survived without the constant flow of donations and endowments it received. The collective impact of merchant contributions is immeasurable but must have been considerable. The Church taught that prayers for the dead had a redemptive value and that the benefit which the living and the dead received varied in direct proportion to the numbers of masses said, and the amount of offering made for each.[110] The majority of testators invested in their future redemption in one or more of three ways: by making a single donation; by making provision for a simple obit and mass at their funeral; by providing for a longer-term chantry endowment or cash payment for masses over a period of months or years.

Certain regular bequests were made in a formal way. After the merchant had commended his soul to the Virgin Mary and all saints he expounded his personal thoughts on the weakness of the flesh and on eternal life.[111] The parish clergy were rarely omitted. The priest would always receive a small sum, 6s. 8d. or under for forgotten tithes, and a further sum for himself of 5s. or under. The parish clerk would be given 4d. or so. The best gown would be left for the mortuary, and a small sum would be left to the church fabric.[112] Robert de Preston of Hull exceptionally left his horse for his mortuary in 1347.[113] In addition to the parish church the testators remembered the fabric funds of major churches: invariably St. Peter's at York, often St. John's, Beverley, and occasionally St. Mary's at Southwell and St. Wilfrid's Ripon.[114] Small cash sums were always left to the friars, rarely more than a mark for each order, often only 4d. and these donations did not significantly fall away in the fifteenth century.

John Gregg of Hull (d.1437) departed from the usual gift of a lump sum when he left money in his will to be paid in installments to the Carmelite and Augustinian friars of Hull so that they should receive 6d. per week for 5 years.

The local religious houses attracted fewer endowments, and those which were made were usually attached to a specific request for masses. Well travelled merchants also left money to religious houses outside their own towns, scattered throughout the immediate region and occasionally further afield throughout the north of England. Such bequests must in part reflect a merchant's area of business activity. Robert Colynson of York (d.1485), for example, left money for masses to the priories of Carlisle, Bolton-in-Craven, Richmond, Appleby, Penrith, Northallerton, Knaresborough, Nunmonkton, and Watton, as well as to parish churches in some of those places. William Goodknapp of Hull (d.1504) left money to the hospital of Harfordlithe (possibly Staxton, E.R.), and the abbeys of Greenfield (Lincs), Ledburn, Nun Cotham (Lincs.), Ferriby (E.R.), and Hornby (Lancs.), and to the churches of Harfordlithe (? Staxton), Drypool, Benbroke, Barton, Grimsby, and Sutton.[115] A merchant who made such extensive bequests as these must have made them in remembrance of his personal and business relationships with a religious house or parish.[116]

Perpetual chantries were either endowed with specific rents or with a cash lump-sum to be invested in property. A licence to alienate the necessary property had to be purchased from the crown either by the benefactor before his death or by his executors.[117] The total number of licences declined in the fifteenth century for the country as a whole, and in York it has been estimated that most of the perpetual chantries were established by citizens between 1310 and 1340. Chantries continued to be founded, however, throughout the late fourteenth and fifteenth centuries[118] and confirmed the pattern of one chantry to each of many of the large number of parish churches in the city. Exceptionally Roger de Moreton jnr. endowed a chantry outside York at Rievaulx Abbey.[119] In Beverley and Hull too few perpetual chantries were endowed for there to be any discernible fluctuation, and the small number of churches available, two in Hull and two and a chapel in Beverley, meant that chantries were more concentrated than in York. In all three towns the few citizens who endowed perpetual chantries were nearly all members of the merchant group. In Hull there was a marked tendency for merchants to endow a combined hospital or almshouse with their chantries. Beverley's biggest chantry, that of John Ake on the Crossbridge, was of this type. In York, citizens preferred either to endow a chantry or an almshouse but the two were not often combined.

The size of the initial endowment of perpetual chantries varied, although the average annual salary in the fifteenth century for a chantry priest was £4. 13s. 4d. In 1390–1 the executors of William Grantham and William de Santon, both merchants of York, alienated rents worth £5 per annum but had to pay £20 for the licence.[120] There seems to have been no preference for a direct property endowment instead of cash or *vice versa* as land values fluctuated. The wealthiest merchants of York left enormous lump sums for chantry foundation from the late fourteenth to the late fifteenth century. Robert Holme left £400 in 1396, Richard Wartre left £336. 6s. 8d. in 1465, and John Gyllyot jnr. left £400 in 1509, each wishing to endow one chantry.[121] Richard Russell of York left both specified properties and instructions to acquire property to endow his chantry at his death in 1435. In addition to a perpetual chantry he left extensive bequests for short-term prayers and further property for a thirty-year chantry. His executors took twenty-five years after his death to obtain a licence to alienate, and possibly would have abandoned the scheme had not one of them, John Thirsk, wanted to share the chantry.[122] Occasionally executors would find that the testator's endowment was inadequate for the scale of his proposed chantry. John Gisburn of York left £40 for two chantry priests in 1390 but his executors had to reduce the establishment to one priest.[123] Similarly the £30 left by Richard Thoresby of York in 1405 and the £66. 13s. 4d. left in 1415 by Thomas Rolleston of Beverley must have been insufficient to maintain a chantry priest in perpetuity.

Once a perpetual chantry was endowed and established, its income could be regularly supplemented by cash gifts or the income of grants of land from succeeding generations of townspeople. John Gyllyot jnr. in addition to founding a new chantry for himself, left property worth 4 marks a year to the chantry priest of St. Thomas' altar in All Saints, Pavement.[124] By far the largest number of gifts to perpetual chantries in the fifteenth century were augmentations of this nature and it is probable that most chantry priests supplemented their income by singing masses for short-term endowments.

In Hull nearly all perpetual chantries were established by merchants who made the mayor and aldermen residuary legatees of
the property and rents involved. In this way no licence to alienate
had to be obtained, and the administration of the chantry was in
the city's hands.[125] The benefactor could also use the establishment of his chantry for patronage. Thus Joan Gregg of Hull named
John Wilde as the first priest of her chantry and Richard Russell of
York named John Turner as priest of his chantry. John Gyllyot
jnr. left the patronage of his chantry to each of his sons
in succession,[126] probably hoping that his family would look
after the chantry and that it would not revert to the care of the
city.[127]

Since the establishment of a perpetual chantry was complicated,
time-consuming and above all expensive, most merchants preferred to distribute money for obits and masses amongst a variety
of religious institutions and priests, and to endow a short-term
chantry. Benefactors seemed to prefer to endow a chantry for one,
three, or seven years, and endowments for periods over ten years
were unusual. William Bowes (d.1439), and John Gyllyot snr.
(d.1484), both of York, left money for chantry priests to sing
masses for twenty years,[128] but this was exceptional as short-term
chantries were always endowed with a lump sum from which the
yearly salary was to be paid, and the provision of masses for a long
period required a large initial cash outlay. Frequently merchants
would leave money for certain chaplains, anchorites, and recluses
to say a mass.[129] Richard Wartre of York (d.1465) was anxious lest
it were forgotten for whom the masses were to be said. He wanted
his name and those of his parents and two wives to be written
down on 'bills' so that all the chaplains could have the names in
front of them as they sang. Since he left £50 for the purpose his
fears are understandable.[130]

The less wealthy, who could not afford an independent endowment, might share in an established collective chantry sponsored by a religious guild. These were established by royal licence,
and they could own property for maintaining their religious services. Their chaplains, paid by the guild, regularly celebrated
masses in a particular church for the members of the guild, who
usually paid an annual subscription. When a member died he
would leave a small cash bequest to the guild for a special mass.
York had three large religious guilds, about ten smaller guilds in
parish churches, and one or two in religious houses. Hull had four
or five large religious guilds which were for specific crafts, and

about fourteen smaller guilds in the two parish churches. Beverley had three large religious guilds, and five small ones.[131]

Merchants were involved in the establishing of many of these guilds. William Craven and John Kirkham, both York merchants, were recipients of the foundation licence for the St. George's Guild of York in 1447. Thomas Crathorn, William Bell, Thomas Cotys, and Richard Thornton, all merchants of York, were active in reforming the St. Anthony's Guild as the St. Martin's Guild.[132] As with perpetual chantries, religious guilds depended upon a steady flow of gifts, and these were common in merchants' wills.[133]

A further act of piety, not uncommon in the later middle ages, was for benefactors to pay for a pilgrimage to be made by proxy.[134] One York merchant, William Vescy (d.1407) left elaborate provision for at least nine separate pilgrimages to be made on his behalf to English holy places including Walsingham, Bury St. Edmunds, and Canterbury. The fee to be paid for each journey was carefully worked out and varied from 2d. for the journey to St. Paul's, London, to 5d. for the journey to Walsingham. Two Hull merchants, Geoffrey Hanby and Thomas de Santon, actually acquired permits to travel abroad as pilgrims in 1350, but it is not known if they went.[135]

Most merchants asked to be buried in their own parish church, sometimes in front of a specific altar, but some, John Pettyclerk of York (d.1426) among them, left it to God's will to be buried wherever they died. Several asked to buried away from their town of residence, probably because they were ill and expected to die while away. Alexander Wharton of Hull died in London in 1506 and wanted to be buried in St. Mary Magdalen, Old Fish Street.[136] John Yarom and John Grantham, both of York, were taken ill in London and had to be buried there in 1347 and 1391 respectively. John Aton of York, however, wanted to be buried in Holy Trinity, Hull, in 1394, for no apparent reason, though he had perhaps been born in Hull.[137]

For some merchants their place of burial reflected the warmth as well as the formality of lifetime relationships. Families were traditionally buried in the same church unless the children had moved away to another parish. Thomas Bracebridge of York (d.1437) wanted to be buried in St. Saviour's next to his wife and children, who had predeceased him, and John Esingwold wanted to be buried in the Austin Friary next to his brothers. Robert Howell of Hull (d.c.1513) wanted to be buried as close as possible to his wife Margaret, in Holy Trinity. Women who had had more than one spouse might have had to decide which to be buried near. Joan, who outlived her third husband, Sir Richard York, chose to be buried next to her second husband in Holy Trinity, Hull.[138]

Most merchants were content with a simple tombstone, but one or two aspired to greater glory. Thomas Rolleston of Beverley left 10 marks for a marble slab in 1415, and in 1485 Stephen Coppendale, also of Beverley, left 6 marks for a marble slab with his arms carved upon it. Elias Casse of Beverley, a business man to the last, left £1 to St. Mary's, Beverley, in 1501 for a 'proper tombstone', but declared that the money was to be halved if no tombstone was provided.[139]

Those merchants who wanted to leave a lasting impression upon the minds of their friends and on acquaintances, provided money to buy wax for candles to burn at their funerals and throughout the period of mourning, as well as for additional masses to be sung, and for alms to be given to the poor. With an eye for detail and a good knowledge of costs, Richard Russell of York (d.1435) left 40lbs. of wax for 3 candles and 48s. for 12 torches. Eight of the torches were to be given to three altars in his parish church of St. John, Hungate, and the rest were to be carried at his death by poor men, who were always willing to supplement their income by forming part of a burial procession and by carrying torches and candles. Most commonly twelve or thirteen torchbearers were employed in this way and they were sometimes partly paid by being allowed to keep the new clothes they were given for the occasion. Robert Jakson of Beverley (d.1480) left caps and gowns to the thirteen poor men who were to attend his funeral, and Richard Russell of York also left £3 to buy bread for his torchbearers.[140]

One or two merchants planned more elaborate funerals.[141] In 1454 Thomas Wilton of Beverley wanted virtually all the members of St. John's staff—the chancellor, sacrist, precentor, seven parsons, nine vicars, nine chaplains, eight clerks, two treasurers, and eight choristers—to sing a mass for him at his funeral. He also left 13s. 4d. for the bells to be rung. Thomas Barton of York similarly remembered all the personnel of his church, St. Michael's, Spurriergate, and in 1460 left £25 for suits of white damask with gold fringe for the chaplains, deacons, and choir. Such splendour was exceptional and was accompanied with massive almsgiving, involving the distribution of over £20. Contemporary society would remember an individual after such an occasion, particularly if accompanied by a funeral feast. William Vescy (d.1407), Bertram

Dawson (d.1516) and John Beesby (d.1538), all of York, thought-fully left money for such a meal for their neighbours.[142]

A less expensive and popular form of memorial was a con-tribution to the lights of one or more specified altars.[143] Parish churches had several altars dedicated to individual saints, in addi-tion to the high altar, and a light was kept burning over each. Bequests in wills for this purpose were usually small; 4d. or 6d. in cash, candles, or a quantity of wax. A benefactor could leave money for the lights of several altars in one or more churches, like John Carre of York in 1487, and thus spread the investment as he might spread his goods between several ships on a commercial venture. In 1433 Margaret, the thrifty widow of Nicholas Black-burn snr., wanted the remains of her eight funerary candles to be distributed between four different churches in York and hers was not an unusual request.[144]

Although no distinction was made in the middle ages between alms and bequests to religious institutions,[145] since it was the act of giving that was thought to be important, society as a whole depended upon the charity of its wealthier members for a variety of needs. The economic success of merchants was beneficial to the urban community, not simply through the employment it created for others, but through the extensive charitable welfare it made possible. Without merchants' donations, religious care of the needy would not have been possible, and their own direct gifts to the poor were considerable. Professor W. K. Jordan has estimated that in London the merchant group comprised 36 per cent of all charitable donors, but was responsible for over 56 per cent of all charitable donations.[146] No precise figures have been calculated for these three Yorkshire towns, but in the variety of ways de-scribed below, their merchant groups accounted for a steadier flow, and a larger proportion of charitable donations, than any other group.

The care of the sick, of the aged, and of the poor, were the areas commonly endowed. Generally such charity took the form of cash distributions at funerals and some merchants left very large sums for this purpose. Richard Russell of York left £13. 6s. 8d. for distribution at his funeral, a similar sum for the most needy in three York parishes, a further £20 for the poor in the rest of York and £10 for the sick. John Brompton of Beverley (d.1444) left £18 in cash for funeral distribution and £10 to buy bread for 80 pau-pers. Nicholas Blackburn snr., of York (d.1432), left money in instalments for the poor of York: £100 at Easter, £100 at All

Hallows, and £60 at the feast of the purification of the Virgin Mary in the year following his death. John Gregg of Hull (d.1437) also favoured instalments and left over £43 for the poor of Hull at 20d. per week for ten years, and over £21 for the poor of Beverley at the same rate for five years. John Garton of Hull (d.1455) stipulated that £20 of the £50 he left for the poor should be given towards the marriage of pauper girls.[147] Bequests of this nature, and those which required the executors to continue to act for many years after the testator's death, must have been very difficult, if not impossible to put into effect. The prayers of the grateful poor on behalf of the testator must often have been won at the expense of the executors' fond memories of him.[148]

Another common form of charity was to leave or make provision for certain goods, usually food and clothes, to be given to the poor. Joan Gregg of Hull left £40 for wool and linen cloth for the poor of Hull in 1438, whereas Richard Wartre of York (d.1465) wanted his executors to have 100 gowns made and distributed together with bread. John Gyllyot jnr., of York (d.1509), left precise instructions that fifty new beds each worth 10s., and a new mattress and two new blankets and sheets for each bed should be given to paupers in the city, that £10 should be given to the most needy married couples in the city, and that £10. 6s. 6d. should be given for dowries for forty poor maidens.[149]

In York it was also customary to leave money to the main prisons, the Kidcotes (civic prisons on Ouse Bridge),[150] the castle and the archbishop's prison. William Bowes (d.1439), left 5s. to each prison, whereas William Chimney (d.1508) left 2d. to each prisoner. Such widespread generosity was no doubt a further burden on executors. Few such bequests occur in Beverley or Hull wills although there was a prison in each town. Occasionally the York prisons would be remembered by Beverley or Hull people. For example Joan Gregg of Hull (d.1438) left 6s. 8d. to the prisoners in the archbishop's prison in York.[151]

Probably the most necessary and effective form of lay charity was the foundation and maintenance of hospitals and maisons-dieu, the latter was a combination of hospital and almshouse. There were at one time and another six main hospitals and about thirteen maisonsdieu in York; four small hospitals, the Charterhouse, and nine maisonsdieu in Hull; and five hospitals and at least three maisonsdieu in Beverley.[152] Several of these institutions were founded by individual merchants and maintained by continuing lay charity. Thomas (d.1406) and Robert Holme of York (d.1396), for example, each established a maisonsdieu in the city, and John Craven (d.1415) established another near Layerthorpe.[153] The four small Hull hospitals were established by merchants; one in the fourteenth century by Robert Selby, and three in the fifteenth century respectively, by John Alcock, John Bedford, and John Gregg. John Armstrong of Beverley (d.1504) established a trust to administer £20 annual income from rents, to maintain the St. John the Baptist maisonsdieu and five others in Beverley,[154] of which no other record has been found. Bequests to such institutions usually took the form of a small cash gift to each incumbent, or to each house, and although such gifts are difficult to evaluate, because we do not know exactly how many recipients there were, some testators' total donations must have been considerable.

The evidence from wills, suggests that some merchants lived in considerable comfort. Bequests of mattresses, feather-beds, tapestries, cushions, quantities of household utensils, and bequests of spoons, dishes, goblets made of pewter, gold, and silver, make familiar reading. There is also evidence to suggest that merchants acted individually and collectively as councillors, to create a healthier, better serviced, and altogether more pleasant environment for the community at large.

Individual merchants who had travelled to London[155] and abroad, had seen examples of physical orderliness and no doubt visiting aliens drew loud and partisan comparisons. Practical considerations led many merchants into financing public works such as highway maintenance, the provision of a water supply, bridge repairs, and street paving.[156] Good communications were close to commercial interests and the repair of roads and bridges regularly attracted donations from testators. Such benefactions had a double advantage, in that they also earned the approval of the Church. One version of a bidding prayer, encouraged the congregations to pray for 'thaim that brigges and stretes makes and amendes that God grant us part of thare gode dedes and thaim of oures'.[157]

The majority of donations were towards the upkeep of roads and bridges close to a merchant's home. Richard Russell of York left money in 1435 for the repair of roads and bridges within a ten league radius of the city. Other merchants favoured the Hull-Beverley road, the Hull-Drypool road, Hull bridge in Beverley, or more distant roads and bridges which were regionally important, including the road across Hessay Moor, the bridge at Stamford Bridge, Caterick bridge, and Frodsham bridge in Cheshire.[158] The

repair of the internal roads and bridges was generally paid for
from pavage grants and tolls. All the same, Thomas Neleson of
York (d.1484) felt that the provision was inadequate and left £10
for the purpose.[159]

Once in a while a merchant would take upon himself responsibility for a major public project. William Todd of York paid for
work on a long stretch of the city walls near Fishergate Bar during
his mayoralty in 1486–7. Robert Holme of Hull contributed the
materials for the construction of a lead conduit in the city, and
when it was pulled up and the lead sold in 1462, the council paid
for a perpetual mass to be sung for him.[160]

During the later middle ages, many councils grappled with the
problems of an expanding population and inadequate public facilities, and devoted time and energy to the day-to-day improvement of
the environment. The provision of a public water supply became
more common. Cleaner streets were encouraged by the regulation
of domestic rubbish dumps and councils tried to protect the structure of streets by prohibiting the encroachment of buildings on to
the highway, and the traffic of carts with iron-bound wheels.[161]
The desire for a cleaner less unhealthy environment was supported by repeated council regulations in York, Beverley, and Hull,
concerning the supervision of pigs (an important scavenging
agency), and other animals. Beverley and York were still closely
involved in husbandry by virtue of extensive common grazing in
their town fields, and Beverley annually appointed swineherds
and other officials to supervise grazing along the town's verges.[162]
The disposal of offal and of waste from industrial processes such
as dyeing and tanning, called for constant vigilance on the part of
councils. The frequency with which councils reissued regulations
specifying where dumps were to be located, down rather than
upstream of a community's water supply, and outside the town
walls rather than in public thoroughfares, suggests that not all
townsmen shared the same concern for their environment.[163]

The late middle ages was a time when a collective sense of civic
pride was increasingly manifested in the building of new
guildhalls,[164] enterprises possible only through collective effort.
Four substantial halls were built in York,[165] three of which have
survived: the Merchant Adventurers' Hall, built in the late fourteenth and early fifteenth centuries by the guild of Our Lord and
the Blessed Virgin; Merchant Taylors' Hall built before 1400; and
St. Anthony's Hall built sometime between 1446 and 1453. The
fourth or common hall, now the Guildhall, was originally built in

the mid-fifteenth century by the guild of St. Christopher and the corporation. It was largely destroyed in the 1939–45 war and subsequently restored.[166] All four halls attracted individual donations towards the initial building costs and upkeep.[167] York was unusual in having several large halls of this type and it was clearly important for a community to have the financial resources as well as a taste for the fashionable. Council guildhalls were recorded in Beverley and Hull, and were probably of fourteenth-century origin, but we know little about them. Hull possibly had in addition two religious guildhalls; the famous Trinity guildhall was started in the 1460's and was probably a two storied half-timbered building with some brickwork.[168]

We have little idea either of the scale of private architectural embellishments to the townscape. Neither York nor Beverley boasted grandiose domestic buildings. Although numbers of large multi-storied houses survive in York, the majority are timber houses in a box frame tradition, built with the minimum of decoration.[169] In Hull the enormously wealthy de la Pole family was responsible for a Humberside *palazzo* which became known as Courthall. It was a capacious house which stood on a large site between Beverley Street and Marketgate, and was possibly re-built by Michael de la Pole in the 1380's. Names suggest other substantial merchant properties in Hull, for example, Snayton Place, Hellward Place, but the name 'place' may have been a fashionable term.[170]

Late medieval townscapes were inevitably dominated by ecclesiastical buildings and the steady flow of benevolence from the laity helped to maintain these. During the late-fourteenth century and in the fifteenth century, lay donations enabled much new building. In Hull and Beverley lay donations made possible the building of three churches, of which Holy Trinity, Hull, is the largest parish church in England, and St. Mary's, Beverley, has a strong claim towards being one of the most beautiful.[171] In York the appearance of most of the parish churches was totally changed in the course of the fifteenth century through lay donations.[172] At least seven churches were wholly or in part rebuilt; aisles widened, chancels extended, and towers built. During the same period, the present fabric of the Minsters of Beverley and York were completed. The economic surplus invested in the beautification of these three towns was considerable.[173]

Merchants seem to have felt a certain responsibility for the churches with which they were associated, and although it is clear that the intention of the donors was to purchase prayers, the careful thought that went into some of the bequests reflects a close involvement and knowledge of their parish churches. The majority left a small sum 'to the fabric' of their own parish church, but some left money for specific repairs and improvements. Richard Russell made provision for the completion of the belfry in his church of St. John, Hungate, for which he had been paying before his death. He also arranged to pay for the bell-frame and ladder, the repair of three altars, and the glazing of three windows. William Goodknapp of Hull left £3. 6s. 8d. in 1504 towards the building of a steeple on St. Mary's, Hull, a church which had already received merchants' bequests over a period of years to establish its peal of bells. John Haynson (d.1458) and John Swan (d.1476) had both left money towards the church's bells. Guy Maliard of Beverley left the materials needed to repair the stalls of St. Mary's Beverley; thirty squared trees and wainscots.[174]

Individual merchants made a significant contribution to the cultural life of their communities through their patronage of the arts. To modern scholars, stained glass is the ecclesiastical art held in highest esteem. The York glass painters evolved a distinctive style, even though they worked from different workshops. They were flourishing in the fifteenth century when many parish churches acquired new windows. The Minster glass must take pride of place in the city, but the glass painters often produced work of an extremely high standard in parish church windows, of a kind not practical in larger windows. Some of the finest late medieval examples surviving were commissioned by merchants. The window made for Nicholas Blackburn jnr. (d.1447) in All Saints, Northstreet, and the 'Yorke window' made for Sir Richard York (d.1498), later moved from his parish church, St. John's Mickelgate, to the north transept of the Minster, are of the highest quality.[175] Other surviving windows owed their existence to the gifts of merchants and it is likely that as many more have been lost. In Beverley and Hull, most of the medieval glass is in fragments, but merchants there left money for memorial windows. Robert Crosse and John Swan of Hull, both left money for windows in Holy Trinity, in 1395 and 1476. Robert Garner, also of Hull, preferred to pay for a window for himself and his wife in the cloister of Swine priory c.1505.[176]

Church furniture and vestments are further examples of ecclesiastical art. Altar cloths and vestments in particular were often of rich fabrics such as velvet or damask embroidered with intricate designs.[177] William Goodknapp of Hull, left to St. Mary's £2 for an altar cloth and £6 for new vestments in 1504. He also left £20 for the purchase of two new altar tables. Richard Russell of York made a similar bequest of vestments, chasubles and altar cloths to St. John the Baptist, Hungate, in 1435.[178]

There was another important area of cultural patronage open to the laity in York and Beverley, and that was the production of the play cycles. There were at least three in York; the Creed play, the Paternoster plays,[179] and the Corpus Christi plays. The most important was the last, staged by the craft guilds.[180] In Beverley two cycles were performed, the Paternoster plays and the Corpus Christi plays.[181] Whatever the relative literary merits of these play cycles, they were a dramatic event which involved the whole community and attracted crowds of visitors. In York, members of the craft guilds paid a compulsory contribution, pageant silver, towards the presentation of the particular play associated with the guild.[182] Each guild or group of guilds grappled with the practical problems of props, the choice of actors, and the manhandling of the pageant wagons from station to station.[183] The council assumed overall responsibility; it discouraged violence, ensured that the streets were cleaned and decorated, and by 1476 was concerned that the competent actors performed 'to the honour of the city and the worship of the said crafts'.[184] In addition, the mayor and council were responsible for the pageant of the Coronation of the Virgin in the fifteenth century.[185] In Beverley similar arrangements existed and each craft was responsible for a play and by 1411 the council supervised the overall performance.[186]

The performance of the plays was seen by the councils in both Beverley and York as an opportunity to entertain visiting notables. York entertained Richard II in 1397 to a performance of the Corpus Christi cycle, and in 1483 entertained Richard III to a performance of the Creed play. Beverley council had members of the Percy family, the local magnates, as guests to a performance of its play cycle in 1423.[187] The plays were also the occasion for profit[188] to shop and innkeepers, and from time to time the commercial and rowdy element threatened the religious purpose of the festival. From 1426, the York plays were performed on the vigil of Corpus Christi, to ensure that people were not distracted from the religious purpose of the festival.[189] Nonetheless, a contemporary writer could claim that the York plays moved spectators to tears, and one recent commentator has seen them as a reflection of the 'personal and quite emotional' spirituality of the city, repeated in the support given to the ecclesiastical arts and church rebuilding of the fifteenth century.[190]

In different circumstances, the York council displayed impressive talent in mounting a flamboyant series of events to greet Henry VII on his first visit to the city in 1486. The King was to be met by the assembled council and officials, correctly robed according to rank, some burgesses, also formally robed, and a number of children calling joyfully, 'King Henry'. He was then addressed from set tableaux, by a personification of the city, 'Ebrauke', by Solomon, David and the Virgin Mary and showered, weather permitting, with rose-water and sweetmeats. The occasion was to be a glorious mixture of a festival atmosphere, spiced with protestations of York's loyalty, Henry's nobility, and his legitimacy as King of England.[191] Like the play cycles, this event was intentionally staged at a popular level; although some of the versification may not have impressed the throng, the council had to consider its own image as a cultural if not cultured elite. There must have been literate merchants in the discussions of the programme for Henry's visit when reference was made to Bartholomew's encyclopedia *De Proprietatibus Rerum* as an authority on the pre-eminence of the rose among flowers: an appropriate allusion.[192]

Literacy is a difficult skill to identify in the middle ages,[193] even though it has been claimed that towns were the nurseries of literacy;[194] men or women able to read could not always write. Wills were often drawn up by scribes,[195] and few personal records such as diaries, letters, or account books have survived. The incidence of book ownership as a reflection of literacy is not reliable; books may have been extremely ornate and valued as artefacts rather than as reading matter.[196] Very few of the wills read contained bequests of books,[197] and without exception those books were religious:[198] psalters, missals, primers,[199] a bible, and a book *Oracione Dominica et Stimulus Conscientiae in Anglia*.[200] An unusual item was an English translation of the Scriptures left by William Ormeshead of York to his nephew Nicholas Blackburn jnr. in 1437. Richard Wartre of York clearly valued books himself, and left books worth £10 to his parish of origin, Bugthorpe, in 1458. Richard Russell, also of York, left an extremely fine collection of books to his parish church, St. John the Baptist, Hungate, in 1435. Russell's origins are not known, but it seems likely that he was brought up or educated by the monks of Durham,[201] and his private library was clearly that of a well-educated man, with literary interests beyond those of the average merchant.

Opportunities for education were available. Ecclesiastical centres such as York and Beverley did not lack educated men who could tutor children, and all three towns had some provision for organized teaching. There is evidence of a school in Hull, later the grammar school, from the late fourteenth century, and it is probable that a school existed in York from the same period and possibly earlier. Beverley had a salaried schoolmaster as early as 1366.[202] Some merchants probably sent their sons away for a fuller education to established schools. John Stockdale of York left £1 in 1506 to his nephew, who was attending Eton College. Certainly merchants' sons went up to Oxford and presumably to the Inns of Court. In 1435 Richard Russell of York left £30 to his nephew Robert to enable him to go to Oxford, and John Brompton of Beverley and John Day of Hull left rents and £20 respectively for their sons' exhibitions, presumably at Oxford.[203]

Occupying as they did the top rung of the urban ladder, it might be supposed that merchants cherished social ambitions. The elevation of the de la Pole family of Hull to the peerage was atypical and was only possible in the context of fourteenth-century wool fortunes and the favouritism of Richard II. Migrations to the country and gentility seem to have been more a characteristic of the sixteenth[204] rather than the fifteenth century. It may have been that the Yorkshire merchants' estates were too small but, as elsewhere, in the midst of community depression, there were one or two extremely wealthy individuals, such as John Northeby of York who left over £700 in 1432, John Brompton of Beverley who left over £900 in 1444, John Gyllyot jnr. who left over £1100 in 1509.[205] Three merchants of York were knighted: John Gyllyot, William Todd, and Richard York. The grandson of William Bowes (d.1476) became Lord Mayor of London in 1546–7, and Bartholomew York became free of the city of York in 1526 as a merchant,[206] following his grandfather's occupation. A handful of merchant families became armigerous,[207] and a few individuals styled themselves gentlemen. Some merchants' sons moved into the professions, mainly the church,[208] and some merchants' daughters married into gentry families.[209]

For the majority the most they could hope for was status within their own communities, and in spite of the economic set-backs of the fifteenth century, merchants survived as a cohesive social and political class in York, Beverley, and Hull. Between 1390 and 1500 there was little perceptible change in personal attitudes or ambitions; a merchant making his will in 1500, ordered his affairs in much the same way as his predecessors, giving priority to his family and to his spiritual future. In public affairs, by accepting the responsibilities of civic office, merchants were involved in improving the quality of urban life; providing social welfare, encouraging physical orderliness, and maintaining political stability within their communities. These public responsibilities were apparently increasing during this period, a consequence perhaps of the sharpening perception, by merchant officials, of their role as civic leaders.

NOTES

1. I am grateful to Professor Barrie Dobson and to Dr. Michael Power for reading and commenting on an earlier draft of this article.

2. For a comparative study see Sylvia Thrupp's *The Merchant Class of Medieval London*, Ann Arbor, Michigan, paperback ed., 1962, which has yet to be surpassed. Good biographies of individual merchants include, M. K. James, 'A London Merchant in the Fourteenth Century', *Economic History Review* [hereafter cited as *Ec.H.R.*], 2nd ser., viii (1955–6); C. M. Barron, 'Sir Richard Whittington', in *Studies in London History*, A. E. J. Hollaender and W. Kellaway, (eds.), London, 1969. E. Power, 'Thomas Betson. A Merchant of the Staple in the Fifteenth Century', in *Medieval People*, London, 10th ed., 1963.

3. H. Pirenne, *Early Democracies in the Low Countries*, New York, paperback ed., 1971, pp. 108–124, made a similar assessment of the urban elites in the thirteenth century.

4. Contemporaries were aware of distinctions between one group and another, and records abound in terms such as *inferiores, mediocres, probi, homines* and so on. These distinctions were reflected in the social status of different religious guilds; in York and Hull, for example, the Corpus Christi guild and Holy Trinity guild were the most exclusive. Similarly in the craft guilds differentials were established and fiercely maintained between masters, journeymen, and apprentices. Such was the finesse with which contemporaries could assess each other that in Hull in 1462, and in York in 1495, it was possible for the council to identify 'those likely to become sheriff'. Hull BRB. 1 f.77v., cited in note 20; A. Raine, (ed.), *York Civic Records*, in 3 vols., Yorks. Arch. Soc., Record Series, York (vol. xcviii, 1939; vol. ciii, 1941; vol. cvi, 1942); vol. ii, p. 121. This work is hereafter cited as Y.C.R.

5. E. Miller, 'Medieval York', in *Victoria History of the County of Yorkshire, City of York*, P. M. Tillott, (ed.), London, 1961, pp. 44, 69, 84. J. C. Russell, *British Medieval Population*, Albuquerque, 1948, p. 142. E. Miller, 'The Fortunes of the English Textile Industry during the Thirteenth Century', *Ec.H.R.* 2nd ser., xviii (1965), p. 69.

6. G. Poulson, *Beverlac*, Beverley, 2 parts, 1829, i, pp. 26–34; A. Raine (ed.), *Historians of the Church of York*, i, Rolls Series, London, 1879, pp. Iiv–Iix. H. Heaton, *The Yorkshire Woollen and Worsted Industries*, London, 1920, pp. 3–4, 29–31; M. Bateson, Review of 'Beverley Town Documents', *E.H.R.*, xvi (1901), p. 566. Russell, *Medieval Population*, cited in note 5, p. 143.

7. Russell, *Medieval Population*, cited in note 5, p. 143. K. J. Allison, 'Medieval Hull', in *Victoria History of the County of Yorkshire, East Riding*, i, K. J. Allison, (ed.), London, 1969, pp. 28–9, 41, 55–6.

8. J. N. Bartlett, 'The expansion and Decline of York in the Later Middle Ages', *Ec.H.R.* 2nd ser., xii (1959–60), pp. 17–33; *V.C.H. York*, cited in note 5, pp. 100–106; *V.C.H.E.R.* cited in note 7, pp. 59–70; E. M. Carus-Wilson and O. Coleman, *England's Overseas Trade, 1275–1547*, Oxford, 1963, pp. 140–1, 146–7.

9. *V.C.H. York*, pp. 70–2, 79; *V.C.H.E.R.*, i, pp. 31–2. In Beverley it is difficult to identify all officials or their occupations, but according to the Account Rolls and Great Gild Book lists of the 12 keepers (councillors) the merchants predominate.

10. It was possible for a woman to engage in such trade. Marion Kent of York continued her husband John's business after his death in 1468, and exported lead in 1471; P.R.O. E122/62/13, 17. No distinction has been made between merchants and mercers, those merchants who specialized in the trade in fine quality cloths, and the term merchant has been used to include both.

11. *V.C.H. York*, p. 108. Not everyone chose to do so, and a man could work as a non-burgess on payment of a regular fine in York, ibid. p. 95, and in Hull. Resident non-burgesses were exempt in Hull after 1467, *V.C.H.E.R.*, i, p. 56; Hull BRE: 1 f.170, BRB: 1 f.108v., cited in note 20.

12. The other most common rights were: the right to hold property in burgage tenure, that is for a cash rent and relative freedom from feudal services; the right not to be tried for specific offences in courts outside the borough; exemption from the payment of specified tolls on goods; the right to trade with aliens; and the right to choose and purchase goods in the borough markets before non-burgesses had access to the markets. A. Ballard, *British Borough Charters, 1042–1216*, London, 1913, pp. xliv–xlv, lxxxviii–lxxxix, 115, 180–191, 211. M. Beresford, *New Towns of the Middle Ages*, London, 1967, pp. 198–221.

13. *V.C.H.E.R.*, i, pp. 56–7. See also for York, *Calendar of Charter Rolls* [hereafter cited as *C.Ch.R.*] 1300–26, p. 187; for Beverley, Bev. Cart. f.11v., cited in note 20.

14. R. B. Dobson, 'Admissions to the Freedom of the City of York in the Later Middle Ages', *Ec.H.R.* 2nd ser., xxvi (1973), pp. 1–22. Entry by apprenticeship was not separately or consistently recorded until 1482. F. Collins, (ed.), *The Register of the Freemen of the City of York*, i, Surtees Society, vol. xcvi, Durham, 1897, p. 204. In Hull, entry by patrimony and apprenticeship were recorded from 1392. Hull BRE: 1 f.240, cited in note 20.

15. Maud Sellers, (ed.), *York Memorandum Book* [hereafter cited as *York M.B.*], ii, Surtees Society vol. cxxv, Durham, 1915, pp. 49, 86, 200. Y.C.R., i, pp. 17, 24, cited in note 4; Bev.G.G.B. ff.6, 21v., cited in note 20.

16. J. Leggett, 'The 1377 Lay Poll Tax Return for the City of York', *Yorks. Arch. Jnl.*, xliii (1971), p. 130. The estimate must be further qualified in the light of R. B. Dobson's appraisal, 'Admissions to the Freedom of the City of York', cited in note 14.

17. E. M. Veale, 'Craftsmen and the Economy of London in the Fourteenth Century', in *Studies in London History*, cited in note 2, p. 136.

18. Based on J. N. Bartlett's figures printed in *V.C.H. York*, pp. 115–116.

19. W. G. Hoskins, 'English Provincial Towns in the Sixteenth Century', in *Provincial England*, London, 1965, pp. 84–5.

20. The following MSS. abbreviations have been used, York corporation House Books—York HB: Beverley Town Records, Account Rolls—Bev. Acct.;

Cartulary—Bev. Cart.; Great Guild Book—Bev. GGB.; Hull Corporation Records, Bench Books—Hull BRB: 1; BRE: 1; BRG: 1.

21. See C. I. A. Ritchie, *The Ecclesiastical Courts of York*, Arbroath, 1956, pp. 13, 19, for a fuller discussion of this court.

22. The Probate Registers and the Archbishops' Registers are in the Borthwick Institute of Historical Research, York, and the Dean and Chapters' collection of wills are in the Minster Library, York. The following MSS. abbreviations have been used; probate registers—Prob. Reg., archbishops registers—Arch. Reg. Printed indexes have been published by the Yorkshire Archaeological Society, Record Series: *Wills in the York Registry, 1389–1514*, vol. vi, 1889; *Dean and Chapter Wills, 1321–1636*, vol. xxxviii, 1907; *Wills in the Registers of the Archbishops of York, 1316–1822*, vol. xciii, 1936.

23. A. K. McHardy, 'Some Late-Medieval Eton College Wills', *Jnl. Eccl. Hist.*, xxviii (1977), pp. 387–8.

24. The high survival rate in the York Diocese was probably due to the greater formality and clerical efficiency which existed in archiepiscopal administrations.

25. McHardy, 'Eton College Wills', cited in note 23, pp. 387–8.

26. In fact, in so far as the size of estates can be calculated from testamentary evidence (see this essay p. 11), most large cash bequests made were by merchants before 1450. *V.C.H. York*, cited in note 5, p. 105.

27. For example Prob. Reg. IV f.181 (Bennington); V. f.8v. (Fisher).

28. M. M. Sheehan, *The Will in Medieval England*, Toronto, 1963, p. 279; J. M. W. Bean, *Decline of English Feudalism, 1215–1540*, Manchester, 1968, pp. 104–5, 148–55.

29. See this essay, p. 33.

30. This is discussed briefly in M. G. A. Vale, *Piety, Charity and Literacy among the Yorkshire Gentry, 1370–1480*, Borthwick Papers No. 50, York, 1976, pp. 114–5. Dr. Vale concludes that wills cannot be used by themselves as evidence of Lollard sympathies.

31. See this essay, pp. 12, 23.

32. T. F. T. Plucknett, *A Concise History of the Common Law*, London, 5th ed., 1956, pp. 743–5; W. S. Holdsworth, *History of English Law*, III, London, 1909, p. 434.

33. G. D. Lamb, (ed.), *Testamenta Leodiensia*, Thoresby Society, xix, Leeds, 1913, pp. vi–vii.

34. The *testamentum* strictly dealt with personal property, chattels, money, and debts. The *ultima voluntas* dealt with real estate and had come to be regarded as a means of conveying instructions to feoffees in the fifteenth century. By the fourteenth century, both sections were usually contained in one document. F. Pollock and F. W. Maitland, *The History of English Law*, II, London, 2nd ed., 1898, p. 331. See also E. F. Jacob, (ed.), *The Register of Henry Chichele*, vol. ii, Canterbury and York Society, xlii, Oxford, 1937, pp. xix–xxi for this development in the Prerogative Court of Canterbury.

35. *York M.B.*, ii, cited in note 15, p. 253; *C.Ch.R.* 1257–1300, pp. 475–6.

36. In smaller communities it is easier to identify scribes. M. Spufford, 'The Scribes of Villagers' Wills in the Sixteenth and Seventeenth Centuries', *Local Population Studies*, no. 7 (autumn 1971), pp. 28–43.

37. Cf. R. B. Dobson, 'The Residentiary Canons of York in the Fifteenth Century', *Jnl. Eccl. Hist.*, xxx (1979), pp. 159–160, where the individual phraseology of the religious preambles to the canons' wills is discussed.

38. For example Thomas Gare of York gave his son all his property in 1427 in return for a life pension. Thomas was dead by 1435. York Corp. B/Y f.47; R. H. Skaife (ed.), *The Register of the Guild of Corpus Christi in the City of York*, Surtees Society, Durham, vol. lviii, 1872, p. 248. Cf. G. A. Williams, *Medieval London, from commune to capital*, London, 1963, p. 316.

39. G. D. Lamb, *Testamenta Leodiensia*, cited in note 33, p. vii.

40. Dobson, ' Residentiary Canons ', cited in note 37, p. 169.

41. E. F. Jacob found that the Canterbury wills were proved within two months on average. *Register of Henry Chichele*, cited in note 24, p. xxv.

42. Holdsworth, *English Law*, cited in note 32, p. 350; Prob. Reg. I f.100.

43. Real estate was not subject to legitim. S. J. Bailey, *The Law of Wills*, London, 7th ed., 1973, pp. 12, 21.

44. Prob. Reg. III f.235. Thomas Aldestonemore of York (d.1435), and John Dalton jnr., of Hull (d.1496), both specified bequests to be made from their own portions, ibid. f.413, V f.484. Margaret Blackburn, widow of Nicholas jnr. in 1435 asked for her portion to be used to supplement one of the bequests in her husband's will if necessary, ibid. III f.417.

45. Ibid. V f.401.

46. Joel Rosenthal, *The Purchase of Paradise*, London, 1972, p. 81. See also Vale, *Yorkshire Gentry*, cited in note 30, pp. 6–7.

47. Ibid. II f.96 (Aldwick); III f.530 (Cliff)

48. This is assuming an age at entry to the freedom of twenty-two, and in the fifteenth century where the dates of entry and of death are known for more merchants, 66 per cent lived over thirty years after becoming free, and 22 per cent lived for over forty years. Death most commonly occurred between thirty and forty years after entry, that is between the ages of fifty and sixty. By way of comparison, it is worth noting that Sylvia Thrupp has estimated that the median age of death for a group of fifteenth-century London merchants was forty-nine or fifty. Thrupp, *Merchant Class*, cited in note 2, pp. 93, 194. An average life-expectancy for a male was about thirty years. Russell, *Medieval Population*, cited in note 5, p. 374.

49. Prob. Reg. III f.487 (Kirkham); VIII f.34 (Gyllyot).

50. Prob. Reg. II f.393v. (Haynson); VI f.175 (Gill).

51. Not all husbands viewed the likelihood with equanimity and some threatened disinheritance, e.g. John Stockdale of York (d.1507), Prob. Reg. VI f.62a.

52. Prob. Reg. II f.233v (Bille); VIII f.81v. (Taillor).

53. Ibid. II ff.220–221v (Bedford); VI f.107 (Goodknapp); VIII f.105 (Garner).

54. Sheehan, *Medieval Wills*, cited in note 28, p. 264.

55. Prob. Reg. II f.386 (Brounfleet); VIII ff.32–4 (Gyllyot).

56. Ibid. V f.271v. (Coppendale); VIII ff.32–4 (Gyllyot); Arch. Reg. 18 ff.384v.–385 (Frost).

57. Hull BRE: 1 f.283 (Gregg). Roger de Moreton jnr. of York (d.1390), had a niece at St. Clement's Priory, York. Ibid. I f.14. John Coppendale of Beverley (d.1343), had a daughter at Walton. Arch. Reg. 10 f.310.

58. Jacob, *Register of Henry Chichele*, cited in note 32, p. xxxviii, notes that Chichele strictly observed this distinction. Holdsworth, *English Law*, cited in note 22, pp. 425–8; Sheehan, *Medieval Wills*, cited in note 28, pp. 234–5.

59. Prob. Reg. I f.98 (Peter Stellar); III f.71v. (Baker); Arch. Reg. 12 f.64 (Joan Stellar).

60. John Russell of York for example, Prob. Reg. II f.68.

61. Ibid. II f.595 (Portington); III ff.76 (Chase), 507v. (Gregg); V f.148v. (Whitfield).

62. The executors were given wide discretion, particularly when the testator left the residue of his estate 'to be disposed of for my soul as my executors see fit'. Cf. McHardy, 'Eton College Wills', cited in note 23, p. 393; Jacob, *Register of Henry Chichele*, cited in note 34, pp. xxiv–xxv.

63. In spite of admonitions that priests should not act as executors. J. V. Ballard and H. C. Bell, (eds.), *Lynwood's Provinciale*, London, 1929, pp. 64–5.

64. Prob. Reg. VI f.107.

65. Ibid. V ff.87v. (Bushel snr.); 350v. (Doughty snr.); IX f.17b (Doughty jnr.); XI f.352 (Bushel jnr.).

66. Ibid. IV f.79 (Day); *C.C.R.* 1466–76, p. 44.

67. P.R.O. Chancery Miscellanea, C1/10/296, 14/25, 15/86.

68. Prob. Reg. V f.484 (Dalton); IV f.116 (Wartre).

69. A similar situation obtained in London, Thrupp, *Merchant Class*, cited in note 2, pp. 202–4.

70. Prob. Reg. III ff.265 (Louth); 580–3 (Bowes); V ff.212–3 (Thomas Neleson); IX f.203 (William Neleson).

71. Ibid. I ff.100v.–103v. (Holme snr.); III f.365 (Holme); VI f.185 (Stockdale).

72. Ibid. I f.38v. (Carleton snr.); II f.84 (Girlington); V f.8v. (Fisher, Hull); f.13 (Fisher, Beverley); Arch. Reg. 16 f.141 (Carleton jnr.).

73. Prob. Reg. III ff.254–255v. (Holme); ff.406–8 (Aldestonemore); V f.147 (Pollington).

74. Ibid. III ff.487–490 (Bracebridge); V f.138 (Tilson).

75. Williams, *Medieval London*, cited in note 36, p. 75 and Tables a–d, between pp. 322 and 323.

76. Prob. Reg. III ff.71v. (Baker), 580 (Bowes); *C.C.R.* 1435–41, p. 40; Hull Deeds 324.

77. Prob. Reg. II f.70 (Markett); V ff.184 (Alice Beverley), 419 (Anne Beverley).

78. See on page 49.

79. J. Raine snr. and J. Raine jnr., (eds.), *Testamenta Eboracensia* [hereafter cited as *Test. Ebor.*], 4 vols., i–iv, Surtees Society, Durham, vol. iv, 1836; vol. xxx, 1855; vol. xlv, 1865; vol. liii, 1869; iii p. 196n.

80. Prob. Reg. II f.220 (Bedford); IV f.96v. (Middleton); Skaife, *Corpus Christi Guild*, cited in note 38, p. 11n.

81. *Test. Ebor.*, iv, p. 121n; Skaife, *Guild of Corpus Christi*, cited in note 38, p. 18n.; Arch. Reg. 18 f.357 (Katherine Tutbury).

82. An astute marriage could rapidly advance the fortunes of an ambitious merchant. For example, William Stockton of York married the widow of Robert Collinson, Richard Wartre married John Moreton's daughter Alice, John Metcalfe married John Ferriby's daughter, and as Metcalfe was said to be 'comen lightly up' his marriage at least was clearly advantageous. Each of these was marrying into a successful merchant family, and each in turn obtained thereby a thriving business in trade. Skaife, *Guild of Corpus Christi*, cited in note 38, p. 29n.; Prob. Reg. IV f.115; V. f.418; Y.C.R., ii, p. 156.

83. See on page 49.

84. Prob. Reg. V ff.148v (Whitfield), 483v.–485 (John Dalton).

85. Collins, *Freemen of York*, cited in note 14, pp. 97, 143, 144, 175, 178, 200, 205, 211, 232, 237, 244.

86. This was the major obstacle to most ambitious young merchants. For some

their inheritance was sufficient; others sold rural property to raise cash. e.g. John Romondby, free in 1367. W. Brown, (ed.), *Yorkshire Deeds*, i, Yorks, Arch. Soc. York, vol. xxxix, 1909, p. 145. Others borrowed from established merchants or elsewhere. Individual merchants often stood as surety for each other in commercial ventures, e.g. *C.C.R.* 1381–5, pp. 94, 575; P.R.O. Chancery Miscellanea C1/16/163. Collectively merchants acted through the York Mercers and Merchant Adventurers' Company to finance ventures, M. Sellers, (ed.), *The York Mercers and Merchant Adventurers*, Surtees Society, Durham, vol. xxix, 1918, pp. 40, 68, 72–3, 195. In Hull similar financing was available through the Guild of the Virgin Mary, and personal loans could be obtained from the Corpus Christi Guild. *V.C.H.E.R.*, i, pp. 58–9; L. and L. T. Toulmin-Smith, (eds.), *English Guilds*, Early English Text Society, orig. ser. vol. xl, London, 1870, pp. 156–7, 160–1.

87. *Y.C.R.*, i, cited in note 4, pp. 163–4.

88. Hull BRE: 1 ff.246, 252, 254, 256, 258, 265; BRG: 1 ff.23–26v.; Prob. Reg. III f.267 (Vescy).

89. Collins, *Freemen of York*, cited in note 14, p. 206; Sellers, *York Mercers*, cited in note 86, p. 323; Prob. Reg. V f.434 (Beverley).

90. *C.P.R.* 1391–6, p. 711; Prob. Reg. V f.473 (Hancock).

91. Hull BRG: 1 f.29; Prob. Reg. V ff.483v–5 (Dalton); IX f.112 (Harrison).

92. Prob. Reg. III f.413 (Aldestonmore).

93. Thomas Scotton was fined for refusing to become an alderman in 1490. York House Book vii, ff.2v., 4. See also *Y.C.R.*, i, p. 37.

94. *V.C.H. York*, p. 70; *York M.B.*, ii, cited in note 15, p. 256; Bev. GGB f.6v.

95. *V.C.H. York*, p.58.

96. *Y.C.R.*, i, pp. 103–4; ii, pp. 115–6.

97. *V.C.H. York*, p. 70; *York M.B.*, ii, pp. 86–7; *V.C.H.E.R.*, i, pp. 30–2.

98. C. Phythian-Adams, 'Ceremony and the citizen: the communal year at Coventry, 1450–1550', in P. Clark and P. Slack, (eds.), *Crisis and Order in English Towns, 1500–1700*, London, 1972. Susan Reynolds, *An Introduction to the History of English Medieval Towns*, Oxford, 1977, p. 180, suggests that such processions encouraged unity, which may have been true of the Corpus Christi feast, but not of other occasions.

99. *Y.C.R.*, i, pp. 2, 5–6; ii, pp. 55, 59, 89, 145–6.

100. *Y.C.R.*, i, pp. 52, 146, 155; ii, p. 25.

101. *C.P.R.* 1436–41, p. 430.

102. For the most famous dispute between John Harper and William Todd in 1486. *Y.C.R.*, i, pp. 155–170; *Test. Ebor.*, iv, cited in note 79, p. 212n.

103. *Y.C.R.*, ii, pp. 70, 90, 96–8.

104. *V.C.H. York*, p. 70; Bev. GGB, ff.6, 7v.

105. *Y.C.R.*, i, pp. 87–8, 91, 169–70; ii, p. 148; *V.C.H.E.R.*, i, p. 30.

106. *Y.C.R.*, iii, p. 10; York House Book, ix f.20v; Hull BRE: 2 ff.13, 21–22v., 77v.–78.

107. In Norwich for example, F. Blomefield, *An Essay towards a Topographical History of the County of Norfolk*, III, Norwich, 1806, p. 129.

108. *Y.C.R.*, i, pp. 104–5, 112–3.

109. See this essay, p. 31.

110. B. L. Manning, *The People's Faith in the Time of Wyclif*, London, 1919, p. 73; Rosenthal, *Purchase of Paradise*, cited in note 46, p. 11.

111. While not a common occurence, an example is the preamble to the will of John Dalton, jnr., of Hull written in 1487, Prob. Reg. V f.483v.

112. According to *Lyndwood's Provinciale*, cited in note 63, p. 6, mortuary was to be paid by the testator 'for and in recompense and satisfaction of such tithes and offerings as he hath taken or kept from the parson'. In the Yorkshire wills, however, mortuary and tithe were often paid as two separate items. Cf. Norwich, where the incidence of tithe bequests increased after 1490. N. P. Tanner, 'Popular Religion in Norwich, 1370–1532'. Oxford University, unpublished D. Phil, thesis, 1973, pp. 28–9. See also A. McHardy 'Eton College Wills', cited in note 23, p. 390, where she describes such payments as conscience money.

113. Arch. Reg. 10 f.323.

114. Each year the masters of the fabric of Lincoln cathedral would send out *nuncii* to publicise the episcopal indulgences offered to benefactors of the fund. K. Edwards, *The English Secular Cathedrals in the Middle Ages*, Manchester, 2nd ed., 1967, p. 231.

115. Prob. Reg. II ff.378–380 (Colynson); III f.507v. (Gregg); VI f.107 (Goodknapp).

116. A good example where such a remembrance is made explicit is the 1420 will of John Lyndwood, a Lincolnshire woolman, in which he differentiated between those parishes in which he had or had not been accustomed to buy wool. Jacob, *Register of Henry Chichele*, cited in note 34, pp. 183–4. See also Prob. Reg. III ff.439–40 (Russell).

117. T. F. T. Plucknett, *The Legislation of Edward I*, Oxford, 1949, pp. 94–102, 109; S. Rabin, 'Mortmain in England', *Past & Present*, 62 (1974), pp. 3–26.

118. Rosenthal, *Purchase of Paradise*, cited in note 46, p. 128; R. B. Dobson, 'The Foundation of Perpetual Chantries by the Citizens of Medieval York', in *Studies in Church History*, G. J. Cuming, (ed.), iv, Leiden, 1967, p. 29.

119. *C.P.R.* 1377–81, p. 458.

120. Bev. Deeds, schedule III; *C.P.R.* 1370–4, pp. 41–2.

121. Prob. Reg. I f.102 (Holme); IV f.116 (Wartre); VIII f.33 (Gyllyot).

122. Ibid. III ff.439–40 (Russell); *C.P.R.* 1452–5, p. 632.

123. Prob. Reg. I ff.15v–16; *C.P.R.* 1401–5, p. 496.

124. Prob. Reg. III f.245 (Thoresby); VIII f.34 (Gyllyot): Arch. Reg. 18. f.34v. (Rolleston).

125. See for example Arch. Reg. 10 f.322v. (Preston); Prob. Reg. II f.383 (Brounfleet); 486v. (Spencer); III ff.507v.–508 (John Gregg).

126. Ibid. III ff.556v. (Joan Gregg); 439 (Russell); VIII f.34 (Gyllyot). Cf. Vale, *Yorkshire Gentry*, cited in note 30, pp. 18–19.

127. Eventually the York city council found that its responsibilities as trustee incurred the city in considerable expense. In 1528 it was claimed that this expenditure was an important factor behind the city's inability to pay the fee farm. By act of parliament in 1536, the city was released from its maintenance of chantries. *V.C.H. York*, p. 123.

128. Prob. Reg. III ff.580–583 (Bowes); V. f.237 (Gyllyot).

129. Richard Russell left money in 1435 for three recluses in York and two in Hull. Ibid. III ff.439–40.

130. Ibid. IV f.116.

131. *V.C.H. York*, p. 482–3; *V.C.H.E.R.*, i, pp. 58, 289, 295; Poulson, *Beverlac*, cited in note 6, pp. 612, 726.

132. *C.P.R.* 1446–52, p. 80; 1446–52, p. 442.

133. For example, *V.C.H. York*, p. 111; *V.C.H.E.R.*, i, p. 58; John Gregg of Hull left money in 1437 for the guild of St. Mary in St. Brigid's church, London. Prob. Reg. III f.507v.

134. For similar acts see Jacob, *Register of Henry Chichele*, cited in note 34, p. xliii.

135. Prob. Reg. III f.268 (Vescy); *C.C.R.* 1349–54, p. 272.

136. Prob. Reg. II f.494 (Pettyclerk); VI, f.216 (Wharton).

137. Ibid. I ff.69 (Aton), 85 (Grantham); Arch. Reg. 10 f.320 (Jarum).

138. Prob. Reg. III ff.487 (Bracebridge), 599 (Esingwold); VIII f.109v. (Howell), XI f.57 (York).

139. Arch. Reg. 18 f.34v. (Rolleston); Prob. Reg. V. f.271 (Coppendale); VI f.12a (Casse).

140. Prob. Reg. III ff.439–440 (Russell); V f.99 (Jakson), and see also VIII f.32 (Gyllyot).

141. The majority, however, were content to leave the funeral arrangements to the discretion of their executors. No contemporaries could justifiably have claimed that the money spent in funerals was excessive: a criticism that was made of Bristol merchants' funerals in the seventeenth century. P. V. McGrath, 'The Wills of Bristol Merchants in the Great Orphan Books', *Trans. Bristol and Gloucestershire Arch. Society*, lxviii, Gloucester, 1949, p. 101.

142. Prob. Reg. II ff.309 (Wilton), 451 (Barton); III f.266v. (Vescy); IX f.147 (Beesby).

143. This was equally popular elsewhere. See A. McHardy, 'Eton College Wills', cited in note 23, p. 391.

144. Prob. Reg. III ff.415–416v. (Blackburn); V f.327v. (Carre). See also Thomas Bracebridge (d.1437), ibid., III ff.487v.–490.

145. M. G. A. Vale concluded that piety and charity cannot be considered separately. *Yorkshire Gentry*, cited in note 30, p. 28.

146. W. K. Jordan, *The Charities of London, 1480–1660*, London, 1960, p. 48. In spite of criticism, his general thesis is supportable. See J. A. F. Thompson, 'Piety and Charity in Late Medieval London', *Jnl. Eccl. Hist.*, xvi (1965), p. 178.

147. Prob. Reg. II ff.86v. (Brompton), 237v. (Garton), 605 (Blackburn); III ff.439 (Russell), 507v. (John Gregg).

148. Some good examples of complicated wills, which must have taxed the executors' patience, are described by E. F. Jacob, *Register of Henry Chichele*, cited in note 34, p. l. Some of these wills involved the distribution of charity to hundreds of paupers in different categories described at great length by the testators.

149. Prob. Reg. III ff.555v.–556 (Joan Gregg); VI f.116 (Wartre); VIII f.33 (Gyllyot).

150. A. Raine, *Medieval York*, London, 1955, p. 217.

151. Prob. Reg. III ff.555v.–556 (Joan Gregg), f.581 (Bowes); VIII f.3 (Chimney).

152. Ibid. I f.38v. (Carleton); II f.342(i)v. (Bridekirk); *V.C.H. York*, pp. 363–5; *V.C.H.E.R.*, i, pp. 333–5; D. Knowles and N. Hadcock, (eds.), *Medieval Religious Houses in England and Wales*, London, 1953, p. 254.

153. Prob. Reg. I ff.16 (Gisburn), 103 (Robert Holme); III ff.254v. (Thomas Holme), 607 (Craven).

154. *V.C.H.E.R.*, i, pp. 333–5; Prob. Reg. VI f.117 (Armstrong).

155. In early fifteenth-century London, the public were accustomed to a certain standard of public hygiene, and it has been argued that there was in fact only a small minority of the citizens who did not co-operate. E. L. Sabine, 'City Cleaning in Medieval London', *Speculum*, xii (1937), pp. 25–7.

156. Cf. Jordan, *The Charities* ..., cited in note 146, p. 21, for the situation in

late fifteenth-century and early sixteenth-century London, where similar bequests, although not unusual, were only a small proportion of all charitable
bequests.

157. Quoted in T. P. Cooper, 'The Medieval Highways, Streets, Open Ditches
and Sanitary Conditions of the City of York', Yorks. Arch. Jnl., xxviii, Leeds, 1913,
pp. 280–1.

158. Arch. Reg. 10 ff.309v.–310 (Coppendale); Prob. Reg. I ff. 15v. (Gisburn),
100v.–103v. (Holme); II ff.327v. (Garton), f.605 (Blackburn); III ff.263 (Kelk), 439v.–
440 (Russell), 507v. (John Gregg), 555v.–556v. (Joan Gregg); V ff.308 (Ince), 327–9
(Carre).

159. Prob. Reg. V f.212 (Neleson). According to Cooper, cited in note 142, pp.
270–86, York's Streets were appalling and in spite of personal donations and
pavage grants, little improvement was made until Elizabeth's reign.

160. Test. Ebor., iv, cited in note 79, p. 213; Hull BRE: 1 f.95.

161. C. Platt, The English Medieval Town, London, 1976, pp. 69–73; V. Parker,
The Making of King's Lynn, London, 1971, pp. 159–162.

162. Bev. Cart. ff.8, 20v.; A. F. Leach, (ed.), Beverley Town Documents, Selden
Society, London, vol. xiv, 1900, pp. 25–7, 46–7.

163. V.C.H. York, pp. 107–8; York M.B. i, pp. 15, 17, 39, 164; Leach, Beverley
Town Documents, pp. 22–3; V.C.H.E.R., i, pp. 74–5, 371, 374–7; Bev. Cart. f.31.

164. The London guildhall was rebuilt in the first half of the fifteenth century.
C. M. Barron, The Medieval Guildhall of London, London, 1974, passim. See also,
Parker, King's Lynn, cited in note 156, p. 12. J. Campbell, 'Norwich', in The Atlas
of Historic Towns, ii, M. D. Lobel and W. H. Johns, (eds.), London, 1975, p. 15.

165. Two others existed, the butchers' and the shoemakers' halls. Raine,
Medieval York, cited in note 150, pp. 65, 186–7.

166. V.C.H. York, pp. 481–3, 542–3; E. A. Gee, 'The Architecture of York', in
The Noble City of York, A. Stacpoole et al., (eds.), York, 1972, pp. 372–3.

167. Thomas Barton and Richard Wartre, for example, left respectively £1 in
1460 and £20 in 1465 towards the York Guildhall. Prob. Reg. II f.451 (Barton); IV
f.116 (Wartre). Similarly in London, Barron, The ... Guildhall, cited in note 164, p.
36.

168. V.C.H.E.R., i, pp. 76, 398, 433; Poulson, Beverlac, cited in note 6, pp.
420–422.

169. Gee, 'The Architecture ...', cited in note 66, p. 368. One elaborate porch
canopy of the late fifteenth–early sixteenth centuries has survived and is now at
Jacob's Well, Trinity Lane. N. Pevsner, Yorkshire: York and the East Riding,
London, 1972, p. 147.

170. V.C.H.E.R., i, pp. 77, 79. In 1388 it had 20 rooms in addition to a chapel,
hall, and tower. A print of c.1541 shows two court-yards and a gatehouse.

171. Ibid. p. 76; Pevsner, Yorkshire, cited in note 169, pp. 17, 180, 268–70.

172. Gee, 'The Architecture ...', cited in note 166, p. 178, 343–4. A similar
rebuilding was underway in fifteenth-century Bristol, E. M. Carus-Wilson, 'Bristol', in Lobel, Historic Towns, cited in note 164, p. 11.

173. V.C.H. York, p. 107; Gee, 'The Architecture ...', cited in note 166, pp.
343–50; Pevsner, Yorkshire, cited in note 169, p. 171.

174. Prob. Reg. II f.393 (Haynson); III ff.436–440 (Russell); V f.7 (Swan), f.309b
(Maliard); VI ff.107 (Goodknapp).

175. P. Gibson, 'The Stained and Painted Glass of York', in Stacpoole, Noble
York, cited in note 166, pp. 69, 137, 164; V.C.H. York, p. 107.

176. Prob. Reg. V. f.7 (Swan); VI f.204v. (Garner); Hull D 179 (Crosse).

177. Individuals left garments to their parish churches, some like the velvet jacket, left by John Petty in 1508, to be altered into vestments; others including 'beds', i.e. hangings, and some garments were also left to be hung near the altar. Reg. Dean and Chapter, ii, f.77v. See also Prob. Reg. IV f.116 (Wartre).

178. Ibid. III f.439 (Russell); VI f.107 (Goodknapp).

179. In the middle of the fifteenth-century the Guild of St. Anthony became responsible for the production of the Paternoster Play, after the guild of that name was absorbed into St. Anthony's. The Mercers' Company performed it in 1488 but in 1496 the Guild of St. Anthony was still putting on an annual performance Y.C.R., ii, p. 118. In the late sixteenth-century it was performed on two occasions in lieu of the Corpus Christi cycle. Raine, Medieval York, cited in note 150, pp. 94–5; K. Young, 'The Records of the York Paternoster Play', Speculum, vii (1932) pp. 540–60. The third cycle, the Creed Play, apparently remained under control of a religious guild. J. S. Purvis, 'The York Religious Plays', in Stacpoole, Noble York, cited in note 166, p. 845.

180. E. K. Chambers, The Medieval Stage, Oxford, 2 vols., 1903, for the dramatic development and literary form of medieval play cycles. For a more provocative interpretation see A. H. Nelson, The Medieval English Stage: Corpus Christi Pageants and Plays, Chicago, 1974.

181. J. R. Witty, 'The Beverley Plays', Trans. Yorks. Dialect Society, part 23, vol. iv (1922), pp. 18–37; A. F. Leach, 'Ordinances of the Beverley Corpus Christi Guild', Proc. Soc. Antiquaries, 2nd series, xv (1894), pp. 103–8.

182. York M.B., i, pp. 134, 136, 185.

183. See for example A. F. Johnston and M. Dorrell, 'The York Mercers and their Pageant of Doomsday, 1433–1526', in Leeds Studies in English, N.S. A. C. Cawley and S. Ellis, (eds.) v (1971), pp. 29–34.

184. York M.B., ii, pp. 64, 146; Y.C.R., i, p. 5.

185. M. Dorrel, 'The Mayor of York and the Coronation Pageant', Leeds Studies, N.S. v (1971), cited in note 183, pp. 34–45.

186. Bev. GGB ff.12b, 16, 26.

187. York Chamberlains' account roll, 1397; Y.C.R., i, p. 81; Bev. Acct. 1423.

188. There were complaints at a public meeting in 1416, that certain individuals were profiteering from the seat-charges paid at the pageant stations. York M.B., ii, p. 64. Thereafter the council was to receive one third of the receipts. On a later occasion in 1432 there were complaints that the crafts were using the plays as a means to advertise. Ibid. p. 172.

189. York M.B., ii, pp. 156–8.

190. C. Davidson, 'Northern Spirituality and the Late Medieval Drama in York', in E. R. Elder, (ed.), The Spirituality of Western Christendom, Kalamazoo, Michigan, 1976, pp. 129–30.

191. Y.C.R., i, pp. 155–9; A. H. Smith, 'A York Pageant, 1486', London Medieval Studies, London, 1939, pp. 382–98.

192. Y.C.R., p. 156.

193. Sylvia Thrupp's estimate of literacy in London; (40 per cent Latin readers and 50 per cent English readers) was based on the recorded literacy of 116 male witnesses before the consistory court, 1467–1476, Merchant Class, cited in note 2, pp. 156–8. Nicholas Orme believes that merchant literacy meant the ability to read Latin without an understanding of the niceties of grammar, and the ability to read and write in English and French. N. Orme, English Schools in the Middle Ages, London, 1973, pp. 47–8.

194. Orme, English Schools, cited in note 193, pp. 43–45.

195. Robert Louth of York paid his clerk for drawing up his will and other documents in 1407. Prob. Reg. III f.265. See also John Carre. *Test. Ebor.*, iii, cited in note 79, p. 300.

196. Cf. Thrupp, *Merchant Class*, cited in note 2, pp. 161–2.

197. This impression is confirmed by other studies. M. Deanesly, 'Vernacular Books in England in the Fourteenth and Fifteenth Centuries', *Modern Language Review*, xv (1920), p. 23. Vale, *Yorkshire Gentry*, cited in note 30, p. 29.

198. An impression borne out by the selection of books available in a city bookshop in 1538. D. M. Palliser and D. G. Selwyn, 'The Stock of a York Stationer, 1538', *The Library*, London, 1972, pp. 207–219. For an account of the city's printing history, R. Davies, *A Memoir of the York Press*, London, 1868; E. G. Duff, *The Printers, Stationers, and Bookbinders of York up to 1600*, York, 1900.

199. Many copies of popular primers in the vernacular survive from the beginning of the fifteenth century and were apparently used by non-Latinists who wished to follow services. J. W. Adamson, *The Illiterate Anglo-Saxon and Other Essays on Education, Medieval and Modern*, Cambridge, 1946, p. 40.

200. Prob. Reg. II f.494 (Pettyclerk); III ff.410–411 (Cateryk), 450 (Louth); *Test. Ebor.*, ii, p. 117.

201. Prob. Reg. II, 19n.; Prob. Reg. III ff.439–440 (Russell); IV. f.116 (Wartre), 503–504v. (Ormeshead); Raine, *Medieval York*, cited in note 150, p. 83.

202. V.C.H.E.R., i, p. 348; Bev. Acct. 1366; A. F. Leach, *Early Yorkshire Schools*, i, Yorks. Arch. Society Record series, xxvii, 1899, pp. xxxix–li, 1, 10–29; Orme, *English Schools*, cited in note 193, pp. 296, 321.

203. Prob. Reg. II f.87v. (Brompton); III f.439 (Russell); IV f.79 (Day); f.185 (Stockdale).

204. Cf. Thrupp, *Merchant Class*, cited in note 2, pp. 279–87, on the problems of definition. W. T. McCaffrey, *Exeter, 1540–1660*, Cambridge, Mass, 1948, p. 261 points to the problems of accumulating sufficient land even in the late sixteenth century.

205. Prob. Reg. II, ff.86v.–90v. (Brompton), 619–20 (Northeby); VIII ff.32–4 (Gyllyot).

206. V.C.H. York, p. 63; Y.C.R., iv, p. 173; Collins, *Freemen of York*, cited in note 14, p. 246.

207. E.g. The Coppendales of Beverley, Prob. Reg. V f.486v; Arch. Reg. 5 f.419; John, son of Simon Grimsby merchant of Hull, styled himself gentleman. Prob. Reg. III ff.398v, 471v.

208. The sons of Thomas Esingwold and William Cleveland of York, became priests. Prob. Reg. II f.531; Sellers, *York Mercers*, cited in note 86, p. 80; Robert, son of William Rolleston of Beverley, became provost of St. John's of Beverley and the son of William Alcock of Hull's son became bishop of Ely. Prob. Reg. II f.370; *Test. Ebor.*, iii, p. 42n.

209. Not many have been traced, but the most extensive gentry marriages were in the York family. See genealogy on page 49.

3

The episcopate

RICHARD G. DAVIES

The invective against the later medieval episcopate handed down by contemporary critics and Protestant apologists as a critique is now little trusted. Yet, by their nature, the surviving records of administration, called in to substantiate or counter such accusations, have not done much more to demonstrate any vigorous spirit within organized religion of the kind that critical observers have expected to see.[1] Some notable historians, seeing the obvious importance of political and other secular factors in the making of bishops in the later middle ages, have discussed the character and working of the episcopate almost entirely, and unfavourably, in such terms. Whilst many studies of individual bishops and dioceses and some perceptive syntheses have indeed promoted more sympathetic conclusions,[2] there is a tendency to discount these as exceptional or purely relative qualifications and to treat the episcopate still as something of a generic term for past and present officers of the Crown, with all that might seem to imply; even, more generally, to dismiss the majority of the bishops as absentee, or, if by chance resident, negligent towards the pastoral and spiritual needs of the dioceses in which they lived; or to assume that, even if they did have some more lively interest in the needs of the Church they ruled, they lacked the requisite experience or understanding of them; or to suppose, accepting the record evidence at face value, that, in any case and at best, they saw their role almost entirely in administrative, judicial or political terms.

All this, however, can become too one-sided, generalized or misconstrued. It would not be far wrong to say that the great majority of bishops were actually highly conscientious and thought they were making a fair job, as they understood it, of the spiritual as well as temporal responsibilities of their episcopal office. Nor indeed—for the defence can even be carried into attack—were they complacent. In the later fourteenth and fifteenth centuries, many clergy, quite as much as laity, and orthodox as much as heretic, did indeed feel that things could be better—or at least

51

different—and even tried to do something about it.[3] Certainly
there was not the simple confrontation of the textbooks between
'reactionary' establishment and 'reforming' critics. Many of the
higher clergy, even whilst adopting a cautious stance in public and
wary of change, saw the need for more positive, perhaps more
individual, spirituality. Predictably enough, they were divided
amongst themselves between some who, seeing no need for
changes in substance, yet wanted greater and closer direction by
the church authorities to prove more obviously the merits of the
status quo, some who did favour a measure of reform, and a few
even who were a good deal more radical. In this, they were, let it be
said, no more divided than their critics, who urged upon them
quite contradictory (and at times frightening) advice and criticism,
most of it well-meant, some of it not, and a good deal of either sort
that was wildly impracticable.[4] This, of course, has not prevented
it appealing to historians.

The ecclesiastical hierarchy had no more desire than most other
authorities to abdicate voluntarily or undermine their own position. But what moved them quite as much was their sense of a
responsibility laid upon them by their office, a responsibility not
hypocritically conceived to justify their own authority or privilege
but one for which they felt they would have to answer in full.
Whilst, too, there is plentiful evidence to justify the charges of
Gascoigne and others of much intrigue, ambition, and corruption
within the higher clergy for the rich plum of episcopacy, this does
not prove a priori that the successful contender would wantonly
neglect his episcopal office once he had obtained it. Far from it.
Contemporary moralists—Bromyard, Gascoigne, and so on—could
convict bishops (too often by rhetoric and affirmation rather than
hard evidence) of every sort of inadequacy, weakness, sin, and vice
by reference to the individual failings of individual men, but many
more prelates showed real care in the execution of their office, and
a personal faith besides. To prove, with certain advantages of
hindsight, that they were misguided is not to prove that they were
malicious or insincere.

In characterizing this period as a time of at least relative intellectual stagnation, academic historians and theologians have had in
mind the highest reaches of theoretical speculation. Even in these
terms this view has not always gone unchallenged. What may be
more important for the present is to note that on a more practical
level there was certainly very lively contemporary debate, embracing all aspects of the form and organization of religion and

reaching out into areas which one might now think of rather as social and political.[5] It would be an anachromism to see this emphasis on the applied rather than the pure, on the practical rather than the theoretical, as intellectual debasement. It is true that such debate failed to provoke really great minds to really great theses. Nevertheless, even if it could be shown that it was generally conducted in over-pragmatic or over-practical terms, it was by no means small-minded or unconstructive. And, by word and deed, the episcopate played a notable part, and sometimes one more positive, certainly less blindly repressive, than has generally been allowed.

Some historians have been surprisingly ready to treat the episcopal hierarchy as monolithic and unchanging in outlook in the century and a half before the Reformation. Bishops came from diverse backgrounds, they won their episcopal promotions in differing circumstances and for different reasons, and they responded to their office differently. All but a relative few had had to make their own way, especially as their path rose higher.[6] They were, therefore, generally able, well-educated, and with a wide range of experience between them. As a whole, they represent no obvious decline from the standards of their predecessors.[7] It is to this diversity of factors that this essay seeks to draw some attention, and in particular, on this occasion, to the intellectual and educational backgrounds of the episcopate. Such basic points need to be established before any wide-ranging implications of the episcopate's cultural persona can even begin to be discussed.

A first consideration is, necessarily, that of their formal education, especially at university. During the period which is to be considered particularly, 1375–1461, bishops were once more recruited in increasing numbers from amongst university-trained clergy, indeed from amongst graduates of the higher faculties.[8] But what exactly did this signify? What aspects of a university education were now being seen as important? Were these seen as directly essential in the making of a bishop, or were there other public needs and careers which stood between, and made the link only an indirect one? How do these aspects and apparently valued qualifications reflect changing priorities within the Church and the realm? And what were the effects, practical or intellectual, of the return of graduates to the leadership of the Church? These are questions raised rather than answered by this essay, but they must be borne in mind.

Before considering the university-trained bishops, however,

there is first an important minority of the bench to be considered:
the non-graduates. In 1375, seven out of the nineteen bishops in
office had not been to university.[9] Six of these held bishoprics of
the first rank, because they were 'Tout's bishops', the royal
administrators.[10] By contrast, the six doctors then on the bench
were not in possession of the more substantial bishoprics, and,
significantly, none owed his promotion primarily to service to the
Crown. Although by September 1399 (the end of Richard II's reign)
no fewer than twenty-one graduates had been promoted (not all of
them, of course, then still alive), and quite a number had enjoyed
important translations besides, non-graduates still occupied several important bishoprics, including Canterbury itself. Whilst several of the fourteen doctors promoted between 1375 and 1399 owed
much to royal favour, none had started his career with the Crown,
and as a body they were not closely tied to its interests.

Henry IV and Henry V, supported by Archbishops Arundel and
Chichele, exercised generally a fairly firm hand over episcopal
appointments so far as they were able, but were thoughtful and
broadminded in their approach to the matter. The menace of Lollardy, perhaps exaggerated by historians and appreciated more
realistically by some contemporaries in authority, provoked no
change in policy in the matter of appointments. Nevertheless, as
many as seven out of twenty-four graduates promoted between
1399 and 1422 were theologians, and more will be said of them.[11]
Only four non-graduates were appointed, namely, two former
keepers of the privy seal and two abbots. A detailed examination
of the careers of the graduate-bishops of these years indicates,
however, that academic distinction was still much less of an essential merit than others, notably professional competence (in particular if it was noted by the Crown).

The domination of the bench by non-graduates had reflected
principally their important services in royal administration, in
which many had made their whole careers. In 1375 they had occupied nearly two-fifths of the episcopal bench, and influential
places at that. Under Richard II they attracted only a quarter of the
promotions, under Henry IV and Henry V less than one-fifth. Between 1422 and 1461, leaving Lewis of Luxembourg (who held Ely
in commendam) aside, and, for the moment, Archbishop William
Booth, the only non-graduates promoted were Thomas Cheriton
and John Wells, the one the duke of Gloucester's confessor, the
other a papal nominee; and both obtained only humble Welsh
bishoprics. Booth was unique as a product of Gray's Inn of Court,

reflecting the new interest amongst the gentry in providing their sons with a more utilitarian training in law, generally without entering holy orders. Booth's career, leading eventually to the see of York, reflected this utilitarian emphasis closely, and his success not unexpectedly incurred the especial wrath of academic observers, Gascoigne at least.[12] Yet only fifty years earlier critics could not have made such surprise sound real. Such was the change that had taken place. Whilst the bench remained as a whole, until 1443 anyway, largely composed of men of primarily administrative experience, as in the period before 1375, such men were, by now, not only graduates in the main but graduates who had achieved the doctorate. Furthermore, few had been lifelong 'civil servants' as so many of the non-graduates had been, but rather they were now being commissioned by the Crown to provide specific duties and services in government and diplomacy, often of an expert kind, whilst still retaining other independent interests and responsibilities.

Between 1375 and 1461 one hundred and twenty-eight bishops held dioceses in England and Wales. Seculars and regulars alike reflect the emphasis in this period upon a thorough academic training. Although twenty-seven bishops had not entered a university, the remainder, once there, had generally persevered to higher degrees. Seventy-six went to Oxford, fifteen to Cambridge, one each to Bologna and Toulouse, with seven whose university is unknown.[13] There was no marked difference between Oxford and Cambridge either in choice of discipline or in level of achievement. Of the one hundred and one attenders upon university, twelve (including, it may be noted, six of noble origins) left during, or after completing only, the basic arts course. Of the remaining eighty-nine, no less than sixty-four achieved a doctorate, far above the average of all known students of higher faculties.[14]

As ever, various talents jostled for recognition within the universities. Obviously the role of universities cannot be discussed only in terms of academic qualifications, even as a substitute for a real appreciation of the intellectual standing of the episcopate. The syllabus of the university may have stunted but it did not prohibit a wide range of intellectual interests. As many an episcopal will can testify, the churchman who was a lawyer by profession often had an additional interest in some aspect of theology or other philosophical discipline, with a good miscellany of other tastes not going unrepresented. Even the real academic interests of some bishops lie concealed behind their formal qualifications; William

Rede, bishop of Chichester (1368), a well-known example, held a doctorate in theology but was principally and eminently a mathematician and astronomer.[15] Nor, of course, was intellectual distinction the only goal of the university student. There were contacts to be made at university which would serve in later life, whether to assist in an administrative career or in a political or social connection. Indeed, political and institutional activities within the universities themselves were externally thought important in themselves and so might win recognition or notoriety. Many bishops had held positions at the head of halls, colleges and the universities.[16]

As in all epochs, the major rival to intellectual and scholarly distinction as the final purpose of a university was the training of useful, vocationally-directed young graduates.[17] Whatever the overall state of graduate employment, it was still those with a training in a vocational or professional discipline who were best-regarded by both secular and ecclesiastical authorities and could find support for their studies and a subsequent career. When the university authorities appealed for more ecclesiastical preferment for their members, they had most earnestly in mind the support of academics. When the English church authorities responded, they did so, in practice if not in intention, in favour of useful administrators.[18] However much they appreciated the benefit to the Church and realm of a scholarly elite, few had the resources to spare for men who could not give them immediately useful service. Such 'useful' graduates rose in turn to become great men and patrons. It was not that the scholar was despised. But the most obvious needs of the Church, which were thought of, at least until the second quarter of the fifteenth century, as administrative and political needs, dictated the policy of recruitment and, in due course, of promotion to the hierarchy. In this respect, high-birth, and the influence this implied, was regarded openly and honourably as a valuable and important qualification.[19] Whilst scholarship or rather, much more broadly, *scientia* was an accepted and conventional attribute in a candidate, it needed evidence of practical application besides.[20] Intellect, theory and idealism, without practical application, must have seemed luxuries to the hard-working rulers of Church and realm. The ideal candidate, such as George Neville, combined all: 'blood, virtue and cunning'.[21]

In the long-term the church leaders may have been misguided. But, in seeing things primarily in the short-term, they were hardly exceptional. What may be more remarkable is the way in which many of even the hardest-headed administrators, even men who had not been to university, kept in touch with the broader theoretical perspectives of their role as leaders of morals and religion, appreciated scholarship, even when they could not relate it to their own pressing immediate tasks, and sought in their private lives and in their episcopacy at least to aim after higher ideals.

If the universities were languishing at this time by the very highest intellectual and academic standards, they remained preeminent in education. Whilst there were facilities and opportunities for both poor scholars and for laymen seeking a basic general education in, especially, legal and business administration, these indeed making up the great proletariat of the university population, the higher faculties, the centres for advanced study, were for the privileged. Within the mass of students seeking, whether or not in the face of difficulty, at least a basic scholastic education, only a few were able to afford, let alone to be sufficient academically, to continue in the higher faculties. Entry into these of itself marked one as a member of a very small elite.[22] Thus, as graduates in the higher faculties came to dominate the episcopal bench, this 'meritocracy' was defined by a common access to education, with commensurate financial support, thus presupposing, happy fortune apart, an advantage in birth in the majority of cases. This is indeed the case, empirically tested: the bench became increasingly dominated by men hailing from what may be very roughly termed 'county society'.

Amongst the university graduates the choice of academic discipline could do much to determine the pre-episcopal career. In particular, a degree in theology was much less likely to lead into a career as a professional administrator, whether in secular or ecclesiastical service. However, it would be rash to guess at the character and opinions of individual bishops simply on the basis of their academic training. It would be unconvincing, for example, to commend the appointment of theologians to the bench as holding better prospects for the welfare of the Church, especially of the dioceses. It cannot, of course, be ignored that lawyers, men who served their pre-episcopal careers in an administrative capacity as such, became increasingly prominent on the episcopal bench in the period before 1443; or that, during the adult years of Henry VI, a reaction in favour of the appointment of theologians took place, which in turn was reversed in 1461. However much one yields to the traditional view that the Church as an institution was now so entrenched in routine and character as to defy any human influ-

ence upon it, the sort of careers to which the particular training
took men of each kind can only have influenced their government
of the Church. However, it seems very likely that an emphasis
upon this variety of approach could easily become exaggerated,
and that overlapping or shared interests, values and experience
could be at least as weighty factors in much that the bishops had
to do. Reaction to the demands of the Crown might be one point,
for example, where differences could be seen, and maybe treatment of religious dissent is another. But classification is an uneasy
business, and academic discipline is but one influence amongst
many.

With such reservations firmly in mind, we may consider first the
forty-one theologians, of whom all but eight were doctors.[23] Their
numbers on the bench increased sharply after 1375, even more so
after 1422, and, qualitatively as well as quantitatively, achieved a
notable peak between 1443 and 1461. There is, however, one important point to be noted at once. In Richard II's reign all nine
theologians were in regular orders, and between 1399 and 1422
five more of such a sort were promoted. It is not possible to say
with certainty how much such men owed to their academic discipline, how much to their religious vocation. It would be unwise
to prefer the first suggestion simply by reason of the promotions
between 1415 and 1419 of three secular theologians, the first since
William Rede in 1368 and all of them (like Rede) scholars of some
distinction. These appointments seem to be individual rewards
and no part of any conscious policy.[24] Between 1422 and 1443, as
appointments became less closely related to service in the public
administration of the Crown, promotions were made of six secular
and three religious theologians, that is to say, nine out of twenty-
two men promoted to the episcopate in that time. Of course, this
meant some change in the character of those promoted and the
type of bishopric they secured. But, more significantly, the bishoprics they obtained remained generally of a modest kind. Of the
overall total of thirty-six episcopal appointments held by theologians between 1375 and 1443, thirteen were in Wales (all but one
being held by religious) and thirteen more (involving only four
seculars) at Chichester, Rochester, and Carlisle, the least well-
endowed of English bishoprics. Even when theologians secured
translation, their positions improved only relatively.

In those few cases before 1443 where theologians—usually
seculars—did do very well, their academic qualification certainly
determined the character of their subsequent distinction, but gen-

erally there were more critical factors in the gaining of their promotion. Most notably, they were all able, in a personal or public way, to place their talents at the service of the Crown. Certainly, however, more eminent promotions of theologians did increase in number after 1399, before which time only Archbishop Waldby of York (1396–7) had achieved real distinction. With the possible (but debatable) exception of Waldby, again, all such promotions were of men who were thorough-going churchmen, as indeed were nearly all the theologians. It is worth remarking, however, on the relatively modest rewards of so many of the theologians who served the Crown in purely ecclesiastical ways. Successive royal confessors (for whom episcopacy was by no means automatic) and favoured chaplains in fact did little better in respect of the quality of their promotions than those of their colleagues promoted independently of royal influence. On the other hand, it may be said in passing that the pope did little with the opportunities he had to promote such men.

Without going into further detail, one may characterize the theologians thus far. Before 1443, nineteen of the theologians were in regular orders, most of whom first achieved a certain degree of prominence through their own orders or in their own houses but then attracted the notice of the government in some way. Of these, six became confessor to the king before their promotions. Of the seculars, four had entered the royal chapel, four were long-term university scholars, and John Rickingale (Chichester, 1426) was confessor to John, duke of Bedford. Evidently, reward by promotion to the episcopate was restricted in the case of theologians to very few careers and positions. Promotions were, furthermore, neither rapid nor lavish. Even theologians of eminence must needs be men of vocation rather than ambition.

The period between 1443 and 1461 was, however, a notable one for the theologians and needs a little explicit attention. In these years sixteen of the twenty-five bishops promoted to the bench were theologians.[25] Including now both seculars and religious, they took a virtual monopoly over appointments to middling and lesser sees. Furthermore, theologians were appointed to Norwich in 1446, Lincoln in 1450, Coventry and Lichfield in 1452, and Ely in 1454. Winchester, and Coventry and Lichfield, had never before had a graduate in theology as their bishop, Norwich none appointed since 1343, Ely none since 1361. And, in 1454, Thomas Bourgchier, albeit only a scholar in the faculty and promoted for distinctly political reasons, became the first archbishop of Canterbury with any sort of formal university training in theology since the great Thomas Bradwardine (d.1349).[26] Furthermore, whereas between 1443 and 1449 eight promotions or translations were made of theologians as against seven of lawyers (including William Booth), from 1450 to the end of the dynasty fifteen promotions or translations of theologians (including the scholars, Bourgchier and George Neville) were offset by only seven of others. True, amongst these latter were major appointments to Canterbury, York, Durham, Lincoln, and Salisbury, but the seven make up so miscellaneous a group as actually to confirm that the long-standing opportunities for lawyers in the service of church and realm were now much less abundant.[27]

Before 1450 the promotion of confessors and chaplains associated with the court accounts for much of the theologians' numerical and even qualitative importance.[28] However, whilst it was court notice and employment which singled them out for promotion, they were essentially churchmen, not politicians, and indeed a group of considerable distinction. Reginald Boulers, Abbot of Gloucester (Hereford, 1450; Coventry and Lichfield, 1453) was, however, a case apart, an unequivocal politician. Two masters of influential London hospitals, John Carpenter (Worcester, 1444) and Reginald Pecock (St. Asaph, 1444; Chichester, 1450), both well-known for their pastoral work amongst the better-educated laity, and the former a respected figure in Oxford and the province of Canterbury generally, also had promotions, and, after a struggle with a reluctant government, Cardinal Kemp secured London for his nephew and client, Thomas Kemp, in 1450, perhaps one of the least deserved of any promotions in these later years. However, it is an interesting point that the two regulars, Stanbury and Boulers, were regarded, probably correctly, as much more politically-implicated than any of their secular colleagues. For, of the four further regular-theologians who were promoted, all to Welsh sees, after 1450, three were also subsequently regarded, or at least treated, as intransigently Lancastrian and politically unacceptable after 1461 in a way that few of their fellow-bishops were to be.[29]

Whilst, in fact, only four secular theologians were promoted to the bench after 1450, all were of considerable distinction. John Chedworth (Lincoln, 1451) and John Hales (Coventry and Lichfield, 1459) were both men of established reputation at the universities and in the Canterbury province. Both attracted the attention of the Crown, the one as the first effective provost of King's College, the other as chaplain and chancellor to Margaret of Anjou, and both

served the House of Lancaster until its fall. Each, however, was
also to prove an outstanding diocesan and neither suffered political recriminations under the new dynasty.

Of even greater intellectual lustre were two theologians promoted during, and probably by reason of, the Duke of York's pro-
tectorates, William Grey II (Ely, 1454) and George Neville (Exeter,
1456). Both of most notable birth, cousins indeed, they shared a
lively interest in both traditional and novel approaches to scholarship. Grey had served some years as king's proctor in the papal
curia, whilst Neville, still only twenty-three, was already the chancellor and current star of the University of Oxford. It was after
their promotions that their careers diverged. Grey, initially not in
sympathy with the ruling house, stood almost entirely detached
from political life and remained the bibliophile and patron. Neville,
formidably, had more than enough talent to exploit the opportunities given him by his birth, but it was in the end his birth
which blighted his career just as it had inspired it. Eloquent,
sharp-witted, practical, fiercely orthodox and devoted to Oxford,
the turbulent politics of his family were to allow only glimpses of
the great administrative and religious reforms he might have
achieved as a bishop and, later, archbishop.

There is, overall, nothing to suggest that Henry VI's government
was looking to theologians explicitly for theoretical or practical
contributions to some distinctive kind of rule. Edward IV was to
reverse the favour once more, to promote lawyers more freely as in
times past. Whether it was wise of the Lancastrian government to
use so much of its best ecclesiastical patronage in favour of
churchmen rather than politicians or administrators is a moot
point, which would require some wide enquiry to be answered at
all objectively. What should be emphasized, however, is that the
Lancastrian leaders were taking up men of established calibre as
their religious and ecclesiastical advisers and then finding them
preferment to which they were certainly equal. Whilst this perhaps did little for the strength of the government, it promised
considerable value to the Church.

The regulars continued to be confined to the lesser sees. They
attracted, too, the greater political hostility as confidants of an
unpopular regime, but in this respect they could quote many
equally unfortunate predecessors over the years and it is no certain reflection upon them. It may be doubted, too, whether Grey
and Neville, whilst obviously benefiting from political favour, were
appointed with primarily political motives in mind in the first

instance. Grey certainly made no political payment, whilst Neville had virtually a birthright to a bishopric, like every comital son in orders before him. What might be remarked upon, however, is the actual existence of such well-born students of theology. Bourgchier and Beaufort, amongst others, provide parallel instances of young noblemen who could be confident that their careers would start 'at the top' and that they would, with hardly a doubt, be leaders of the Church. They too—if probably with less dedication than Grey or Neville—studied theology rather than law in preparation for their office. If law was the discipline for those with a career to make in the Church, theology seems to have been the choice for those with no ambition to make a career and for those who had it made.

Until 1443, however, and after 1461 the lawyers were very much the dominant group amongst graduate-bishops. It is probably more important to note this dominance and the possible effect it had on the character of the episcopate than to scrutinise closely the precise levels of academic attainment of members of the group. Forty-four lawyers sat on the bench before 1461. Twenty of these had a qualification in both the canon and civil law, sixteen in only the civil law, eight in only the canon law. These last were a miscellaneous group, of whom two (Thomas Appleby and Thomas Brinton) had been promoted before 1375. William Barrow was a university administrator, but, like Benedict Nicoll and Lawrence Child, both of whom had worked in the Curia, he probably owed his promotion to the pope. Late in the period, the cases are rather different. John de la Bere and John Langton filled financial offices under the Crown and in swift succession, in 1446–7, were appointed to the bishopric of St. David's. As for Richard Beauchamp, a case apart, he himself said he 'grew up almost from the cradle' under Henry VI's patronage, and time spent at Oxford and then prominently in government preceded his promotion to Hereford (1448) and Salisbury (1450). All the canon lawyers, save only Beauchamp, had had only very modest episcopal promotions, and they play no significant part in the present discussion. One might merely note that they did have a minor revival in that same latest part of the period when theologians were doing so well. More generally, it is worth remarking how those qualified only in the canon law yielded place in the later fourteenth century to those who had studied both laws. These latter more than compensated numerically for the disappearance for sixty years of the pure canonist, which may have coincided with the sharp reduction in men

promoted by the pope from amongst officials in his curia. At all
events, the miscellaneous character of the group, and their individual careers, suggests no strong continuing influence of canonistic
thought upon the bench as a whole, even though, of course, the
practical implementation of the canon law, as William Lyndwood
showed, remained of basic importance to the episcopate as a
whole.

Had the young cleric examined, cynically, the best prospects for
promotion, especially rapid promotion, in the last quarter of the
fourteenth century, he would have concluded that success was
most likely to go to those who were of distinguished blood or who,
from an early age, excelled in royal service. Administrative service
to the Church, but especially at mere diocesan level, was, by contrast, not only unremunerative in terms of episcopal promotions
but also did no more than afford a very slow means of ascent even
for those who did at last achieve the episcopate. However, as the
period went on, more and more bishops were appointed who had
entered ecclesiastical, and even especially diocesan, service.[30] This
represented, in effect, a return to the pattern of earlier times.[31]
Apart from the religious, who favoured theology, the majority of
these successful ecclesiastical administrators were men with a
training in both civil and canon law. Nevertheless, they could not
suppose from precedent that their ecclesiastical service was but a
showpiece either for recruitment to royal service or directly for
promotion to episcopacy. Despite any current ' recession ', academic achievement would probably, if applied practically, bring in time
a comfortable accumulation of diocesan and capitular preferment,
but most certainly, so it seemed, it would not lead to swift episcopal promotion. Although after 1416, at latest, graduates virtually
monopolised promotions to the episcopate, this was especially because such men had, in the end, given service to the Crown. It was
not the direct result of their academic training and qualifications
as such, and, indeed, it was often fortuitous.

Between 1399 and 1443 the numbers of lawyers on the bench
rose from a quarter of the total to two-fifths. More impressive, their
promotions were to more eminent sees. By this time more experienced diocesan and provincial administrators were being recruited
directly for high office and external commissions under the
Crown.[32] Such a development is one of the most important points
to emerge from a study of the episcopate by academic groupings.
The trends which it represents had already been evident under
Richard II in the promotions of experienced churchmen with a

training in both civil and canon law like Edmund Stafford, Walter Skirlaw and Richard Scrope, but under Henry IV and Henry V a whole generation of men, exemplified by Robert Hallum, Henry Chichele, Philip Morgan, John Kemp, Thomas Polton, John Catterick, and Henry Ware, came into prominence. Then and thereafter, until 1443, whilst certainly the sons of magnates continued to enjoy a share of the well-worthwhile and best appointments, as did the occasional careerist officer of state, such as William Alnwick (a civil lawyer), a training in law, preferably in both laws, and service in ecclesiastical administration came to offer one of the best opportunities to rise, *in time*, to episcopal status. Most of the lawyers who were successful in this way could not have thought of their training so explicitly in such terms. First, however, the strain imposed upon the royal administration by Henry V's war effort necessitated recruitment of officials out of the Canterbury administration. Then the rule by a regency council that included several bishops in the years following encouraged further secondments of men from ecclesiastical to royal administration and, in addition, the episcopal promotions of such men in due course. Thus such men came to unexpected eminence, and brought with them a wealth of experience in both the administration of the Church and the needs of the state.

Bishoprics differed greatly in value and character. Although there was, of course, much more to a candidate for promotion than the fact that he possessed a university degree, it is nonetheless interesting to relate academic distinction and discipline to the kind of bishoprics secured. Those men promoted who had studied only the basic arts course did very well because, by definition, they had needed weighty distinction of other kinds to reach the episcopate at all, that is, distinction by birth or service to the Crown. Generally speaking, also, non-graduates outside the religious orders who reached the bench also did very well in the type of see they secured. And this, too, was for other reasons: they had to be, as indeed they were, men of particular talents in service. Contrary to what is often said, very few men destined for greater bishoprics were first placed for convenience or as a kind of 'probation' in lesser bishoprics.[33] Although there was indeed a much greater turnover in the lesser sees, this was due much less to translations than to the kind of bishop promoted. Men of long, devoted service in the dioceses, the curia, the universities or the regular orders, or even men who had served the king's spiritual needs, were rewarded with these humbler bishoprics late in life, with correspondingly fewer years left to them. Perhaps not surprisingly, therefore, there were only thirteen translations in the whole period which carried a bishop from one of the 'lesser' to one of the 'greater' bishoprics.[34] Although seven of these involved lawyers, there were twenty-two other such graduates who had to be satisfied with their humbler promotions. These were, in the main, the men of their kind with least connection with the Crown.

The civil lawyers and the graduates in both civil and canon law have certain well-defined characteristics. Nearly all were of quite substantial birth. Their origins, education, and eventual handsome promotions might together suggest strong advantages leading ine- vitably to success, but a closer view of individual careers tends to cast doubt on such a conclusion. Not only did virtually all (save Henry Despenser and Marmadule Lumley, men of noble birth) engage in a pre-episcopal career of some importance and duration, but in many cases this was primarily in ecclesiastical service. As has been suggested, it seems incorrect to suppose that this was intended only as a means whereby to attract the Crown's attention as soon as possible. Certainly men such as Robert Braybrooke (for particular reasons of royal kinship), Roger Harwell, William Aln- wick, Thomas Bekynton, and Lawrence Booth soon entered secular employment, but others such as Chichele, Ware, Kemp, and Morgan achieved positions of authority in the Church before trans- ferring to the service of the Crown. In short, whilst these were certainly men who undertook a university training with a view to making themselves useful in a potentially-rewarding adminis- trative career, they were not as a rule aiming directly for secular advancement, wherein ecclesiastical preferment was only a con- venient 'stop-gap' affording profitable remuneration meantime. If they gave to the episcopate an administrative character, they brought also a collective awareness of the nature of the institution they were to rule and of their obligations towards it. Beyond this basic assessment, we are moving into the realms of subjective opinion.

For most bishops, obviously a quite unrepresentative sample of graduates, time at university had provided a vocational training for useful (if not invariably highly-remunerative) service to the Church or realm. Thus they brought to the bench a professional expertise and expert appreciation of the functioning of the Church as a jurisdictional and/or theological entity. Far fewer bishops, however, were intellectual contributors in their own right, and the two qualities seldom overlapped. Adam Moleyns was virtually unique in his excellence in both respects.[35] The English episcopate has customarily included a leavening of active scholars, particularly so long as the universities were closely tied to the clerical orders, although the cares of episcopal office have often been at the expense of any continuing scholarly interests. In considering a period of intellectual and social uncertainty, sometimes expressed in a conservative reaction but tending towards profound upheaval in the long term, there is, indeed, a particular interest in the extent to which the episcopate did include men of positive scholarly and intellectual attainments. For whilst in practical terms it was the actions of Arundel, William Courtenay and like-minded bishops that made the most significant impression upon theological and intellectual thought, if only of a repressive nature and temporary effect, these were, whatever their authors' personal capacity, more the deeds of worried administrators and rulers than of intellectual leaders. They should not be taken as typical of the episcopate's attitude and quality.

It is very easy to find involvement in controversy and debate of a polemical nature and even appreciation of scholarship in others. Only a handful of bishops, however, were themselves (so far as is known) distinguished by active scholarship beyond their necessary exercises in the university schools, and such scholarship was rarely of itself enough to gain even the humblest promotion. Of course, even from this relatively late period in time much scholarship has left little or no trace of its nature or very existence. Nor is this necessarily a reflection on its quality. Some very notable scholars amongst bishops as amongst other writers may now be quite unrepresented or even unrecognized. Edmund Bromfield of Llandaff (1389), a Benedictine, who was recognized as a notable theologian and teacher, is one case in point. Reputedly a prolific author, not even the titles of his works have survived.[36] Similarly, John Stanbury of Bangor (1448) and Hereford (1453), Henry VI's confessor, was credited by John Bale in the sixteenth century with a whole series of treatises, and certainly did write, but we have no sample of his work.[37]

The interests of most of the identifiable scholars were such as cannot be related easily or directly to the wider social and religious challenges of the time. This, of course, is hardly unusual. It would be anachronistic to expect too obvious a relevance, and, in fact, the gulf between scholars and laymen was maybe no wider than it has ever been. As regards theology, the bishops' surviving contributions are often from their early work in the university schools, which, being specifically useful in the education of others coming behind, had a chance of survival or notice, for example in a college library. The *Reportorium argumentorum* of Stephen Patrington, better-known for his hostility to Wycliffitism, has survived, for example.[38] Perhaps he was also the author of an *expositio* on Numbers and Ruth in the possession of Bishop Fitzhugh.[39] Thomas Peverel, who like Patrington contributed material to Thomas Netter's *Fasciculi Zizaniorum*, worked up, at least according to Bale, *Questiones theologicae*.[40] The canon lawyer, William Lyndwood, was known to Bale also as the author of a commentary on certain of the psalms, which too sounds like a product of early days at Oxford rather than of later interests. John Lowe of St. Asaph (1433) and Rochester (1444), a vigorous theologian certainly and an author with some reputed interest in humanist studies, is said by Bale to have composed *disputationes theologicae* and *lecturae ordinariae*.[41] No doubt he did in the course of his time at Oxford, but what their quality and why they were remembered one cannot say. Perhaps the contribution most intimately connected with the schools was Richard Fleming's development of a new form of the *quaestio*, a refinement of the established methodology of academic study that enjoyed considerable prestige and use in subsequent years.[42]

Whatever may have been lost, it seems clear that the bishops generally did not continue their scholarly work or contribute as authors after the completion of their studies at university. Here, as in other respects, Bale was to lay claim to knowledge and sources which otherwise have left little trace. Roger Whelpdale of Carlisle (1419), a mathematician according to more immediate authorities, is attributed by Bale with one treatise, perhaps of a popular sort, *de rogando Deo*. Robert Mascall of Hereford (1404) was also singled out (surely from amongst many) for his charge *ad Herefordenses et Salopienses*.[43] (Maybe, to be fair to Bale, it was of some singularly ambitious or original nature.) More certainly, Edmund Lacy of Exeter (1420), a churchman and scholar who seems only narrowly to have missed true greatness, fame and reverence both in his life and after his death, did compose a treatise of a probably more scholarly sort, *de quadruplici sensu Sacre Scripture*.[44] But, again, this has not survived. More influential at the time was his office for St. Raphael, which was quickly adopted in several dioceses.[45]

The 'fact' that the ecclesiastical authorities responded with indignation, prohibition and persecution to the criticisms and ideas

of the Lollards in particular, rather than by measured discussion
and programmes for education or reform, is well-enshrined. To
many historians the prelates' chief offence has appeared to be their
simple failure to be persuaded by Lollardy. Yet Wycliffe, it must be
remembered, was confounded by intellectual argument, both directly in debate and by refutation in counter-treatises.[46] And the
Lollards soon found their criticisms of the Church answered by
strong counter-criticisms of their own ideas.[47] Arundel (not without some justification) found Lollards self-righteous and even hyp-
ocritical in manner.[48] Reginald Pecock could see the nature of their
appeal to educated laymen but thought their case illogical and
invalid, even on its own terms. Indeed, he thought their methods
and values only provided a yet stronger case for orthodoxy and, in
numerous writings for lay consumption, he was quite successful in
proving as much.[49]

In the early days of Lollardy, Patrington and Peverel had both
played a part in opposing Wycliffite ideas by preaching and
disputation and, as has been said, by contributing material to
Netter's *Fasciculi Zizaniorum*.[50] John Swaffham of Bangor (1376),
again on the testimony of Bale, wrote directly *Contra
Wiclevistas*.[51] However, with the possible (but at most only par-
tial) exceptions of Patrington, Pecock, and Lowe, it is unlikely that
any episcopal appointments were made in order to promote men
who would make it their first duty to deal with Lollardy, or indeed
of men who had made their name in such a cause. Nor did youthful
dalliance with heresy debar Repingdon or Fleming from promotion, even though, in the first case at least, the bishop continued
to have some sympathy (as did so many, in all probability) with the
moral views of the Lollards. Only rarely was vigorous opposition
to heresy offered explicitly as a virtue in a candidate for promotion, and even then it does not ring true.[52]

Many bishops probably did take a hand in preaching. Certainly,
whatever critics supposed (and do suppose), matters of religion
did occupy their interest as well as their professional obligation. In
regulating the intellectual standards of their clergy, the episcopate
generally accepted quite minimum standards of decency, which,
whilst obviously disappointing in absolute terms, is not the same
thing as saying that they set no standards at all.[53] It was at least
as much a matter of practical limits as of actual disinclination
towards anything better. However, whilst a good deal of the
bishops' efforts, by word, example or written instruction, would
be, by definition, transient and leave no trace, circumstantial evi-

dence does suggest, of course, that much of their work was regulatory and judicial, aiming to maintain existing practices and standards by discipline, rather than being more positive or innovatory
in intention. In fact, however, a surprising number of bishops were
well thought-of in their dioceses. The criteria may have been other
than we would wish but at least such bishops were meeting contemporary criteria. If the cultural content of these was low, the
bishops had plenty of justification for approaching their task in
the way they did.

On the administrative side, of course, the bishops were vastly
more experienced, and, being conscientious as a body, a great deal
of consolidation and improvement of efficiency was achieved
which, whilst it might not be counted scholarly or directly pastoral
or culturally-enhancing, left a clear mark—sometimes good, sometimes not—upon the life of the Church. Necessity and tradition
imposed this role of ' holding the ring' upon them, and whilst some
critics deplored their failure to do more, a majority of their flock
probably did not directly disparage them. It is in their encouragement of others to undertake more specific roles in ministry rather
than in personal contribution that their case may be made. The
greatest intellectual achievement within this administrative frame-
work, and one most influential on the Church, was that of William
Lyndwood, whose celebrated *Provinciale*, completed in 1430, some
years before his episcopal promotion, codified and commented
comprehensively upon the canon law as interpreted in the Canterbury province.[54] Lyndwood's excellence lay not only in scholarly
or theoretical imagination but in his great practical experience of
administering the canon law in the province.[55] Many other
bishops, too, had made their careers as practitioners of law, rather
than theorists. One formal exercise to survive, however, is John
Trefnant's *repetitio* on a book of the Digest, composed in his graduate days at Oxford. However, his episcopal register of Hereford
suggests that Trefnant stood out amongst his colleagues in invok-
ing directly the letter of the canon law in his administration.[56]
Whether there is more than a coincidence here is an interesting
question.

The wills of the bishops do show certainly that at least some
had a broad taste in literary, cultural, and intellectual matters.[57]
However, their personal contributions to subjects beyond theology
and law were no greater than their contributions within those
fields. They led busy, useful lives, competitive in their careers and
unlikely to win advancement by the pursuit of letters *per se*. True,

there are notable exceptions to the rule. The excellent scholarly fame of William Rede was perhaps greatest as an astronomer, although he was indeed a polymath.[58] It is notable, however, that his promotion, to Chichester in 1368, was owed to Archbishop Islip, a zealous patron of his college, Merton. Roger Whelpdale, principal of Queen's College, Oxford, and a notable preacher, was the author of works of logic and mathematics.[59] Such scholarship played its part in his career but hardly more than the fact of his being a native of the Carlisle diocese, for which see alone, as the head of the Oxford college associated with it, he was a strong candidate in a relatively uncompetitive field. It seems probable, besides, that his writings were directly utilitarian manuals, designed for those seeking vocational training in Oxford. One, more famous, example in this genre is the *De Moderno Dictamine* of Thomas Merk, the monk of Westminster and scholar who began a potentially notable career in public life in the last years of Richard II's reign but fell abruptly and forfeited his see of Carlisle when he would not accept the revolution of 1399. His manual on the art of letter-writing lay so firmly in the scholastic tradition yet was so fresh in style and catholic in inspiration and content as to be a considerable success.[60]

There is little sign of interest in historical works or annals in the bishops' wills,[61] and virtually nothing survives to testify to authorship of such work by themselves. Several works have, indeed, been attributed to them, but in ways which seem at best tentative, often very dubious. There is no certainty at all, for example, that William Rede wrote the brief historical studies, including lives of popes, emperors, and archbishops of Canterbury, ascribed to him, but these in any case would be little compared to his greater compositions in other fields.[62] Thomas Rudbourne at least collected historical material, as did John Langdon, according to Rudbourne's nephew, whose *Historia Minor*, which used their evidence, has, however, not survived.[63] Both may even have composed a chronicle of their own. Rudbourne and Edmund Lacy are, by circumstantial evidence, amongst the stronger candidates for the authorship of that skilful propaganda piece, the *Gesta Henrici Quinti*, but the latest editors conclude, 'we doubt whether they have any valid claims'.[64] Roger Walden probably did not write the *Historia Mundi* of MS. Cotton Julius B. XIII.[65] John Lowe, according to Bale, wrote *Temporum Historiae*, but again even the existence of the work remains putative.[66] An attempt has been made to attribute to John Trevor of St. Asaph (1395), amongst much else, the *Continu-*

atio Eulogii Historiarum and the altogether antithetical chronicle
usually (and correctly) attributed to Jean Creton, but such attributions are groundless.[67] And, finally, 'Giles's Chronicle' *might*
have been the work or inspiration of Robert Fitzhugh, but it is
most unlikely.[68]

Although, especially as a consequence of the ecclesiastical diplomacy of the Great Schism and the Conciliar Period, English
bishops and scholars were not unaware of changes in cultural and
intellectual interests on the continent, it was to be near the end of
our period before any serious students of the newer modes were
achieving promotion to the bench. Of course the classics, for example, had long been recognized in England, certainly by scholars
like William Rede, but 'approach and attitude' remained un-
changed in essence.[69] Rede had works by Aristotle and Cicero in
his great library for their content, not for their method or style.[70]
Merk could refer to Horace and (incorrectly) to Cicero, just as he
was not afraid to introduce an English aphorism into his style. But
in either case these were mere incidents by comparison with his
use of medieval Latin examples. More important, his approach to
his subject and his uncritical use of his sources as quarries of fine
phrases declared him a staunch medievalist, if not an inflexible
one, in his approach.[71] In this respect he was not untypical of his
own contemporaries or even of those who followed for several
decades; nor, indeed, of some who were elsewhere thought of as
humanists.[72]

Either side of 1400, exactly at Merk's time, other bishops, Ralph
Erghum and Richard Clifford, thought it politically useful to have,
in Gilbert Stone, an *amanuensis* who could capture the latest supposed epistolary fashion in the papal curia.[73] And Archbishop
Arundel, neither academic nor avowedly intellectual, yet found it
interesting to meet the more progressive Italian scholars such as
Coluccio Salutati whilst in exile in 1397–9, although he imbibed
nothing of their newer approaches to learning.[74] A generation
later, the abbot of St. Albans, John Whethamstede, could still enjoy
a reputation in England for such 'fine writing' as was thought to
appeal in Italy, and was used accordingly by Archbishop Chichele
to plead his cause to an inimical curia.[75] But, in truth, such crude
mimicry was soon being shown up for the verbiage and florid
vulgarity it was by the clear and fluent latinity that more acute and
practical students such as Thomas Bekynton, Adam Moleyns and
William Grey II, all future bishops, were learning from their contacts in the papal curia, with its potential to make a fundamental

contribution not only to pure learning but even to the theory and practice of government.[76] Their true antecessors in England were bishops such as Hallum, Fleming and Fitzhugh, who, whilst Whethamstede obfuscated, were impressing successive international councils of the Church with their cogency and clarity of argument. In this, as in much else, England's best fruit grew on practical rather than consciously aesthetic boughs.

The bishops, in short, like other patrons, took note of 'humanism' slowly, and through individual interest, for these two identifiable but overlapping reasons, the one aesthetic, the one practical. The political advantages to be gained from being 'in fashion' at the papal curia were obvious. The patronage of modern scholarship, or more specifically literature, apparently seemed rewarding. Hallum and, less predictably, Bubwith, for example, sponsored a translation of Dante's *Divine Comedy* into Latin verse whilst they were at the Council of Constance.[77] But whilst Hallum at least probably had more than a connoisseur's interest in the scholarship he found abroad, there is no sign that he was particularly impressed by it. Political and social factors, too, persuaded Bishop Beaufort to recruit Poggio Bracciolini to his household in 1418. Poggio duly sought out classical texts and, meeting the more utilitarian purpose of his contract, interested one or two of the bishop's officers in classicizing their style, but he found neither inspiration nor real interest in England, and particularly not from Beaufort, whose perennial interest in impressing the papal curia did not extend to achieving any real cultural sensitivity himself.[78]

However, the secretariat of the papal curia had adopted plainly a more classically-influenced style, and envoys to England during the Conciliar Period such as Cesarini and especially Pietro dal Monte were making it more obvious to those in English public life that in both form and content there was something more than aesthetic pleasure to be noted in the new style.[79] The most eminent patron of letters, the duke of Gloucester, being avowedly catholic in taste, had been, in any case, very willing to receive books and scholars illustrative of the new learning, and in time provided a link to Oxford. Whilst such an aesthetic response was not immediately significant, one at least of his own officials, Thomas Bekynton, grasped the opportunity to equip himself for an influential and rewarding career in government and diplomacy. It was, indeed, this practical application of the classical style to forms of correspondence and diplomacy which was the more important facet of the reception of 'humanism' into England. Bekynton saw perfectly well, besides, the political and administrative value of cultivating the leading intellectuals in the papal curia.[80] Likewise, English scholars actually in the curia who could grasp the style *and sense* of the new learning and could work within it were now proving the most valuable amongst proctors and were taken up into royal service. The civil lawyer, Adam Moleyns, was notably adept and, combining an outstanding intellect with both quick practical sense and genuine cultural sensitivity, he alone of Englishmen of the time acquired real respect amongst Italian intellectuals. Yet at the same time he became so invaluable to the English government that he forfeited his leisure for study and eventually, in 1450, met a notorious fate as a disgraced politician.[81]

William Grey II found similar intellectual distinction rather differently. He had travelled as a wealthy young scholar to Cologne, Padua, and Ferrara with the admirable but conservative ambition of widening his study of theology and philosophy. Without losing his principal interests, he found humanist studies and methods attractive. Thus equipped, he too came to be used for several years by the Crown as its proctor in the curia. However, unlike Moleyns, he had no need to be a careerist, and humanism did not make him a fascinated politician or yet move him to innovation as a church leader. Avoiding ensnarement in politics after his return to England and after his achievement of episcopacy, he continued a patron and bibliophile.[82] As such, he may be compared with his cousin, George Neville, who, although less personally experienced in humanistic modes, was interested enough to include practitioners amongst the scholars whom he maintained in his household.[83] Possibly Neville's interest was largely utilitarian, looking for epistolary style first, aesthetic pleasure second, and conceptual depth only last. Maybe, too, he lacked Grey's more scholarly appreciation, but he gave the new studies serious room, not a perfunctory acknowledgment. Although humanist studies remained only a relatively minor interest to both, it was from the lead and patronage of these two (amongst a few others) that scholars like Bishop John Shirwood of Durham (1484) emerged, for whom the new studies were not merely chance contributions to basically traditional scholarship but principal determinants.[84]

However, both in pure scholarship and in practical application to the life of church, government, and society, it must be concluded that by the mid-fifteenth century humanistic interests had as yet played no part of true substance. There seems no evidence, for example, that Moleyns or Bekynton brought anything new in the way of theory to their practice of government.[85] In matters ecclesiastical, too, the debate was still one employing authorities and concepts of medieval descent rather than one inspired by the infusion of any substantially new or rediscovered values.

As to whether the bishops encouraged cultural and intellectual interests in others, and of what kind, and whether rarefied or in direct application to the practice of religion or, indeed, of government, these are big and as yet unanswerable questions. They had their share in new collegiate foundations at Oxford and, more widely and commonly, in the protection and encouragement of the established colleges and of the universities as a whole. In the later part of the period especially, more of them, if still a minority in number and limited in their generosity, encouraged education through bequests and scholarships. They had a part to play in the founding of schools, if not a very notable one and by individual acts rather than as part of any co-ordinated policy. Later in the period a few do seem to share some appreciation of useful education seen apart from any immediate religious or ecclesiastical application, but any such change was slow and hemmed in by the more traditional concepts of charity which so dominated the bishops' thinking.

The caution of the bishops, their understandable reluctance to contemplate the possibility of popular cultural or educational reformation, their nagging belief that education and learning were almost inappropriate and certainly dangerous outside the circle of the carefully trained, and that such training was for specified and controllable ends, may perhaps be seen, too, in their consideration of the use and provision of books. In this respect, the evidence of wills comes to mind at once, but this is evidence notorious in its problems. Of the sixty-four episcopal wills surviving from the period (which vary greatly in detail and content), exactly half make mention of books other than works of practical devotional or liturgical use.[86] One use to which such evidence clearly *cannot* be put is as a full reflection of the real quality or quantity of bishops' libraries or of their own breadth of taste: John Gilbert, Patrington, Fleming, Langdon, and Morgan, academics or intellectuals all, did not mention a book between them; Robert Hallum included only a *liber decretorum* and a book of rosaries. Indeed, only a handful of wills record more than a few books. Several others, improbably, deal with books in only one discipline, and then sometimes only generically. Speculation upon such evidence, in the present context, must be cautious.

Although many bishops retained a close interest in the universities, as has been said, and in particular in their own colleges, and showed as much by their wills, books, at least in the recorded evidence, still did not figure as much as might be expected in their benefactions.[87] Bishops tended to hand on their own basic books to clerical associates and kinsmen rather than deposit them with institutions for common use. Only eight bishops are known to have made bequests of books to universities or colleges, and Dr. Emden's researches have identified few such gifts by bishops in their own lifetime.[88] Some donations, however, were notable. William Rede's enormous but carefully-organized bequests, notably to Merton College (his own *alma mater*), but to five other colleges as well—some 250 books in all, from his library of at least 400—reflected his own wide interests which ranged far beyond the defined syllabus of the university.[89] Having donated, as usual, his basic reference works to his own clerical protégés and, handsomely, to New College, which needed them, he sought to encourage in fellows of other colleges his own breadth of taste. Fleming and Chichele (who both died intestate) had a more basic objective in mind in providing their own foundations, Lincoln and All Souls respectively, with a solid library nucleus.[90] But Fleming, true to his intention to establish a pillar of orthodoxy, did include, alongside treatises of academic theology, works on the art of preaching, model sermons and the second part of Netter's *Doctrinale*.[91] In 1423 Roger Whelpdale bequeathed to Balliol College *inter alia* works by Gregory, Augustine and Giles of Rome.[92]

Some years earlier, in 1404, Walter Skirlaw, J.U.D., had bequeathed to University Hall a sound set of texts for the student of laws, whilst to New College he gave a part of Augustine's *Summa*.[93] In like fashion, bequests by John Bottlesham (to Peterhouse), by the non-graduate Brantingham (to Merton and Stapledon's, the latter his own diocese's Oxford connection), by Lowe, who was actually a distinguished theologian (to the Austin friars at Oxford), by Lyndwood (to the University of Oxford itself) and by Fitzhugh (to the University of Cambridge) were all centred upon canon law texts. This is a feature perhaps to be remarked upon, given the relatively small numbers of professional canonists amongst the episcopate. The needs of ecclesiastical administrators meant that all bishops, whatever their background, had to have at least a procedural understanding of canon law, and not a few apparently built up a small reference library. Finally, the dispositions of Langley merit some particular note: to Oxford University two volumes of the *Reductorium Morali*; to Cambridge the complete lectures of Nicholas of Lira and *Lectura Moralis*; to Durham College, Oxford, St. Augustine on the Psalms; to University Hall St. Augustine's *De Civitate Dei*. All these were drawn from the considerable and wide-ranging library of a bishop with obviously sensitive intellectual and cultural tastes. Langley, it should not be forgotten, was not a graduate.[94]

No less than nineteen of the thirty-two bishops who mentioned appropriate books left specific works or collections to clerical associates, sixty in all, usually their own employees. Some of the clerical legatees were very probably also kinsmen of the testator. Hardly surprisingly, and clearly not contemned at the time, many bishops aimed to establish their younger kinsmen in the Church, usually in their own diocesan administrations. At least seven did bequeath books to such kinsmen identifiably, and this is very much an under-statement. A majority of all the bishops' bequests were of basic texts and commentaries in law or theology, and most of these predictably reflected the particular academic background of the testator. Nevertheless, fourteen bishops explicitly mentioned works relating to more than one discipline: in some cases these were lawyers with pastoral or theological interests, in others bishops owning some work on the canon law, presumably for its practical administrative value. It is a point worth noting, however, that works of academic theology are only occasionally found in hands other than those of bishops with degrees in theology. For official purposes the bishops could rely on the services of experts, but it is an interesting point that they themselves probably had a personal theology based on much the same footing as that of the more educated of their lay congregation, drawing heavily on works of devotion and to no great extent on the expositions of the learned.

Although cathedral churches did well in terms of service books, they received only eight immediate bequests of other books, all but two from their own bishops. These were rather miscellaneous gifts, some to be used, some to be prized.[95] Whilst there were obviously other gifts made during a bishop's lifetime, which must as always encourage caution in any consideration of will-evidence and leave open the question of the bishops' generosity in quantitative terms, such a miscellany does suggest that the bishops gave no great thought to the idea of cathedrals as centres for libraries and learning specifically, and regarded them much more exclusively as places where liturgy and devotion could be practised at their most excellent.

Even some of the best-known of the schools established by bishops, such as Chichele's Higham Ferrers or Kemp's Wye, were really each only a small ancillary part of a much larger pious project, intended primarily for the commemoration of the founder. In itself the educational role was not at all significant in either case. We should not really expect handsome bequests of books to them, even by their founder, but neither, again, should gifts, such as those by Chichele to his school during his lifetime, be forgotten. Winchester College stands quite apart as a foundation and, comparably, its founder, Wykeham, did leave it a handful of improving works of pastoral theology. William Rede made a tactful gift to the earl of Arundel's college in his diocese. These apart (and the educational function of the latter is doubtful anyway), schools had no known bequests of other than liturgical or devotional books from the episcopate. Nor, with exceptions, did religious houses or other non-cathedral churches do much better. Again we must be cautious. John Lowe, for example, established a remarkable library for the Austin Friars in London in his lifetime, from which, after its dispersal in the sixteenth century, a mere three books are known to have survived.[96] But there are only six actual bequests. Robert Rede left the residue of ' all my books save missals and chorals of the use of Sarum ' and all his ' quires ' to form a chained library in the Dominican friary at King's Langley, which may well have been the house where he himself was educated.[97] Archbishop Sudbury, hastily dictating the themes of his will under the immediate threat of death, left all the books of his chapel *tout court* to his collegiate church at Sudbury, most of which were presumably liturgical in any case, but, even so, one wonders whether greater leisure would have made him more discriminating in his bequests.[98] Lyndwood left the principal copy of his masterpiece, the *Provinciale*, to St. Stephen's Chapel, Westminster, which meant more to him than ever did his bishopric of St. David's.[99] Polton bequeathed Pagula's *Summa Summarum* to St. Margaret's Priory, Marlborough, one of the principal agents of his complicated scheme for permanent memorials, and a volume of *decreta* and Cassiodorus on the Psalms to Bisham Priory, with which, again, his association was a personal one.[100] Amongst the many recipients of his books, Langley included the collegiate churches of Manchester (of which he was co-founder) and St. Mary's, Leicester.[101] It was yet another non-graduate, John Wakering, who made the most notable contribution to parochial education through books, and that only in very relative terms.[102] Such individual cases apart, there is little sign that bishops thought that much in their own libraries was best-suited to the use of monks, parish clergy or laity.[103] Certainly, insofar as one can tell, it is true that most of their collections were too academic or advanced for the parishes. Even so, as Wakering, and maybe Robert Rede as well, indicated, there were sorts of works which could have had a wider appeal and value. In this respect, the bishops appear, at least in their wills, to have taken a narrow view. They were, by contrast, generous with works of liturgy and devotion and broadcast these, but most else seemed to them relevant to only a restricted circle.

Something of the same attitude might be seen, finally, in the bishops' attitude to popular preaching. By 1400, if not a good deal earlier, new demands had promoted this to a probably unprecedented volume, and, difficult to control as it was, it was now seriously worrying to the authorities.[104] They could not define to their own satisfaction even the function of the sermon. Responding to the contemporary emphasis in religion away from the penitential towards the pastoral and educational, they accepted, without enthusiasm maybe, the efficacy and even necessity for preaching even within an essentially sacramental religion, but clearly they had many, and often well-founded, qualms about the content of much of it. In this regard, the greatest problems were the reliability and competence of even their most well-meaning preachers and the capacity for understanding and degree of benevolence of their lay audience.[105]

Whilst the hierarchy were no doubt particularly concerned at the volume of criticism of themselves and other contemporary religious institutions that was coming from the pulpit, there is little evidence that, within the bounds of orthodoxy, they really tried to stifle it. As to preaching to the laity generally, perhaps the church authorities were indeed uneasy that this should become so influential an aspect of religious life. But what was good for themselves could not easily be forbidden to at least the more educated of the laity. And, rightly or wrongly, more and more laity were regarding themselves as adequately trained for the opportunity. Unless carefully controlled, the implication was always there that the substance and form of faith, supposedly eternal truths, were to be not merely explained and clarified, as with traditional preaching and religion, but proved by continuing judgment by the lay body of the Church. Nevertheless, there is little sign that the hierarchy scorned (or feared) to allow it. In short, the Church, as has been said, had more delicate, certainly more difficult problems.

Concern for quality and true instruction (we must allow the subjectivity) is the keynote to the Church's attitude to preaching: its provincial legislation was avowedly regulatory, not prohibitive. Heterodoxy apart, which had to be purged uncompromisingly, it was not uncritical loyalty but competence and suitability in the preacher which was the goal. Even Archbishop Arundel, who led the most extreme assault on unlicensed preaching, guarded the opportunities, albeit by regulations so strict as to be impossible really to enforce and liable to throttle the supply of preachers if kept to the letter.[106] Whilst, according to Dr. Gascoigne, Arundel's successors at Canterbury, Chichele, and John Stafford, tried to maintain this regulation, yet, in mid-century, the veteran critic could still regard preaching as perhaps the most controversial religious issue of the day.[107] He found a good deal to object to in modern styles of preaching, in particular the friars' vulgar debasement of established standards and modes to satisfy popular taste.[108] Heretical preaching, as such and by comparison, was a problem of little consequence, but he condemned the hierarchy for failing to provide proper orthodox preaching, either by example or by any willingness to license freely those able to preach (by which Gascoigne meant academics in fact).[109] To conservative idealists proper preaching meant the simple passing on of timeless, unqualified truths: in practice, preaching had now become both commercialized and the most powerful means of public information and persuasion, inevitably involving the promotion of sharp opinion.

We do not hear much of bishops preaching in person. The charges of critics and Pecock's defensive reaction suggest that this was indeed because they did not do much. Given the nature of episcopal registers and most other surviving material, it is unlikely that such work would be regularly recorded, but there are limits to how much can be argued from silence. It is fair to say, however, that at least some of the religious, in particular, who achieved episcopacy did so after being noticed for some distinguished public churchmanship and the active promotion of religion. Certainly they would dominate any list of known preachers amongst the bishops, albeit generally from evidence associated with their pre-episcopal rather than episcopal careers. The corollary of their being in religious orders was that such known preachers were often promoted to less eminent, often remote Welsh, sees, with the implication, justified in terms of both contemporary thinking and practicality, that they were not expected to lead by example within their dioceses. Indeed, there is some stronger implication that their churchmanship was expected on a more general stage.

The demand in the later fourteenth century for more positive religious instruction, especially of the laity—not so much to counter explicitly any prevalent errors and dissent as to quench the growing thirst for more intellectually-satisfying *orthodox* religion—brought the episcopate under further pressure, not as irrelevant and inadequate figures to be undermined or replaced by better, but rather as the obvious source of improvement in teaching, principally by organization but also by the contribution of their own talents: 'if a bishop or a doctor stands up to preach the word of God, many people will draw thither to hear him; and if he reproves vice and sin, the people will not grouch at all against him nor will they forget his words'.[110] Probably the episcopate (and there is evidence, albeit fragmentary) could and did preach and teach when need and opportunity arose, perhaps even did so well in many cases. Brinton is the most famous,[111] but Repingdon and Lacy were in their own time hardly behind him.[112] Both Brinton and Repingdon, in the sermons we have, preached moral values most strongly and demonstrate the fallacy of establishing any firm division between the orthodox and the heterodox on this issue. Moral reformation did not imply any social or institutional reformation, and outspokenness in this regard was no sin.

Really, however, the whole question is a far bigger one. In respect of the general organization of pastoral education, even hostile observers of the hierarchy have accepted that manuals and aids for parish priests were legion and that, however misleading or corrupted, faith and religion were still not only available but enjoined to even the humblest of laymen. If it can be established that bishops resided for the most part in their dioceses, that they, for example, made visitations more regularly than historians have sometimes supposed, and that the generality of the laity still found many means of expression for their faith within ecclesiastical orthodoxy, then surely it is not unreasonable to suppose that the bishops themselves played a positive, not obstructive, part in religious life and, drawing upon their own knowledge of more sophisticated cultural conceptions, managed at least some response to demands for more information and instruction from a laity with whom they themselves had much in common. And, adding all the diverse evidence together, it seems likely that, in their own way (however erroneous), they did.

NOTES

* For economy I have assumed easy recourse to Emden, *Oxford* and *Cambridge* for references omitted in this essay. Biographical detail and support for general observations may be sought also in my own unpublished Ph.D. thesis, 'The Episcopate in England and Wales, 1375–1443 ', Manchester, 1974.

1. The gulf between the expectation of most contemporary observers, who often had good words for the bishops, and that of subsequent critics is notable. For just a few examples, relating to bishops whose careers before and during episcopacy might not suggest at once that they would be good diocesans, see *The Obituary Roll of William Ebchester and John Burneby*, Surtees Society, xxxi, 1856, pp. 56–8 (on Walter Skirlaw); *Anglia Sacra*, H. Wharton, (ed.), I, London, 1691, p. 570 (on Nicholas Bubwith); B. L. MS. Harley 431 (Letter Book of John Prophete) f.97v (on Roger Walden), and *Historiae Dunelmensis Scriptores Tres*, Surtees Society, ix, 1839, pp. 137–9 (on Thomas Hatfield). Many other examples could be cited. Reasoned petitions to the pope or recommendations to cathedral chapters may seem special pleading but make provocative reading about contemporary criteria.

2. Fourteenth-century bishops have received more attention than the fifteenth: Kathleen Edwards, 'Bishops and Learning in the Reign of Edward II', *Church Quarterly Review*, cxxxviii (1944), pp. 56–86; J. R. L. Highfield, 'The English Hierarchy in the Reign of Edward III', *T. R. Hist. S.*, 5th series, vi (1956), pp. 115–38; W. A. Pantin, *The English Church in the Fourteenth Century*, Cambridge, 1955, especially chapter II, 'The Social Structure of the English Church'. For administration, see A. H. Thompson, *The English Clergy and their Organization in the Later Middle Ages*, Oxford, 1947, especially chapter 1, 'The Episcopate', and R. L. Storey, *Diocesan Administration in the Fifteenth Century*, St. Anthony's Hall Publications no. 16, York, 2nd edition, 1972. M. D. Knowles, 'The English Bishops, 1072–1532 ', in *Medieval Studies presented to Aubrey Gwynn, S. J.*, J. A. Watt, et al. (eds.), Dublin, 1961, p. 296, made a general defence of the later medieval episcopate, whilst more specific intercession on behalf of the fifteenth-century bishops is contributed by R. M. Haines, 'The Practice and Problems of a Fifteenth-Century Bishop: the Episcopate of William Gray', *Medieval Studies*, xxxiv (1972), pp. 436–40.

3. 'The church and churchmen were showing themselves more aware of the needs of congregations whose understanding was limited by vernacular horizons, even if partially illiterate'; Margaret E. Aston, 'Lollardy and Literacy', *History*, lxii (1977), p. 350. See also the important general statement by G. Leff, 'Heresy and the Decline of the Medieval Church ', *Past & Present*, no. 20 (1961), pp. 36–51.

4. It is sometimes forgotten that much of the criticism of contemporary religion and church authority was not well-founded in truth or practicability, and that the reforms and alternatives proposed often lacked conviction and were rarely irresistible. Historians have found it too easy to attribute the failure of Lollardy, for example, simply to repression. Its own weaknesses have received less attention.

5. Dr. Anne Hudson has recently done a good deal to consolidate the reputation of Lollardy as a positive and thoughtfully-founded creed in its own right, much more than a simple reaction to specific abuses in Catholicism. There is no good reason to believe that 'popular religion' of an orthodox kind was, by contrast, moribund. Critics of the day have been taken too much at face value. Indeed, their own evidence suggests much more vigour in contemporary dis-

cussion and practice than they would care to admit. See now the excellent general account by J. R. Lander of 'Religious Life', chapter 4 in his *Government and Community: England 1450–1509*, London, 1980.

6. Eighteen bishops were directly of families of baronial status or higher, of whom twelve probably owed their promotions immediately to their birth. Only the sons of earls appear to have had well-nigh 'automatic' promotion at an early age. No more than four of the eighteen bishops, however, could be deemed unsatisfactory in performance or ability, and there was a decided credit side for the Church in having men with such illustrious political and social connections amongst its leaders.

7. For comparative studies, see the works cited in notes 2 and 31.

8. T. H. Aston, 'Oxford's Medieval Alumni', *Past & Present*, no. 74 (1977), pp. 27–8, 31–2, and T. H. Aston, G. D. Duncan, and T. A. R. Evans, 'The Medieval Alumni of the University of Cambridge', ibid., no. 86 (1980), pp. 83–4, have cast serious doubt upon the thesis of G. F. Lytle, cited in note 18, pp. 122–34, that general employment prospects for graduates in the different parts of public service deteriorated from the mid-fourteenth century until at least 1430. As regards episcopacy specifically, several particular factors favouring graduates are suggested in the following pages: diplomatic activity involving church interests during the periods of the Great Schism and the General Councils necessitated greater use of experienced churchmen by the Crown; the strain upon the king's own 'civil service' during Henry V's reign led to the secondment of officials of the Canterbury province and encouraged their subsequent episcopal promotions; the influence of bishops on the regency council after 1422; the interest of Henry VI and the duke of Suffolk in later years, who may have shared in some sort of 'reformation spirit' at that time, with promotions deliberately going to churchmen proper at the expense of those engaged in secular administration. In any case, the laity were taking over some of the offices held by clerics in the royal administration in times past, leaving episcopal promotion free for others. All these factors brought graduates originally in the service of the Church to an episcopacy for which they might not have hoped. The change is in routes to the bench rather than in graduates taking over non-graduate positions lower down.

9. Excluding Robert Wyville, who died in September 1375, after forty-five years on the bench, but including Henry Wakefield, who was then *en route* to Worcester.

10. They held Durham, Winchester, Lincoln, Exeter, Coventry and Lichfield, Worcester, and Llandaff, with Thomas Arundel (a B. A. at best) at Ely.

11. See this essay p. 58.

12. T. Gascoigne, *Loci e Libro Veritatum*, J. E. Thorold Rogers, (ed.), Oxford, 1881, pp. 47–8, 52, 194. But note also the fierce popular criticism of Booth for his aggressive ambition and secular career and talents, in, e.g., *Political Poems and Songs*, Thomas Wright, (ed.), II, Rolls Series, 1861, pp. 225–9, 232.

13. Probabilities are included. Henry Beaufort, Robert Fitzhugh, John Chedworth, and George Neville are all accredited to Oxford. William Grey II is too, although he obtained his doctorate of theology at Padua and also attended Cologne and Ferrara.

14. See T. H. Aston, cited in note 8, pp. 3–20, and Aston, Duncan, and Evans, cited in note 8, pp. 58–9 for general statistics, although Aston does not divide off the doctors. Of the episcopate, three-fifths of the civil lawyers were doctors, four-fifths of the theologians, two-fifths of the canon lawyers. Nearly a half of the

graduates in both civil and canon laws were doctors in both, and a further quarter in one or the other.

15. See this essay p. 70. Bishops are identified hereafter by their sees and the date of their promotion.

16. For bishops and future bishops who were chancellors of Oxford University, see *Snappe's Formulary, etc.*, H. E. Salter, (ed.), Oxford Historical Society, lxxx, 1923, pp. 330–4; *Registrum Cancellarii Oxoniensis*, H. E. Salter, (ed)., I, Oxford Historical Society, xciii, 1930, pp. xxxv–viii. Cambridge also had several future bishops holding the office.

17. A. B. Cobban, *The Medieval Universities*, London, 1975, pp. 8–20.

18. John Flitcroft, 'Constitutions for the promotion of university graduates in England, 1417–38 ', unpublished M.A. thesis, Manchester, 1937, is still useful, but see now the important discussions by G. F. Lytle, 'Patronage Patterns and Oxford Colleges, *c.*1300–*c.*1530 ', in *The University in Society*, L. Stone, (ed.), I. Princeton, 1975, pp. 111–49, and R. L. Storey, 'Recruitment of English Clergy in the period of the Conciliar Movement ', *Annuarium Historiae Conciliorum*, vii (1975), pp. 290–313. J. W. Bennett, 'Andrew Holes ...', in *Speculum*, xix (1944), p. 314, is more optimistic about the bishops' patronage of 'learned men ', but the evidence does not seem to bear him out. Lay patrons appear to have made little response at all in respect of scholars, one or two notable exceptions apart.

19. If an episcopal candidate's birth was at all distinguished, this would not fail to be pointed out by his promoters. After ten years as a bishop, Robert Neville's claims for a translation to so notable a see as Durham could still be proposed first on the grounds of his ' birth and kinsmen, the which are of very great and notable estate '; Durham, Prior's Kitchen: *Locelli* nos. 96, 96x.

20. T. H. Aston, cited in note 8, p. 35, overstates but illustrates the point: ' there was no such thing as an academic profession as we understand it ... There were fine scholars ... but they did not normally spend their lives at the game '.

21. *Rot. Parl.*, V, p. 450.

22. T. H. Aston, cited in note 8.

23. Beaufort, Bourgchier and George Neville are relegated here to the group of graduates in arts. It should be noted, however, that Neville, especially, and Bourgchier both resided at Oxford for some time after their episcopal promotion, and the former at least had the intellectual perception of one well-versed in the higher faculty.

24. Edmund Lacy (Hereford, 1416; Exeter, 1420), Richard Fleming (Lincoln, 1419) and Roger Whelpdale (Carlisle, 1419).

25. Here George Neville is included because, although holding no degree in theology for certain, by graduate study and by later interests he certainly showed his interest and quality, even with distinction. However, although in 1457, at the age of 25, he supplicated for the doctorate, this was evidently a step owing more to the distinction of his birth than of his mind; Gillian I. Keir, 'The Ecclesiastical Career of George Neville, 1432–76 ', unpublished B. Litt. thesis, Oxford, 1971, pp. 27–8. Graduates in both laws, who had accounted for almost one quarter of all promotions for some seventy years past, and major promotions at that, disappeared. Three civil lawyers, three canon lawyers, two masters of art of noble birth, a doctor of medicine (unique in the period), and the first episcopal graduate of the inns of court completed the new appointments.

26. Simon Langham (1366–8) did study at Oxford but apparently did not graduate even in arts; Emden, *Oxford*, p. 1095. 'Nothing in his later activity

suggests that he had literary or speculative talent beyond the ordinary'; M. D. Knowles, *The Religious Orders in England*, II, Cambridge, 1961,

27. William and Lawrence Booth, firmly established with Margaret of Anjou, account for York and Durham; Salisbury went to a canon lawyer, Richard Beauchamp, who had been a court protégé all his life; and Lincoln and Canterbury itself were given to two political veterans, Marmaduke Lumley and John Kemp respectively, when both had in effect been recalled from a past age in a time of crisis to take up the great offices of state. The young aristocrat, William Percy, took the minor northern see of Carlisle in 1452 by reason of family influence or at least of the royal court's wish to flatter the family. John Arundell, a royal physician so favoured that he had even been recently proposed by the king for Durham, had Chichester.

28. The point is made by J. M. George jnr., 'The English Episcopate and the Crown, 1437–50', unpublished Ph.D. thesis, Columbia, 1976, pp. 40, 51–2. Bishops who may be included in this category are Richard Praty, dean of the chapel royal (Chichester, 1438), William Waynflete, headmaster of Eton College and the king's most intimate spiritual adviser (Winchester, 1447), John Stanbury, the king's confessor (Bangor, 1448; Hereford, 1453), Nicholas Close, first effective warden of King's College, Cambridge (Carlisle, 1450; Coventry and Lichfield, 1452), and Walter Lyhert, confessor to Margaret of Anjou and the then marquis of Suffolk (Norwich, 1446).

29. Thomas Bird (St. Asaph, 1450); John Hunden (Llandaff, 1458); Robert Tully (St. David's, 1460). The fourth bishop was James Blakedon (Bangor, 1453), a long-serving suffragan in the south-west.

30. R. G. Davies, cited in note * (see this essay, p. 81) pp. 496–7.

31. See, e.g., Marion Gibbs and Jane Lang, *Bishops and Reform, 1215–1272*, Oxford, 1934, part I; Kathleen Edwards, cited in note 2.

32. See note 8. The small group of purely civil lawyers remained fairly constant during the period.

33. John Catterick's appointment to St. David's in 1414, however, was explicitly such an instance. He needed episcopal status quickly but was promised a 'pinguior' see by the pope as soon as any such should become available. Usually, however, a candidate with a collection of lesser benefices would want to wait for a really worthwhile vacancy. John Stafford's is the classic example.

34. 'Lesser' and 'greater' may seem arbitrary and vague as a definition, but there is a quite obvious line in practice.

35. See this essay p. 73.

36. *D.N.B.* (A. Miller) II, 1306, and references.

37. The putative works are listed by Emden, *Oxford*, p. 1756 and in *Registrum Johannis Stanbury*, J. H. Parry, (ed.), Canterbury and York Society, 1919, p. v, both relying cautiously on John Bale. The list includes public sermons and a good deal on the application of canon law and ecclesiastical authority. Whilst a bishop, he did compose an *expositio in symbolum fidei*, in 1463.

38. St. John's College, Cambridge: Crawshaw MS.103, cited by Emden, *Oxford*, p. 1435.

39. *Register of Henry Chichele, Archbishop of Canterbury, 1414–43*, II, E. F. Jacob, (ed.), Canterbury and York Society, 1938, p. 541.

40. In 1408 an ambiguous reference to the bishop of Worcester by an opponent as 'a simple man, ignorant of the law and insufficient in letters', might just, by hostile interpretation, be applicable to Peverel, but possibly applies better

(but hardly more fairly) to his predecessor, Richard Clifford; Bodleian Library, Oxford: Arch. Seld. B.23 (Letter Book of William Swan, part 1), ff.113v.–4.

41. For Lowe, see F. Roth, *The English Austin Friars, 1249–1538*, I, New York, 1966, pp. 104–8, 430.

42. *Snappe's Formulary*, cited in note 16, p. 139; T. Gascoigne, *Loci e Libro Veritatum*, cited in note 12, pp. 182–4.

43. The problems of using John Bale's treasure-houses of dubious information have been much discussed. Margaret E. Turner, 'Some Aspects of the English Carmelites in the first half of the fifteenth century', unpublished M.A. thesis, Manchester, 1933, remains as useful a guide as any, whilst May McKisack, *Medieval History in the Tudor Age*, Oxford, 1971, chapter I, 'Leland and Bale', provides a more recent general synopsis.

44. R. Weiss, 'Henry VI . . . ', in *E.H.R.*, lvii (1942), p. 104.

45. G. R. Dunstan, 'Some Aspects of the Register of Edmund Lacy, bishop of Exeter', *Journal of Ecclesiastical History*, vi (1955), p. 41, who notes the introduction of the office to York and Hereford, to which may be added Salisbury and the English Franciscans.

46. John A. Robson, *Wyclif and the Oxford Schools*, Oxford, 1961, pp. 162–70, 218–46; *Fasciculi Zizaniorum*, W. W. Shirley, (ed.), R. S., 1858, especially pp. 1–103 (John Kenyngham's counters), 241.

47. See, e.g., Anne Hudson, *Selections from English Wycliffite Writings*, Cambridge, 1978, pp. 19–25 ('Sixteen Points upon which the Bishops accuse Lollards'); *E.H.R.*, xii (1907), pp. 292–304 ('The Twelve Conclusions of the Lollards', with Roger Dymmok's refutations).

48. According to the memoir of William Thorpe, who was cross-examined by the archbishop in 1407, Arundel had a good deal of criticism to make about the heretics' personal attitudes, much of which, whether or not fair, seems at least understandable. The whole text is printed, not from the best manuscripts, by A. W. Pollard, *Fifteenth Century Prose and Verse*, Westminster, 1903, pp. 107–67.

49. E. F. Jacob, 'Reynold Pecock, Bishop of Chichester', *Proceedings of the British Academy*, xxxvii (1951), pp. 121–53 (reprinted in *Essays in Later Medieval History*, Manchester, 1968, pp. 1–34), still seems much the best discussion in spite of various subsequent contributions of unequal value; V. H. H. Green, *Bishop Reginald Pecock*, Cambridge, 1945, is a useful general account of his career.

50. For Patrington's work against Wycliffitism see, in particular, *Fasciculi Zizaniorum*, pp. 289, 292–5, 316; Diocesan Record Office, Lincoln: Chapter Act Book A.2.27 (1384–94), f.35v. records his appointment as preacher and reader at the cathedral in 1391.

51. Emden, *Cambridge*, p. 569.

52. The most interesting example was in December 1433, when the monks of Worcester, at the Crown's bidding, pressed the twenty-two year old Thomas Bourgchier on the Pope on such grounds. This was clearly intended to neutralize the claims of the rival candidate (and papal provisor), Thomas Brouns, who had played a leading part in the formulation in the convocation of Canterbury of lists of questions to be asked of suspected heretics and *was* recognized (by virtue of his legal offices, in fact) as a leading prosecutor. Bourgchier's strength really lay in his birth and connections, and he did little about heresy after he gained the appointment, which is discussed in my Ph.D., cited in note *, (see this essay, p. 81), pp. 389–96. For examples of Brouns's reputation, see *Epistolae Academicae Oxoniensis*, I, pp. 50–1, and for his career, E. F. Jacob in *Essays in British History*

presented to Sir Keith Feiling, H. R. Trevor-Roper, (ed.), London, 1964, pp. 61–84. In 1407 Richard Dereham, a royal servant, was proposed by the Crown for Norwich. It was pointed out *inter alia* that heresy was rife in the diocese, so a theologian and good preacher was needed in order to put down the sects before they waxed strong. The candidacy failed, for other reasons; Bodleian Arch. Seld. B.23, ff.112–3, 113v–4, for his cause.

53. Peter Heath, *The English Parish Clergy on the Eve of the Reformation*, London, 1969, especially pp. 75–7, 104–34.

54. W. Lyndwood, *Provinciale, seu constitutiones Angliae ...*, Oxford, 1679. In absolute terms, this great work has hardly begun to be examined, and certainly a new edition is needed, but see C. R. Cheney, 'William Lyndwood's *Provinciale*', *The Jurist*, xxi (1961), pp. 405–34 (reprinted in *Medieval Texts and Studies*, Oxford, 1973, pp. 158–84), and F. W. Maitland, cited in note 55.

55. F. W. Maitland, 'Canon Law in England. I. William Lyndwood', *E.H.R.*, xi (1896), p. 449 (reprinted in *Canon Law in England*, London, 1898, p. 5), comments upon Lyndwood's extensive library and his familiarity with contemporary thought amongst Italian and French canonists.

56. Emden, *Oxford*, p. 1901, which draws attention to *Registrum Johannis Trefnant, Episcopi Herefordensis*, W. W. Capes, (ed.), Canterbury and York Society, 1916, pp. 53–5, 73–90, 103–14, 131–5.

57. The unexpected breadth of interests of such differently educated and experienced men as William Rede, Lacy, Wakering, and Langley, for example, is impressive.

58. His reputation was noted by a continuator of the *Polychronicon Ranulphi Higden*, J. R. Lumby, (ed.), ix, R.S., 1886, p. 65. See F. M. Powicke, cited in note 70, pp. 28–32.

59. Emden, *Oxford*, p. 2031, with addition in *Bodleian Library Record*, vi (1957–61), p. 685.

60. J. J. Murphy, 'Rhetoric at Oxford in the Fourteenth Century', *Medium Aevum*, xxxv (1965), pp. 1–20.

61. Copies of Ranulf Higden's *Polychronicon* are mentioned by Langley and Lowe. Robert Rede referred to a book of Welsh and English History. Whelpdale left Queen's Hall, Oxford, Vincent of Beauvais's *Speculum Historiale*.

62. C. L. Kingsford, in *D.N.B.*, xvi, p. 819, and Emden, *Oxford*, p. 1560, accepted the ascription inserted in B. L. MS. Cotton Julius B. iii, but James Tait, *Chronica Johannis de Reading et Anonymi Cantuariensis*, Manchester, 1914, pp. 73–5, pointed out that the manuscript is an abbreviation of Lambeth MS. 99, which is not ascribed to Rede, and was written up after the bishop's death and originally without the ascription.

63. *Anglia Sacra*, I, pp. 287, 380; Emden, *Oxford*, pp. 1093–4.

64. *Gesta Henrici Quinti*, J. S. Roskell and F. Taylor, (eds.), Oxford, 1975, p. xxii.

65. Discussed by James Tait, in *D.N.B.*, XX, p. 482.

66. F. Roth, cited in note 41, I, p. 557.

67. The attributions are by E. J. Jones, in 'The Authorship of the *Continnatio ...*', *Speculum*, xii (1937), pp. 196–202 and ibid., xv (1940), pp. 460–77, but see J. J. N. Palmer's refutation in 'The Authorship ... of the Chronicles ...', *Bulletin of the John Rylands University Library of Manchester* (hereafter *B.J.R.L.*), lxi (1978–9), pp. 145–81, 398–421.

68. M. V. Clarke and V. H. Galbraith, 'The deposition of Richard II', in *B.J.R.L.*, xiv (1930), p. 152.

69. R. Weiss, *Humanism in England during the Fifteenth Century*, Oxford, 3rd ed., 1967, p. 3. Some recent scholarship has again warned against too clear an idea, as Weiss perhaps had, of sharply opposed 'scholastic' and 'humanist' approaches to learning, and has indicated the degree of pragmatism and eclecticism on both sides; but in England it was a long time before even this came to pass. Bishop Merk and his contemporaries were not in possession, or even conscious, of a choice or collection of approaches.

70. The library is listed by F. M. Powicke, *The Medieval Books of Merton College*, Oxford, 1931, pp. 164–73, and, for an assessment of Rede, see pp. 28–32.

71. J. J. Murphy, cited in note 60, pp. 17–20.

72. Thomas Gascoigne, for example, showed much the same incidental knowledge of the classics.

73. E. F. Jacob, *Essays in the Conciliar Epoch*, Manchester, 3rd ed., 1962, p. 206, commenting on Bodleian MS. 859 (Gilbert Stone's Letter Book).

74. R. Weiss, cited in note 69, p. 11.; J. H. Wylie, *History of England under Henry IV*, London, 1884, pp. 294–6; Margaret E. Aston, *Thomas Arundel*, Oxford, 1967, p. 374.

75. On Whethamstede, see E. F. Jacob, cited in note 73, chapter XI, 'Verborum Florida Venustas', especially pp. 189–92 for Chichele's use of his skills, and for some trenchant observations upon them; and Weiss, cited in note 69, pp. 30–8.

76. Bekynton obviously knew how proud the abbot was of his latinity and took a malicious delight in offering him a grammatical correction; *Official Correspondence of Thomas Bekynton*, G. Williams, (ed.), I, R.S., 1872, p. 116.

77. B. L. Egerton MS. 2629, cited by Emden, *Oxford*, p. 855.

78. R. Weiss, cited in note 69, pp. 11–21.

79. Dal Monte's opportunity to play upon the intellectual and cultural curiosity and aspirations of his English acquaintances for political advantage is an important theme in his own reports of the mission; Johannes Haller, *Piero da Monte, ein gelehrter und päpstlicher Beamter des 15. Jahrhunderts*, Rome, 1941, prints the correspondence and is a very under-appreciated source of information on the politics of the 1430s.

80. R. Weiss, cited in note 69, pp. 71–3; A. F. Judd, *Life of Thomas Bekynton*, Chichester, 1961, pp. 71–2.

81. R. Weiss, cited in note 69, pp. 80–3.

82. R. A. B. Mynors, 'William Gray and his Books', in *Catalogue of the Manuscripts of Balliol College, Oxford*, Oxford, 1963, pp. xxiv–xlv; more generally, R. M. Haines, cited in note 2, pp. 435–61, and especially p. 441.

83. R. Weiss, cited in note 69, chapter IX, 'George Neville and his Circle'; Gillian I. Keir, cited in note 25, is an excellent study of all aspects of Neville's career, and for his interest in humanism within the context of very strong commitment to traditional authority, see pp. 64–6.

84. R. Weiss, pp. 142–5.

85. Political theory in the fifteenth century is not a well-researched field, certain figures such as Sir John Fortescue apart, so conclusions must be very provisional. But did Thomas Rushook in the 1390s perhaps write the *De Quadripartita Regis Specie*, printed in *Four English Political Tracts of the Later Middle Ages*, J.-P. Genet, (ed.), Camden Fourth Series, xviii (1977), pp. 22–39?

86. On inspection, it seems unlikely that as many bishops' wills have failed to survive for this period as might appear at first sight. References to particular wills are generally omitted in what follows, for brevity's sake; those of graduates are noted in Emden, *Oxford* and *Cambridge*, whilst J. T. Rosenthal, cited in note 87, p. 117, n. 5, locates all those after 1399. I have not made too much here of the evidence of either wills or book-ownership as such, because the present methods of usage by scholars of such evidence seem to me in need of considerable further refinement before conclusions can be developed. I am mindful, for example, of R. B. Brentano's chiding comment in *Speculum*, li (1976), p. 737, that 'intellectual history' can be 'too much the careful reconstruction of the library'.

87. See J. T. Rosenthal, 'The fifteenth-century episcopate: careers and bequests', *Studies in Church History*, Derek Baker, (ed.), X, Oxford, 1973, pp. 117–21, for the general question of episcopal bequests to universities.

88. Of those bishops whose wills survive, John Bottlesham had already given works by Aquinas and Gregory to Pembroke Hall, Cambridge; and John Rickingale had given *libri phisicorum commentati* and *commentum super metaphysicam* to Clare Hall. Thomas Rudbourne, who died intestate, gave certain books to Merton College, and John Kemp gave the *Postils* of St. Hugh to Durham College, Oxford; Emden, *Oxford*, pp. 1583, 1032.

89. The will is printed by F. M. Powicke, cited in note 70, pp. 87–90.

90. A contemporary list of the books given by Chichele is printed by E. F. Jacob, in *B.J.R.L.*, xvi (1932), pp. 469–81.

91. Emden, *Oxford*, p. 698. Here the gift was being put together deliberately by the bishop rather, so far as we know, than being drawn exclusively from his own library, but no doubt it reflected his own idea of what was valuable.

92. *Reg. Chichele*, II, p. 238.

93. *Testamenta Eboracensia*, I, Surtees Society, iv, 1836, pp. 323–4.

94. *Hist. Dunelm. Script. Tres*, cited in note 1, pp. ccxlv–vi.

95. Lacy, perhaps an extreme example, left works of theology, astrology and medicine to Exeter. His will, and with it a full record, has not survived; Emden, *Oxford*, p. 1082.

96. F. Roth, cited in note 41, I, p. 557.

97. *Reg. Chichele* II, p. 38.

98. *Sede Vacante Wills*, C. E. Woodruff, (ed.), Kent Archaeol. Soc., Kent Records, iii, 1914, p. 81.

99. *Archaeologia*, xxxiv (1852), pp. 418–20.

100. *Reg. Chichele*, II, pp. 487, 490.

101. *Hist. Dunelm. Script. Tres*, p. ccxlv. They received, respectively the *Flores* of St. Bernard and *Racionale Divinorum* (and the bishop's personal missal).

102. *Reg. Chichele*, II, pp. 312–3. Even here, most of his bequests to parish or prebendal churches were of works of liturgy or devotion, the rest of his interesting collection, which apparently included several works by Grosseteste, being distributed, as usual, amongst his individual associates. Orpington received, however, *Legenda Aurea* and *Dieta Salutis*, whilst St. Michael's collegiate church, Coventry, which had a library, was given Prior Bartholomew's sermons and *Racionale Divinorum*. See the comments by C. R. Cheney, in *Medium Aevum*, ix (1940), p. 52.

103. See Margaret E. Aston, cited in note 3, pp. 354–5.

104. G. R. Owst, *Preaching in Medieval England*, Cambridge, 1926, and *Literature and the Pulpit in Medieval England*, Oxford, 1933, were the seminal works

which emphasized the need for recognition and edition of the many extant texts before any confident analyses could be attempted. Such work has been disappointingly slow and remains piecemeal. Thus, sermon literature is referred to extensively and respectfully in general terms by historians, but can rarely be with conviction.

105. Pecock, as generous as any in sharing religious thinking with the laity, wrote, ' the highest and subtlest and hardest truths ... ought not to be delivered to laymen '; Margaret E. Aston, cited in note 3, pp. 350–1.

106. D. Wilkins, *Concilia Magnae Britanniae et Hiberniae*, III, London, 1737, p. 314, clause 1: ' that no-one shall preach without licence unless he be lawfully so-privileged '. See also W. Lyndwood, *Provinciale*, p. 133, note f, that the function of preaching was explicitly allocated to bishops and those obliged in cure of souls, or their deputies when so licensed; and to others who might be approved, ' as are doctors of theology ' ... ' not that everyone who desires to preach should be admitted to that office '.

107. On Stafford, cf. *Political Poems and Songs*, cited in note 12, p. 231: ' the devel's sheparde ', ' he wolle not suffre the clerkes preche/ Trowthe in no wise he wille not teche '.

108. T. Gascoigne, *Loci e Libro Veritatum*, cited in note 12, pp. 44–5.

109. Ibid., pp. 34–5, 44–5, 128.

110. B. L. Royal MS. 18. B. xxiii, f.75, quoted by Owst, *Preaching*, cited in note 104, pp. 169–70.

111. *Sermons of Thomas Brinton*, M. A. Devlin, (ed.), C. S., 3rd series, lxxxv–vi, 1954.

112. MSS. listed by Emden, *Oxford*, pp. 1082, 1567. A manuscript simply called ' Repyngton ' (apparently a sufficient description for recognition) was in the possession of two consecutive vicars of St. Stephen's, Norwich, in 1462 and 1472. Probably a sermon collection, it was then bequeathed to Gonville Hall, Cambridge, ' if they do not have it ', which suggests that the testator thought it a quite common work and of academic repute; N. P. Tanner, ' Popular Religion in Norwich, with special reference to the evidence of wills, 1370–1532 ', unpublished D.Phil. thesis, Oxford, 1973, pp. 75, 76, 79.

4

Gentleman-bureaucrats

R. L. STOREY

From the reign of Henry V formal records show an increasing number of men described as gentlemen. The adoption of this personal description appears to have been a consequence of the Statute of Additions of 1413 which required that in original writs and indictments names of defendants should be followed by 'additions of their estate or degree, or of their mystery, and of the towns and counties where they were living'.[1] Previously many names were entered in common law records without any addition to denote rank or occupation, and no instance has been found of a man styled gentleman in these sources prior to 1414. This description, usually in the English form 'gentilman', thus came into use to meet the new statute's demand for precision in the identification of defendants, and the practice was soon being followed in certain categories of administrative records. This was a new usage. In more literary contexts, gentleman, generosus, and other equivalent forms, had for many years been synonymous with noble, and this meaning, with its implications of idealized standards of behaviour, was to have a long future; lords, even princes, would not cavil at being called a gentleman in this sense.[2] The gentlemen who answered in the courts and transacted business in Lancastrian England must be defined by other, more mundane, criteria.

This latter class of gentleman has not yet been satisfactorily identified.[3] Two groups of evidence are helpful in this respect. One consists of discussions reported in the Yearbooks of Henry VI's reign. Here there are four cases which give some indication of contemporary understanding of the meaning of the description, at least by judges and serjeants-at-law. They date from the years 1436–49, and as no other such cases have been traced, it would appear that in this span of time the professional judiciary became familiar with the new usage of gentleman and accepted criteria for its definition. The second body of evidential material are those numerous categories of administrative and judicial records in which individuals are named as gentlemen and which provide

further information about their careers. The main point to emerge
from this evidence is that these gentlemen did not belong to a
single occupational group. Many lived in the country, but it cannot
be assumed that all such men were occupying land and supported
by agriculture. Other gentlemen were town-dwellers with professions or certain other kinds of employment, some of which are
the subjects of other chapters in this volume. The main purpose of
this chapter is to consider one category of men described as gentlemen in the first half of the fifteenth century, namely laymen
holding administrative offices under the crown. It will not be
claimed that any individual members of this group may be credited
with notable cultural attainments. On the other hand, the emergence of this class of lay civil servant was in itself a development of
far-reaching cultural significance, because it helped to accentuate
the distinction between civil and ecclesiastical institutions of government.

Before the adoption of the description of gentleman by civil
servants can be considered, it is necessary to examine the available evidence of contemporary definitions of this 'degree', what
kinds of men were recognized as gentlemen, and eventually how
civil servants met the accepted criteria for thus styling themselves.
The first case reported in the Yearbooks certainly shows that the
post-1413 type of gentleman bore little resemblance to the butt of
the couplet of 1381:

> When Adam delved and Eve span
> Who was then the gentleman?

A defendant ('C.') in 1436 claimed that he should have been styled
'gentilhom' in a writ for debt even though both he and his sons
often drove his ploughs. His counsel argued that it was incorrect to
describe 'C.' as a husbandman because he had considerable earnings ('grand gainage'). This was the only argument 'C.'s' counsel
advanced: he said nothing about his client's birth and ancestry, his
conduct or social repute in any respect other than for his wealth,
nor about the conditions of his tenure of land, whether it was
freehold, at farm, or by any other form of tenancy. None of the
others present disputed that a gentleman could work with his
hands; indeed, Justice Strangways remarked that a gentleman
could engage in husbandry. Perhaps it was assumed that such gentlemen were self-employed, working only on land held in their own
names or to their use, and possibly it was their income alone, and
hence their standards of living and display, which allowed them to

claim to be regarded as gentlemen by their neighbours. This conclusion is not certain, however, because in this and the other three
cases the judges and serjeants revealed their understanding that a
gentleman held a clearly definable position.

This definition appears in the counter-argument by Richard
Newton, counsel for 'C.'s' opponent. If he were to sue a writ of
debt against a serjeant of the kitchen in the king's household, he
said, he would have him named him as a cook, and his writ would
be valid even though the serjeant had a collar [of livery] and was a
gentleman. Chief Justice Inyn observed that officers of the king's
household would be aggrieved to be described in this way, but
Justice Paston said that the writ would accord with the Statute of
Additions because it would be naming the defendant's mystery: in
such a case, the defendant would be both gentleman and cook. It
was accepted, therefore, that a gentleman could have an occupation. What gave gentlemanly status was the household in
which the occupation was held. In 1436 Newton also stated that he
would describe his own yeoman as a husbandman, even though
his clothing was the clothing of a gentleman and he passed for a
gentleman with others. Newton's colleagues disagreed on this
point, and six years later, when he was chief justice of Common
Pleas, there was unanimous assent that the household servant of
another judge should have been described as a gentleman: on this
occasion a writ against a servant of Sir John Fortescue was traversed because it did call him a husbandman. Later in 1442, the
judges were told that Martin Prideaux had been retained by the
abbot of Buckfast to serve in a gentleman's office called 'carver'.
Finally, in 1449, there is a case when an outlawed debtor claimed
not to be a gentleman. He admitted to being a gentleman when he
contracted the debt, but by the date of the writ's issue he was a
merchant. To show that it was possible to lose gentlemanly
status, the outlaw 'J. B.' referred to officers in households of the
king and lords: they were gentlemen while they held office, but
when they were dismissed they became yeomen.[4]

It thus appears that the judiciary accepted that men holding
positions of some standing in the royal household and in the
households of great men—including abbots and judges—might be
styled gentlemen.[5] In this sense the usage of gentleman is similar
to the contemporary usage of yeoman. Both kinds of men appear as
members of households, where the yeomen occupied a lower
order.[6] In collective indictments the order of status is clear:
knights, esquires, gentlemen, yeomen, and finally men with occu-

pational descriptions. Judicial records are naturally the first after the Statute of Additions to describe men as gentlemen, and yeomen also begin to appear more frequently in these sources.[7] When King's Bench was at Lichfield in 1414 it received many indictments against Hugh Erdeswick, esquire, his associates and enemies. The description of gentleman was reserved for Erdeswick's brothers and for the sons and other kinsmen of the armigerous ringleaders. Their followers were mostly called yeomen. The charges include the granting of liveries of cloth to these men by Erdeswick and his neighbours although they were not their household servants and legal counsel, and thus contrary to statute. Some of these recipients of liveries were described as tradesmen of Lichfield.[8] Presumably it was because they became liveried followers of knights and esquires that these men could subsequently be described as yeomen, and this is why instances can be found of yeomen also known to have mysteries.[9]

It is apparent that gentlemanly standing was achieved in the same way by men probably of higher original social rank than the like of Erdeswick's yeomen and in more prestigious entourages. There was, however, no permanent social barrier between the two categories: many instances can be found of men described as gentleman *alias* yeoman. Nearly as common are examples of men termed gentleman *alias* esquire. As Newton said in 1436, gentleman and esquire were 'names of worship', not 'a name of dignity' like knight, and his preference to call his own yeoman a husbandman suggests that he also thought of yeoman as 'a name of worship'. He argued, therefore, that occupational descriptions should be given in judicial records for men who claimed 'names of worship' because the latter were not sanctioned by the Statute of Additions. Newton was apparently mistaken in generally equating the usage of esquire with that of gentleman, because unknighted heads of armigerous families—like Hugh Erdeswick—were described as esquire in judicial records. On the other hand, there was a second usage of esquire. Chancery letters refer to certain royal domestic servants as the king's esquires.[10] This usage contradicts the Yearbook discussions in 1436 and 1449, where it was said that these officers were held to be gentlemen, but it supports Newton's contention that esquire was 'a name of worship'. While royal letters might prefer to style such men as esquires, common estimation was based on how they appeared in public, and there was seemingly no visible means of distinction between esquires and gentlemen.

Personal appearance was obviously taken as indicative of a man's status. A plaintiff in Chancery alleged that his adversary had deceived the court when he brought in four men to provide security for him dressed 'in the similitude of gentlemen or of thrifty merchants' while 'none of the four of his own goods was worth four pence'. The trappings of gentility may be illustrated: when John Woodcock of Black Moor, Yorkshire, gentleman, was sentenced to death in King's Bench in 1424, it was recorded that he had no lands but he did possess a horse with saddle and reins, a black gown furred with beaver, a silver belt, a baselard with a silver hilt, and a two-handed sword.[11] In the discussion of 'C.'s' case, the collars of the king's servants and the clothing of Newton's servant were cited as reasons why these men were commonly reputed to be gentlemen. Their visible signs of gentility, therefore, were the liveries provided by their masters. With the failure of statutory regulation of retaining in the fifteenth century, others beside baronial domestics received liveries. It is not unreasonable to suppose that a good proportion of the men styled gentlemen in records of Henry VI's reign were liveried retainers and that their claims to be so reputed rested on their connections with greater men and their consequent ability to achieve a gentlemanly appearance by wearing suits of livery. Social pretension, therefore, may well have been another cause of the growth of 'bastard feudalism'.[12]

The most fruitful record source for identifying soi-disant gentlemen are royal letters of pardon, many in the rolls of letters patent but still more numerous in the unpublished supplementary series known as Pardon Rolls.[13] Consequent to the Statute of Additions, recipients of royal pardons came to appreciate that they should be described in these letters in every form by which they were known. Some recipients of pardons thus provided outlines of their careers. The first pardon roll of Henry V's reign (for 1413–14) shows few aliases; indeed, many of the recipients of this general pardon are shown without any descriptive particulars: there are no gentlemen, although *chivaler* and *armiger* are not rare.[14] The next roll (for 1414–17) still shows many men undescribed: of some 5,000, however, about 50 are called *gentilman*, three with the *alias* of esquire and three more with other descriptions.[15] In the last years of the reign, gentlemen were appearing quite frequently in the Close and Patent Rolls. They were to be found, seemingly, in most English counties, some in London and other towns.[16] When Henry VI resumed granting general pardons in 1437, the practice of giving multiple descriptions was well-established. An extreme example is the general pardon for Peter Cuncliffe in 1438: it quotes seventeen aliases to include various spellings of his surname, his residence at Clitheroe and three other places in that district, and his personal descriptions as bastard, husbandman, yeoman and gentleman.[17]

These records thus sometimes indicate the actual occupations of gentlemen. The earliest examples, from 1416 onward, include men retained to serve in lords' companies in Henry V's French campaigns.[18] Merchants who victualled castles in France and in the marches towards Scotland sometimes had the alias of gentleman.[19] Both the soldiers and the victuallers may have received liveries from the lords they served. Other merchants appear as gentlemen of places far from their businesses. This may have been because they had country estates where they could live in another style: in 1462, for instance, two London merchants, John Colville, apothecary, and Richard Pierrepoint, stockfishmonger, had the respective aliases of gentlemen at Ryarsh, Kent, and Meering-on-the-Hill, Lincolnshire.[20] It is still possible, however, that they were also baronial clients. A pardon in 1423 to Henry Rafman, merchant of Norwich, and his son describes the latter as a gentleman.[21] William Wisbech, a fishmonger of Southwark, was called a gentleman when he was convicted in Staffordshire in 1434 and 1437.[22] These two mercantile gentlemen probably owed their status to noble patronage, because they are not known to have been men of property in the country. A possibly similar case is that of Hugh Venables of London, indicted in 1430 as gentleman *alias* 'common cutpurse'.[23] His may have been one of the examples the parliamentary commons had in mind in 1433 when they asked the lords to swear that they would not keep felons as members of their households.[24]

Members of the profession of common lawyer also came to describe themselves as gentlemen. The description 'man of law' which figures in the *Canterbury Tales* rarely appears in records of the first half of the fifteenth century. There is one instance in the pardon rolls of Henry V's reign, as an alias of Robert Warcop of Melsomby, Yorkshire, esquire, and a solitary example, of a Norfolk man dated 1424, in the Chancery rolls of Henry VI.[25] Other specific descriptions of lawyers are scarcely more plentiful: apprentices of law in 1426 and 1440 (two); attorneys in 1429, 1433, 1438, 1439 (two) and 1447; man of court in 1438 and 1442. Most of the attorneys and men of court have the alias of gentleman.[26] Through-

out the country, however, the practice—and malpractice—of the
law gave employment to considerable numbers. A parliamentary
petition alleged in 1455 that there were in Norfolk and Suffolk 80
'attorneys or more, the most part of them not having any other
living but only their winning by their said attorneyships'.[27] The
extent of such 'winning' is suggested by the ruins of John
Heydon's spacious moated manor-house at Baconthorpe, Norfolk,
and by the substantial personal wealth of Nicholas Radford of
Devonshire, described after his murder in 1455 as 'one of the most
famous apprentices of law in the country'.[28] General pardons
identify other provincial lawyers: in 1446, Thomas Drakes of Ray-
leigh, gentleman, clerk of the peace for Essex and under-sheriff of
Essex and Hertfordshire; John Doding of Gloucester, Worcester
and London, gentleman, clerk of the peace and former under-
sheriff of Gloucestershire, and burgess for Gloucester in the parliament of 1455.[29] Robert Sheffield of Butterwick, Lincolnshire, is
described as gentleman in letters patent of 1443 exempting him
from holding various offices including serjeant-at-law.[30] Lawyers
may have opted to be called gentleman instead of by a professional
description for reasons of self-esteem; some, though not all, did
hold estates. It is no less likely, however, that many lawyers owed
their 'worship' as gentlemen to noble patronage. The laws against
retaining allowed the grant of liveries to legal counsel, and all
lords spiritual and temporal usually retained several lawyers with
fees and robes. Radford was counsel to Lord Bonville, Heydon to
the duke of Suffolk.[31]

It is doubtless impossible to identify a sufficiently high proportion of those called gentleman in Henry VI's reign to support an
argument that this description was only adopted by domestic officers and liveried counsel and clients of the crown and nobility. The
upper strata of Henry's subjects were much concerned with social
distinctions, occasionally seeking statutory delineations to defend
their 'worship' against encroachment from below. Most notable in
this connection was the statute of 1429 limiting the parliamentary
franchise in the shires to freeholders worth 40s. p.a. or more. The
commons petitioning for this measure distinguished between *les
gentils* and *autres gentz*, the latter being persons of little substance
whose large numbers and tumultuous behaviour threatened the
peace at elections. The establishment of this property qualification
was designed to exclude these plebian troublemakers.[32] If it is
assumed that every man with an income from land of 40s. was a
gentil, the total number of English gentlemen must have been very

considerable, far more than are likely to have been baronial retainers.[33] It seems equally improbable that every forty shilling freeholder would have styled himself a gentleman. Even if many did so, however, it cannot be maintained that this was a new social category: this was the element in county society which, as Fortescue wrote, had sufficient means, leisure and independence to serve as jurors in the law courts; it was the direct descendant of those communities of the shires which had for centuries served the local administration of royal justice.[34] Undoubtedly there were newcomers in these communities in the fifteenth century, county natives of humbler origin who had prospered by agricultural enterprise, merchants and lawyers converting their profits into real estate, but *parvenus* in the counties were not a novel phenomenon in this period.[35] Baronial households and the legal profession were no less well-established features in medieval English society. The use of the description gentleman by men of these kinds did not signify the arrival of a new social class; their adoption of the description is the only real novelty.

A more momentous development in English public life was the expansion of another occupational group whose members also adopted the description of gentleman. These were laymen employed in administrative work; their appearance in the departments of state at Westminster is particularly significant, but they are also to be found in clerical offices in the king's household and engaged in both royal and other administrative employment throughout the country. As medieval government was personal to a ruler, its officers could of course be regarded as members of his extended household: the king granted liveries of cloth to the officials of departments of state.[36] They would thus have met the criteria for gentility previously shown to have been accepted by legal opinion. The earliest example found of a man of this group so described in a formal record is the grant in 1419 of an Exchequer farm of lands to Simon Yerll of Cornwall, 'gentilman'. Yerll's name appears in a list of Exchequer clerks in 1422.[37] The first member of the other great department found described as 'gentilman' is Thomas Haseley of Oxfordshire, as a mainpernor for Thomas Chaucer. Haseley had entered Chancery in Henry IV's reign and was appointed one of the two clerks of the Crown in 1415, an office he held until his death in 1449.[38]

What is important about the use of the style gentleman to describe these civil servants is that it denotes that they were laymen. It is well known that many of the more prominent officials in

English medieval administration were ordained clergy whose services were rewarded by presentation to church benefices. An ordinance for Chancery attributed to 1388–9 required that its clerks should not be married and it sought the king's confirmation of the ancient custom allowing the chancellor to uphold the court's honour by presenting its clerks to all benefices in crown patronage up to the annual value of twenty marks.[39] Until the end of the first quarter of the fifteenth century, the normal personal description of a man employed as a scribe or accountant was clerk; in the case of a civil servant being mentioned in a record of central government, he would be called the king's clerk. In fact, the word clerk was applied to any man with some learning, who had the skills of literacy and numeracy; a distinguished scholar or poet would be 'a great clerk'.[40] Such personal descriptions, therefore, do not make it clear whether a clerk was an ecclesiastic or effectively a layman in that, although possibly in minor clerical orders, he may have been married and in his daily life and social standing in no particular way differed from his entirely lay associates and neighbours.

Fourteenth-century examples of *clerici uxoriati* are not easily found. Master Thomas Harpham described himself as an advocate of the court of York in his will of 1341, which made bequests to his wife and children; he had previously been ordained and beneficed, but seemingly resigned his rectory on becoming a notary.[41] The first clerk of Chancery known to have been married was John Tamworth, a clerk of the Crown until his death in 1375. Although his successor Geoffrey Martin was also described as the king's clerk, his appointment to the commission of the peace for Middlesex indicates that he was not in holy orders; while Martin's colleague Edmund Brudenell was subsequently appointed the king's attorney in the two benches and presumably must have been a common lawyer.[42] The Chancery ordinance did in fact exempt the two clerks of the Crown, and their four clerks, from remaining unmarried. The next married clerk appointed to Chancery was dispensed from this restriction by letters patent. This was in 1411 when Ralph Greenhurst, doctor of civil law, was appointed protonotary of Chancery; he also was elsewhere referred to as clerk and the king's clerk.[43] When the ordinance was revised in Henry V's reign, five other clerks were specifically allowed to remain in Chancery despite being married, a total now of eleven exceptions from the staff of 101 clerks indicated by the ordinance.[44] Richard Coleman, one of the five named exceptions, is described as clerk in private deeds of 1426 and 1429, and in his will proved in 1430.[45] His best known contemporary *clericus uxoriatus*, Thomas Hoccleve the poet and clerk in the Privy Seal Office, was likewise styled clerk until his death in 1426.[46]

The minority of Henry VI (1422–36) was the period when the king's married clerks began regularly to adopt the personal description of gentleman, although in official records they continue for some time to be described as clerks. John Ardern was the king's clerk in his letters patent as clerk of the works in 1421; he was both gentleman and esquire in records of 1423, when he was also under-treasurer of the Exchequer, and he was the king's esquire in 1439.[47] Robert Leversedge, a clerk in the Great Wardrobe from Henry IV's time, described himself as *generosus* in his will of 1434.[48] In addition to Simon Yerll, thirteen of the Exchequer clerks listed in 1422 were subsequently described as gentlemen, mostly in records of commitments of crown farms when they mainperned for each other or for other Exchequer colleagues.[49] In Chancery, Thomas Haseley was still being described as a clerk up to 1430, when he received attorneys, although by now he was regularly called esquire in other notices.[50] The second clerk of the Crown, from 1415, Richard Sturgeon, was a less prominent figure; once a fellow of New College reading civil law (1399–1405), he was described as ' of London, gentilman ' in his will dated 1456, where the main legatee was his daughter Joan, wife of Thomas Frowick, citizen and mercer of London.[51] The James Kelom of London, gentleman, who appears from 1434 and as married in 1439, was presumably the same as the Chancery officer of 28 years' standing exempted from service as sheriff and other lay subjects' duties in 1449.[52] Peter Aumener, clerk of Chancery, had a wife in 1440 and was referred to as a gentleman in 1444.[53] Three of the eight clerks of the almonry of Chancery were given licence to marry in 1448 and 1449 and a fourth married man was dispensed to hold another of these clerkships despite the ancient prohibition. Thomas Ashcombe had held this office for over 25 years, but declared he was not disposed to take holy orders and preferred marriage.[54] By this time it is apparent that many of the junior clerks of Chancery were styling themselves gentleman in their private transactions; although some also appear as clerks of Chancery, it is clear now that this term refers to their employment and is not evidence of ecclesiastical status.[55] In short, it had apparently become normal practice for a married clerk to assume the personal description of gentleman. The writ against a husbandman in 1442 had been traversed because he was a 'wedded man' serving Sir John Fortescue as a clerk and should therefore have been referred to as a gentleman.[56] Nor, indeed, does it seem that possession of a wife is a necessary qualification for a bureaucrat to claim gentility. The 'Robert Walsham of Chancery, gentilman', in a deed of 1442, is doubtless the same as the clerk of the almonry of Chancery who, after fifteen years' service, received permission to marry in 1449.[57] A prominent official position was no more essential: John Croft, for instance, was a clerk of one of the chamberlains of the Receipt, and William Slingsby had been clerk to two engrossers of the Exchequer, but both were known as gentlemen.[58]

The adoption of this description makes it possible to establish that a substantial number of men serving in bureaucratic positions in the second quarter of the fifteenth century were laymen. Earlier, it is less easy to discover how many civil servants were not ecclesiastics because all were called clerks. Some of the many obscure clerks charged with administrative duties in the reigns of Henry IV and Henry V may have been laymen.[59] On the other hand, the king's clerks who held more senior positions in his administration enjoyed his patronage and thus were, if canonically qualified, given ecclesiastical preferment. By tracing the occupants of offices throughout the period of the Lancastrian kings it can be shown that ordained clergy were replaced by laymen. In the first decade of the century, all the major positions in the Exchequer were held by beneficed clergy; so too were the main financial offices in the king's household and chamber, and also the offices of keeper of the Great Wardrobe and clerk of the Works. Before Henry IV's death, some of these positions were being held by laymen, and by 1430 it was the exception instead of the rule for ordained clergy to occupy any of these financial offices.[60] The secretarial offices of Chancery, Privy Seal, and Signet were apparently slower in succumbing to this tide, perhaps because their heads remained ecclesiastics. For the conduct of international diplomacy, the king continued to require the expert knowledge of doctors of laws who had usually been ordained and beneficed before their entry to royal service, and it was normally from these graduate-entrants to his administration that the king chose his secretarial ministers, most of whom were promoted to bishoprics.[61] The senior clerks of Chancery also continued to be well-beneficed clergy, but they had a growing number of lay colleagues in the second quarter of the century.[62] Unlike Chancery, the Privy Seal and Signet Offices were apparently not subject to an ordinance requiring celibacy. In 1441, five clerks in these two departments were exempted from holding office and jury service, a clear indication of their secular status.[63] In the administration of the Duchy of Lancaster, the reign of Henry VI witnessed the disappearance of ecclesiastics: whereas John of Gaunt had employed clergy as receivers and auditors, and in the financial offices of his household, their fifteenth-century equivalents were laymen; Walter Sherrington was the Duchy's last clerical chancellor (1431–49).[64]

Unlike lawyers, baronial retainers and landed merchants, lay bureaucrats were largely a new category of gentlemen in fifteenth-century England. They were new, not because their duties were created by recent developments in administrative practice, but because they had supplanted the ordained clergy who had previously discharged the same functions. Naturally there were differences in the roles in public administration which could be exercised by the king's clerks and the gentlemen of Westminster, but the essential point is that offices once held by clergy now passed into lay hands. The consequences of this transformation of the civil service were of no little importance, both immediately and in the long term, to the Crown, to the Church, and by the creation of a new social group. The causes of this development also demand consideration, but the initial problem is to establish when this preference for lay status first became common in the administrative class. It must be presumed that individuals chose to be laymen rather than proceed to holy orders. There is no evidence that it was ever official policy to discourage civil servants from being ordained. Indeed, as shall be shown, it was by no means to the king's advantage that his clerks should be ineligible for ecclesiastical perferment. When Henry IV appointed Ralph Greenhurst protonotary of Chancery in 1411, he expressed his unwillingness that other married men might be so promoted.[65]

Another reason for discounting the possibility of any directive by the crown is that the process of laicization took place over a considerable passage of time. It can be shown that some individuals began their careers in royal service in the traditional way, as aspirants for ecclesiastical promotion, but later abandoned their clerical character. Two of the gentlemen already noticed may be the same as the Robert Leversedge presented to a rectory in 1401 and the Thomas Haseley similarly presented in 1405, and in 1409 ratified as prebendary of St. Chad's, Shrewsbury, and warden of two free chapels.[66] John Hanham, clerk of the poultry in Henry IV's household, was granted custody of a hospital in 1411, when he was aged about twenty. He resigned the hospital in 1424, and from six years later was described as esquire until 1449, when he ceased to be serjeant of Henry VI's catery.[67] Peter Aumener and Henry Garstang of Chancery received crown presentations to several benefices between 1421 and 1427; next year, both resigned their livings and are subsequently to be found described as gentlemen.[68] Thomas Kent, doctor of laws, was beneficed when he was appointed clerk of the King's Council in 1444, but he married soon afterwards.[69] An earlier example of desertion from the clerical ranks is that of William Loveney, described as the king's esquire in 1399 when he was appointed keeper of the Great Wardrobe, another office usually held by beneficed clergy; as a clerk in Henry of Derby's household, Loveney had been presented to a rectory in 1387, but he was married eight years later.[70] The replacement of clergy by laymen in the Exchequer and household offices in the first thirty years of the fifteenth century was presumably the final stage in a longer process. These were senior positions to which their incumbents had often been promoted after years in more junior grades; it may be observed from the careers of individuals that a working life of 40 years was not exceptional. It may be presumed, therefore, that the older beneficed officers had as potential successors a younger generation of colleagues containing a substantial proportion of laymen. Only two of the thirty Exchequer clerks listed in 1422 were and remained ecclesiastics.[71]

The preference for lay status may therefore have first become marked among civil servants recruited in the first decade of the fifteenth century, if not slightly earlier. This supposition may be confirmed from the evidence of ordinations of clergy in the dioceses of southern England: this points to a general change in public opinion about the clerical profession. The ordination lists show a striking decline in the numbers of men receiving orders as secular priests in the last quarter of the fourteenth century, a reduction which cannot be attributed solely to the overall demographic consequences of the Black Death of 1348–9 and its further outbreaks; although it is perhaps possible that celibacy became socially less acceptable in a period of population decline. A further explanation must be that the vocation of priest was no longer as attractive as it had been earlier in the century, and it is less remarkable that this should have been the case when the authority of the established Church was undermined by the scandal of the Great Schism, challenged by the polemical work of John Wycliffe, and criticized in anti-clerical parliaments and in the literature of

Langland, Chaucer, and other religiously orthodox writers. This climate of anti-clerical opinion must have been particularly strong in London, and prelates who conducted ordinations in its neighbourhood saw its results in the reduced numbers of candidates appearing before them. Ordination lists of the diocese of London are particularly important with regard to the civil service because it was doubtless here, where they worked, that many king's clerks chose to be ordained. Bishop Sudbury ordained over 100 secular priests annually in 1369–73, but the next surviving lists of London ordinands show average annual totals of 29 in 1384–1401 and 43 in 1408–48, of whom a minority were natives of the city and diocese.[72]

King's clerks cannot be regarded as genuine recruits to the priestly profession. Many appear to have proceeded to major orders only when this became canonically necessary. The junior clerk's first gain from the king's ecclesiastical patronage was normally his nomination to a newly created prelate for a pension until the prelate could provide him with a benefice. The next stage was crown presentation to a minor benefice without cure of souls, custody of a hospital or chapel, or a prebend in a royal free chapel. Parish churches at the crown's disposal might come later, and only then was it essential to proceed to major orders in order to retain possession. Another notable contrast between late fourteenth and early fifteenth-century London ordination lists is that in the former a high proportion, at times nearly a quarter, of the candidates were already beneficed; later such ordinands were few and are often identifiable as canon lawyers, not civil servants, as in the earlier period. Even after being beneficed with cure of souls, some king's clerks were able to defer assumption of orders by papal licence. Robert Rolleston, for instance, was already rector of Mablethorpe in 1403, when he was a clerk in the Privy Seal Office. In 1407 he became clerk of the king's works. He was still a subdeacon two years later, when the pope authorized him to retain the rectory without proceeding to further orders for seven years.[73] John Stopingdon of Chancery had a rectory and four prebends in 1422, when the pope required him to proceed from minor orders to the subdiaconate but excused him from going further for five years.[74] Such evidence of reluctance by king's clerks to become priests before they were beneficed suggests that some who were unsuccessful in the pursuit of ecclesiastical preferment remained unordained. Hoccleve records his years of waiting for a benefice and eventual resort to the consolation of matrimony.[75] Frustrated ecclesiastical ambition may therefore be a reason why some civil servants opted for lay status, but clerks holding prominent office in all three Lancastrian reigns rarely failed to become pluralists on a considerable scale.[76]

It is therefore unlikely that higher civil servants became gentlemen through any reduction in the opportunities for ecclesiastical preferment. Of course marriage did account for some clerks turning their backs on the priesthood, but it can hardly be supposed that the king's clerks were massacred by Cupid's arrows: why should the civil service have been struck by an 'epidemic of matrimony'[77] at this particular time? Indeed, some lay bureaucrats appear to have remained unmarried even though they held positions which would have earned ecclesiastical preferment had they chosen to receive clerical orders.[78] The general decline in recruitment to the priesthood suggests that civil servants were influenced by contemporary opinion. One element in popular criticism of the Church establishment was resentment of the ecclesiastical promotion heaped on king's clerks. Being fully engaged in royal service, they neglected their spiritual responsibilities and their only interest in their benefices was financial. They were suitors of 'Lady Meed', they were 'Christes false traitours', while their outstanding colleagues who attained bishoprics were the Caesarean prelates of Wycliffe's invective.[79] Moreover, Richard II's and Henry IV's clerks aggravated the abuse by their resort to administrative malpractice and chicanery, sometimes dispossessing incumbents in their unscrupulous quest for advancement.[80] It is not unlikely that some civil servants were repelled by the abuse of the crown's ecclesiastical patronage and, as pious laymen, accepted that it was indecent to hold benefices they would not serve. Some may have been more directly influenced by anti-clericalism. The adoption of the personal description of gentleman, when it was gaining currency in the 1420's, may in some cases have arisen from reluctance to be identified with the ecclesiastical profession.

The most obvious consequence of the secularization of administrative personnel was that other forms of reward and support had to be found: senior officers had never regarded their wages as adequate, and now some substitute had to be found for the practice of supplementation by ecclesiastical preferment. So far as employers were concerned, this meant that instead of rewarding servants at no cost to themselves, by presenting them to benefecies, they had to divert sources of revenue to their lay administrators.

This may well be a reason why more gentlemen were prominent in the Exchequer at a somewhat earlier stage than in Chancery. While the crown's ecclesiastical patronage was dispensed through Chancery, much of it at the command of its clerks' departmental master, the clerks of the Exchequer, under a lay treasurer, had greater access to temporal benefits like farms of escheats and the ulnage; perhaps the occasional widow of a minor tenant-in-chief was induced to marry an Exchequer clerk. There were also opportunities for profit by assisting the crown's debtors and creditors: the latter, for instance, would wish to secure assignments on reliable sources of royal revenue, or they might seek the aid of Exchequer officials in selling or converting 'bad tallies'. The deterioration of the king's revenues obliged his creditors to resort to these expedients.[81] It must be asked how far this deterioration was due to the practices of Exchequer officials who, instead of seeking ecclesiastical advancement, were now supporting families and ambitious to establish themselves as gentry. Certainly the quality of administration in the Exchequer cannot have been improved in one respect: senior clerical officials reaching advanced age usually retired to live on their benefices, but for obvious reasons their lay successors could not afford to go when age was impairing their efficiency. Some obtained life-grants of their offices and were then able to sell either immediate occupation or their reversion to others. Certain Exchequer offices thus became the freeholds of their nominal occupants, and the crown's freedom to appoint its own officials was accordingly reduced.[82]

The practice of granting life-interest in other offices became quite common after Henry VI began his personal rule. Very often these grants were made to officers of his household or servants of his central administration at Westminster. Like grants of pensions and other sources of profit, also numerous in Henry VI's time, they were obtained by the usual process of submitting petitions to the king. The stream of such bills was rapidly swollen from October 1436, when the application of the royal sign-manual shows that Henry himself was now dispensing crown patronage.[83] Henry's notorious liberality must have favoured the aspirations of crown servants now seeking secular instead of ecclesiastical benefits. Robert Sherrington had been controller of the works since 1423, but in 1438, after he had been reappointed for life and given a Duchy receivership which was exercised by a deputy, he resigned his prebends in two royal free chapels in favour of Walter Sherrington.[84] John Thorley of the household, assigned a pension

until he should be beneficed in 1427, was styled the king's esquire
in 1437 when he was appointed steward of Langley Marsh.[85] His
colleague the ex-clerk John Hanham had a life-grant of the office of
porter of the castle of Newcastle-upon-Tyne in 1437, and later a
second temporal sinecure held since 1432 was converted into a
joint grant in survivorship with a fellow household-man.[86] John
Claydon, a Privy Seal clerk since 1415, had also once been beneficed; in 1432 he was granted charge of fisheries in Caernarvon-
shire, had this converted to a life-grant in 1438, and in the next
year ceded his title in favour of Thomas Bateman, Queen
Katharine's cofferer.[87] The brothers John and Richard Merston,
successively treasurer of the Chamber and clerk of the king's
jewels, were regular recipients of Henry's patronage. Again, these
were offices previously held by clerical pluralists.[88] A noteworthy
instance of the diversion of the crown's patronage in temporal
benefits to its bureaucrats is the custody of Sarum castle by John
Nayler, the gentleman-clerk of Chancery.[89]   Two outstanding
careers in the central departments were crowned with the confer-
ments of knighthoods on Thomas Haseley of Chancery (1445) and
Thomas Thorp of the Exchequer (1460), both of whom had risen to
considerable wealth by the accumulation of offices, other crown
grants, and doubtless also by exploiting their opportunities for
further profit in the course of their duties. Haseley, Thorp, and
Thomas Kent, clerk of the Council, were presumably men of equivalent calibre to the king's clerks of previous generations who ultimately became bishops.[90]

Crown patronage was always a sensitive issue in medieval politics. Henry VI attracted much criticism for his prodigality. Not
only his lack of acumen should be blamed, however, for in his
reign crown patronage was under the additional strain of having
to provide for a new category of legitimate suitors, that of officials
who in past times could have been rewarded by presentation to
church benefices but now sought benefits appropriate to laymen.
The coincident decay of the Exchequer and decline of crown revenues obviously increased the pressure of grants providing personal incomes. Moreover, the inanity of Henry VI resulted in the
real exercise of his patronage falling into the hands of his most
influential courtiers.[91] The bureaucrats who achieved most success apparently did so by attaching themselves to these favourites.
At an early stage in his career, Thomas Haseley was closely associated with Thomas Chaucer, naturally enough as both had Oxfordshire connections, and later with Chaucer's son-in-law, William de

la Pole, then earl of Suffolk.[92] Several of the Exchequer gentlemen increased their stakes in their native counties by acquiring crown farms, occasionally serving as escheators, and perhaps also by connections with local 'good lords'. William Stanlow of Lincolnshire doubtless owed his Exchequer office to the treasurer, Lord Cromwell, whom he had previously served as an attorney.[93] The Yorkshireman Thomas Stockdale, a teller of the Receipt by 1420, established his personal fortune in Essex but often acted as agent for north-country lords, the earl of Salisbury in particular.[94] Thomas Thorp was employed in the Exchequer by 1434, when he was privately a gentleman of London; his outstandingly successful and profitable career—he rose to be a puisne baron, king's councillor, and speaker of the Commons—was obviously aided by the patronage of the dukes of Suffolk and Somerset; he attracted the enmity of the rebels under Cade and later of the duke of York, finally losing his life while trying to escape from prison in 1461.[95] Thorp shows how lay bureaucrats could become dangerously compromised in political faction.

In contrast to the crown under Henry VI, the consequences to the Church of the emergence of this new kind of civil servant were arguably more advantageous. Episcopal appointments were still made only on the initiative of the king or his council, and clerical officers of state and councillors continued to be nominated for papal provision. These ministers, however, were now almost exclusively graduates, some with previous experience as ecclesiastical administrators and judges. They were accordingly better qualified for episcopal office than the like of those 'unlearned' bishops of the fourteenth century who had risen from service in Edward III's wardrobe.[96] John Wakering of Norwich (1415–25) was the last non-graduate bishop to earn episcopal rank after lifelong service in Chancery, followed by one year as keeper of the Privy Seal.[97] With the death in 1437 of Thomas Langley of Durham the episcopate lost its last member whose ecclesiastical promotion was the reward of administrative service to the house of Lancaster 'from the days of his youth'.[98] Similarly at a lower level, the Church lost the major proportion of civil servants masquerading as priests who had battened on its emoluments. A notably disgraceful instance is that of Robert Watton. A Chancery clerk, he procured a crown presentation to an occupied rectory and, by starting common law proceedings to prove the king's title, frightened its incumbent into surrendering him a prebend; but Watton later married and so lost the fruit of his extortion.[99] Presumably such malpractices became rarer as king's clerks diminished in number. Exchanges of benefices, a practice deplored by Archbishop Courtenay in 1392 but much used by king's clerics, became comparatively uncommon in the second quarter of the fifteenth century.[100] With fewer royal clerks requiring benefices greater opportunities for preferment would have been available for more genuinely committed members of the ecclesiastical profession. Graduates had good cause to complain earlier in the century that their prospects of obtaining benefices had been severely reduced. Their meagre prospects then were at least partly due to the successful importunities of the king's clerks: the chapter at York, for example, had a substantial contingent of members engaged on royal service. The situation altered after 1430, and from then until the end of the century an increasing majority of cathedral benefices were held by graduates.[101] Presumably there were also now more parish churches with incumbents really following spiritual vocations instead of absentee rectors employed at Westminster. For the Church, the near extinction of the ordained clerk in secular administration provided a notable opportunity to improve the quality of its ministry.

On the other hand, there are grounds for claiming that the rise of the class of gentlemen-administrators worked to the ultimate advantage of the crown and the ruin of the Church establishment. Under a king more masterful than Henry VI, lay civil servants could be employed to further his interests by undertaking duties which clergy could not have performed; they could strengthen his influence in the localities where they were developing their own standing as men of property, and they could be elected to parliaments.[102] The king could exploit their entire dependence on his continuing favour for their material well-being, they were far more exposed to his possible displeasure than beneficed clerks enjoying ecclesiastical immunities and sources of income independent of the crown. Conversely, the disappearance of ordained clergy from administrative offices led to a reduction in clerical influence in the king's council: a valuable compensation for the exploitation of church livings by royal ministers was that these well-placed representatives of the clergy were able to uphold the interests of their order against the pressures of temporal interests.[103] In the sixteenth century, ecclesiastical representation in the higher levels of government was no longer strong enough to withstand these pressures. Westminster's last bastion of celibacy fell in 1523 when a statute authorised marriage by the last six clerks of Chancery still bound by its ancient prohibition.[104] There were no clerical ministers in the council which prepared the legislation of the Henrician Reformation.

Appendix

The full citations are provided in the notes to the essay.

1. THE EXCHEQUER

Treasurer
All were laymen except in 1401–3, 1407–8, 1421–6 and 1446–9 (*Handbook of British Chronology* (cited in note 61), pp. 102–3).

Treasurer's clerk
Henry Somer was the first certain lay clerk, 1408–10, 1411–13. All were laymen from 1422, save for Robert Rolleston, 1443–6 (J. L. Kirby, 'The Rise of the Under-Treasurer of the Exchequer', *E.H.R.* lxxii (1957), pp. 666–75).

Barons
The chief baron, being a common lawyer, was necessarily a layman. All four puisne barons were termed king's clerks in their appointments on 30 September 1399. Three were beneficed, *viz.* Laurence Allerthorpe, Thomas Feriby and William Ford, but John Staverton was probably a layman.

Allerthorpe, first appointed in 1375, vacated on becoming treasurer, 1401–2; he died in 1406 as dean of Wolverhampton royal free chapel and canon of Hereford, London and York (*C.P.R. 1405–8*, p. 206; *Fasti*, II, p. 48; V, p. 25; VI, p. 85). Succeeded as second baron by Thomas Tutbury, dean of Wells and archdeacon of Buckingham, who died 1403 (Ibid., I, p. 15; VIII, p. 4). Next was Roger Westwood, 1403–23; canon of Lincoln, Lichfield, and Dublin, he died in 1432 as master of Charing Cross hospital (*Visitations of Religious Houses in the Diocese of Lincoln*, A. Hamilton Thompson, (ed.), Canterbury and York Society, 1915–27, i, p. 209).

Feriby, a new appointment, ceased as third baron in 1402; he died in 1432 as canon of Salisbury and Hastings royal free chapel (*Fasti*, III, p. 91; *C.P.R. 1429–36*, p. 192). His successor Thomas Overton was rector of St. Magnus, London, who died in office, 1407; his bequests included bibles, a 'best book of statutes of the realm' (to Thomas Stockdale, q.v., p. 107 above) and the king's livery (P.R.O.: Prob. 11, no. 2a (Marche), f.97). Replaced by Henry Merston, who retired in 1421 and died in 1433 as canon of London,

York, and St. Stephen's, Westminster (*Fasti*, V, p. 24; VI, p. 93; *C.P.R. 1429–36*, p. 268; P.R.O.: Prob. 11, no. 3, f.142). William Hesill, who replaced him, 1421–3, had been an auditor of the Exchequer. His wife Agnes was daughter of John Appleton of Dartford, auditor of the Exchequer (d.1392–3), whose sons Richard (d.1432) and Roger (retired by 1447) were also auditors (P.R.O., Prob. 11, nos. 1 (Rous), f.51, 3, ff.24v, 131v; C. 67, no. 37, m.12; *C.P.R. 1417–22*, p. 117; *1446–52*, p. 70).

Ford was baron from 1384 to 1407, dying that year as canon of York (*Fasti*, VI, p. 37). Henry Somer succeeded until 1410, when he became chancellor (below, p. 113). His immediate successors Richard Bank, previously L.T.R. (below, p. 114), Robert Sandford, 1417–18, and Roger Waltham, 1418–22, are not known to have been beneficed.

Staverton, another new appointment in 1399, is also not known as beneficed while in office. A John Staverton was presented to the church of Binfield, Berks., in 1388 (*C.P.R. 1385–9*, p. 401), but another of this name was J.P. in Suffolk from 1387 to 1422. This was probably the baron, as Exchequer farms of the alien priory of Creeting St. Mary, Suffolk, were granted to him for indefinite terms in 1378 and 1399 (*Calendar of Fine Rolls*, IX, p. 79; XII, p. 16; see also *C.P.R. 1399–1401*, p. 517). A clerical baron succeeded Staverton in 1413. Robert Malton had received crown presentations to minor benefices in 1393 and 1398, and was clerk of the pipe in 1400. He died in office and as rector of St. Martin the Martyr, London, in 1426 (*C.P.R. 1391–6*, p. 329; *1396–9*, p. 327; *1399–1401*, p. 257; P.R.O.: Prob. 11, no. 3, f.40).

There were two clerical barons at Henry VI's succession (Westwood and Malton). There were only five more in his reign. Nicholas Dixon, previously under-treasurer replaced Westwood in 1423. He retired in 1434 and died in 1448 as canon of Chichester, Lincoln, London, and Salisbury, and rector of Cheshunt (*Lincoln Visitations*, I, pp. 198–9). Followed, as third baron, by William Derby, 1435–8, when he died as archdeacon of Bedford and canon of Lincoln and Westminster (Ibid., I, pp. 178–9).

Malton was replaced by William Ward, previously K. R. (below, p. 114), in 1426. He is not known to have had a benefice but his will, dated and proved in 1428, describes him as clerk; it shows he had a breviary and vestments and does not mention a wife or children. He was later referred to as a chaplain (P.R.O.: Prob. 11, no. 3, ff.75–6; *C.P.R. 1446–52*, p. 33).

By 1430, three of the barons were laymen, perhaps all common lawyers. John Fray, formerly recorder of London, was third baron from 1426, second baron in 1435, and chief baron 1436–47 (*C.P.R. 1422–9*, p. 534). William Babthorp, 1430–43, had been the king's attorney in Common Pleas, 1420–9 (see also Somerville, *Lancaster*, p. 563; P.R.O.: Prob. 11, no. 3, f.261). Robert Frampton, 1429–45, was twice married (*C.P.R. 1436–41*, p. 394; *C.C.R. 1441–7*, p. 461).

Before Derby's death, however, a second clerical baron was appointed on Fray's promotion in 1436. William Fallan was an Exchequer clerk in 1418. Beneficed as a subdeacon in 1421, when he was excused further ordination for three years. He resigned as third baron, in favour of Thomas Thorp, 1453. Fallan was treasurer of the household, 1454–6. He died in 1466 as archdeacon of London (*Cal. Fine Rolls*, XIV, p. 232; *Cal. Papal Letters*, VII, p. 223; *Rot. Parl.*, V, p. 342; *Fasti*, V, p. 9). There was briefly a second clerical baron during his term of office. Thomas Lewisham, 1447–9, had been K. R. since 1426 (below, p. 114). He had been in the Exchequer in 1410. As a priest, he obtained a benefice by simony in 1431, was collated to a canonry of Lanchester, Co. Durham, in 1437, and was also canon of Hereford, 1442–61 (*Cal. Fine Rolls*, XIII, pp. 191, 208; *Cal. Papal Letters*, VIII, p. 328; *Register of Thomas Langley*, Surtees Society, 1956–70, v, p. 21; *Fasti*, IX p. 50).

Fallan was the last clerical baron. At the end of the reign, the second baron was Thomas Thorp (above, p. 107). The other puisne barons were Brian Roucliffe, 1453–79, presumably a 'Yorkist' as he was dismissed as J.P. for the West Riding in 1459; John Holme, 1446–62, and John Durham, 1448–70), both of whom had been Exchequer clerks in 1422 (see note 49, p. 125); they were also J.P.s, Durham in Buckinghamshire from 1453 and Holme in Yorkshire from 1458. The last two were described as gentlemen in 1462 (Pardon Rolls, no. 45, mm. 5, 45).

(For barons generally, see lists and biographical notes—not quite complete or correct—in E. Foss, *The Judges of England*, London, 1848–57, IV; most appointments in *C.P.R.*; and wages in *Warrants for Issues*, cited in note 63).

King's Chamberlain
John Godmanston, appointed 1396, died in 1401 as chancellor of St. Paul's and canon of Hereford and Chichester (*C.P.R. 1391–6*, p. 695; *Fasti*, V, p. 19; II, p. 46; VII, p. 28). Succeeded by John Icklington, 1401, who was dismissed in 1403 and replaced by John Legbourne, who had been Gaunt's receiver-general (1394–9) and the king's cofferer of the household (1399–1401) and receiver of the

chamber; he died c.1430 as archdeacon of Leicester and canon of Lichfield (*C.P.R. 1399–1401*, p. 501; *1401–5*, p. 259; Somerville, *Lancaster*, p. 368; *Fasti*, I, p. 13; X, p. 54). Icklington, meanwhile treasurer of the prince of Wales' household, was reappointed in 1413; he retired in 1415 and died as archdeacon of Wells, 1419 (*C.P.R 1413–16*, pp. 2, 433; *Fasti*, VIII, p. 14).

The office was thereafter held by laymen, presumably employing deputies as they were engaged elsewhere: John Woodhouse, esquire, 1415–31 (Somerville, *Lancaster*, p. 389); John Hotoft, esquire, treasurer of the household, 1431, with life-appointment as chamberlain, 1439, who died 1443 (Roskell, *Parliament of 1422*, p. 191). In 1440, reversion of the office was granted to James Fiennes, esquire, who ceded it to Lord Cromwell in 1442 (*C.P.R. 1436–41*, p. 423; *1441–6*, p. 158).

Warwick Chamberlain
John Oudeby, B.C.L., confirmed in office, 1397; died as archdeacon of Derby and canon of Lichfield, 1418 (*C.P.R. 1396–9*, p. 196; *Fasti*, X, pp. 16, 21). In 1414 replaced by Nicholas Calton, canon of Salisbury 1413–40 (P.R.O. E. 159 (K. R. Memoranda Rolls), no. 190, Trin. Rec. rot. 2; *Fasti*, III, pp. 71–2). Laymen followed: John Throckmorton, 1419–45, John Nanfan, John Brown, Thomas Colt (Roskell, *Parliament of 1422*, p. 225; Wedgwood, *Parliament*, II, pp. 621–2, 120, 208–9).

Chancellor
John Nottingham, 1399–1410, died in 1418 as treasurer of York and canon of London (*C.P.R. 1399–1401*, p. 5; *Fasti*, VI, p. 14; V, p. 30). Under Henry Somer, former baron and sometime under-treasurer (above, pp. 110, 111), 1410–39, the office presumably became a sinecure. His successor, John Somerset, 1439–53, was Henry VI's physician (Emden, *Oxford*, III, pp. 1727–8). For intrigue to secure the reversion, see Storey, *End of Lancaster*, pp. 50–1. Thomas Witham, 1454–69, seems to have in the service of the duke of York before then and may have been the duke's nominee for the office (*C.P.R. 1452–61*, pp. 158, 161; *Cal. Fine Rolls*, XIX, p. 119; but cf. Roskell, Speakers (cited in note 95), pp. 250, 366. For wages of all chancellors, see *Warrants for Issues*).

King's Remembrancer
Robert Thirsk, 1398–1419, was dead in 1420, having been canon of St. Stephen's, Westminster, and vicar of St. Michael's, Coventry

(*C.P.R. 1416–22*, p. 254; *Reg. Langley*, II, p. 177). William Ward, clerk, appointed 1419; promoted baron, 1426 (above, p. 111). Succeeded by Thomas Lewisham, clerk; promoted baron, 1447 (above, p. 112). John Durham granted office in survivorship with Lewisham, 1447; also succeeded Lewisham as baron, 1449 (above, p. 112). In 1447 the office was granted in survivorship to the king's esquires, Thomas Daniel and William Troutbeck, which suggests that it was being regarded as a sinecure; but the next incumbent was William Essex, 1450–80, who was to be under-treasurer, 1478–80 (Kirby, 'Under-treasurer', p. 675; Wedgwood, *Parliament*, II, pp. 302–3).

Lord Treasurer's Remembrancer

Held from before 1399 by Walter Malet, who died in 1404 as canon of London (*C.P.R. 1396–9*, p. 173; *Fasti*, V, p. 39). None of his successors can be identified as beneficed clergy or even described as clerks. They were Richard Bank, 1399, until promoted baron, 1410; Thomas Broket, 1411–35; John Serf, 1436–43 (called gentleman in *Cal. Fine Rolls 1430–7*, pp. 72, 95, 237, and as citizen of London in his will, 1444, P.R.O.: Prob. 11, no. 3, f.226); Thomas Thorp, 1444–52; and Richard Ford, 1454–75. The last had been clerk of the pipe, was described as gentleman in 1450, and was married (*C.P.R. 1446–52*, pp. 127, 312; *C.C.R. 1447–54*, p. 312. Appointments of all remembrancers are shown in *C.P.R.* and their wages in *Warrants for Issues*).

2. THE HOUSEHOLD

Treasurer
This officer, also known as Keeper of the Wardrobe, had been a
beneficed clerk throughout the thirteenth and fourteenth centuries
and until 1406. Thereafter all were laymen except for Thomas
More, in 1413, and William Fallan, 1454–6 (*Handbook of British
Chronology*, pp. 77–9; for Fallan, as baron of the Exchequer, see p.
112 above).

The three following lists of accounting Household officers may
be incomplete save for the reign of Henry IV, which is examined in
A. Rogers, *The Royal Household of Henry IV*, unpublished
Nottingham Ph.D. thesis, 1966 (hereafter cited as 'Rogers').

Cofferer
John Legbourne, clerk, 1399; later chamberlain of the Exchequer
(above, p. 112).

John Cranborne, 1401 (?); farmer of Eltham manor, 1402–9; Exchequer pension, as 'the king's servitor' (not 'clerk'), 1405, but
probably the same man as the John Cranborne, chaplain of Os-
pringe hospital, Kent, by the king's grant, 1401–11, because the
last warrant for the pension is also dated 1411 (Rogers, p. 680; *Cal.
Fine Rolls*, XII, p. 176; XIII, p. 162; *C.P.R. 1399–1401*, p. 528; *1409–
13*, p. 301; *Warrants for Issues*, p. 77).

Robert Tunstall, bachelor of laws, 1406; died 1419, as rector of
Great Dunmow and prebendary of Tamworth (Rogers, p. 680;
Emden, *Oxford*, III, pp. 1915–16).

John Spenser, esquire, 1413; briefly, until keeper of the Great
Wardrobe (below, p. 120).

William Kinwolmarsh, 1413. In 1407, when clerk of the treasurer
of the Household, and only tonsured, became rector of Keyston,
Hunts., and excused further ordination for seven years. Actually
ordained acolyte and subdeacon in 1421. Under-treasurer of the
Exchequer, 1417, and treasurer, 1421. Died 1422, as dean of St.
Martin-le-Grand, provost of Beverley, and also holding two rectories and three cathedral prebends (*The Register of Henry Chichele*, E. F. Jacob, (ed.), Cant. and York Soc., 1937–47, II, p. 660; IV, p.
346; *Cal. Papal Letters*, VI, p. 132).

John Feriby, esquire, 1419. A clerk in Henry IV's household
by 1400; granted hospitals, 1406, 1408 (the first revoked as the

benefice was already occupied); pensions until beneficed, 1409, 1410; crown pension, as 'the king's clerk', 1415 (surrendered 1440). Perhaps now married: his wife died in 1475 but her father died in 1417. As esquire retained for the Agincourt campaign. Controller of Henry VI's household by 1430, until 1440(?); sheriff of Surrey, 1426, 1436, and M.P., 1425, 1429, 1433; steward of Knaresborough, for life, 1437–41 (*C.P.R. 1399–1401*, p. 355; *1405–8*, pp. 223, 291, 395; *1413–16*, p. 272; *1436–41*, p. 486; *C.C.R. 1405–9*, p. 487; *1409–13*, p. 170; J. H. Wylie, *The Reign of Henry the Fifth*, Cambridge, 1914–29, vol. II, p. 31; *Warrants for Issues*, p. 101; *Reg. Chichele*, II, p. 652; Somerville, *Lancaster*, p. 524).

Thomas Gloucester, a clerk of accounts, 1430; served Henry IV, Henry V, and Henry VI; as esquire, receiver-general of Duchy of Cornwall, 1439; described as 'late cofferer', 1452 (*Warrants for Issues*, p. 117; *C.P.R. 1436–41*, p. 345; *1452–61*, p. 30).

John Everton, a clerk of accounts when granted pension until beneficed, 1432; parker of Brigstock, 1437; receiver of Guines for life, by deputy, 1440; cofferer in 1452 (*C.C.R. 1429–35*, p. 230; *C.P.R. 1436–41*, pp. 68, 488; *Warrants for Issues*, p. 98).

Clerks and under-clerks of the kitchen

Robert Tunstall, clerk, 1403–6; later cofferer (Rogers, p. 683; above, p. 115).

John Tilton, under-clerk, 1405, when nominated for pension until beneficed (Storey, *Langley* (cited in note 98), p. 18).

Thomas Brigges, clerk, 1406; ceded corrody, 1435 (*C.C.R. 1435–41*, p. 44).

Thomas Lilbourne, under-clerk, 1408, still in 1423; corrody, 1433; pension of Henry IV confirmed, 1433 (*C.P.R. 1422–9*, p. 114; *1429–36*, p. 265; *C.C.R. 1422–9*, p. 451).

Robert Allerton, B.C.L., under-clerk, 1415; beneficed from 1416 but dispensed, as subdeacon, from further orders for five years, 1422; clerk of the kitchen, 1427; died 1437, as rector of Amersham and canon of Ripon and Windsor (Emden, *Oxford*, I, p. 25).

William Balne, clerk, 1416, when pensioned; died 1417 (*C.P.R. 1416–22*, pp. 9, 62).

Richard Reston, under-clerk, 1415; presented to rectories, 1414, 1416 (*Warrants for Issues*, p. 233; *C.P.R. 1413–16*, pp. 235, 385).

William Brewster, under-clerk, 1425; clerk, 1430; retired by 1446; died 1465, as canon of Lincoln, London, Chichester and (?) Exeter (*Warrants for Issues*, p. 40; *C.P.R. 1422–9*, p. 268; *1446–52*, p. 2; *Fasti*, I, p. 84; V, p. 50; VII, p. 16; IX, p. 51).

John Hardwick, under-clerk, 1437; clerk, 1446; corrodies, 1431–2; pensions until beneficed, 1433; offices in duchies of Cornwall and Lancaster, and Irish Exchequer, 1435, 1437 (*C.C.R. 1429–35*, pp. 111, 182, 257, 292; *C.P.R. 1429–36*, p. 447; Somerville, *Lancaster*, pp. 618–19).

Ralph Legh, under-clerk, 1437; pension until beneficed, 1437; king's esquire, serjeant of catery, 1441; marshal of hall (in Household), 1444–55; M.P. six times, 1442–67 (*C.C.R. 1435–41*, p. 124; Wedgwood, *Parliament*, II, pp. 533–4).

John Brown, under-clerk, 1445–59; corrody, 1452 (*C.P.R. 1441–6*, p. 372; *1452–61*, p. 514; *C.C.R. 1447–54*, p. 356). [Grants to the last three were excepted from the act of resumption, 1450 (*Rot. Parl.*, V., pp. 192, 194, 195).]

Clerks of the Spicery
William Glym, 1399–1400; his attempts to enter Salisbury chapter frustrated, 1400–10; resident as vicar of St. Nicholas, Newcastle-upon-Tyne, 1418–36 (Rogers, p. 684; Storey, 'Clergy and common law' (cited in note 80), pp. 402–4; *Reg. Langley*, II, p. 177; V, p. 8; and *passim*).

John Breche, 1402–6, when rector of Ewell, Surrey, and canon of Westminster; canon of London, 1406–18; still rector of Orpington, Kent, 1432 (*C.P.R. 1399–1401*, p. 26; *1413–16*, p. 118; *Fasti*, V, p. 24; *Reg. Chichele*, I, p. 274).

Roger Woodley, under-clerk, 1406; clerk, 1407; pensions until beneficed, 1399, 1406; hospital granted, but revoked, 1402; pardon for papal provision, 1406; dean of Bangor, 1413–16 (*C.C.R. 1399–1401*, p. 99; *1402–5*, p. 18; *1405–9*, p. 125; *C.P.R. 1401–5*, p. 61; *1405–8*, p. 190; *Fasti*, XI, p. 6).

William Peck, under-clerk, 1415; previously in Prince of Wales' service; clerk of Spicery by 1430, until 1454; constable of Northampton Castle, for life, with 12*d.* daily, 1439 (*Warrants for Issues*, p. 215; *C.P.R. 1413–16*, p. 390; *1436–41*, pp. 305, 487; *1452–61*, p. 204).

3. THE CHAMBER

Receiver (or Treasurer) and/or Keeper of the King's Jewels
John Elvet, 1399; died 1404, as archdeacon of Leicester, canon of Lincoln and Salisbury (*Warrants for Issues*, p. 95; *C.P.R. 1401–5*, p. 29; *Fasti*, I, pp. 12–13, 81; III, p. 56; XII, p. 15).

John Legbourne, clerk, 1401; later king's chamberlain of the Exchequer (above, p. 112)

William Pilton, 1403; king's secretary, 1406–13; died 1435, as archdeacon of York, canon of Exeter, York and (?) Chichester (*Warrants for Issues*, p. 220; Otway-Ruthven, *King's Secretary* (cited in note 61), pp. 153, 165–7; *Fasti*, VI, pp. 18, 45; VII, p. 18; IX, p. 46).

Simon Flete, esquire, 1406; keeper of the Privy Wardrobe in the Tower for life, 1407–30 (*Warrants for Issues*, p. 104; *C.P.R. 1405–8*, pp. 387, 411; *1429–36*, p. 79).

Thomas Ringwood, esquire, 1411; later keeper of the Great Wardrobe (below, p. 120)

Richard Courtenay, bishop of Norwich, 1413–15 (Emden, *Oxford*, I, pp. 500–1).

Thomas Chittern, esquire, 1415(?), 1417 (*Warrants for Issues*, p. 63; *C.P.R. 1416–22*, p. 107).

John Butler, 1420; usher of the chamber, constable of Liverpool Castle for life, 1417–21 (*C.P.R. 1416–22*, pp. 69, 338; Somerville, *Lancaster*, p. 498).

Nicholas Merbury, esquire, 1421; esquire of the earl of Northumberland, 1402; king's esquire by 1411; master of the ordnance, 1414; chief butler, 1418; [nominal] chirographer of Common Pleas until death, 1421 (*C.P.R. 1401–5*, p. 121; *1408–13*, p. 308; *1413–16*; p. 241; *1416–22*, pp. 175, 340; *1422–9*, p. 194; *Warrants for Issues*, p. 189).

John Merston, esquire, 1423; constable of Pleshey, 1437–61; knight, 1459 (*C.P.R. 1436–41*, pp. 91, 591; *1452–61*, pp. 557, 679; *Warrants for Issues*, p. 190; Somerville, *Lancaster*, p. 611).

Edward Grimston, esquire, in survivorship with John Merston, on the latter ceding life-grant, 1448. Grimston was the king's envoy to France, Burgundy, etc., 1440–8; married three times, died 1478 (*C.P.R. 1446–52*, p. 130; *Warrants for Issues*, p. 124; *Complete Peerage*, XI, p. 106).

Richard Merston, 1453; clerk of the jewels, 1437; with his brother John, constable of Pleshey, 1439–61; joint controller of king's works, 1441–6; married, although not found described as esquire or gentleman (*C.P.R. 1436–41*, p. 65; *1452–61*, p. 293; Somerville, *Lancaster*, p. 611; Wedgwood, *Parliament*, II, p. 587).

[Richard Davy, clerk of the jewels in 1453 and 1455, is doubtless the same as the gentleman of Horton, Surrey, who mainperned for John Merston and his wife in 1451 and 1453 (*Warrants for Issues*, p. 85; *Cal. Fine Rolls*, XVIII, p. 210; XIX, p. 23; cf. Wedgwood, *Parliament*, II, p. 262).]

William Grimsby, esquire, 1456(?); life-appointment, 1458; under-treasurer of the Exchequer and M.P., 1459; attainted, 1461 (*C.P.R. 1452–61*, pp. 293, 360, 432; *Warrants for Issues*, p. 123; Wedgwood, *Parliament*, II, pp. 400–1).

4. KEEPERS OF THE GREAT WARDROBE

William Loveney, esquire, 1399; as clerk of Henry, earl of Derby, presented to church of Stratton, 1387, and pardoned for homicide, 1388; married in 1395–6; regularly employed in Henry IV's household. M.P. for Middlesex, 1401, 1407, 1413; died 1435 (*C.P.R. 1385–9*, pp. 267, 531; *1399–1401*, p. 267, and *passim*; Rogers, pp. 755–8; Somerville, *Lancaster*, p. 386).

Richard Clifford, junior, 1408; died 1422, as archdeacon of Middlesex, canon of St. Paul's and rector of Biddenden, Kent (*C.P.R. 1405–8*, p. 425; Emden, *Oxford*, I, pp. 441–2).

Thomas Ringwood, esquire, 1412; yeoman of robes in Henry (IV)'s households, 1396–1407; with his wife, granted corrody, 1412; Duchy receiver in Hants., etc., 1415–37 (Rogers, pp. 781–2; *C.P.R. 1408–13*, p. 390; *C.C.R. 1409–13*, p. 397; Somerville, *Lancaster*, p. 622).

Thomas Carnica, 1413; previously (Prince) Henry's receiver-general; died 1413, as dean of Wells, canon of Lincoln and York (*C.C.R. 1409–13*, p. 76; *C.P.R. 1413–16*, p. 14; *Fasti*, I, p. 111; VI, p. 81; VIII, p. 5).

John Spenser, esquire, 1413; pensioned as 'the king's clerk', 1391 and 1398, and granted free chapel, 1397; esquire by 1403, when controller of Prince of Wales' household; cofferer of household, 1413; died 1421; his widow married John Tirell, later treasurer of the household (*C.P.R. 1388–92*, p. 398; *1396–9*, pp. 204, 333; *1413–16*, pp. 103, 121; *1416–22*, p. 337; *1422–9*, p. 268; *Warrants for Issues*, p. 261).

Robert Rolleston, 1418; clerk in the Privy Seal Office, 1401; clerk of the works, 1407–13; under-treasurer of the Exchequer, 1443–6; died 1450/1, as archdeacon of Durham(?), provost of Beverley, canon of Lincoln and York (*C.P.R. 1416–22*, p. 150; *Warrants for Issues*, p. 238; *Fasti*, I, p. 45, VI, pp. 45, 113; *Testamenta Eboracensia* (Surtees Society, 1855), II, pp. 138–41; above, p. 103).

John Norris, esquire, 1444; usher of the chamber, 1429; squire of the king's body, 1441–60; died 1466 (Somerville, *Lancaster*, p. 569; Wedgwood, *Parliament*, II, pp. 637–9).

Thomas Tuddenham (1446), William Cotton (1450), Henry Fillongley (1453) and Thomas Vaughan (1460) were all laymen who probably held the office as a sinecure, as they were employed elsewhere; all died by violence (q.v. in Wedgwood, *Parliament*, II).

5. CLERKS OF THE WORKS

Their careers are discussed in *The History of the King's Works*, general editor H. M. Colvin, I (London, 1963), pp. 194–5. Again the pattern is of laymen replacing clergy. The first lay clerks were Roger Elmham (1388–9) and Geoffrey Chaucer (1389–91). Ordained clergy held the office thereafter until 1419. After then all the clerks of the works were laymen with the exception of Master William Cleve (1444–51). The appointment of an ecclesiastic was now exceptional and was presumably connected with Henry VI's foundation of Eton and King's Colleges.

6. CHANCERY

The senior clerks who witnessed the first *act* of new chancellors in 1450–5 (*C.C.R. 1447–54*, pp. 194, 509; *1454–61*, p. 71) were the following:

Thomas Kirkby, keeper of the rolls, 1447–61; a beneficed priest by 1438; died 1476, as treasurer and canon of Exeter (A. F. Pollard, ' Fifteenth-Century Clerks of Parliament ', *Bulletin of the Institute of Historical Research*, XV (1938), pp. 148–50; *C.P.R. 1436–41*, p. 160; *C.P.L.* IX, p. 8; *The Register of Bishop Lacy*, F. C. Hingeston-Randolph, (ed.), part I (Exeter, 1909), p. 392; *Fasti*, IX, pp. 11, 54).

John Fawkes, clerk of Parliament, 1447–71; beneficed, dispensed to defer ordination, 1426; died 1471, as dean of Windsor, canon of Lincoln and Lichfield (Pollard, pp. 150–2; *Fasti*, I, p. 75; X, p. 50).

William Hill, master of Chancery, 1449–54; pension until beneficed, 1431; rector of Whittington, Salop, 1436; dispensed to hold a second benefice, 1437; presented to prebend of Westminster, allegedly vacant by death of William Fallan (q.v., this essay p. 112), 1450; presumably died 1454 (*C.C.R. 1429–35*, p. 106; *1447–54*, pp. 138, 497 (but not again in this source); *C.P.R. 1436–41*, p. 26; *1446–52*, p. 401; *Cal. Papal Letters*, vol. VIII, p. 656).

Richard Wetton, D.C.L., master of Chancery, 1448–65; died 1465, as canon of Wells and rector of Ditcheat, Somerset (Emden, *Oxford*, vol. III, pp. 2027–8).

Robert Kirkham, keeper of the hanaper, 1450–61; keeper of the rolls, 1461–70; died 1471, as precentor of Salisbury and dean of Westminster (*C.P.R. 1446–52*, p. 307; *1467–77*, p. 259; *Warrants for Issues*, p. 161; *Fasti*, III, p. 16).

Richard Freston, clerk of the petty bag, 1447–71; described as clerk of Chancery and gentleman of London, 1446–54; pension until beneficed, 1453; canon of Lincoln, 1456–62; died 1477, as canon of London (*Warrants for Issues*, p. 111; *C.C.R. 1447–54*, p. 415; *Fasti*, I, p. 39; V, p. 26).

William Normanton, master of Chancery, 1450–7; born c.1391; priest, beneficed from 1423; under-clerk of the hanaper in 1428–9; died 1459, as archdeacon of Chichester and canon of Salisbury (*C.C.R. 1447–54*, p. 189; *1454–61*, p. 372; *Cal. Papal Letters*, vol. X, p. 608; *Reg. Lacy*, part i, p. 69; P.R.O., E.101/215/9; *Fasti*, III, p. 50; VII, p. 12).

John Derby, LL.D., protonotary of Chancery, 1448–60; beneficed, 1432–68(?); died 1474 (*C.P.R. 1441–6*, p. 285; *C.C.R. 1447–54*, p. 142; Emden, *Cambridge*, p. 184).

NOTES

1. *Statutes of the Realm*, Record Commission, 1810–28, II, p. 171.

2. F. R. H. Du Boulay, *An Age of Ambition*, London, 1970, pp. 65–6, 69. See also D. Defoe, *The Compleat English Gentleman*. K. D. Bülbring, (ed.), London, 1895, pp. xxxii–xlv.

3. Sir George Sitwell argued that he was 'a freeman whose ancestors have always been free' ('The English Gentleman', *The Ancestor*, i (1902), pp. 58–103). Professor Du Boulay identifies him as a member of the rural middle-class improving its fortunes in the fluid land-market consequent to the Black Death, a class which developed its own standards of gentility (*Age of Ambition*, pp. 61–71).

4. *Les Reports des Cases*, J. Maynard, (ed.), London, 1678–80, VII: 14 Hen.VI, Trin. no. 52; 20 Hen.VI, Pas. no. 28; 21 Hen.VI, Mic. no. 30; 28 Hen.VI, Mic. no. 10.

5. For a servant of the dean of York styled gentleman, see *C.P.R. 1441–6*, p. 256.

6. The *O.E.D.*'s examples of the use of yeoman in this period all refer to 'menial men' of the great. The earliest example quoted showing a yeoman as a man holding a few acres is that of Bishop Latimer's father (1549). For distinction between liveries of clothing for gentlemen and yeomen, see *C.C.R. 1435–41*, pp. 384–5. A testator's distinction between 'gentlemen's sheets' and 'yeomen's sheets' in 1415 is thus not 'absurd' (Du Boulay, *Age of Ambition*, cited in note 2, p. 71). See also Carole Rawcliffe, *The Staffords, Earls of Stafford and Dukes of Buckingham, 1394–1521*, Cambridge, 1978, pp. 68–9.

7. Of nearly 10,000 recipients of general pardons in 1377–99, only two are described as yeoman (*valettus*), both being servants in households. There are no gentlemen in these rolls. See *Index to Pardon Rolls 1377–99* (unpublished Public Record Office index, 1973), pp. 61, 65.

8. *Collections for a History of Staffordshire*, William Salt Archaeological Society, original series, xvii (1896), pp. 5–11.

9. E.g. William Beddenhall of Lichfield, tailor *alias* yeoman, 1446; John Parmenter of Trent, Somerset, mason *alias* yeoman, 1452 (P.R.O.: C.67 (Pardon Rolls), nos. 39, m.29, 40, m.22).

10. E.g. master-cooks (*C.P.R. 1441–6*, pp. 259, 343).

11. P.R.O.: C.1 (Early Chancery Proceedings), bundle 16, no. 520 (of 1443–56); K.B. 27 (Coram Rege Rolls), no. 651, Rex, m.19.

12. Cf. R. L. Storey, *The End of the House of Lancaster*, London, 1966, pp. 16–17.

13. Discussed ibid., pp. 212–13.

14. P.R.O.: C.67, no. 36.

15. Ibid., no. 37. Thomas Gardyner of Brantingthorp, Leics., also ploughman, labourer, husbandman and yeoman (m.53); John Gamel, late bailiff of Shrewsbury (m.52); Philip Trembras of Trelawney(?), Cornwall, franklin (m.2).

16. Sir George Sitwell observed that in the lists of those substantial men required to take the oath against retaining evil-doers in 1434, only forty-two (*recte* forty-six) were described as gentlemen, in six of twenty-eight (*recte* twenty-nine) counties (p. 74, cited in note 3). The shire-knights who compiled these lists obviously interpreted their instructions with more liberty than consistency: esquires were described in sixteen counties, abbots and priors included in eleven. There was also great variation in numbers: over 400 were sworn in Kent, Norfolk, and Oxfordshire, under fifty in Rutland, Middlesex, Northumberland and Shropshire. Only a small proportion of those sworn were described, knights alone in every county (*C.P.R. 1429–36*, pp. 370–412).

17. P.R.O.: C.67, no. 39, m.6. Was he the defendant 'C.' in the Yearbook of 1436?

18. *C.C.R. 1413–19*, p. 322; *1419–22*, pp. 206, 227–9, 255–6; *1422–9*, p. 197. In retinues for war, men-at-arms were apparently gentlemen and archers were yeomen (*C.C.R. 1435–41*, pp. 384–5).

19. E.g. *C.P.R. 1422–9*, pp. 537, 538; *1436–41*, p. 125; John Bere, gentleman of Dunstanburgh, merchant of Berwick-upon-Tweed, and gentleman and esquire of Carlisle, 1455, (C.67, no. 41, m.15).

20. C.67, no. 45, m. 44.

21. *C.P.R. 1422–9*, p. 114.

22. He then read and so gained benefit of clergy. *C.P.R. 1436–41*, p. 260.

23. P.R.O.: K.B.27, no. 675, Rex, m.18.

24. *Rot. Parl.*, IV, pp. 421–2.

25. C.67, no. 37, m.53; *C.C.R. 1422–9*, p. 183.

26. *C.P.R. 1422–9*, p. 308; *1429–36*, pp. 23, 268; *C.C.R. 1435–41*, pp. 249–50, 383; *C.P.R. 1436–41*, p. 195; *1441–6*, p. 117; *1446–52*, p. 105 (attorney *alias* husbandman). I have found no examples in Henry VI's pardon rolls, C.67, nos. 38–43.

27. *Rot. Parl.*, V, p. 326.

28. Storey, *End of Lancaster*, cited in note 12, pp. 168–70.

29. C.67, nos. m.5, 41, m.18; J. C. Wedgwood, *History of Parliament*, London, 1936–8, vol. II, p. 277.

30. *C.P.R. 1441–6*, p. 228. He is presumably the second of three successive Robert Sheffields, all 'men of law' (see Wedgwood, *Parliament*, cited in note 29, II, pp. 759–60).

31. Heydon is gentleman in several indictments of Suffolk's henchmen in 1450 (P.R.O.: K.B.9 (Ancient Indictments), files 267, no. 24, 272, mm.1–5; see also Wedgwood, *Parliament*, cited in note 29, II, pp. 452–3).

32. *Statutes of the Realm*, cited in note 1, II, pp. 243–4, discussed in Du Boulay, *Age of Ambition*, cited in note 2, p. 71. See also *Statutes*, II, p. 309, of 1439, requiring J.P.s to have lands worth £20 p.a.

33. 10,000 is the estimate for the electorate of H. L. Gray, 'Incomes from Land in England in 1436', *E.H.R.*, xlix (1934), p. 631. Cf. numbers attesting shire elections cited in J. S. Roskell, *The Commons in the Parliament of 1422*, Manchester, 1954, pp. 9–14.

34. Sir John Fortescue, *De Laudibus Legum Angliae*, S. B. Chrimes, (ed.), Cambridge, 1942, pp. 68–9.

35. S. L. Thrupp, *The Merchant Class of Medieval London*, Chicago, 1948, pp. 118–30; J. H. Hexter, *Reappraisals in History*, London, 1961, pp. 78–80.

36. E.g. P.R.O.: E.101 (Exchequer, Various Accounts), box 407, no. 4 (Great Wardrobe account-book, 1420–21), ff.10v.–14, 36–40; and see note 68.

37. *Calendar of Fine Rolls*, H.M.S.O., 1911–62, vol. XIV, p. 293; P.R.O.: E.403 (Exchequer, Issue Rolls), no. 658, m.9.

38. *Cal. Fine Rolls*, XIV, p. 371; XIII, p. 242; *C.P.R. 1413–16*, p. 362; *1436–41*, p. 188.

39. Bertie Wilkinson, *The Chancery under Edward III*, Manchester, 1929, pp. 217–22.

40. *O.E.D.* The term king's clerk was also applied in Chancery letters to indicate, presumably, that a clerk was favoured by the king although not actually in his service: e.g. John Bath, Archbishop Arundel's secretary, once called king's

clerk in 1412, when Arundel was chancellor; Thomas Chichele and Thomas Kemp, nephews of the two archbishops, both called king's clerks only in 1443 (*C.P.R. 1408–13*, p. 370; *1441–6*, pp. 151, 162; cf. Emden, *Oxford*, I, pp. 131, 412–13; II, pp. 1032–3). In this chapter king's clerk is used to denote a man known to have been employed by the crown.

41. *Testamenta Eboracensia*, Surtees Society, I (1836), pp. 2–3; Emden, *Oxford*, II, p. 879. See also C. R. Cheney, *Notaries Public in England in the Thirteenth and Fourteenth Centuries*, Oxford, 1972, pp. 87–8.

42. T. F. Tout, *Collected Papers*, Manchester, 1934, II, pp. 162–3, 169; *C.P.R. 1370–4*, p. 414; *1374–7*, pp. 209, 491; *1377–81*, pp. 47, 104, 537; *1385–9*, p. 25.

43. *C.P.R. 1408–13*, p. 272; *1413–16*, pp. 18, 115; *Cal. Fine Rolls*, XIII, p. 185; *C.C.R. 1413–19*, p. 70; Emden, *Oxford*, II, p. 816.

44. Wilkinson, *Chancery*, pp. 65, 220. It is unlikely that 101 was the full total: the ordinance does not mention the protonotary, for instance, or the almonry of Chancery (see this essay, p. 99).

45. *C.C.R. 1422–9*, pp. 316, 432; P.R.O.: Prob.11 (Canterbury Prerogative Court Registers), no. 3 (Luffenham), f.102, which mentions two sons, a daughter, and deceased wife.

46. A. L. Brown, 'The Privy Seal Clerks in the Early Fifteenth Century', *The Study of Medieval Records*, D. A. Bullough and R. L. Storey, (eds.), Oxford, 1971, p. 270.

47. *C.P.R. 1416–22*, p. 374; *1422–9*, pp. 57, 184; *1436–41*, p. 281; *Cal. Fine Rolls*, XV, pp. 49, 63.

48. P.R.O.: E.101 (cited in note 36), boxes 405, no. 22, f.31, and 407, no. 4, f.14; Prob. 11 (cited in note 45), no. 3, f.159v.

49. The list is cited in note 37. All but one of the following first notices as 'gentilman' are in *Cal. Fine Rolls*, XV–XVII:

1424: John Denton of Lincolnshire

1427: John Derham of Buckinghamshire (baron of the Exchequer, 1448–70); John Santon of Essex; Henry Southwell of Nottinghamshire.

1428: William Scarborough of Surrey (*C.C.R. 1422–9*, p. 394); John Holme of Yorkshire (baron, 1446–62).

1429: John Aglyon of Yorkshire.

1430: Roger Byrne of Selby, Yorkshire.

1431: William Elyot of Devon; Robert Shireokes of Derbyshire.

1433: Henry Lynby of Hertfordshire; Gerard de la Hay of Yorkshire (described in his will, 1465, as *indignissimus peccator*; married. P.R.O.: Prob. 11, no. 5 (Godyn), f.101).

1438: Robert Mildenhale of London.

[Surnames spelt as in indexes of the *Calendars*.]

50. *C.P.R.* and *C.C.R.* for 1422–36, passim.

51. Emden, *Oxford*, III, p. 1810; P.R.O.: Prob. 11, no. 4. (Stokton), f.65; Wedgwood, *Parliament*, II, pp. 358–9.

52. *Cal. Fine Rolls*, XVI, p. 203; XVII, pp. 7, 73; *C.C.R. 1435–41*, pp. 247, 284; *C.P.R. 1446–52*, p. 301.

53. *C.C.R. 1435–41*, p. 369; *1441–7*, p. 221.

54. *C.P.R. 1446–52*, pp. 153, 185, 264, 309. Ashcombe was married at his death in 1466 (P.R.O.: Prob. 11, no. 5, f. 114).

55. *C.P.R.* and *C.C.R.* for 1436–61 show the following as (i) members of Chancery and (ii) of London, 'gentilman', on the dates quoted. There may be some

cases here of two men with the same name, but such coincidence is unlikely for the majority.

John Louth: (i) 1436 ... 1457; (ii) 1436 ... 1458.

John Broke: (i) 1443 ... 1459; (ii) 1456.

Thomas Buk: (i) 1444; (ii) 1456.

Thomas Morker: (i) 1446; (ii) 1448.

John Nayler: (i) 1446 ... 1459; (ii) 1444 ... 1459.

John Hill: (i) 1447; (ii) 1451 (? *Cal. Fine Rolls*, XVIII, p. 204).

Richard Cabull: (i) 1448; (ii) 1443–7.

William Bolton: (i) 1449 ... 1460; (ii) 1451, 1458.

William Goodyng: (i) 1449; (ii) 1437–53.

Master John Bekyngham; (i) 1452; (ii) 1453.

John Payn: (i) 1452, 1459; (ii) 1442, 1452 ... 1461.

Hugh Wynkley: (i) 1452; (ii) 1446–60.

Thomas Tetisworth: (i) 1453–5; (ii) 1458.

Richard Loy: (i) 1454; (ii) 1451 (*Cal. Fine Rolls*, XIX, p. 217).

Henry Upton: (i) 1454, 1460; (ii) 1448 (Ibid., vol. XVIII, p. 93), 1455.

Henry Wyndesore: (i) 1455–8; (ii) 1456–60.

John Toller: (i) 1457; (ii) 1454–9.

[Surnames spelt as in indexes of the *Calendars*.]

56. *Reports*, cited in note 4, 20 Hen.VI., Pas. no. 28. Many notaries were married by this time (Cheney, *Notaries Public*, cited in note 41, pp. 79–81). Robert Percy, a married notary who was registrar of the archdeaconry of Westminster, was called a gentleman in 1457 (*C.C.R. 1454–61*, pp. 42, 213, 447). He would have been a member of the household of the abbot of Westminster.

57. *C.C.R. 1441–7*, p. 64; *C.P.R. 1446–52*, p. 264. See also note 78 below.

58. P.R.O.: C.67, cited in note 9, nos. 41, m.30 (1455), 44, m. 47 (1462).

59. E.g. collectors and controllers of customs. Under Henry IV, about twenty (a minority) are called clerks in notices of appointments in *Cal. Fine Rolls*; there are six under Henry V. After 1422, they are rare and probably ordained clergy: Robert Dixon and Richard Lumbard at Boston in 1423, and Nicholas Clerk at Hull in 1429, seem to have been rectors of nearby churches (*C.P.R. 1429–36*, p. 387; *C.C.R. 1422–9*, p. 301; *1429–35*, p. 354). The last appointments of (four) clergy as customers were in 1438–9, possibly at the instance of Cardinal Beaufort (*Cal. Fine Rolls*, XVII, pp. 58–60). See also A. Steel, ' The Collectors of the Customs in the Reign of Richard II ', *British Government and Administration* ', H. Hearder and H. R. Loyn, (eds.), Cardiff, 1974, pp. 27–39.

60. Appendix to this essay, pp. 110–20.

61. The only fifteenth-century lay chancellors were Thomas Beaufort (1407–9) and Richard Neville, earl of Salisbury (1454–5). Keepers of the privy seal and secretaries were all ecclesiastics (*Handbook of British Chronology*, F. M. Powicke and E. B. Fryde, (eds.), Royal Historical Society, 1961, pp. 85–6, 92–3; J. Otway-Ruthven, *The King's Secretary and the Signet Office in the Fifteenth Century*, Cambridge, 1939, pp. 153–5, 160–79. See also R. L. Storey, *Diocesan Adminis-tration in Fifteenth-Century England*, Borthwick Papers no. 16, York, 2nd. ed., 1972, pp. 16–7).

62. Appendix to this essay, p. 122. Cf. note 55 above.

63. *C.P.R. 1436–41*, p. 567. Crosby, Gedney and Osbern were signet clerks (Otway-Ruthven, cited in note 61, pp. 185–6). Osbern's wife was an heiress and he

is described as esquire (*C.P.R. 1441–6*, p. 136; *1446–52*, p. 320). Henry Benet and Thomas Frank were in the Privy Seal Office from c.1418, to 1453 in Frank's case, and longer for Benet (Ibid., *1436–41*, pp. 197, 521; *1452–61*, pp. 79, 143, 195; *Warrants for Issues 1399–1485*, P.R.O. Lists and Indexes, Supplementary Series, no. IX, 2, 1964, pp. 25, 110, 178). Frank and his privy seal-colleagues William Alberton and John Claydon were granted pensions until beneficed, 1423–6. All later received secular offices in Wales (*C.C.R. 1422–9*, pp. 56, 260, 266, 314; *C.P.R. 1422–9*, pp. 205, 537; *1429–36*, pp. 144, 196). Alberton was called gentleman, of London, 1448. Frank's widow occurs 1455 (*C.C.R. 1447–8*, p. 97; *1454–61*, p. 66).

64. R. Somerville, *History of the Duchy of Lancaster*, I, London, 1953, pp. 99, 119, 190–4, and lists of officers from p. 364.

65. *C.P.R. 1408–13*, p. 272.

66. This essay pp. 97, 99. *C.P.R. 1399–1401*, p. 445; *1405–8*, p. 86; *1408–13*, p. 24.

67. Ibid., 285, *1422–9*, p. 264; *1429–36*, p. 254; *1446–52*, p. 325. For the similar case of John Feriby, see the Appendix to this essay at pp. 115–16.

68. *C.P.R. 1416–22*, pp. 397, 401; *1422–9*, pp. 7, 345, 383, 463, 474. For Aumener, see this essay, p. 99. For Garstang, see Somerville, *Lancaster*, p. 478; *C.C.R. 1435–41*, pp. 333, 456. His will, dated 1464, shows he was married; he was born at Garstang, Lancs., and settled at Cirencester, Glos.; his bequests included a royal livery 'de SS' (P.R.O.: Prob. 11, no. 5 (Godyn, f.41v.).

69. Emden, *Oxford*, vol. II, pp. 1037–8; A. L. Brown, *The Early History of the Clerkship of the Council*, Glasgow University Publications N.S. 131, 1969, pp. 33–4.

70. Appendix to this essay, p. 120.

71. *viz.* Fallan and Lewisham, see this essay p. 112. Cf. note 49, p. 125 above.

72. R. L. Storey, 'Recruitment of English Clergy in the Period of the Conciliar Movement', *Annuarium Historiae Conciliorum*, vii, 1975, esp. pp. 307–10.

73. *C.P.R. 1401–5*, p. 305; *C.P.L.*, VI, p. 153; and the Appendix to this essay. p. 120.

74. Otway-Ruthven, *King's Secretary*, 44, m. 47 cited in note 61, pp. 171–2. For other examples of deferred orders, see the Appendix to this essay, pp. 115, 116, 122.

75. A. L. Brown, 'Privy Seal Clerks', cited in note 46, pp. 267–8.

76. Appendix to this essay, pp. 110–3, 115–8, 120, 122.

77. Tout, *Coll. Papers*, cited in note 42, II, p. 169.

78. No wives or children are mentioned in the wills of Robert Shireokes of the Exchequer, 1439 (P.R.O.: Prob. 11, no. 3, f.214; above, note 49, p. 125), and William Crosby, esquire, of the signet office (Prob. 11, no. 4, f.141v.; Otway-Ruthven, *King's Secretary*, cited in note 61, pp. 130–1, 185). See also the Chancery clerks Ashcombe and Walsham, this essay, pp. 99–100.

79. G. M. Trevelyan, *England in the Age of Wycliffe*, reprinted London, 1972, pp. 106–13.

80. R. L. Storey, 'Clergy and common law in the reign of Henry IV', *Medieval Legal Records*, R. F. Hunnisett and J. B. Post, (eds.), H.M.S.O., 1978, pp. 350–2, 363–5, 391–5, 402–3.

81. Storey, *End of Lancaster*, cited in note 12, pp. 52–3.

82. This essay, pp. 113–4.

83. P.R.O.: E.28 (Council and Privy Seal), file 58; Storey, *End of Lancaster*, cited in note 12, p. 31.

84. Otway-Ruthven, *King's Secretary*, cited in note 61, pp. 183–4; Somerville, *Lancaster*, cited in note 64, p. 607; *C.P.R. 1436–41*, pp. 154, 172.

85. *C.C.R. 1422–9*, p. 326; *C.P.R. 1436–41*, pp. 69, 193 (life-grant).

86. *C.P.R.*, 93, *1441–6*, p. 373; this essay, pp. 101–2.

87. Ibid., *1422–9*, p. 332; *1429–36*, p. 196; *1436–41*, pp. 195, 362–3; and note 63 above.

88. This essay, pp. 118–9.

89. *C.P.R. 1452–61*, p. 513; and note 58 above.

90. Haseley's will, 1449, describes him as knight, under-marshal of England, clerk of the crown in Chancery and J.P. for Middlesex; it shows he was born at Great Haseley, Oxon., and was twice married (Lambeth Palace Library: Register of Archbishop Stafford, ff.174–5). He admitted to an income of £100 from land in 1436 (Gray, 'Incomes', cited in note 33, p. 638; see also *C.C.R. 1447–54*, pp. 134–5; *Cal. Fine Rolls*, XVIII, p. 97). Kent (this essay, p. 102) was able to bequeath his (second) wife £800, including £100 owed by the earl of Warwick (P.R.O.: Prob. 11, no. 5, f.205). For Thorp, see this essay, p. 107.

91. Storey, *End of Lancaster*, pp. 37–42, which does not mention this added burden on patronage.

92. This essay, p. 97, and note 90; *C.P.R. 1422–9*, p. 330; *1429–36*, pp. 156, 336, 346; *1441–6*, p. 130.

93. Wedgwood, *Parliament*, II, p. 801.

94. P.R.O.: E.101 box 407, no. 4, cited in note 36, m.10v., *Cal. Fine Rolls*, XIII, p. 245; XIV, p. 124; XV, p. 272; XVI, p. 95; XVIII, p. 268; *C.C.R. 1429–35*, p. 228; *1435–41*, p. 93; *1447–54*, pp. 26, 487; *1454–61*, pp. 307–8; *C.P.R. 1422–9*, p. 127; *1452–61*, p. 320. His career apparently began as clerk to Thomas Overton, baron of the Exchequer (d.1407. This essay, p. 110).

95. J. S. Roskell, *The Commons and their Speakers in Medieval Parliaments*, Manchester, 1965, pp. 248–54, 366–7; 'Thomas Thorpe, Speaker in the Reading Parliament of 1453', *Nottingham Medieval Studies*, VII (1963), pp. 79–105.

96. W. A. Pantin, *The English Church in the Fourteenth Century*, Cambridge, 1955, pp. 11–13.

97. *Register of Henry Chichele*, Canterbury and York Society, 1937–47, II, p. 681.

98. R. L. Storey, *Thomas Langley and the Bishopric of Durham*, London, 1961, pp. 219, 1–22. At the time I was not aware of this significance in Langley's career.

99. Storey, 'Clergy and common law', cited in note 80, p. 351.

100. R. L. Storey, 'Ecclesiastical Causes in Chancery', *Study of Medieval Records*, cited in note 46, pp. 244–54. Royal presentations in exchanges appear frequently in *C.P.R.* There were between thirty and forty p.a. in 1399–1407 and then a decline in numbers; after 1425 the annual total was usually in single figures.

101. Kathleen Edwards, *The English Secular Cathedrals in the Middle Ages*, Manchester, 2nd. ed., 1967, pp. 85–9; Barrie Dobson, 'The Later Middle Ages, 1215–1500', *A History of York Minster*, G. E. Aylmer and R. Cant, (eds.), Oxford, 1977, pp. 66, 74; G. F. Lytle, 'Patronage Patterns and Oxford Colleges c.1300–c.1530', *The University in Society*, Lawrence Stone, (ed.), Princeton, 1974, vol. I, pp. 122–5, 129–34.

102. Roskell, *Speakers*, cited in note 95, p. 338.

103. Pantin, *English Church*, cited in note 96, pp. 39–46; Storey, *Diocesan Administration*, cited in note 61, pp. 19–20, and cf. 29–33.

104. *Statutes of the Realm*, cited in note 1, vol. III, part 1, p. 216.

5

The cultural interests and achievements of the secular personnel of the local administration

HELEN M. JEWELL

The medieval English governmental policy of running local administration inexpensively through the often nominally unrewarded labours of a wide range of local men, impressed *ad hoc* for some specific administrative duty, makes difficult any overall classification of local secular administrators.

By the early years of the fourteenth century, hundreds of men were unprofessional civil servants in their localities, commissioned occasionally to levy taxation in their area, or to supervise the array of armed men there, or to buttress a commission of justices from the central courts on itinerant visitations of assize or oyer and terminer. Some of these individuals were apparently only employed in these ways in an area once or twice; others were repeatedly commissioned by the government for particular types of task in an area, but not across the whole range of local administration; and some were repeatedly commissioned for a wide variety of tasks in one or more counties: these men were apparently flexible administrators who could apply themselves equally well to raising taxes or levying troops, settling arbitrations, sitting on judicial commissions, conserving the peace, and sometimes representing their locality in parliament.[1] Such men were not retained in permanent office by the government, but were practically professional in their almost habitual employment for one task or another.

It is clear that any grouping together of the secular personnel of the local administration is bound to be unwieldy in numbers if everyone who ever held at least one local administrative commission, for however short a period, is included, and a single classification might well seem too broad to be meaningful if so rarely commissioned a person is treated as the equal of administrators with a much greater degree of familiarity with varied administrative tasks, over many years, in one or more geographical areas. Moreover, what the local administrators had in common, namely some government commission, and responsibility to the government, may seem hardly enough to hold together men from widely differing social environments, for the local administrators of the medieval counties were very widely ranging in social stratification. The local administration employed so many levels of society from the friends of kings and members of the nobility to the remotest township constables, that to group these together in any single way might seem a mockery of classification. There were among the holders of local administrative commissions members of the nobility,[2] and also clerical personnel, performing administrative tasks at other times entrusted to laymen.[3] There were individuals holding local commissions who worked at times in branches of the central civil service, exchequer, royal household, or central judicial benches,[4] and others who held local government offices during a career which included working for a private employer.[5]

It is, therefore, admitted that the grouping selected for study is unwieldy in numbers, widely varied in social composition, and difficult to define. However, some degree of focus can be achieved by limiting the survey geographically, and for this reason the following investigation will be concentrated on the medieval county of Yorkshire, with parallel illustrations from neighbouring counties. Men only, save in a few exceptional cases,[6] held local administrative commissions, but female relatives of administrators will be included in this study.

The large group of men who are under consideration enjoyed varying degrees of government employment, and had experience of both governing and being governed. When commissioned to administer, they would learn the desirability of power, necessary to expedite the king's business. When left to suffer being administered they would want protection from arbitrary treatment by officials. It was this healthy balance in the administrators' minds between the minimum amount of power which could reasonably be allowed to officials for the purpose of carrying out the government's requirements efficiently, and the maximum degree of governmental control which free men would tolerate, which made medieval bureaucracy the flexible and pragmatic machine it was. Red tape and the rule book did not yet dominate.

Among so many men with different personal backgrounds, and

employed at various levels, a wide range of cultural attainments may be expected. Attempting to study the cultural interests and achievements of a group of such diversity involves first establishing proofs of basic literacy among members of the group. Then only may one look for signs of more advanced education, and cultural interests, such as the possession of books, (and, more valuably still, indications of their owners having read them), and self expression in writing, including letters. Evidence of patronage of the various arts must also be considered, and it proves rewarding to look for indications of awareness of the value of education.

As to literacy, the clearest indication that the government actually required this in some of its local agents at least comes from those commissions of appointment which state that the official is to keep the records 'in his own hand'. Geoffrey Chaucer's commission in 1377 to keep the customs counter-roll in London was one such commission; Chaucer was a most untypical controller of customs, but similar requirements were asked that year of the controllers of other ports, including in the north Henry Briggesle, described as chaplain, at Hull, and John Paxton and later John Eghton at Newcastle-upon-Tyne.[7] The wording of these commissions presupposes controllers were expected to be literate in the 1370s, and perhaps most controllers were. But Chaucer's career reveals how much more than the basic qualification of literacy such an appointee might have. No other controller is considered to have been a literary genius, though a Boston (Lincolnshire) one, John Bell, managed to write 'pedestrian Latin verse' on exchequer venality in the early years of Henry IV's reign.[8] Chaucer's career included many activities which were out of the normal sphere of local officialdom, but he also held posts well within the more usual range of customs officials. As a justice of the peace, and member of parliament for Kent, he would have fitted in with the career pattern of his contemporaries at Newcastle-upon-Tyne.[9]

Another indication of literacy, and indeed of more academic education, can be found in government record in the giving of a title suggestive of formal intellectual training, such as *Magister* before a name, or the description 'king's clerk', or 'clerk', or 'chaplain' after it, showing that some men employed in tasks at other times performed adequately by laymen were clerics.[10] Hull's Briggesle, described above as chaplain, was one such, and in Hull in the early fourteenth century *Magister* John Barton was at different times collector of customs, member of parliament for the borough, mayor, and coroner. However, not all the references give

John Barton the *Magister* title, and as the name is hardly distinctive in Humberside, it is impossible to be sure that this is the career of only one man.[11] Two knights of the shire for Yorkshire in early fourteenth-century parliaments were described as clerks, Roger Clotherum, and Hamo Alverthorp.[12]

Sometimes it is possible to discern that an administrator was actually a trained lawyer. William Eland, for example, member of parliament for Hull in 1450, 1459, 1461, 1467, 1469, and 1470 was a lawyer, and was a justice of the peace, and Archbishop Neville's seneschal of Beverley. He was sheriff of Hull, in 1458, and resided there, but Jalland considers him ' more of a country gentleman than a burgess '.[13] Richard Drax, member of parliament for Carlisle in 1422, and John Forster, member for Appleby in the same parliament, were both members of Lincoln's Inn; Forster had been made a forester for life in Inglewood forest from 1394.[14] At Newcastle-upon-Tyne, Richard Weltden, member of parliament 1450–1 and 1467, was a lawyer, and commissioner of the peace; his family lived in the borough but is classed by Jalland as ' a local Northumberland county family '.[15]

These instances demonstrate literacy in some identified administrators. But the identification of some literate controllers, members of parliament, justices of the peace, and a collector of customs who was also a coroner and a mayor, does not mean that all such officials may be assumed to be literate even at the time of the reference. It is hard to pin down the actual government requirements for any level of office in the local administration. The use of the tally at the exchequer, once seen as indication of the illiteracy of medieval accountants, is not now seen as such proof. A recent history of the sheriff's office states categorically that the tally ' was not used by the exchequer or the sheriffs because they were unable to read or write or make mathematical calculations ', citing Ralph Glanvill, William Fitzstephen, and Gervase of Cornhill as early examples of cultured and financially skilful sheriffs.[16] Admittedly, these were exceptionally talented men. But when more ordinary men, of the shire-knight class, became the typical sheriffs in the thirteenth century, the sheriffs' judicial duties ' required a good knowledge of the common law ', and their fiscal responsibilities to the exchequer required financial expertise, for which reason some apparently began to employ professional accountants at their own expense if they were not confident of their own abilities.[17] By the end of the fourteenth century, the sheriffs are seen as country gentlemen, holding land from the local lord and sending their sons to the lord's household to learn of tournaments and war skills.[18] What part reading, writing, or arithmetic had in this education is not clear. As for coroners, the first record of these officers, from 1194, implies that a clerical coroner would be needed to keep the records his knightly colleagues might not be able to read. Clerical coroners soon disappeared, and knightly ones gave way to coroners from the non-knightly gentry. Coroners had clerks, so their personal literacy is not to be assumed too readily. The government seems to have been more concerned to enforce landed status than education as the qualification for office; however, there was one occasion when lack of literacy seems to have been regarded as a disqualifying factor in the fifteenth century. That he was 'an illiterate man, altogether unqualified to serve in that office' was one reason for replacing a Derbyshire coroner in 1443.[19]

A mixture of inference from general requirements and specific statement or information about particular cases takes the question of basic literacy this far and no further. But what of further cultural interests and attainments?

The most accessible evidence of book ownership in this period comes from wills. Very many of the books mentioned in Yorkshire wills were left, as might be expected, by ecclesiastics, and usually either to other clerics or to churches or to ecclesiastical libraries. However, books do appear in the wills of lay persons from time to time. Out of 148 wills examined in Dr. Vale's recent study, only twenty-four mentioned books.[20] It must be made clear that, judging from their wills, many lay people possessed only religious books, and that they regarded these simply as part of the furniture of their chapels, and left them to local churches, often along with vestments and plate. In a will proved in 1378, Marmaduke Constable, knight, sheriff of Yorkshire 1360–2 and 1366–7, and a justice of oyer and terminer and of the peace in Yorkshire and other northern counties, left a bible to the prior and Convent of Warter.[21] In 1379 Robert Swillington, knight, left to Swillington church two missals, a large portable breviary (*portiforium magnum*) and other equipment of the chapel.[22] There was more than one Robert Swillington active in government record around this time, but since in the will this Robert calls himself Robert Swillington, knight, junior, his tentative identification with the Robert Swillington the younger, knight, who was given a commission of oyer and terminer to investigate the breaking of a close at Creskeld in Wharfedale in May 1375 seems reasonable.[23] In 1404

Agnes St. Quintin, widow of John St. Quintin, a keeper of Scarborough castle and knight of the shire for Yorkshire, left a missal to Sigglesthorne church.[24] Richard Russell of York, merchant, a sheriff of the city in 1412 and mayor in 1421 and 1430, left in 1435 a large Antiphonary, a *Legenda* of the York Use, three notated books of anthems (*gradalia*), a notated book *De Invitatoriis cum versibus et collectis cum processionario*) and a large missal (*magnum missale*) to St. John's, Hungate, York.[25]

In other wills, books were left by laymen to specific churchmen. Joan Walkingham, widow of John, a knight of the shire for Yorkshire in 1325, in a will proved in 1347, left to the parish church of St. Felix, Ravensthorpe, a missal and a silk cope, but singled out two named recipients for other books. One, *Dominus* Peter Riccall, was left Joan's old portable breviary (*vetus portiforium*). The other, *Dominus* Walter Creton, rector of Cowthorpe and one of those present at the making of the will, was to receive a psalter and a book in English (*psalterium cum littera grossa et quendum librum scriptum littera anglicana*).[26] In 1405 Thomas Graa of York, eight times member of parliament for York city, and son of a York member of parliament, left to John Horsley, chaplain ' unum librum vocatum Tyxt'.[27]

It is of more interest in the present study when a testator disposes of several identified books to lay persons, whether or not books were also left to churches or churchmen in the same will. Henry Percy, keeper of Scarborough castle, commissioner of oyer and terminer in Yorkshire, commissioner of array and keeper of the marches, whose will was made in 1349, left his daughter Isabel a collection of goods ending with ' unum librum de Natura Animalium in gallico'.[28] This Isabel married William, son of Gilbert Ayton, both of whom are mentioned in the will. Isabel's husband was a justice of oyer and terminer, of the peace, and of labourers, in the North and East Ridings, and sheriff of Yorkshire 1368–70 and 1372–3.[29] The womenfolk of the Percy family and circle evidently had at least the opportunity to read. In a will proved in 1394, Mary Roos, widow of John Lord Roos of Hamlake, joint warden of the West March and a commissioner of the peace in the North Riding, daughter of Henry, third baron Percy, a warden of the marches and governor of Berwick, left money and clothing to Isobel Percy, along with ' libro gallico de Duce Lancastriae, et [meum] primerium viride, quod quondam fuit domini patris [mei]'.[30]

Robert Roos, who died in 1392, is identifiable as a commissioner of oyer and terminer, and of the peace, and as an arrayer, sheriff of Yorkshire, collector of subsidies, and knight of the shire for the county.[31] He left a missal, two portable breviaries, and a book of anthems to the chapel of St. Mary, Ingmanthorpe, a small psalter to his son Thomas, a French book 'de veteribus historiis' to Thomas's wife, Joan, a French psalter to his own daughter Eleanor, along with a bible and a French Legenda Sanctorum, and the sapphire ring with which he had married her mother; to his daughter Katherine, a nun, went a small psalter which had been her mother's, and a French book Sydrak was left to Elizabeth Stapleton.[32] John Depeden, knight, in a will proved in 1402, left a newly bought missal with silver-gilt clasps to the chantry priests of Healaugh Park, and two newly bought books of anthems, and to the church of Healaugh he left the missal he used daily in his own chapel (missale quo utor cotidie in capella mea). Among many beneficiaries of this will, Joan, wife of William Beckwith, received a large primer with illuminated letters (primarium magnum cum litteris illuminatis). Depeden was a justice of the peace in the West Riding in 1394, and had a commission to arrest two men and bring them before the king and council in 1396, and an oyer and terminer commission to investigate a plaint of Fountains the same year. He and his wife Elizabeth had licence to alienate lands in Caterton and the advowson of Healaugh into mortmain for the benefit of the prior and convent of Healaugh Park.[33]

Sir John le Scrope, knight, brother of Archbishop Scrope and a commissioner of the peace, of walls and ditches, and of array, and keeper of the temporalities of the archbishopric, and knight of the shire for Yorkshire in 1401, died in 1405, leaving to his daughter and coheiress Joan 'unum librum de gallico vocatum Tristrem', and to his other daughter and coheiress Elizabeth a French book called Grace Dieu.[34] One of his daughters married Sir Richard Hastings, knight of the shire for Yorkshire, sheriff of the county, constable of Knaresborough castle, arrayer, peace commissioner and assessor of subsidies.[35]

Eleanor Roos, daughter of Robert Roos and a beneficiary of his will cited above, left in 1438 a psalter to Robert Roos, knight, her nephew, and 'unum librum Anglicanum vocatum primum librum Magistri Walteri' to Robert's wife.[36] In the same will, Isabel Roos was left a 'primarium de Sancto Spiritu', and Richard Roos, the testatrix's great nephew, a book 'de passione Domini', while his wife was left Credo in Deum. A book called Maulde Buke was left to Joan Courtenay. Meanwhile, the Thomas Roos who received the small psalter in 1392 left a psalter to the rector of Kirk Deighton church, where he hoped to be buried; to *Dominus* William Healaugh he left a book called *Maundevyl* and the book *Prick of Conscience*; to William Pukston he left his '*primarium* [*meum*] *nigrum cum orationibus*' and to Elizabeth Redman his *Legenda Sanctorum*.[37] This Elizabeth was the daughter of William Aldeburgh, lord of Harewood, and was married first to Sir Brian Stapleton, by whom she was the mother of Sir Brian Stapleton, knight of the shire for Yorkshire in 1416, and secondly to Sir Richard Redman of Levens. Redman, or Redmayne, was a noteworthy administrator who held 'at one time or another practically every position open to a man of his class and calibre', including the shrievalties of Cumberland and Yorkshire, the escheatorship of Yorkshire, membership of parliament, where he was Speaker in 1415, commissions of oyer and terminer, of the peace, of array, a commission to bring to trial and execute rebels in Yorkshire, and surveyorship of weirs.[38] A later Yorkshire sheriff, Sir John Savill, sheriff 1454–5 and appointed again in 1460, left in 1481 'unum librum vocatum Missale' to John Savill, with other goods, 'pro le heirelomes'.[39]

One case where a cleric thought fit to leave books to laymen emerges from the will, made in 1432, of John Raventhorpe, priest of St. Martin's, Aldwark, York. He left a small library of books, mainly to be divided between ecclesiastics and churches, but including a missal left to Thomas Bracebrigg of York, who had been a sheriff of the city in 1416 and its lord mayor in 1424. John Raventhorpe also left an English book of fables and stories, the only specifically English work detailed in his will, to one Agnes Celayne, who had been his servant for many years.[40]

This examination of wills has shown that books were owned by northern administrative families, and that they were in some cases valued by them not merely as chapel furniture. That any of the administrators crossed the barrier from enjoying others' work to producing their own seems much less likely. Henry, first duke of Lancaster, wrote his *Le Livre de Seyntz Medicines* in 1354, a copy of which Mary Roos left to Isobel Percy, but Lancaster must be ranked as socially above the administrative class treated here.[41] A nearer candidate for inclusion is the Lancastrian poet Sir Richard Roos (c.1410–82). His family had long connections with Helmsley, and his biographer suggests that the poet probably lived there in his infancy, before joining his elder brothers at Belvoir, where his father, William, sixth Lord Roos, treasurer of England 1403–4, had founded a chantry with, as one of its purposes, the education of his younger sons in 'discipline and grammar'.[42] Sir Richard held a few administrative commissions in his lifetime, but not in the northern counties. The Roos family was well connected and culturally active. Sir Richard's aunt Elizabeth married Thomas, sixth Lord Clifford, and their daughter Matilda married Richard earl of Cambridge, and bequeathed several primers distinguished as '[meum] primarium viride', 'unum parvum nigrum primarium' and 'magnum primarium optimum', a portable breviary, and two French books called Gyron le Curtasse.[43] Sir Richard's uncle John married Mary Percy, whose bequeathed books have already been detailed.[44] The Roos family erected the St. William window in the north transept in York Minster in 1422, in memory of the sixth lord, and Sir Richard and his brother Sir Robert are portrayed in the glass.[45]

There is no known evidence of Yorkshire administrative families commissioning the copying of texts, as occurred in the East Anglian Paston family. Nor is there evidence of these families commissioning writings, and though there would appear to be an element of commissioning in the guild texts of miracle plays, insufficient is known about the original authorship and degree of later adaptation to make it possible to know what part individuals had in writing, adapting or commissioning plays in the northern cycles. If the northern administrative families were not writing or commissioning books, a few members of them were certainly writing letters, even though the surviving correspondence may not be holograph. Indeed, none of the Plumpton correspondence is, for the whole collection only survives in early seventeenth-century transcriptions made for Sir Edward Plumpton; however some of the letters were originally in the correspondents' own writing and state this.[46] Medieval private correspondence is a rare treasure, and the few collections which survive have on the whole been closely scrutinised by scholars, particularly the letters of the Pastons of East Anglia. Of the four major collections from the fifteenth century, the Plumpton correspondence from the West Riding of Yorkshire is the least well known.

The main series of the Plumpton correspondence in the Plumpton Letterbook begins in the time of Sir William Plumpton (1404–80), who was sheriff of Yorkshire in 1447–8 and of Nottingham and Derby in 1452–3. He was a retainer of the Percies and seneschal of their Yorkshire estates; he held crown office as constable of Knaresborough castle and master forester of Knaresborough forest; he also served as a commissioner of the peace in the West

Riding.[47] There are however isolated earlier letters, among which, from the Plumpton Coucher Book, is the earliest of them to be written in English, from some citizens of York to Sir William's father, Sir Robert Plumpton, in 1416.[48] This Sir Robert, who died in 1421, was a knight of the shire for Yorkshire in 1411 and 1416, and for Nottinghamshire in 1414, and great grandson of an earlier Yorkshire knight of the shire, Sir William Plumpton who died in 1361. The range of the Plumpton family's marital connections, from townsfolk to titled nobility, is interesting. Sir William Plumpton who died in 1361 was married to Christiana, widow of Richard Emeldon, intermittently mayor of Newcastle-upon-Tyne from 1305–6 to 1332; this Sir William founded a chantry at Ripon.[49] His son, Sir Robert, who died in 1407, was married to Isabella Scrope, sister of the archbishop of York executed for treason in 1405. Sir Robert's son, Sir William, married Alice, daughter of John Gisburn, mayor of York in 1371, 1372, and 1380. This William was also executed for his part in the Scrope rebellion, and left at least nine children. The eldest, Sir Robert Plumpton (1383–1421) was a knight of the shire for Yorkshire and for Nottinghamshire and married the heiress Alice Foljambe. Another son, George, became an ecclesiastic, and in 1447 was presented to the rectory of Bingham (Notts), the gift of Sir Thomas Chaworth, whose daughter had married John, Lord Scrope of Masham.[50] A letter to George from his sister Katherine Chadderton is preserved in the Letterbook, mentioning an apparently ill-received earlier request for a psalter or primer, wanted by Katherine's daughter.[51] Sir Robert Plumpton's son Sir William (1404–80) married Elizabeth, daughter of Sir Brian Stapleton. This Sir William was commissioned with Sir William Gascoign and Sir Robert Waterton, knights, and others, to array men in the West Riding in 1435. William and Elizabeth were admitted to the fraternity of St. Christopher's guild in York in 1439.[52] Their eldest son, Robert, was married to Elizabeth, daughter of Thomas Lord Clifford, but since Robert died before the consummation of the marriage, she was married to the next brother, William, who was killed at the battle of Towton in 1461. Sir William had another son called Robert (1453–1523), by his secret marriage to Joan Wintringham, and this Sir Robert married Agnes, daughter of Sir William Gascoign of Gawthorpe. An illegitimate son of Sir William Plumpton, also called Robert, was elected common clerk of York in 1490.[53]

The Plumpton letters do not really provide much information about the family's cultural interests, being much taken up with litigation over land. They do, however, reflect the well tried formulae of laboured letter writing, and on the legal side it appears that the Plumpton writers and recipients of letters understood a wide range of law terms in Latin.[54] They also reflect an interest in current affairs.[55] Through the correspondents they show that other administrators communicated by letters. Among the Plumptons' friends and relations whose letters survive in the collection from the period up to 1500 were Sir Ralph Ryther, who became sheriff of Yorkshire in 1503, and Sir Brian Roucliffe, a justice of the peace and baron of the exchequer.[56] Correspondence with the earls of Northumberland shows the level of patronage and clientship. Edward Plumpton, a lawyer and attorney for Sir Robert, described himself in a letter as 'secretary to my lord Straung'.[57] From the correspondence 'there is almost no evidence of books' in the family's possession.[58] George Plumpton's brothers Brian and Richard inherited money and plate from their cousin Stephen le Scrope, Archdeacon of Richmond, and Richard was left a black psalter by Matilda Mauley, widow of Peter Mauley VIII.[59] Richard left his small psalter to his brother George, a psalter covered with red velvet to 'the minister of the house of St. Robert', and a primer covered in red satin to Ellen Crosse.[60]

To speak of the patronage of the arts in this period is to use the term in a rather restricted sense. It is clear that people had an appreciation of the work of woodcarvers, stonemasons, goldsmiths, and other craftsmen, and that they had respect for scholars, though in this latter case perhaps more as men of religion than as men of learning. One case where a northern administrator exercised protection over a young man of promise had very great consequences, for the protégé was Richard Rolle, ultimately one of medieval England's most read authors. Rolle was born at Thornton-le-Dale around 1300, and studied at Oxford, under the sponsorship of Thomas Neville, later Archdeacon of Durham. About 1320 Rolle abandoned his studies, with the idea of becoming a hermit. It was at this point that he found protection from John Dalton, then constable of Pickering castle, who gave food and shelter to this mystical youth. A recent editor of Rolle's *Fire of Love* described Dalton as 'squire of the village of Dalton and constable of Pickering, a self made man and ruthless character', who lost his post at Pickering after the failure of Lancaster's rebellion in 1322.[61] Duchy of Lancaster Ministers' Accounts refer to John Dalton as bailiff and receiver of Pickering in the early years of the fourteenth century, and he rendered account in this capacity for

the year from Michaelmas 1313 before the earl of Lancaster's auditors, Sir Simon Balderstone and Robert Silkstone, at Pontefract.
Dalton was named as a late constable of Pickering castle in the
forest eyre of 1334, and with this role went the wardenship of the
forest of Pickering. His wages were £10 per year.[62] An idea of
Dalton's alleged ruthlessness can be gleaned from the petition of
Nicholas 'At the bridge' of Pickering that Dalton as bailiff had
detained him in prison at his house for over six weeks in 1319,
claiming that Nicholas owed the earl of Lancaster over £100, and
had forced him to surrender his lands to Dalton to obtain release.[63]
Dalton having been removed from office in 1322, he was delivered
from prison and his chattels were restored to him at the request of
Henry Percy and Eleanor (Henry's mother).[64] A John Dalton paid
5s. in the taxation of the soke of Pickering in 1327, and 5s. $0\frac{3}{4}d$. in
1333.[65] In the Pickering forest eyres of the 1330s he was convicted
of giving away does and hinds, and delivering felled oaks without
authorisation.[66] Whether he was literate or not is unproven. Accounts show him allowed 5s. for parchment for rolls of the wapen-
take and forest attachment courts, but it is clear that he had, as
constable, at least one clerk, Roger Long, who seems to have acted on
the financial side.[67] Dalton emerges from the administrative records
as a hard, even ruthless man, and since he is known to have resisted
the agistment claims of the Abbot of Rievaulx, he was obviously
capable of standing up to men of religion.[68] It seems therefore rather
curious to find him as the saintly Rolle's protector.

Evidence of artistic commissioning by private persons is now
most clearly testified by commemorative monuments. The previously mentioned stained glass St. William window in York Minster, erected by the Roos family, was a handsome memorial,[69] and
another, smaller commemorative window in the Minster from this
period is the Tunnock window in the north aisle. Richard Tunnock
was a bailiff of York, in 1320–1, and a member of parliament for
the city in 1327, and founded a perpetual chantry in the Minster in
1328. He had himself portrayed in the window, presenting a model
of it to St. William of York. Tunnock was a bell founder and
goldsmith and the window is decorated with bells.[70] Sir Edmund
Mauley, killed at Bannockburn in 1314, has his arms in a commemorative window in the nave of the Minister, and in the aisle
window below is the figure of Stephen Mauley, Archdeacon of
Cleveland, who died in 1317 and is thought to be the person who
commissioned the windows.[71] Commemorative windows are, however, rare survivals; more memorials have survived in stone.

The Percy tomb in Beverley Minster is described by Pevsner as 'the apogee of fourteenth-century funerary sculpture, and of fourteenth-century sculpture altogether', and 'the most splendid of all British Decorated funerary monuments'.[72] It is not even certain who is here commemorated: likely contenders for the honour are Eleanor Percy, who died in 1328, and her daughter-in-law, Idonea or Immania, née Clifford.[73] What is clear is that admiration of this tomb spread quickly, and it is held to be the inspiration behind the monument to Sir Edmund Mauley at Bainton, and one of the de la Pole monuments in Holy Trinity, Hull.[74] Several effigies identifiable with administrators have survived on tombs from this period. Sir Peter Middleton, who died in office as sheriff of Yorkshire in 1335, reposes in effigy in Ilkley Parish Church, in mail armour with his shield. It is thought that this effigy was made at York some time before Middleton's death.[75] Sir William de la Pole, who died in 1366, and his wife Katherine, who died in 1381, are represented in effigy in Holy Trinity, Hull. He was a mayor of the city, five times its member of parliament, and became a baron of the exchequer.[76] Sir Richard Redman, whose career was noted above, is probably one of the Redmans lying in effigy with his wife in the parish church at Harewood, where there are alabaster tombs of six fifteenth-century couples.[77] Another fine set of alabasters is to be seen in St. Oswald's, Methley, where Robert Waterton, who died in 1425, is portrayed wearing his **SS** collar, his wife Cecily lying beside him. Waterton was a justice of the peace in the West Riding in 1405, sheriff of Lincolnshire in 1410, and constable of Pontefract in 1424. He was employed by Henry IV on diplomatic service, and was the king's master of horses (1399) and of hart-hounds (1404). He was also an executor of the king's will in 1413. In 1417 he had to escort the Duke of Orleans, the poet, from Windsor to Pontefract, and in 1420 was employed by Henry V to persuade Yorkshire gentry to serve in France, replying to this commission in a letter dated 12 April 1420 'at zour awne logge of Methelaye'.[78] The chapel he provided for in his will was not built until 1483–4, but the monument was probably made at Waterton's death.[79] Stone attributes this alabaster to the York alabasterers around 1425, and points to several features of the face, notably the bulging eyeballs and spiral tufts of the beard, as evidence that the same carvers were working on alabaster tombs and panels at this date.[80] These examples bear out Stone's view that 'the smaller landed gentry together with a scattering of business and professional men were growing in importance as artistic patrons' in the later fourteenth century.[81] Some administrators are also commemorated by brasses, a Yorkshire example being Sir John St. Quintin, who died in 1397, and whose brass is in Brandesburton Church.[82]

Aesthetic appreciation of the artistic work of goldsmiths is impossible to detect. Precious stones and plate are mentioned in wills, but one cannot tell whether the emeralds and rubies and engraved cups were prized simply for their financial worth, like the woolman's stock or the cattle and horses on estates. Where plate is described as engraved with the family, or some other family's arms,[83] this decoration may be valued merely as an identifying mark, or may be something of a status symbol. Some jewellery was precious for sentimental reasons, as is surely indicated by Robert Roos' bequest to his daughter of the 'sapphire ring with which [he] married her mother', cited above.[84] One will is a little more informative, and is, significantly, the will of a goldsmith who might be expected to be explicit in his instructions from his own knowledge of the trade. Sir Edmund Shaa, founder of Stockport grammar school, whose career took him to London where he became Lord Mayor, commissioned sixteen mourning rings to be 'of fine gold, graven with the well of pity, the well of mercy and the well of everlasting life'; he noted that John Shaa (the testator's nephew) and Ralph Latham 'understonden right well the makying of them'.[85]

Architectural commissioning by guilds in the towns has some relevance to this study since the leading men of the guilds were not uncommonly mayors and bailiffs in the towns. In York there are four halls which preserve in parts fifteenth-century civic architecture. The Guildhall, restored after severe bomb damage in the second World War, was built by Robert Couper in 1447–8 for the mayor, commonalty and guilds of St. Christopher and St. George; St. Anthony's Hall was built for the guild of that saint in the mid-fifteenth century and later in the century doubled in size; the Merchant Adventurers' Hall was built for the mercers, and the Merchant Taylors' Hall contains a hall of c.1400 within its brick exterior.[86] The setting up of chantry chapels by guilds and private individuals also promoted architectural patronage, though the establishment of a chantry did not always involve new building or even alteration of existing structures.

The chantry, 'the institutionalized expression of late medieval popular piety par excellence'[87] was a favourite form of commemoration in the late Middle Ages, and in York city alone there were some 140 different chantry foundations by the time of the dissolution, over half of these being in the city's parish churches. Mayors of York were active as founders: six of York's early fourteenth-century mayors were founders of chantries.[88] One of them at least, Andrew Bolingbroke, was not always so pious.[89] The Vavassour, Percy and Scrope families founded perpetual chantries in York Minster,[90] and other administrators who founded chantries include Sir William Plumpton (at Ripon), Sir Robert Waterton (at Methley), and Sir Simon Balderstone (at Hemsworth).[91] These foundations tell more about the piety of the founders than their culture, but at least they indicate receptiveness to church teaching.

The final point to be considered concerns the educational facilities in the area. From Dr. Orme's lists one may identify in the northern counties forty-two places with schools or schoolmasters mentioned in records at some date or dates between 1250 and 1500.[92] In some cases there is only a single reference known—for Kelk and South Dalton the only references are to the suppression of the schools which were there and which were breaching the chapter of Beverley's monopoly of education in 1305 for Kelk and in 1304 and in 1306 for South Dalton.[93] Other places have recurrent evidence of institutional schools. But the demonstrable existence of a school in a place at any time does not prove that the local administrators in its area had received their own education at it, or were in any way cognisant of its activities. However, there are some instances where it can be shown that the local administrators had some involvement or connection with the school.

It is not unusual to find some part of the management of a school given over to town officials. Thus the 1448 licence for the foundation of the chantry at Alnwick, Northumberland, of which one chaplain was 'to teach poor boys in grammar without payment, and to do other works of piety' stipulated that the two chaplains of the foundation were to be nominated by the burgesses of Alnwick to the earl of Northumberland and his heirs.[94] In Lancaster the burgess John Gardyner, mayor in 1467, apparently intended to establish a chaplain to celebrate in St. Mary's and 'to instruct and inform boys in grammar' in 1469. However in his will made in 1472 and proved in 1483 he separated the chantry from 'a certain grammar school in the town of Lancaster' which was to be maintained freely at his expense; in 1500 his executor granted the nomination, election and correction of the chantry priest and schoolmaster to the Mayor of Lancaster and the chantry priest of Gardyner's almshouse.[95] In 1478 the mayor and burgesses of Appleby (Westmorland) granted three chantries in their patronage to a single chaplain, who agreed to keep a grammar school while he held them.[96]

In Kingston-upon-Hull the relationship between town officials and the school was rather more involved. The borough records of the fifteenth century show that the corporation was paying out money for the school, for example for repairs to the schoolhouse, benches and master's desk, and when there was no schoolmaster at Hull in 1444, it was the mayor who sent a messenger to Scarborough, presumably to entice one from there to Hull.[97] Corporation ordinances of 1454 gave the master of the grammar scholars a livery gown at the council's pleasure, and the monopoly of teaching all scholars in the town except the little ones learning alphabets and graces, and in 1459 an ordinance established that the master should have two marks a year salary, a gown, and a rent free house worth 13s. 4d.[98] In 1479 a distinguished son of Hull, John Alcock, then bishop of Worcester, secured letters patent to alienate lands into mortmain to found a perpetual chantry with one chaplain in Holy Trinity Church, and though schoolmastering is not mentioned in the records surviving from this time, it is plain from the later chantry investigations that the keeping of the grammar school at Hull was the responsibility of this chaplain.[99] After Alcock's death, appointment was to lie with the mayor and burgesses, who were the ultimate trustees responsible for reducing both the subsidiary payments to a parish clerk teaching singing to the children, and the exhibitions for the ten best scholars, should the revenues diminish.[100] The burgesses of Alnwick, mayor of Lancaster, mayor and burgesses of Appleby, and mayor and corporation and burgesses of Hull are thus seen to have been involved in the maintenance of their local schools as part of their official responsibilities. The evidence cited thus far does not tell us that any of these individuals, except John Gardyner, had any personal connection with schooling, or interest in it. But in Hull individual connections between the school, and educationists in the county, and borough officials can be discovered. Nicholas Gysburgh, the first actually identified Hull schoolmaster, from 1477, became town clerk in 1484.[101] The Hull mayor and sheriff Robert Benyngton, was brother-in-law, through his wife Emmota, to the schoolmaster of St. Peter's School, York, John Hamundson. Benyngton was one of the executors of Hamundson's will, made in 1472, in which he was left 'the best gold ring'; his wife Emmota was left another gold ring, and the Benyngtons' son Nicholas was left 'a book called Horshede'.[102] Maybe the effects of available schooling can be discerned in Hull: Thomas Dalton, an alderman, wrote his will in 1487 in his own hand,[103] John Aldwick, another alderman, left his son Geoffrey 'his best primer',[104] and it has been suggested that the stylized handwriting and clear, grammatical and systematically abbreviated Latin of the corporation archives 'were obviously the result of long and careful schooling, and there is no reason to suppose that the clerks who wrote these documents were schooled elsewhere than in Hull'.[105]

Hull definitely had administrative families who showed benevolent interest in local education. Bishop Alcock was the second son of William Alcock, a Hull merchant, and the bishop's brothers, Thomas and Robert, were both Hull aldermen, sheriffs, mayors and members of parliament for the city. How the bishop was channelled into his different career is not known, nor where he received his own early education. It may be significant that he obtained the letters patent to found his chantry the year after the mayoralty of Thomas Alcock.[106] In 1484 Elena, widow of alderman William Burgh, left four houses to Alcock's chantry; these had been lost sight of by the time of the chantry commissioners' investigation in 1546,[107] but the endowment may indicate further generosity towards educative charity by an alderman's family at Hull.

Two more Yorkshire born bishops founded schools in the county in the late fifteenth century, at Acaster and Rotherham. There is nothing to connect these bishops, Robert Stillington and Thomas Rotherham, with local administration, but the founders' remarks about the curriculum make these schools significant in the discussion of educational opportunities for laymen. Stillington's father was John Stillington, esquire, and his grandfather is thought to have been the John Stillington who was admitted to the freedom of York in 1363 as a mercer. The Acaster school was to have 'three dyvers maisters and informatours in the facultees underwritten: that is oon of theym to teche grammer, another to teche musyk and song, and the third to teche to write and all suche thing as belonged to scrivener craft'.[108] There was a very slight connection between this school and the civic officials of York in its early years, for when dispute arose over enclosure of rights of common on the site of Acaster college in 1483, the mayor and aldermen of York were appointed to adjudicate on compensation claims.[109]

Thomas Rotherham was the son of another Thomas Rotherham, 'an obscure Yorkshire knight',[110] and had been educated in the parish apparently rather fortuitously by a travelling grammarian temporarily settling there; this lack of any permanent provision of education in the town the bishop intended to remedy. At Rotherham, as at Acaster, there was a triple curriculum, with masters for grammar, music, and writing and accounts, this final branch being defended thus:

'*quia multos, luce et ingenii acumine preditos juvenes profert terra illa, neque omnes volunt sacerdocii dignitatem et altitudinem attingere, ut tales ad artes mechanicas et alia mundum concernencia, magis habilitentur, ordinavimus tercium socium in arte scribendi et computandi scientem et peritum.*'[111]

The first grammar master of Rotherham College, John Bocking, was a married man, who wished to be buried in the south chancel of Rotherham church, by the pew in which his own wife Margaret and the wife of Richard Lylle, bailiff of Rotherham, sat.[112] It is from the positioning of a grave that another Yorkshire schoolmaster earlier in the century comes to be recorded. Robert Wardall, burgess of Scarborough, wanted to be buried in 1457 near the font in Scarborough parish church '*ubi Hugo Rasen quondam magister scolarum grammaticalum sepultus fuit*'.[113] It is not explicit that Rasen's grammar teaching took place in Scarborough, but he certainly had Scarborough connections, and he has been identified as the bailiff of that name in 1421–2 and member of parliament for the borough.[114]

Hull's schoolmaster-town clerk is somewhat paralleled at Beverley, where *Magister* William Harding can be traced in the Beverley Town Minute Books from 1436 to 1456. In 1436 *Magister* William Harding, schoolmaster, was a collector of assessments in Beverley to pay for archers and armed men to fight in Scotland. He was disfranchised in 1440, for breach of town pasture regulations, but readmitted to the franchise six months later, and in 1446 he was elected one of the twelve governors of the town. In 1448 he was assigned to ride to greet Henry VI on his visit to Beverley, and as 'seneschal of the great guild of St. John of Beverley', with his colleague John Middleton, loaned the governors £10 towards £89. 6s. 8d. given to the king as a present. In 1450 Harding reached the final eighteen from whom the twelve governors for the year were chosen, and he was a governor again in 1456, when he was one of three entrusted with a key to the common chest. Here clearly was a schoolmaster whose extra-mural activities benefited his whole community.[115] Two of the York grammar school masters are known to have been admitted as freemen of York, John of York in 1380 and *Magister* Walter Hericz in 1397.[116]

Occasionally the will of a layman bequeathed money to educate a particular person or persons, often relatives or acquaintances of the testator, but in general there are few references to schooling in the wills of Yorkshire layfolk which are in print. John Depeden, whose will was cited above, left £20 to John son of John 'fitz Richard', born in Healaugh, with the specification that the boy and the money be in the custody of *Magister* John Newton, treasurer of St. Peter's, York, or Robert Wycliff, parson of Rudby, the custody to last until the boy knew how '*intelligere et scribere*'. Then he was to be sent to London to learn the art of fishmonger, grocer or mercer.[117] Richard Russell, sheriff and mayor of York, whose will was also cited above for its bequest of books, left £30 to his nephew Robert '*ad exhibendum ipsum ad scolas in universitate Oxoniensi*'.[118]

There were pre-Reformation benefactors to the cause of higher education who wished to provide for specifically northern, but individually unspecified, scholars. Queen's College, Oxford, founded in 1341 by Robert Eglesfield, chaplain to Queen Philippa, a Cumberland man, rector of Brough-under-Stainmore, made preference for inhabitants of Cumberland and Westmorland 'on account of the waste, desolate, and illiterate condition' of those counties; the scholars 'distinguished in character, poor in means, and apt for the study of theology' who were to benefit have been assumed to be 'the sons and protégés of the minor gentry, yeomen and burghers.'[119] Thomas Rotherham, while Bishop of Lincoln, revised the statutes of Richard Fleming's foundation, Lincoln College, to assign four fellowships to the York diocese, one at least being for the Rotherham area.[120] Though one cannot be sure how strictly tied fellowships were administered at the universities, presumably the motives of their founders were to offer opportunities to advanced, mainly theological, students from a particular area. Clearly there were well informed and influential patrons wishing to offer such opportunities to students from the north, and seeing this provision in some way as the apex of the educational system there—in Bishop Alcock's case he certainly knew the system well.[121]

From the sixteenth century the literacy, literary and cultural tastes, and education of the gentry class, to which many of the descendants of the medieval administrators then belonged, become much more demonstrable, in the north as elsewhere in England.

The student of the earlier period looks a little enviously towards a time when schools as institutions have continuous history, text books can be identified, and old scholars write their recollections of schooling. The education of the gentleman then acquires its post-renaissance classical veneer, and bright boys from the local town grammar schools begin to make their mark on society. The evidence from before 1500 considered in this study is patchy at best, but one can see that the 'desolate and illiterate condition' of the north was being penetrated by the arts, and that the local administrators, as laymen in a still church-dominated intellectual world, quite aptly, with their families, illustrate this development.

NOTES

1. Examples of these three levels of employment may be found in Helen M. Jewell, 'The King's Government in Yorkshire, 1258–1348', unpublished Ph.D. thesis, University of Leeds, 1968, chapter 7; see also Helen M. Jewell, 'Local Administration and Administrators in Yorkshire, 1258–1348', *Northern History*, xvi, 1980, pp. 1–19.

2. Various marcher wardenships, for example, were given throughout the period to the Percies, both as barons Percy of Alnwick and as earls of Northumberland. Great magnates though the Percies undoubtedly became, those of them who were wardens of the marches were not distinctly above the holding of lesser, more ordinary, local commissions; e.g. Henry, second baron Percy, was a warden of Scarborough castle and an arrayer in Northumberland. *D.N.B.*, XLIV, pp. 393–4.

3. For example, of the thirty-two men officiating as escheators in Yorkshire between 1258 and 1348, at least twelve were at some point described as clerks or king's clerks, as appears from the writs of appointment of Richard Havering (*C.F.R. 1272–1307*, p. 411), John Hotham (*C.F.R. 1307–19*, p. 52), Robert Wodehouse (ibid., p. 77), Robert Clitheroe (ibid., p. 232), Gilbert Stapleton (*C.F.R. 1319–27*, p. 15), John Houton (*C.F.R. 1327–37*, p. 192), John Lowther (ibid., p. 284), and John Woodhouse (*C.F.R. 1337–47*, p. 225), and from *de cursu* writs to Richard Clifford (*C.P.R. 1266–72*, p. 18), William Boyvill (*C.F.R. 1272–1307*, p. 21), Philip Willoughby (ibid., p. 28) and Thomas Bergh (*C.P.R. 1321–4*, p. 71), see Jewell, *Northern History*, cited in note 1, pp. 8–11. Clerks were also used for purposes more often performed by laymen, e.g. Richard Moseley, constable of Conisbrough and Sandal castles, and receiver of Pontefract castle and honour after Lancaster's forfeiture, was rector of Fryston and later parson of Dewsbury. (*C.F.R. 1319–27*, p. 322; *C.C.R. 1318–23*, p. 673; *C.C.R. 1327–30*, p. 365.)

4. For example John Darcy 'le neveu', constable of Norham castle in 1317, sheriff of Nottinghamshire and Derbyshire 1319–22, of Lancashire 1323, of Yorkshire 1327–8, justiciar of Ireland intermittently 1323–44, a seneschal of Gascony 1330, steward of the royal household 1337–40, chamberlain to the king 1341–6, and constable of the Tower of London, first in 1337 and for life from 1346. See R. F. Darcy, *The Life of John, first baron Darcy of Knayth*, London, 1933; *D.N.B.*, XIV, p. 46; *Complete Peerage*, IV, pp. 54–8.

5. For example William Scargill, whose career, embracing service of the earl of

Warenne and in local government, is described in A. Gooder, *The Parliamentary Representation of the county of York, 1258–1832*, Yorkshire Archaeological Society, Record Series, xci, 1935, volume I, pp. 79–81. See also the career of Sir William Plumpton, this essay, p. 138.

6. Eleanor Percy, widow of Henry, first baron Percy of Alnwick, had the commission of the corpus of Scarborough castle in 1325, *C.P.R. 1324–7*, p. 192.

7. *C.P.R. 1377–81*, pp. 7, 11.

8. Irene Gladwin, *The Sheriff, the Man and his Office*, London, 1974, p. 256.

9. A. B. Steel, 'Collectors of customs at Newcastle on Tyne in the reign of Richard II' in J. Conway Davies (ed.) *Studies presented to Sir Hilary Jenkinson*, London, 1957, pp. 390–413, and 'The collectors of customs in the reign of Richard II' in H. Hearder and H. R. Loyn, *British Government and Administration: studies presented to S. B. Chrimes*, Cardiff, 1974, pp. 27–39.

10. This essay, note 3.

11. P. R. O. E 372/184 m. 33d (two references); *Return of Members of Parliament*, Part I, 1878, p. 108; L. M. Stanewell, *City and County of Kingston upon Hull, Calendar of Ancient Deeds, Letters Miscellaneous Old Documents etc. in the Archives of the Corporation*, Hull, 1951, p. 8; *C.C.R. 1337–9*, p. 216.

12. Gooder, *Parliamentary Representation*, cited in note 5, pp. 44, 89. Clotherum represented Ripon in parliament in 1307, and Yorkshire in 1315; Alverthorp represented Yorkshire in 1338.

13. Patricia Jalland, 'The "Revolution" in Northern Borough Representation in mid-fifteenth-century England', *Northern History*, xi, 1976 for 1975, p. 36.

14. J. S. Roskell, *The Commons in the Parliament of 1422*, Manchester, 1954, pp. 174, 181. Jalland, *Northern History*, cited in note 13, pp. 43–7 calls Carlisle and Appleby completely rotten boroughs and cites three more lawyer members of parliament there.

15. Ibid., pp. 39–40.

16. Gladwin, *The Sheriff*, cited in note 8, p. 67.

17. Ibid., p. 151. One does not doubt that the sheriffs' duties required legal and financial expertise, but this does not prove that it was the sheriff personally who had acquired these skills. The view taken by R. V. Turner 'The *Miles Literatus* in Twelfth- and Thirteenth-Century England: How Rare a Phenomenon?', *American Historical Review*, lxxxiii, 1978, p. 940 that sheriffs had to be capable of reading and that an illiterate one would have been at a disadvantage is reasonable but does not prove the point.

18. Gladwin, *The Sheriff*, cited in note 8, p. 206.

19. *C.C.R. 1441–7*, p. 97, cited in R. F. Hunnisett, *The Medieval Coroner*, Cambridge, 1961, p. 177. This coroner, however, was also said to have been 'not duly elected' and indeed 'secretly and unlawfully advanced' by the sheriff. The medieval coroner was not required to have legal or medical qualifications.

20. M. G. A. Vale, *Piety, Charity and Literacy among the Yorkshire Gentry, 1370–1480*, Borthwick Papers no. 50, York, 1976, p. 29.

21. *Testamenta Eboracensia*, Surtees Society, i (iv, 1836), ii (xxx, 1855), iii (xlv, 1865), iv (liii, 1869), i no. 73. For Constable's career, see Bertha H. Putnam, *Yorkshire Sessions of the Peace, 1361–4*, Yorkshire Archaeological Society, Record Series, c, 1939, p. xlii.

22. *Test. Ebor.*, cited in note 21, i no. 80.

23. *C.P.R. 1374–7*, p. 151.

24. *Test. Ebor.*, cited in note 21, i no. 232. For St. Quintin's career, with its varied local commissions, see Gooder, *Parliamentary Representation*, cited in note 5, pp. 137–8.

25. *Test. Ebor.*, cited in note 21, ii no. 40, and footnote.

26. Ibid., i no. 13; Gooder, *Parliamentary Representation*, cited in note 5, pp. 60–2, describes John Walkingham's career.

27. *Test. Ebor.*, cited in note 21, i no. 240, and footnote.

28. Ibid., i no. 46. *D.N.B.*, XLIV, pp. 393–4 outlines Percy's career.

29. Putnam, *Yorkshire Sessions*, cited in note 21, p. xxxix gives details of William Ayton's career.

30. *Test. Ebor.*, cited in note 21, i no. 160. For Roos see *Complete Peerage*, XI, pp. 101–2; for Percy, ibid., X, pp. 462–3.

31. Gooder, *Parliamentary Representation*, cited in note 5, pp. 129–30.

32. *Test. Ebor.*, cited in note 21, i no. 145.

33. Ibid., i no. 216. Depeden's commissions are recorded in *C.P.R. 1391–6*, pp. 439, 654, 732. *C.P.R. 1396–9*, p. 248 gives the licence.

34. *Test. Ebor.*, cited in note 21, i no. 239. Scrope's career is described in Gooder, *Parliamentary Representation*, cited in note 5, pp. 157–8.

35. Ibid., pp. 183–4. *Test. Ebor.*, cited in note 21, i no. 239, footnote 1 says Elizabeth married Hastings, and mentions another daughter, Margaret.

36. Ibid., ii no. 49. *Magister* Walter is presumably Walter Hilton.

37. Ibid., i no. 183.

38. Gladwin, *The Sheriff*, cited in note 8, pp. 228–37, 243–4; J. S. Roskell, *The Commons and their Speakers in English Parliaments, 1376–1523*, Manchester, 1965, pp. 162–4; Gooder, *Parliamentary Representation*, cited in note 5, pp. 165–9, and this essay, p. 142.

39. *Test. Ebor.*, cited in note 21, iii no. 107; P.R.O. Lists and Indexes 9, *List of Sheriffs for England and Wales*, 1898, p. 162.

40. *Test. Ebor.*, cited in note 21, ii no. 22.

41. His career is fully described by K. Fowler, *The King's Lieutenant*, London, 1969.

42. Ethel Seaton, *Sir Richard Roos, Lancastrian Poet, c1410–82*, London, 1961, p. 24.

43. *Test. Ebor.*, cited in note 21, ii no. 97.

44. This essay, p. 135.

45. Seaton, *Sir Richard Roos*, cited in note 42, pp. 23, 58–9 and frontispiece.

46. J. Taylor, 'The Plumpton Letters 1416–1552', *Northern History*, x, 1975, pp. 72–87; T. Stapleton, *Plumpton Correspondence*, C. S., London, 1839; ibid., p. 14 provides an example of a letter originally in its author's own hand.

47. Taylor, *Northern History*, cited in note 46; Stapleton, *Plumpton Correspondence*, cited in note 46; Shirley M. Walker 'The Plumpton Correspondence, an historical and social survey', unpublished M.A. thesis, University of Leeds, 1962; *C.P.R. 1467–77*, p. 638.

48. Taylor, *Northern History*, cited in note 46, p. 79. The author is grateful to Mr. Taylor for clarifying this point.

49. Stapleton, *Plumpton Correspondence*, cited in note 46, p. xxi. For Emeldon's career, see A. M. Oliver, *Early Deeds relating to Newcastle upon Tyne*, Surtees Society, cxxxvii, 1924, pp. 209–12. *C.I.P.M.* vii, 1909, p. 444 records the assignment of dower to Christiana, wife of William Plumpton, late wife of Richard Emeldon. The Ripon chantry is described in W. Page, *Certificates of the*

Commissioners appointed to survey the chantries, guilds, hospitals etc. in the county of York, Surtees Society, xci–ii, 2 vols, 1894–95, ii p. 360.

50. Stapleton, *Plumpton Correspondence*, cited in note 46, p. xxxvi. Chaworth left an interesting library including several mass books, 'a litel portose, the which the saide Sir Thomas toke with hym alway when he rode', an English book 'which begynnyth with ye lyffe of Seynt Albon and Amphiabell', an English *Grace Dieu*, an English *Polychronicon* and a Latin one, an *Orilogium Sapienciae* in English, and a 'Graile', *Test. Ebor.*, cited in note 21, ii no. 179.

51. Stapleton, *Plumpton Correspondence*, cited in note 46, p. xxxix. Katherine's sister, Joan, married William Malory; their grandson Thomas is suggested as a possible author of *Le Morte Darthur* in W. Matthews, *The Ill-Framed Knight: a skeptical inquiry into the identity of Sir Thomas Malory*, Berkeley and Los Angeles, 1966, chapter 4. This work also probes the connection of Cambridge University Additional Manuscript 7071 (two romances) with the Mauleverers of Ribston in the later fifteenth century.

52. *C.P.R. 1429–36*, p. 522; Stapleton, *Plumpton Correspondence*, cited in note 46, p. lxii.

53. Taylor, *Northern History*, cited in note 46, p. 84.

54. Stapleton, *Plumpton Correspondence*, cited in note 46, e.g. pp. 5, 9.

55. Taylor, *Northern History*, cited in note 46, p. 82.

56. *List of Sheriffs*, cited in note 39, p. 163 (Ryther); *C.P.R. 1452–6*, p. 683 (Roecliffe). From a letter of Roecliffe's we learn that his daughter-in-law, Margaret, née Plumpton, then aged four, was making progress 'and speaketh prattely and french and hath nearhand learned her sawter', Stapleton, *Plumpton Correspondence*, cited in note 46, p. 8.

57. Ibid., p. 89. Strange was the earl of Derby's son.

58. Taylor, *Northern History*, cited in note 46, p. 87.

59. *Test. Ebor.*, cited in note 21, i no. 275; ii no. 50.

60. Stapleton, *Plumpton Correspondence*, cited in note 46, p. xxxiv. This was St. Robert's at Knaresborough.

61. C. Wolters, *The Fire of Love*, Harmondsworth, 1972, p. 14. *D.N.B*, XLIX, p. 164 places Dalton near Rotherham and says John Dalton's sons had known Rolle at Oxford. C.f. Frances M. M. Comper, *The Life of Richard Rolle together with an edition of his English Lyrics*, London, reissued 1933, pp. 57–61.

62. R. B. Turton, *The Honour and Forest of Pickering*, North Riding Record Society, New Series, i–iv, London, 1894–7, ii, pp. 25–7, 57, 121.

63. Ibid., iii pp. 240–1.

64. Ibid., iv, pp. xxxii, 203. This is the Henry whose will is referred to in this essay, note 83, and p. 134. Eleanor was the castellan of Scarborough, this essay, note 6, and may be the person commemorated at Beverley, this essay, note 73.

65. Ibid., iv, pp. 145, 160.

66. Ibid., ii, pp. 121–30.

67. Ibid., ii, p. 26, iii, p. 63.

68. Ibid., iii, p. 94.

69. This essay, p. 138.

70. D. E. O'Connor and J. Haselock 'The stained and painted glass' in G. E. Aylmer and R. Cant, *A History of York Minster*, Oxford, 1977, pp. 350–1.

71. Ibid., p. 343. This is the Edmund whose tomb is at Bainton, this essay, p. 142.

72. N. Pevsner, *The Buildings of England. Yorkshire: York and the East Riding*, Harmondsworth, 1972, pp. 30, 175.

73. Ibid., p. 30. Pevsner favours Eleanor, who died in 1328, as the likeliest candidate, though acknowledging that the heraldry makes a date earlier than 1339 impossible. There is a Clifford shield among the heraldic decorations, however, ibid., p. 175. L. Stone, *Sculpture in Britain, the Middle Ages*, Harmondsworth, 2nd ed. 1972, pp. 171–2, thinks this is not a tomb at all, and is more likely to be an Easter Sepulchre, erected at Lady Idoine Percy's expense.

74. Pevsner, *York and the East Riding*, cited in note 72, pp. 30, 165, 270.

75. J. Le Patourel, *Ilkley Parish Church*, Gloucester, 2nd ed., 1968, p. 11.

76. Pevsner, *York and the East Riding*, cited in note 72, p. 270. *D.N.B.*, XLVI, pp. 49–50 outlines Pole's career.

77. This essay, p. 137. N. Pevsner, *Buildings of England. Yorkshire: West Riding*, Harmondsworth, 2nd ed. 1967, pp. 243–4, identifies the six medieval alabaster tombs at Harewood with Sir Richard Redmayne (d. 1426) and wife; Sir William Ryther (d.1425) and wife; Sir William Gascoigne (d.1419) and wife; a Gascoigne couple (d.c1470–80), Sir John Nevil (d.1482) and wife; and Sir Richard Redmayne (d.1476) and wife. The Redmayne who died in 1426 is, however, believed to be buried at York, see Roskell, *Speakers*, cited in note 38, p. 164 n. 2; Gladwin, *The Sheriff*, cited in note 8, p. 244. M. D. Anderson, *History and Imagery in British Churches*, London, 1971, p. 193 waxes lyrical over Sir William Gascoigne's effigy in its judicial robes, calling it 'the most striking memorial to medieval law'.

78. Pevsner, *West Riding*, cited in note 77, p. 364. For Waterton's career, see H. Armstrong Hall, 'Some Notes on the personal and family history of Robert Waterton of Methley and Waterton', Thoresby Society, xv, *Miscellanea*, Leeds, 1909, pp. 81–102, and H. S. Darbyshire and G. D. Lumb, *The History of Methley*, Thoresby Society, xxxv, Leeds, 1937 passim.

79. Pevsner, *West Riding*, cited in note 77, p. 364.

80. Stone, *Sculpture in Britain*, cited in note 73, p. 200.

81. Ibid., p. 178.

82. Pevsner, *York and the East Riding*, cited in note 72, p. 195. In St. Quintin's will he left 20 marks to buy a marble tombstone and to have three images of brass representing himself and his wives Lora and Agnes, *Test. Ebor.*, cited in note 21, i no. 168. (Agnes' will is cited in note 24.) Only two brasses were put on the tomb, however, see Vale, *Piety and Charity*, cited in note 20, p. 9.

83. E.g. in Henry Percy's will, cited in note 28, a good deal of plate and jewellery is described, including a cup (*ciphum*) enamelled with the arms of France and England, and a salt (*vas pro sale*) with a shield of the arms of Percy and Arundel, two enamelled basins depicting respectively the judgement of Solomon and the wheel of fortune, gold rings, a gold clasp, two separately mentioned rubies, a sapphire, and an emerald.

84. This essay, p. 136.

85. B. Varley, *The History of Stockport Grammar School*, Manchester, 2nd ed. 1957, p. 26.

86. Pevsner, *York and the East Riding*, cited in note 72, pp. 136, 150, 144, 141; G. Benson, *Later Medieval York*, York, 1919, p. 106.

87. J. T. Rosenthal, 'The Yorkshire Chantry Certificates of 1546: an analysis', *Northern History*, ix, 1974, p. 27.

88. Roger Basy, Andrew Bolingbroke, Nicholas Langton, Nicholas Flemyng, Robert Meke and Richard Wateby, identified in R. B. Dobson, 'The Foundation of

Perpetual Chantries by the citizens of medieval York ', in G. J. Cuming (ed.), *Studies in Church History*, iv, Leiden, 1967, pp. 33–4.

89. G. O. Sayles, ' The Dissolution of a Guild at York in 1306 ', *E.H.R.*, lv, 1940, pp. 83–98.

90. R. B. Dobson, ' The Later Middle Ages, 1215–1500 ' in Aylmer and Chant, *York Minster*, cited in note 70, p. 96. *Certificates*, cited in note 49; pp. 40, 21, 25. The Percy chantry belongs, however, to the sixteenth century.

91. Ibid., ii, pp. 360, 317, 281.

92. N. Orme, *English Schools in the Middle Ages*, London, 1973, pp. 293–325.

93. A. F. Leach, *Early Yorkshire Schools*, Yorkshire Archaeological Society, Record Series, i. xxvii, 1899, ii. xxxiii, 1903; i, pp. 81, 80m–81, 88, 92.

94. *C.P.R. 1446–52*, p. 170.

95. *V.C.H. Lancaster*, II, 1908, pp. 562–3. A. L. Murray, *The Royal Grammar School, Lancaster*, Cambridge, no date, says that Gardyner was the school's first and greatest benefactor, but that ' the very school which he endowed ' had been in existence two centuries before, pp. 1, 12–19.

96. E. Hinchcliffe, *Appleby Grammar School, from chantry to comprehensive*, Appleby, 1974, p. 18.

97. J. Lawson, *A Town Grammar School through six centuries*, London, 1963, p. 16.

98. Ibid., pp. 17–18.

99. Ibid., pp. 25–7; Page, *Certificates*, cited in note 49, ii, p. 340.

100. Ibid., cited in note 97, p. 29. Page, *Certificates*, cited in note 49, ii, p. 340 leaves this to the mayor and vicar.

101. Lawson, *Town Grammar School*, cited in note 97, p. 21.

102. Leach, *Early Yorkshire Schools*, cited in note 93, i, p. 28; *Test. Ebor.*, cited in note 21, iii no. 56.

103. Ibid., iv no. 15.

104. Ibid., ii no. 86.

105. Lawson, *Town Grammar School*, cited in note 97, p. 15.

106. Ibid., pp. 22–34.

107. Ibid., p. 28.

108. Leach, *Early Yorkshire Schools*, cited in note 93, ii, p. 89.

109. Ibid., ii, p. 91.

110. Dobson, ' The Later Middle Ages ' cited in note 90, p. 98.

111. Leach, *Early Yorkshire Schools*, cited in note 93, ii, p. 110.

112. Ibid., ii, p. 141.

113. *Test. Ebor.*, cited in note 21, ii no. 163.

114. Jean W. Rowntree, ' The Borough, 1163–1500 ' in A. Rowntree, *The History of Scarborough*, London, 1931, p. 139.

115. Leach, *Early Yorkshire Schools*, cited in note 93, i, pp. 102–9.

116. Ibid., i, p. 26.

117. This essay, p. 136.

118. This essay, p. 135.

119. Hinchcliffe, *Appleby Grammar School*, cited in note 96, p. 16.

120. Leach, *Early Yorkshire Schools*, cited in note 93, ii, pp. 103–4.

121. He is now believed to be the author of a revealing sermon illustrating educational theory and practice, composed for the boy bishop of St. Paul's School, between 1489 and 1496, edited by J. G. Nichols in *Camden Miscellany*, C. S. vii, 1875, pp. 1–13, cited in Lawson, *Town Grammar School*, cited in note 97, p. 23.

6

The civil lawyers

C. T. ALLMAND

At first sight the civil lawyer may appear to have but little claim to a place in a book of studies devoted to cultural groups in late medieval England. In a country with its own common law, what could men whose legal studies embraced one, often two, seemingly alien systems, Roman and Canon law, have to offer distinctive enough for them to be regarded as a group worthy of consideration? The law which they professed had little in common with that practised by the large majority of courts in the land. Furthermore, the civil lawyers, trained as they were in the two universities in England, and in others abroad notably those of northern Italy, seemed to lack what their common law counterparts achieved through study at, and membership of, the Inns of Court—that measure of cohesion which brought influence and, in its turn, served to further the careers of individual members of the group. So much may be admitted. But on closer inspection the first general impression will be seen to have been wrong. For the fact remains that at both Oxford and Cambridge, from the end of the thirteenth century into the sixteenth, an ever-increasing number of young men studied civil law not simply, one may be sure, in the hope of acquiring some small theoretical knowledge of the subject but, in a very large number of cases, with the intention of applying it. It would be a gross error to think of the English student of civil law as one interested in legal knowledge merely as an intellectual exercise. Even in a country of common law, an expertise in civil law had a strong practical value. For if, by the fifteenth century, the theologian trained in the universities was finding it increasingly difficult to secure the patronage which his position as a graduate seemed to merit, it will be seen that the same was not always true of his legal counterpart. This may be one reason which helped to account for the steady rise in the popularity of civil law studies in English universities in the later middle ages.[1]

Civil lawyers contributed to English culture, taking that word in its widest meaning, in two ways. One was through their involvement in the practice of law, government and administration. Traditionally, the academic lawyer could find employment in a judicial function in the service of the Church. Since all canon lawyers had, in theory, at least a smattering of civil law, some a good knowledge of it, and others still degrees in both laws, ecclesiastical courts provided many opportunities.[2] Some of these were positions of semi-permanent employment, in the tribunals of archdeacons, officials-principal, and bishops, perhaps as proctors in the smaller consistory courts or, with greater rewards, as advocates in, or in a few cases, as dean of, the court of Arches.[3] Service in the Church could lead to Avignon or Rome; individuals, churches, corporations both lay and ecclesiastical, as well as kings, sought representation either on an *ad hoc* or permanent basis at the papal curia, and many a career in royal employ was begun by successful pleading before such high ecclesiastical tribunals, where a number of English doctors sat as auditors during this period.[4]

Such employment, although important, was traditional. More novel and an important contribution to legal culture in England, was the role played by English civil lawyers in certain judicial developments of the late middle ages, notably in the growth of new courts and jurisdictions. The courts to which the civil lawyers were, above all, called, were those of Admiralty and Chivalry, both dispensing a law which, although based upon Roman law and, as such, not part of the law of the land, none the less was recognized by it.[5] The court of Admiralty concerned itself mainly with disputes over shipping and merchandise, piracy and other crimes committed at sea, cases frequently involving foreigners who did not recognize a court of common law, and on whose behalf justice had to be expedited as rapidly as possible.[6] The court of Chivalry, the court of the constable and marshal, dealt largely with cases of armorial disputes and of military lore and practice, such as those concerning prisoners and ransoms,[7] as well as some cases of treason.[8] Both courts came to assert themselves in the second half of the fourteenth century; both could attribute their *raison d'être* and development to the changing needs brought about by the long war with France; both were manned by men of whom many owed their appointment as assessors of first instance, or as commissioners to hear appeals, to the fact that they had received a training in the civil law taught at the universities.[9]

The other notable development involving civil lawyers was the emergence of the equitable jurisdiction of the chancellor, already used to suppress disorder in the time of Richard II, which saw its business increase three-fold between 1420 and 1450, chiefly over matters inadequately protected by common law, such as land use and contract. The popularity of such a court in which, as chancellor Stillington enunciated in 1469, 'a man shall not be prejudiced by mispleading, or by default of form, but according to conscience', increased notably in the fifteenth century, much work being delegated by the chancellors, (fifteen of whom, between 1330 and 1515, studied canon or civil law or both) to the master of the Rolls, a post frequently held by a civil lawyer.[10] The emphasis placed on judgements made according to conscience,[11] and on those cases for which the common law had no adequate remedy, reflects the fact that something of a 'reception' of substantive rules and procedures, unknown to common law, took place, a development which was to inject an element of flexibility and the provision of a form of supplementary jurisdiction into the legal system. For all the fears expressed about it, such a development tended towards a more effective implementation of the law in the late middle ages and early modern times.[12] 'It is the glory of the chancellors that they did this.'[13] One could add, too, that it was the positive influence of the canonists and civil lawyers, above all through their different notions on procedure, which was in large measure responsible for bringing about this historic development. To say, as some have said, that the influence of civil law upon English law was either negligible or merely academic, is to fly in the face of the evidence.[14]

In government and administration, in addition to occupying some of the high offices of state, especially the legal ones, the civil lawyers contributed most effectively in the development of the art and practice of diplomacy in the centuries under review. Few embassies (and they were many, especially in times of war) left these shores without a civil lawyer or two in attendance, their task being to offer advice on the presentation of a diplomatic case or to oversee the drawing-up of treaties which were becoming increasingly complex and more than ever in need of expert drafting. It is now widely recognized that the prolonged Anglo-French struggle of the late middle ages greatly favoured the development of English diplomatic practice, especially the preservation and orderly filing of documents for future use in presenting a satisfactory legal case in diplomatic exchanges with the enemy.[15] The drawing up of documents and the copying of them by notaries (here one may emphasise the role of notaries, studied by Professor Cheney)[16] served to emphasise that in the expanding diplomatic activity of the time the civil lawyer, who came closest in concept in this period to that of the present-day international lawyer, had a major role to play, not as a passive observer but as one with an active and positive contribution to make to rapidly developing procedures.[17]

If lawyers are normally men of conservative or traditional attitudes, it must none the less be admitted that many English civil lawyers of this period were not of the kind to let the grass grow under their feet. Some came to be involved in the well-known issues and controversies of late medieval history. They were aware of, and some took active steps to resolve, the difficulties which faced graduates in their search for ecclesiastical advancement.[18] In this they appear to have been reasonably successful; if a mitre was a recognition of success in matters temporal as well as spiritual, then the twenty-three per cent of all Oxford graduates appointed to sees between 1216 and 1499 who had graduated in civil law, or the ten per cent who had studied both laws or, to take another example, the thirty-seven per cent of all Oxonians appointed to cathedral deaneries between 1307 and 1499 who had studied civil law or the sixteen per cent who had read both laws, represent the measure of their success in the search for high ecclesiastical office.[19] The advancement of graduates may be regarded as one of a number of reforms debated at the series of Church Councils which made their mark upon the history of Europe in the first half of the fifteenth century. Certainly, the matter was one which deeply concerned archbishop Henry Chichele, and such a man deserves to be remembered more for his positive contribution to the solution of the problem—the founding of All Souls College, Oxford—than simply as part of the statistic quoted above.[20] Chichele was nothing if not a man of action. But he was also interested in wider questions of reform, and he may be regarded as one of a group of English civil lawyers whom we know to have been deeply concerned, as lawyers could be expected to have been, about the Great Schism which broke out in 1378, and how best to resolve it.[21] To many, the problem of how to cure the spiritual division of Christendom was, at heart, a legal one, and it was natural that the solution should have been widely discussed in these terms. Hope lay in the calling of a Council: but who should call it? It was to this kind of question that Nicholas Ryssheton, a man who had already gained much diplomatic experience in the service of Henry IV, turned his attention in 1409 in a cautious tract in which he showed that a man with his legal training had something constructive to offer, and that he could interest himself in matters of both practical and theoretical importance since they raised fundamental questions regarding political authority.[22] Nor was Ryssheton alone. Both he and Chichele had been members of the reforming chapter at Salisbury when Robert Hallum was bishop; all three were aware of the difficulties facing Christendom in the early fifteenth century, and all worked towards their solution. The collections of documents regarding the Councils made by two other civil lawyers, Thomas Polton, bishop of Worcester and then of Ely,[23] and, a few years later, William Sprever,[24] testify to the interest shown by lawyers in the events going on in the world around them. This evidence is further supported by the tract, *Liber de jure regis Anglie ad regnum Francie*, written by Thomas Bekynton to bolster his royal employer's historical claim to the throne of France,[25] another example of a claim best expressed in appropriate legal language and in the form of a collection of documents not unlike the formulary so beloved of notaries or lawyers wishing to marshal their evidence for future use. This tract constituted but the latest example of the far-reaching influence which lawyers, through the use of written forms sometimes based upon foreign models, had upon the development of English diplomatic method and practice in the two formative centuries following the death of Edward I.

The civil lawyers were not infrequently the beneficiaries of legacies, bequests and other forms of endowment which enabled them to pursue their studies, and they played a significant part both in the setting up of educational foundations and in providing special facilities and opportunities for education. At one level we may note the founding of schools by men of legal, and particularly civil law, training: Hugh Oldham, who helped Richard Foxe to found Corpus Christi College, Oxford, was a major benefactor of Manchester Grammar School,[26] while John Kemp founded a grammar school at Wye, Kent,[27] Thomas Bekynton assisted in the founding of Eton College and John Incent in that of Berkhamstead School.[28] At another level the civil lawyers who founded halls and colleges at the universities displayed a breadth of interest and sympathy which should be remembered. Henry Chichele, in founding All Souls College in 1438, might decide that sixteen of the forty fellowships (forty per cent) should be reserved for civil lawyers, a proportion which in practice rose to eighty-five per cent later in the century, making All Souls into an almost entirely civil law college. This trend is supported by figures for New College, founded more

than fifty years before, for these show that civil lawyers far out-
numbered the canonists with whom the founder had stipulated
they should be on terms of parity.[29] But civil lawyers who supported educational foundations were not always as committed to their
professional subject. In 1361, Michael de Northburgh might leave
an endowment for the maintenance of scholars in both canon and
civil law at Oxford,[30] and in 1536 Richard Nykke could support
canon and civil law studies at Trinity Hall, Cambridge;[31] but in
1403 Walter de Skirlaw preferred to bequeath land to endow three
theologians at University College, Oxford,[32] while Simon Islip and
even Chichele himself could set up centres for monks in Oxford—
Canterbury Hall partly for Black Monks in 1361,[33] and St. Bernard's College for White Monks in 1437—as very few monks ever
studied civil law, evidently neither had the advancement of his
particular professional class in mind. The statutes of two other
Oxford colleges, Brasenose and Corpus Christi, both founded by
civilians in the early years of the sixteenth century, also suggest
that neither was intended to perpetuate their founders' academic
training. At Brasenose, under William Smyth, the emphasis was to
be on traditional, non-legal disciplines, while at Corpus Richard
Foxe and Hugh Oldham moved decidedly in the direction of the
classics and in favour of the interpretation of Scripture following
the Greek and Latin Fathers, rather than the scholastic commentators. The future, as it turned out, lay rather with the college of Foxe
and Oldham, friends of humanists such as Erasmus, Colet, and
More, than with Smyth's foundation a few hundred yards away.

   In terms of civil law, Cambridge was not to be left behind. The
King's Hall was founded by Edward II with the specific aim of
forming 'a cradle of civil law studies within the Cambridge *stud-
ium*', and the large proportion of legists, about a fifth of the university's total in the hundred years from 1350 came from that college,
an indication of the impact which one foundation could have upon
a university. In 1350 William Bateman, a civil lawyer who was
bishop of Norwich, founded Trinity Hall, where twenty scholars
were to be B.A. on admission, and of these ten were to study civil
and seven canon law. Bateman was clearly intent upon perpetu-
ating his own kind, but in the century following this foundation,
Trinity Hall only produced a quarter of the number of civil lawyers
who graduated from the King's Hall, which maintained its position
as the leading foundation in this field.[34]

   The civil lawyers had among their number some notable patrons
of builders. Not surprisingly, their patronage was concentrated on

ecclesiastical buildings: that of Walter de Stapledon in the choir of Exeter cathedral, together with his fine tomb;[35] that of John Harewell who paid for much of the cost of erecting the south-west tower of the cathedral at Wells;[36] the fine chantry chapel at Ely, completed in 1508, which was the burial place of bishop John Alcock, a notable ecclesiastical builder;[37] and the work at Norwich carried out by James Goldwell, notably the reconstruction of the cathedral tower and the erection of a fine tomb for the bishop himself.[38] These are random examples. A larger number could only add weight to the supposition that many civil lawyers were men of devotion, who wished to be remembered,[39] and who built or completed, usually in traditional style, buildings begun by their predecessors. The not infrequent bequests of valuable ecclesiastical furnishings, including precious vessels, copes and chasubles, to churches and colleges is further evidence of the ingrained 'clerical' culture of the men of this group.[40]

Some, however, were interested in furthering secular, indeed even military, architecture. At Wells, Thomas Bekynton was responsible not only for building within the cathedral precinct, 'but the city also was included within the range of his vision', especially when the events of Cade's rebellion appeared to be an actual threat, and works of defence needed to be carried out,[41] At the very end of the fifteenth century, Richard Foxe, when bishop of Durham, added to the fortifications of Norham Castle, reconstructed parts of Durham castle, and was also to improve the harbour of Calais by the construction of sluices, in addition to carrying out work at Winchester cathedral when he was translated to that see.[42] Both these men were men of the Renaissance, open to outside influences; it may not be too fanciful to attribute to this influence the architectural patronage which they extended in practical directions as well as in their more traditionally religious manifestations. A real awareness of stylistic changes in secular architecture was to be shown in the early sixteenth century by William Knyght who, c.1520, enlarged, in the Renaissance style, his prebendal house at Horton in Gloucestershire, building in the grounds an ambulatory 'clearly modelled on the Italian loggia rather than on the Gothic cloister', the whole work being 'thoroughly Italian'.[43]

Naturally, some civil lawyers found themselves drawn to the great law centres of northern Italy, Bologna, Padua, and Ferrara, where they could study both civil and canon law in the hope that an Italian degree would assist them in their professional advancement.[44] But they did more than learn the law. The 'Italian connection', already in existence by the fourteenth century, put lawyers in the forefront of the introduction into England of humanistic ideas and values associated with the Italian Renaissance.[45] William Knyght, the builder of the ambulatory at Horton, had studied law at Ferrara in 1501 and had visited Rome in 1507.[46] John Yonge, Master of the Rolls, an alumnus of that remarkable educational progression, Winchester, and New College, Oxford, which produced so many civil lawyers during this period, had a monument with recumbent effigy by Torrigiano placed over his tomb in the Rolls Chapel when he died in 1516. Yonge, it may be noted, had studied at both Bologna and Ferrara, had patronised Erasmus who dedicated a minor work to him, and numbered among his friends archbishop William Warham, another civil lawyer and patron of humanists who was, likewise, of Winchester and New College.[47] Nor may one forget Cuthbert Tunstal, a student of both Oxford and Cambridge, who held law degrees from Padua, a man widely esteemed for his learning (he, too, received the dedication of a humanistic work) who owned a number of printed works in Greek.[48] He was a friend of Erasmus, as was another sixteenth-century Cambridge graduate, Richard Sampson. He went on to study at Paris and at Siena, wrote commentaries on books of the Bible, composed motets including two in praise of Henry VIII, and was the author of a work in defence of the royal supremacy, *Oratio quae docet Anglos regiae dignitati ut obediant*, printed c.1535.[49]

Others went to Italy to serve as proctors at the papal curia, or to obtain professional employment in the papal service.[50] Among these curialists in the fifteenth century was Adam Moleyns, from Sefton in Lancashire, who spent some years in the early fourteen-thirties as king's proctor at the papal court, also attending the Council of Basel. Moleyns came to know the humanist, Poggio Bracciolini, probably at the curia, and it may have been at Basel that he met Aeneas Sylvius Piccolomini, the future Pius II, who praised his Latin style and classical learning. In the late fourteen-thirties Moleyns returned to England where he became a royal councillor and, in 1444, Keeper of the Privy Seal.[51] Among his contemporaries was yet another alumnus of Winchester and New College, Andrew Holes, a Cheshire man who, already an Oxford graduate in civil law, obtained a doctorate in canon law from Padua and, as a King's Clerk, served as Henry VI's proctor in Rome from 1432 to 1444. A friend of Pope Eugenius IV, an acquaintance of Cardinal Bessarion, Holes was described as a lover of books by the Florentine bookseller, Vespasiano da Bisticci, and can justly be regarded as a distinguished English collector of humanistic works. But his interests and abilities went further. Holes helped to obtain the bulls for the foundation of Eton College, while he and Thomas Bekynton who, as bishop of Bath and Wells, had been active in furthering the foundation of Henry VI's school, combined together to make a reality of the smaller school in St. Anthony's Hospital, London, founded by John Carpenter in 1441. When Moleyns died, by violence, in 1450, it was Holes who was chosen to succeed him as Keeper of the Privy Seal.[52]

One has some evidence of how civil lawyers introduced humanistic values into England. Richard Petteworthe (like so many civil lawyers, a notary public),[53] was secretary to bishop Henry Beaufort by 1415 and, as a member of Beaufort's household, came to know Poggio whom Beaufort had befriended at the Council of Constance. Petteworthe's correspondence with Poggio showed 'a lively interest in modern writings' and through their friendship he was able to introduce Poggio's own works into England, besides showing a great liking for, if no great skill in, an elegant epistolary style.[54] In a similar way, it was through his position as chancellor to Humphrey, duke of Gloucester, that Thomas Bekynton first came into contact with humanists, and it was in the service of the king, and mainly in the cause of England's foreign relations, that he used and developed a good Latin style based on classical models in his diplomatic correspondence. Bekynton, who had been Keeper of the Privy Seal before Moleyns, is the third member of the small but remarkably talented group, which among the civil lawyers also included Moleyns and Holes, whose members actively encouraged educational developments in the form of schools and colleges, and who put their legal and humanistic education at the service of the crown during the middle years of Henry VI's reign. The personal combination of a respect for scholarship and matters academic, coupled to a strong practical streak which enabled these three men to take on the responsibilities inherent in the Keepership of the Privy Seal, is what makes them outstanding contributors to a wide range of cultural developments in their day.[55]

What of their writings? It must first be admitted that no English civil lawyer made any real contribution to the literature of Roman law during this period.[56] Although both John de Acton and William Lyndwood had doctorates in civil law, such original contributions as they made were to canon law, and to English canon law at that; Acton in the thirteen-forties when he wrote a *Glossa* on the Legatine Constitutions of Otho and Ottobone, Lyndwood in the fourteen-twenties with his *Provinciale*, a guide to the English ecclesiastical law of his day.[57] Thus although it has been claimed for Lyndwood that he was well-read in the continental decretalists, his interests were largely English. None the less it must also be admitted that Lyndwood regarded the documents which he collected as living law,[58] and it is this vital interest in living issues and problems, so important for the lawyer if he is to be successful, that is reflected in the writings of the other civil lawyers. The following instances may help to illustrate this point.

We have already noted the interest which certain civil lawyers had in contemporary events such as the Great Schism and the Anglo-French war. It was entirely appropriate, since cases concerning heraldry were heard in the Court of Chivalry in which civil lawyers served, that Nicholas Upton, a lawyer with degrees in both canon and civil law, should be the author of a *De Officio Militari*, a work on heraldry and knighthood which showed the marked influence of the great Italian jurist, Bartolus of Sassoferrato.[59] A lively interest in matters contemporary is likewise evidenced in the original works of three civil lawyers, all of them actively involved in the politics of their day. As eye-witnesses, sometimes as protagonists, they chronicled events: Adam Murimuth, advocate in the Court of Arches, royal envoy and royal proctor at the papal curia, wrote the *Continuatio Chronicarum*, begun in 1325 and carried on until his death in 1347;[60] John Walwayn, treasurer of England in 1318 and royal envoy, was probably the author of the *Vita Edwardi Secundi*;[61] while the Welshman, Adam of Usk, likewise an advocate in the Court of Arches, auditor of causes of the papal palace, notary public and public intriguer, wrote a record of events, much of it concerned with the deposition of Richard II in which he had taken a personal part.[62] In the case of these men an active role in politics and administration led to a determination to record a version of the events through which they had lived— typical of the cast of mind of a lawyer or a notary, perhaps.[63]

The original works so far examined are chiefly legal in character and written in Latin. Yet some of these lawyers moved with the times. If, at the beginning of the fifteenth century, Robert Hallum commissioned a translation of Dante's *Divina Commedia* into Latin verse,[64] by the end of the century John Alcock, already noted as a patron of building, had Wynkyn de Worde print religious works in English whose titles reflect the pietistic movement of the times.

The same printer was to be responsible for producing Richard Foxe's *The Contemplacyon of Synners* in 1499, while in 1516(?) Richard Pynson printed Foxe's translation of the *Rule of St. Benedict*, evidence not only of these men's concern for religious practice but of their appreciation that the new printing processes would make vernacular works more readily available.[65]

The content of personal libraries, and their disposal are an indication of cultural interest. Few civil lawyers appear to have had as many books as John Trefnant who, as bishop of Hereford, died in 1404.[66] The inventory of his manuscript lists ninety-one items, of which sixty-six (nearly three-quarters) were books on canon and civil law; there were a mere ten on theology, and thirteen service books.[67] Trefnant had served for four years as an auditor of causes in the papal service, and this fact doubtless accounts for the predominance of legal texts and commentaries, including Azo, Hostiensis, some of the best thirteenth- and fourteenth-century French and Italian commentators in both laws, and several volumes of the relatively up-to-date Bartolus. That Trefnant was an active lawyer accustomed to pleading and to drawing-up official documents is brought home to us by the presence in his library of Quintilian's *In Declamacionibus* (always a popular text among lawyers), a *Liber de exemplis sacre scripture* and a *Formularium magnum cum diversis formis literarum*; that he might need to look up points of law quickly is further suggested by the presence of a *Tabula terminorum Iuris per litteras alphabeti*. We know, too, that Trefnant was one of the lawyers consulted by Richard II in January 1399 to advise him concerning the Schism;[68] this could account for his possessing a volume with gatherings of paper comprising 'scriptura diversorum super eleccione Urbani VI et scismate sedando'. As a bishop, he had more than his share of troubles with another contemporary problem, the rise of Lollardy and heresy, and his knowledge of canon law, reflected in the treatise 'de censura ecclesiastica' found among his books, could have been useful in dealing with such problems. His theological works were unexceptional: Augustine, Peter Lombard, Hugh of St. Victor, and Aquinas. His interest in general culture was reflected in his possession of the *De proprietatibus rerum* of Bartholomeus Anglicus; an interest in things Roman is seen in his Valerius Maximus, *Super memorabilibus Romanorum*, with a commentary, a popular work which provided a source of *exempla* valuable to the advocate. What is most striking here is that we are in the presence of what is essentially a professional man's working library which must be related to the activities of his career. Trefnant was above all a practising lawyer, accustomed to being asked his opinion on legal matters such as that of the Schism, and who, in consequence, had a professional obligation to be well-informed on the law and its development. The fact that he had a *De decisionibus Rote*, written on papers, suggests that he tried to keep as up-to-date as possible.

This professionalism is reflected in a number of other known libraries. It was appropriate that an advocate such as John Elmer should have owned a *De modo dictandi*,[69] as did John Lecche, who also had a fine library of civil law texts and canonist commentaries which he bequeathed to Llanthony Priory near Hay-on-Wye.[70]

Professionalism is also seen in the way in which a good lawyer kept up with the latest opinion, as in the instance already noted of John Trevenant who kept a record of cases settled in the Roman Rota. The advent of printing made the circulation of such volumes in quantity very much easier, and it is of interest that three late fifteenth- early sixteenth-century lawyers, Richard Nykke, Thomas Mors, and William Warham, should have possessed books of *consilia*, or legal opinions, printed in Italy or France.[71] Nykke and Warham, it should be noted, had had spells in Italy.[72] Everything suggests that such men regarded the civil law as a living law (as Lyndwood had regarded the canon law of England as a living law), not as a body of legal texts to be studied philologically as the more extreme humanists were coming to believe. In this respect it should be emphasized that the concept of the civil law as living law had been that of Bartolus and the post-Glossatorial school,[73] and the evidence which can be mustered for England, in terms both of the commentators studied and of English lawyers' attitude towards the law which they practised, reflects the strong influence of this Italian school of thought.[74]

Another kind of Roman influence was reflected in the libraries of some civil lawyers. Richard Foxe left Corpus Christi College, Oxford, over 100 books and manuscripts. These were of many kinds. If Foxe showed himself to be very 'English' by possessing a copy of works by Acton, Lyndwood, and William Sherwood on English canon law, and largely traditional in his theological tastes (he had originally planned to found his college for monks), it is the presence of works by humanists such as Poggio, works by a large selection of classical authors and, above all, works in Greek, all in print, which shows the remarkable breadth of interest and accounts for the far-reaching cultural influence which this particular lawyer exercised through his patronage and the stimulus which he gave to both classical and theological studies in the 'modern' vein.[75] Foxe, it must be admitted, was perhaps hardly typical. The only lawyer who could approach him on anything like equal terms was Cuthbert Tunstal, who died in 1559, at the advanced age of eighty-five. A student of Padua, as well as of Oxford and Cambridge, he served as an auditor of causes for archbishop Warham, was master of the Rolls, keeper of the Privy Seal and royal envoy, besides which, as a friend of Erasmus, he was in touch with other humanists. Some of these factors are clearly reflected in the manuscripts and books known to have belonged to him; two manuscripts and six books were in Greek, and he possessed a variety of other works, ranging from Quintilian, by way of the *Stratagemata* of Polyaenus, to the Complutensian Polyglot Bible.[76] Languages, one may infer from this and other works in his library, had a great interest for Tunstal. Such was the breadth of his culture that it would be difficult to deduce, from the books which are known to have belonged to him, that he had even had a lawyer's training.[77]

An interest in classical Latin literature was fairly common among the civilians. In this sense they differed from the common lawyer, Thomas Kebell (d.1500) whom Dr. Ives has described as being 'no searcher after the humanists', and resembled more the lawyers of the *Parlement* of Paris of about 1400 and, even more closely, the *légistes* of the Burgundian court in the fifteenth century.[78] Authors such as Cicero, Caesar, Ovid, Seneca, Frontinus (whose *De Aquis* was owned by both John Shirwood and Richard Foxe,[79] whereas one would have expected the *Stratagemata* which John Neuton possessed),[80] Valerius Maximus and Vegetius were to be found in their libraries. Such writers, some of them historians,[81] were probably read not merely for pleasure but more likely for didactic or oratorical purposes, for the *exempla* which they could provide,[82] and for the cultural veneer which the quoting of them could bestow. History, in the more modern form of Higden's *Polychronicon* in Latin (a few had Vincent of Beauvais *Speculum Historiale*, another world history) was owned by some lawyers,[83] while James Goldwell even owned Thomas Elmham's *De vita et gestis Henrici V*.[84] Generally the taste was for 'l'histoire savante', in Latin, a taste shared by lawyers outside England at this time.[85]

We do well to remember that we are dealing with men who were predominantly clerical, a fact clearly reflected in their libraries. Religious works were of various kinds. In addition to the Bible, complete or in parts, were numerous commentators; the Fathers, with Augustine and Gregory probably the most popular; some pre-scholastics and a number of the scholastics themselves, as well as volumes of sermons (a form of oratory)[86]—in brief, the whole gamut of theological writing. It is interesting to observe how, as in the case of works chosen for printing, evident sympathy was reflected for contemporary religious sentiments and practices, as well as for some fashionable authors. Above all one may note the relatively frequent appearance of mystical writers, beginning with the works of St. Bernard. More recent were the *Revelations* of St. Bridget owned, for instance, by John Dygon and Robert Heete who were almost contemporaries at Oxford at the beginning of the fifteenth century;[87] the works, in part or whole, of Richard Hampole, owned by John Neuton, John Dygon, Owen Lloyd, and William Smyth,[88] whose careers ranged over more than a hundred years from the late fourteenth to early sixteenth centuries; John Neuton also possessed some works of Walter Hilton who may have been a civil lawyer by training and a contemporary of Neuton's at Cambridge. In addition John Dygon, who was to become a recluse c.1435, copied out the earliest extant text of what has come to be known as the *Imitatio Christi* in 1438.[89] The fact that Richard Teryndon could leave many of his books, including some sermons of Vincent Ferrer, to Syon Monastery,[90] and that works with such devotional titles as *Tractatus de Passione, De Sanguine Christi* (a work of Pope Sixtus IV) and *De Sacramento Eucharistiae* could be owned by lawyer-bishops of the late fifteenth- and early sixteenth-centuries[91] suggests a strong streak of traditionalism in the religious culture of these men, who were not of the kind to become radical reformers in religious matters.[92]

Yet we have suggested that the civil lawyers were men who were not afraid to face and seek answers to contemporary problems. Their active involvement almost inevitably implied something of a philosophical turn of mind, an interest in what is today called political theory. Mme. Autrand suggests that the clergy, by dint of repetition, must have got to know the psalms by heart and that they had before them an example, in David, of the ideal king;[93] psalters were certainly very common in their libraries. This interest may be taken further. The works of Plato and Aristotle were to be found among the books of a number of civil lawyers. The remarkable bibliophile John Neuton, possessed a manuscript of John of Salisbury's *Policraticon*, a printed copy later being owned by Nicholas Goldwell, brother of the bishop of Norwich.[94] Egidius

Colonna's popular *De Regimine Principum*, written at the end of the thirteenth century, was owned by John Lecche, who was dead by 1361, by John Neuton, who died in 1414, and by Owen Lloyd,[95] who died over a century later; Lecche was clearly interested in this kind of work because he also bequeathed a *De Regimine Dominorum*, while William Warham left All Souls College a work entitled *De origine bonorum regum*.[96] Since some of these titles suggest a latent interest in political thinking, we should certainly note the political influence which the reading of certain French and Italian legal works, by authors who were primarily lawyers not political theorists, may have had upon those who studied them. What the effect was of reading the thirteenth-century Parisian canonist, Guillaume Durand, on sovereignty or, above all, the great Bartolus on this and many other subjects which we might adjudge to be 'political', can never be measured, but that these and other writers had an influence on the formation of political concepts can scarcely be doubted.[97] There were those, chiefly but not solely in the reign of Richard II, who feared that civil law principles were in the process of taking over in England. If they had, much of the responsibility would have been placed at the door of the well-read civil lawyers.[98]

One may perhaps ask what attempts the civil lawyers made to perpetuate their legal culture and to form themselves into an integral professional group to defend the system and the law which they professed. While the civil lawyer with a small library (it might be a very 'professional' library of only a few books, most of which would be basic texts, together with a handful of commentaries) would normally leave these to a single legatee (whether an individual who might be a relative studying law, or a cathedral library where the books might be consulted by future ecclesiastical lawyers, or perhaps most often of all a college at Oxford or Cambridge which specialized in civil law studies)[99] it is possible to discern, in the case of a number of the larger testators, a tendency to divide books up into specialist collections in order to bequeath them to different institutions. A number of legacies, mostly taken from the first quarter of the fifteenth century, illustrate this point. In 1410, William Rolf left five of his books on civil law and 'unam par decretorum' to King's Hall, Cambridge, while at the same time Richard Dunmow was bequeathing 'totum corpus juris civilis', some commentaries and other works, including his copy of Higden's *Polychronicon*, to Pembroke Hall.[100] But when John Neuton, with a big library, came to make his will in May 1414, he

gave some books to Peterhouse and others to York Minster, specifying that his legal books should be placed in a special chest in the
vestry for use by any of his nephews who might study civil law,
and that only after they had had use of them should the books be
placed in the Minster Library; in 1404, John Bottlesham left his law
books to Peterhouse, while Pembroke Hall received his works on
theology; and John Elmer, a Wykehamist who died in Henry V's
reign, left his law books to New College and his others to the
chapel and library at Winchester.[101] A century later Richard Foxe
could endow his college of Corpus Christi with largely humanistic
works, while the bulk of his books on law were bequeathed to the
collegiate church of Bishop Auckland; and William Warham, on
his part, divided his books between New College and All Souls
College, the former receiving works on theology and law, the latter
a collection consisting largely of devotional books, sermons and
other works.[102]

From such evidence it is possible to suggest not only that, in
bequeathing their books, some civil lawyers were helping the new
collegiate foundations of Oxford and Cambridge to acquire basic
texts which would be of use to their members, but also that there
was a similar pattern of intention shared by those who founded
colleges to further the study of civil law (King's Hall and Trinity
Hall in Cambridge, New College and All Souls College in Oxford)
and those who sought, by means of their bequests, to provide them
with libraries which corresponded to those studies, the second
complementing the work of the first. The number of members and
former-members of both New College and All Souls College who
left basic legal texts and, above all, commentaries to their colleges
strongly suggests that specialist institutions attracted specialist
bequests.[103]

Such was one vital way in which the specialist culture of these
lawyers could be perpetuated. The other was through the formation of a professional institution to unite those who had received
their legal education not only in the two English universities, but
elsewhere, mainly in Italy. The common lawyers had their corporations which provided them with their legal training and served to
defend their interests; their Inns had the added advantage of being
established in London, ' over the shop ', so to say. Curiously, it was
not until the end of the fifteenth century that anything appears to
have been done to remedy this deficiency for civil lawyers.[104]
When he died, in 1469, Thomas Kent (as a clerk twice married he
was probably precluded from serving in a church court in spite of

holding doctorates in both laws) left twenty-eight books, over twenty of which were on the civil law, to form a library for the use of the dean, advocates and proctors of the court of Canterbury (the Court of Arches), provided that these could be housed in a suitable building near St. Paul's cathedral, failing which they were to be given to All Souls College.[105] But it is only in 1495 that a reference is found to 'cum doctoribus de arcubus' in Pater Noster Row, when there may well already have existed a 'college' whose earliest surviving record is, however, dated 1511.[106] While it is clear that not all the members were practising advocates, the list, which includes the names of Thomas More, John Colet, Polydore Vergil, and William Grocyn, suggests a strong sympathy for the humanistic culture of the day.

The culture which has been described in these pages presupposed a considerable measure of wealth, in some cases almost riches.[107] The time needed to study to obtain a doctorate had to be paid for; hence the importance of the new collegiate foundations which, in some cases, were like academic chantries established by pious founders. Such was one way around the problem of maintaining students. Many law students, however, appear to have been men of either noble or well-to-do birth, men who may have begun life with a measure of financial security. Certainly everything suggests that even a moderately successful lawyer could do quite well for himself.[108] Their careers could be profitable in terms of revenue. With fees paid for causes pleaded and with retainers paid by both individuals and corporations who might wish for representation, a comfortable income could be gained by practitioners in ecclesiastical courts. Some bought land, but often only to give it to the Church or to endow a fellowship. Unlike the common lawyers who were laymen and for whom legal wealth could be expressed in terms of land and social advancement,[109] the financial investment of the civil lawyers was to be largely in culture.[110] Their wealth, which could be considerable, was placed at the disposal of education through investment in buildings, in sources of learning, and in artefacts, both sacred and profane. This reflects the measure of prosperity enjoyed by many clerical *litterati*, a level of prosperity which Roger Otery, who, in 1366, held six benefices, five of them sinecures, valued at £47. 1s. 4d., thought was appropriate for members of that class.[111] In addition to his books and the endowment of a house of residence for some chantry priests, Thomas Kent left his wife £800 (including some debts which he was owed);[112] John Trefnant's library of ninety-one books was

valued at over £300; other large bequests could be cited in support
of this point.

On what could a prosperous, but celibate, group spend its
money except on religion and culture? In the final analysis we are
up against this fact, which goes a long way towards explaining
how wealth, whether inherited, earned in a professional capacity
as a lawyer, or obtained as a member of the literate, pluralist clergy
was actually spent, whether on assisting members of the 'clan' to
study,[113] or on endowing scholarships,[114] or on establishing bequests of books and the founding of educational institutions. At
least two of the lawyers employed by Philip IV of France, Gilles
Aicelin and Raoul de Presles, became founders of famous colleges
in Paris in the early fourteenth century,[115] a process continued in
England by William Bateman, Henry Chichele, and Richard Foxe.
Foxe founded Corpus Christi College, Oxford, from his private
revenues, being able to do so in spite of a background humble
when compared to that of Chichele, who came from a family of
prosperous burgesses. The cultural contribution of the civil lawyers to late-medieval English society reflects their importance, the
avenues for advancement open to them, and the usefulness they
served in contemporary society which enabled them to earn the
wealth to pay for that culture. If most of them were men of God, it
should not be forgotten that most of them were men of the world as
well.[116]

NOTES

1. On this matter see G. F. Lytle, 'Patronage Patterns and Oxford Colleges,
c.1300–c.1500', The University in Society, L. Stone, (ed.), I, Princeton, 1975, pp.
111–49.

Mr. T. H. Aston has very kindly provided me with the following figures for
students of Civil Law and Both Laws at Oxford and Cambridge:

| | Civil Law | | Both Laws | |
	Oxford	Cambridge	Oxford	Cambridge
Before 1200			4	
1200–1299	54	9	19	2
1300–1399	329	178	148	59
1400–1499	532	330	535	155
1500	17	6	10	4
Totals	932	523	716	220

(Students are arranged according to the first recorded or estimated date of residence.
Those under '1500' covers those known to have been first resident in that year.)

2. K. R. N. Wykeham-George ('English Canonists in the Later Middle Ages: A historical, literary and biographical study', unpublished Oxford B.Litt. thesis, 1937, pp. 214–18) showed that in the fourteenth and fifteenth centuries many canonists were dispensed from following the courses in civil law. The cutting of academic corners could have a bad effect on legal knowledge: 'Canonista sine legibus parum valet, legista sine canonibus nihil', quoted in G. D. Squibb, *Doctors' Commons. A History of the College of Advocates and Doctors of Law*, Oxford, 1977, p. 1.

3. On this, see B. L. Woodcock, *Medieval Ecclesiastical Courts in the Diocese of Canterbury*, Oxford, 1952, ch. III; R. W. Dunning, 'The Wells Consistory Court in the Fifteenth Century', *Proceedings of the Somersetshire Archaeological and Natural History Society*, cv, (1961–2), pp. 46–61; R. H. Helmholz, *Marriage Litigation in Medieval England*, Cambridge, 1974, pp. 141–54; W. Senior, 'The Advocates of the Court of Arches', *Legal Quarterly Review* [hereafter cited as *L.Q.R.*], xxxix (1923), pp. 493–506; T. H. Aston, G. D. Duncan, and T. A. R. Evans, 'The Medieval Alumni of the University of Cambridge', *Past & Present*, no. 86, (1980), p. 76.

4. Men such as John de Ros, Richard Scrope, John Trefnant and Adam of Usk, Emden, *Oxford*, pp. 1590–1, 1659–60, 1898–9, 1900–02, 1937–8.

5. G. D. Squibb, *The Law of Arms in England*, The Heraldry Society, East Knoyle, Wilts, 1953, p. 4; B. P. Levack, *The Civil Lawyers in England, 1603–1641. A Political Study*, Oxford, 1973, p. 143: 'The Admiral jurisdiction is lex terrae to the subject ...'

6. J. L. Barton, *Roman Law in England* (Ius Romanum Medii Aevi), Milan, 1971, pp. 75–6; T. Runyan, 'The Rolls of Oléron and the Admiralty Court in Fourteenth-Century England', *American Journal of Legal History*, xix (1975), pp. 95–111; W. Senior, 'The First Admiralty Judges', *L.Q.R.*, xxxv (1919), pp. 73–83 and 'Admiralty Matters in the Fifteenth Century', ibid., pp. 290–9; *Select Pleas in the Court of Admiralty*, R. G. Marsden, (ed.), Selden Society, vi, 1894. See also N. Pronay, 'The Chancellor, the Chancery and the Council at the end of the fifteenth century', *British Government and Administration. Studies presented to S. B. Chrimes*, H. Hearder and H. R. Loyn, (eds), Cardiff, 1974, pp. 94–7.

7. On this court, in addition to G. D. Squibb's study, *The Law of Arms*, cited in note 5, see his important book, *The High Court of Chivalry*, Oxford, 1959; and A. Harding, *The Law Courts of Medieval England*, London, 1973, pp. 103–7.

8. M. H. Keen, 'Treason Trials under the Law of Arms', *T.R.Hist.S.*, 5th series, xii (1962), pp. 85–103.

9. Squibb, *High Court of Chivalry*, cited in note 7, p. 221; *Select Pleas ... of Admiralty*, cited in note 6, pp. 17–26.

10. M. E. Avery, 'An Evaluation of the Effectiveness of the Court of Chancery under the Lancastrian Kings', *L.Q.R.*, lxxxvi (1970), pp. 84, 87–8, 91; Barton, *Roman Law in England*, cited in note 6, pp. 39ff; H. Coing, 'English Equity and the Denunciatio Evangelica of the Canon Law', *L.Q.R.*, lxxi (1955), p. 238; R. H. Jones, *The Royal Policy of Richard II. Absolutism in the Later Middle Ages*, Oxford, 1958, p. 158. Mr. Pronay ('The Chancellor', cited in note 6, pp. 91–2) emphasizes that it was in the reign of Edward IV that the civil lawyers came to 'take over' the mastership of the Rolls.

11. For 'The Court of Conscience', as men of the time called it, *Select Cases in Chancery, A.D. 1364–1471*, W. P. Baildon, (ed.), Selden Society, x, 1896, p. xxx and

item no. 123. See also Barton, *Roman Law in England*, cited in note 6, pp. 50, 57, 63–4. Andrew Holes and John Middelton possessed a copy of the *Summa de casibus conscientiae* of Bartholomew de S. Concordio, Emden, *Oxford*, p. 950, 1277. As Keeper of the Privy Seal, Holes may have been involved in the hearing of such cases.

12. J. A. Guy, 'The Early-Tudor Star Chamber', *Legal History Studies 1972*, Dafydd Jenkins, (ed.), Cardiff, 1975, p. 124.

13. Coing, 'English Equity', cited in note 10, p. 240. See also Pronay, 'The Chancellor', cited in note 6, passim; S. B. Chrimes, *Henry VII*, London, 1972, pp. 163–6. For one chancellor, see E. F. Jacob, 'Archbishop John Stafford', *T.R.Hist.S.*, 5th series, xii (1962), pp. 1–23.

14. At the beginning of the present century there was a strong tendency to underestimate the role of civil lawyers and the influence of Roman practice upon English law. See, for instance, *Selected Historical Essays of F. W. Maitland*, H. Cam, (ed.), Cambridge, 1957, p. 109 (an essay published in 1902) and C. Kenny, 'Bonus Jurista malus Christa', *L.Q.R.*, xix (1903), p. 328. Today, however, the influence of the existing common law rules is being re-emphasized once more. See *St. German's Doctor and Student*, T. F. T. Plucknett and J. L. Barton (eds.), Selden Society, xci, 1974, p. xliii. As Mr. Pronay 'The Chancellor', cited in note 6, p. 102, says, 'to what extent they actually applied specific civilian doctrines in Chancery, Star Chamber, Admiralty and Requests we do not know and perhaps it is a hopeless quest.'

15. See G. P. Cuttino, *English Diplomatic Administration, 1259–1339*, 2nd edn., Oxford, 1971. The *liber recordorum* referred to by the writer of the *Gesta Henrici Quinti*, F. Taylor and J. S. Roskell, (eds.), Oxford, 1975, was probably one such record.

16. C. R. Cheney, *Notaries Public in England in the Thirteenth and Fourteenth Centuries*, Oxford, 1972, especially pp. 60–2.

17. In addition to the work of Cuttino, cited in note 15, the following may also be usefully consulted: D. E. Queller, *The Office of Ambassador in the Middle Ages*, Princeton, 1967, especially chs. II and VI; F. L. Ganshof, *Histoire des relations internationales: I. Le Moyen Age*, Paris, 1953, ch. XII; G. Schwarzenberger, 'International Law in early English Practice', *British Year Book of International Law*, xxv (1948), pp. 52–90, especially p. 88; P. Stein, *Roman Law in Scotland* (Ius Romanum Medii Aevi), Milan, 1968, pp. 29–31; V. F. Snow, 'The Evolution of Proctorial Representation in Medieval England', *American Journal of Legal History*, vii (1963), pp. 319–39.

18. See Lytle, 'Patronage Patterns', cited in note 1; E. F. Jacob, 'Petitions for Benefices from English Universities during the Great Schism', *T.R.Hist.S.*, 4th series, xxvii (1945), p. 54, n.1. On the strongly-expressed views of one civilian, Roger Otery, see A. Hamilton Thompson, *The English Clergy and their Organization in the Later Middle Ages*, Oxford, 1947, appendix IV, pp. 246–7.

19. T. H. Aston, 'Oxford's Medieval Alumni', *Past & Present*, no. 74 (1977), p. 28. For Cambridge see the more recent article by Aston, Duncan, and Evans, 'Alumni of Cambridge', cited in note 3, p. 70.

20. E. F. Jacob, *Henry Chichele*, London, 1967, ch. 6.

21. Ibid., ch. 3.

22. Margaret Harvey, 'Nicholas Ryssheton and the Council of Pisa, 1409', *Studies in Church History: vol. 7. Councils and Assemblies*, G. J. Cuming and D. Baker, (eds.), Cambridge, 1971, pp. 197–207.

23. B. L., MS. Cotton Nero E.v. See C. M. D. Crowder, 'Constance Acta in English Libraries', *Das Konzil von Konstanz*, herausg. von A. Franzen and W. Müller, Freiburg, 1964, pp. 481–2, 493–4.

24. Bibliothèque Nationale, Paris, MS. Latin 1448. On Sprever, see Emden, *Oxford*, pp. 1745–6. To this, one may add the collection 'scripta Parisius et universit' Oxon' de sismat' owned by Nicholas de Wykeham, Emden, *Oxford*, p. 2111; a work on the *acta* of the Council of Constance by Patrick Foxe, ibid, p. 715, and an 'acta Concilii Basiliensis' left to New College by James Russell at the end of the fifteenth century. Russell was also concerned with another contemporary problem, that of heresy, on which he compiled or possessed works, ibid, p. 1610. On the interest of French lawyers in the Councils, see Françoise Autrand, 'Culture et mentalité. Les librairies des gens du Parlement au temps de Charles VI', *Annales E.S.C.*, xxviii (1973), p. 1233.

25. See A. F. Judd, *The Life of Thomas Bekynton*, Chichester, 1961, p. 40.

26. T. Fowler, *The History of Corpus Christi College*, Oxford Historical Society, xxv, Oxford, 1893, p. 30; Emden, *Oxford*, p. 1397.

27. Emden, *Oxford*, p. 1032.

28. Ibid., pp. 158, 999.

29. Aston, 'Oxford's Medieval Alumni', cited note 19, pp. 14–15. The detailed figures of the pattern of civil law studies at both New College and All Saints College will be published by Dr. A. B. Cobban in his forthcoming contribution to the *History of the Univeristy of Oxford*, vol. II.

30. Emden, *Oxford*, p. 1370; See also Aston, Duncan and Evans, 'Alumni of Cambridge', cited in note 3, pp. 43–4.

31. Emden, *Oxford*, p. 1382; Emden, *Cambridge*, p. 431. One may add that in 1513 Cardinal Bainbridge had had a project to open a school at Bologna where canon law would be the speciality, D. S. Chambers, *Cardinal Bainbridge in the Court of Rome 1509 to 1514*, Oxford, 1965, p. 120.

32. Emden, *Oxford*, p. 1710.

33. Emden, *Oxford*, pp. 1007–8: it was turned into a secular college a few years later.

34. Alan B. Cobban, *The King's Hall within the University of Cambridge in the Later Middle Ages*, Cambridge, 1969, pp. 54–5, 255–8; Aston, Duncan and Evans, 'Alumni of Cambridge' cited in note 3, pp. 52–3.

35. He also helped to found Stapledon Hall, later Exeter College, Oxford, Emden, *Oxford*, p. 1765.

36. Ibid., p. 873.

37. Emden, *Cambridge*, p. 6.

38. Emden, *Oxford*, p. 785.

39. A point strongly emphasised by J. Bartier, *Légistes et gens de finances au XVe siècle. Les conseillers des ducs de Bourgogne, Philippe le Bon et Charles le Téméraire*, Brussels, 1955, pp. 273–4.

40. Such gifts were very numerous; the number of copes bequeathed suggests a deep appreciation of the beauty of *opus anglicanum*. From very many examples, two must suffice: the bequest of valuable vestments by John Southam to Lincoln cathedral in 1441, Emden, *Oxford*, p. 1733, and that of thirty copes by William Smyth to the same in 1514, ibid., p. 1722. Mme. Autrand stresses the very 'ecclesiastical' culture of members of the *Parlement* of Paris, 'Culture et mentalité', cited in note 24, p. 1242. The same would appear to apply to the civil lawyers of England.

41. Judd, *Thomas Bekynton*, cited in note 25, p. 156. See the whole of ch. VII on

'The Bishop as Builder'.

42. Emden, *Oxford*, p. 716.

43. C. Hussey, 'Horton Court, Gloucestershire', *Country Life*, lxxi (1932), pp. 122–7; see R. Fédou, *Les Hommes de loi lyonnais à la fin du moyen âge. Étude sur les origines de la classe de robe*, Annales de l'Université de Lyon, 3ème série: Lettres; fasc. 37, Paris, 1964, plate VI ('La maison des Palmier') for Renaissance influence on the domestic architecture of a legal family in France.

44. See the five articles by R. J. Mitchell: 'English Law Students at Bologna in the Fifteenth Century', *E.H.R.*, li (1936), pp. 270–87; 'English Students at Padua, 1460–75', *T.R.Hist.S.*, 4th series, xxix (1936), pp. 101–17; 'English Students at Ferrara in the XVth Century', *Italian Studies*, i (1937–8), pp. 75–82; 'English Student Life in Early Renaissance Italy', ibid., vii (1952), pp. 62–81; and 'Scottish Law Students in Italy in the Late Middle Ages', *Juridical Review*, xlix (1937), pp. 19–24.

45. Lawyers played a similar role in the Burgundian Low Countries, Bartier, *Légistes et gens de finances*, cited in note 39, p. 280.

46. Emden, *Oxford*, p. 1063.

47. On Yonge, see ibid., pp. 2136–7; H. W. Garrod, 'Erasmus and his English Patrons', *The Library*, 5th series, iv (1949), p. 7. On his tomb, see F. Grossmann, 'Holbein, Torrigiano and some Portraits of Dean Colet', *Journal of the Warburg and Courtauld Institutes*, xiii (1950), pp. 209, 222, and plate 55d.

48. See Emden, *Cambridge*, pp. 597–8.

49. Ibid., pp. 505–506.

50. Cf. Bartier, *Légistes et gens de finances*, cited in note 39, pp. 281–2.

51. On Moleyns, see Emden, *Oxford*, pp. 1289–91, and A. L. Brown, *The Early History of the Clerkship of the Council*, Univ. of Glasgow Publications, NS 131, 1969, pp. 29–30.

52. On Holes, see Emden, *Oxford*, pp. 949–50; J. W. Bennett, 'Andrew Holes: a neglected Harbinger of the English Renaissance', *Speculum*, xix (1944), pp. 314–35.

53. Notaries, whose concepts and professional phraseology owed much to roman and canon law, appear in English society in any significant number from the late thirteenth century onwards. First employed in bishops' chanceries, their historical development was closely allied to the advance in bureaucracy characteristic of the late middle ages. Since one of their chief functions was to authenticate documents and draw up officially-approved records of proceedings, judicial or diplomatic, notaries could find employment in the service of both church and state. The spread of the procedures and terminology of canon and civil law in Europe from the mid-thirteenth century onwards increased their opportunities. In such an historical development, England could not be left behind, and she came to owe much to the particular legal knowledge and expertise of these men, who were probably more numerous than has generally been recognized in the past. See Cheney, *Notaries Public in England*, cited in note 16, passim, and Aston, Duncan and Evans, 'Alumni of Cambridge', cited in note 3, p. 82.

54. On Petteworthe, see Emden, *Oxford*, p. 1471; R. Weiss, *Humanism in England during the Fifteenth Century*, Oxford, 3rd edn., 1967, pp. 19–21. On the whole matter of Renaissance letter collections, see C. H. Clough, 'The cult of Antiquity: letters and letter collections', *Cultural Aspects of the Italian Renaissance. Essays in honour of Paul Oskar Kristeller*, C. H. Clough, (ed.), Manchester-New York, 1976, pp. 33–67.

55. On these men, see Weiss, *Humanism in England*, cited in note 54, ch. V; J. Saltmarsh, *King Henry VI and the Royal Foundations*, Eton: Cambridge, 1972, pp. 5–6; *Four English Political Tracts of the Later Middle Ages*, J.-Ph. Genet, (ed.), Camden 4th series, xviii, Royal Historical Society, London, 1977, p. 42.

56. See Maitland's considered view: 'No medieval Englishman did anything considerable for Roman law', *Selected Historical Essays*, Cam, (ed.), cited in note 14, p. 109.

57. Wykeham-George, 'English Canonists', cited in note 2, pp. iv–v, 96–111; L. Boyle, 'The Curriculum of the Faculty of Canon Law at Oxford in the first half of the Fourteenth Century' *Oxford Studies presented to Daniel Callus*, O.H.S., new series, xvi, 1964, p. 162. On this see Aston, Duncan and Evans, 'Alumni of Cambridge', cited in note 3, p. 64, where the same evidence is quite independently quoted.

58. C. R. Cheney, 'William Lyndwood's Provinciale', *The Jurist*, xxi (1961), pp. 405, 410.

59. Nicholas Upton, *De Officio Militari*, E. Bysshe, (ed.), London, 1654; on Upton, see Emden, *Oxford*, pp. 1933–4. It has also been argued that John Trevaur, bishop of St. Asaph in the late fourteenth and early fifteenth centuries, was Johannes de Bado Aureo who compiled the important *Tractatus de Armis*, the oldest known treatise on heraldry written in Britain. The argument, it should be added, has not won general acceptance. See E. J. Jones, *Medieval Heraldry. Some Fourteenth-Century Heraldic Works*, Cardiff, 1943, which also includes the text of Bartolus's *De Insigniis et armis in vexillis et clypeis portandis*, a copy of which William Spekynton gave to New College in 1509, Emden, *Oxford*, p. 1741.

60. *Ade Murimuth Continuatio Chronicarum*, E. M. Thompson, (ed.), R. S., London, 1889; see Emden, *Oxford*, p. 1330.

61. See the valuable introduction by N. Denholm-Young to his edition of the *Vita Edwardi Secundi*, Edinburgh, 1957, or the same writer's article, 'The authorship of Vita Edwardi Secundi', *E.H.R.*, lxxi (1956), pp. 189–211. See also Emden, *Oxford*, pp. 2224–5.

62. *Chronicon Adae de Usk, A.D. 1377–1421*, E. M. Thompson, (ed.), 2nd edn., London, 1904; see Emden, *Oxford*, pp. 1937–8. Usk owned a copy of Higden's *Polychronicon* (J. Taylor, *The Universal Chronicle of Ranulf Higden*, Oxford, 1966, p. 154). It is possible that another Welsh civil lawyer, John Trevaur (see note 59) may also have written history. See E. J. Jones, 'The Authorship of the *Continuation of the Eulogium Historiarum*: a suggestion', *Speculum*, xii (1937), pp. 196–202, and his 'An Examination of the Authorship of the *Deposition and Death of Richard II* attributed to Créton', *Speculum*, xv (1940), pp. 460–77.

63. On the notion of the cartulary as a form of history, see J.-Ph. Genet, 'Cartulaires, registres et histoire: l'exemple anglais', *Le métier d'historien au moyen âge. Études sur l'historiographie médiévale*, B. Guenée, (ed.), Publications de la Sorbonne, série 'Études', xiii, Paris, 1977, pp. 95–138.

64. Emden, *Oxford*, p. 855.

65. Emden, *Cambridge*, p. 6; H. S. Bennett, 'Printers, Authors, and Readers, 1475–1557', *The Library*, 5th series, iv (1949), pp. 156–8.

66. Emden, *Oxford*, pp. 1900–2. The list of his books was printed by B. G. Charles and H. D. Emanuel, 'Notes on old libraries and books', *The National Library of Wales Journal*, vi (1949–50), pp. 356–9.

67. This was undoubtedly a big law library. In 1356, Bartolus had left sixty-four volumes, of which only thirty were law books, and two years later Robert le

Coq had left seventy-six books, mostly on law, R. Delachenal, 'La bibliothèque d'un avocat du XIVe siècle. Inventaire estimatif des livres de Robert le Coq', *Nouvelle revue historique de droit français et étranger*, xi (1887), pp. 529, 527, while in 1500 Serjeant Thomas Kebell, a successful common lawyer, was to leave thirty-three different works, E. W. Ives, 'A lawyer's Library in 1500', *L.Q.R.*, lxxxv (1969), pp. 104–16. See also Autrand, 'Culture et mentalité', cited in note 24, passim, and W. Senior, 'Roman Law MSS. in England', *L.Q.R.*, xlvii (1931), pp. 337–44.

68. E. Perroy, *L'Angleterre et le Grand Schisme d'Occident. Étude sur la politique religieuse de l'Angleterre sous Richard II (1378–1399)*, Paris, 1933, p. 386.

69. Emden, *Oxford*, pp. 635–6.

70. Ibid., p. 1119.

71. Mme. Autrand, 'Culture et mentalité', cited in note 24, p. 1242, stresses how the lawyers of the *Parlement* of Paris aimed at maintaining good professional standards. In England, common lawyers attempted to do this through the Year Books, see E. W. Ives, 'The Purpose and Making of the later Year Books', *L.Q.R.*, lxxxix (1973), pp. 64–86; reprinted in substance as 'The Origins of the later Year Books', *Legal History Studies 1972*, cited in note 12, pp. 136–51 and R. C. Palmer, 'County Year Book Reports: the professional lawyer in the medieval county court', *E.H.R.*, xci (1976), pp. 776–801, esp. p. 798. Canonists did this by means of volumes such as that owned by Trefnant, by John Wells who bequeathed a *Decisiones Rote* in 1417, *Somerset Medieval Wills (1383–1500)*, F. W. Weaver, (ed.), Somerset Record Society, xvi, 1901, p. 87; Emden, *Oxford*, p. 2010, by Walter Stone who left a *Decisiones Rote nove et antique* to All Souls when he died in 1519, Emden, *Oxford*, p. 1789, and by James Goldwell who owned *Conclusiones sive Decisionum Auditorum Rotae Romanae Collectio*, Emden, *Oxford*, p. 785. See A. Fliniaux, 'Les anciennes collections de "Decisiones Rotae Romanae"', *Revue historique de droit français et étranger*, 4e série, iv (1925), pp. 61–93, 382–410. When John Mottesfont bequeathed 'omnes reportorios meos' to John Norton in 1420, Emden, *Oxford*, p. 1325, he was presumably referring to 'summaries' or works of a similar nature, to which one may add the *consilia* of leading jurists which circulated first in manuscript and, in due course, in print, see M. P. Gilmore, *Humanists and Jurists. Six Studies in the Renaissance*, Cambridge, Mass., 1963, pp. 73ff. In all instances, the aim was to keep abreast of the latest legal opinion and judgements. On the three owners of *consilia*, see Emden, *Oxford*, p. 1381–2, 1315–16, 1988–92.

72. On the importation of foreign books into England during these years, see Elizabeth A. Armstrong, 'English purchases of printed books from the Continent, 1465–1526', *E.H.R.*, xciv (1979), pp. 268–90.

73. M. H. Keen, 'The Political Thought of the Fourteenth-Century Civilians', *Trends in Medieval Political Thought*, B. Smalley, (ed.), Oxford, 1965, pp. 111–2.

74. Gilmore, *Humanists and Jurists*, (cited in note 71), pp. 30–4, 83–6. Dr. Cobban, *The King's Hall*, cited in note 34, p. 251 has underlined that the post-Glossators and their commentators were well represented in the library of King's Hall.

75. Emden, *Oxford*, pp. 717–19.

76. Tunstal was sent Erasmus's New Testament (2nd edn., 1519) specially printed on vellum. I owe this information to Dr. C. H. Clough.

77. Emden, *Oxford*, pp. 1913–15.

78. Ives, 'A Lawyer's Library', cited in note 67, p. 106; Autrand, 'Culture et

mentalité', cited in note 24, pp. 1237, 1242; Bartier, *Légistes et gens de finances*, cited in note 39, p. 278.

79. Emden, *Oxford*, pp. 1693, 718.

80. Emden, *Cambridge*, p. 421.

81. Generally, the 'ancient' historians appear to have been more widely read than the 'medieval' ones, although Higden's *Polychronicon* and a number of other recent historical works are to be found owned by the lawyers. But M. Genet detects a lack of interest in history among university-trained jurists in the late-medieval and early-modern period, J.-Ph. Genet, 'Essai de bibliométrie médiévale: l'histoire dans les bibliothèques anglaises', *Revue française d'histoire du livre*, xvi (1977), pp. 17–22.

82. Autrand, 'Culture et mentalité', cited in note 24, p. 1238.

83. E.g. by Richard Dunmow (Emden, *Cambridge*, p. 198) and William North (Emden, *Oxford*, p. 1368), see also note 62, above.

84. Emden, *Oxford*, p. 785.

85. Autrand, 'Culture et mentalité', cited in note 24, p. 1238.

86. Ibid., pp. 1234, 1236, 1242.

87. Emden, *Oxford*, p. 615, 901.

88. Emden, *Cambridge*, p. 421; Emden, *Oxford*, pp. 616, 1154, 1722.

89. R. Lovatt, 'The *Imitation of Christ* in Late Medieval England', *T.R.Hist.S.*, 5th series, xviii (1968), pp. 114–15.

90. Emden, *Oxford*, p. 1856.

91. The first, printed in Rome in 1473, was owned by James Goldwell; the second by William Warham; the third by Cuthbert Tunstal, who himself wrote a tract *De Veritate Corporis et Sanguinis Domini nostri Jesu Christi in Eucharistia* while confined in London in the reign of Edward VI, Emden, *Oxford*, pp. 785, 1990, 1915.

92. The conventional religious tastes of French and Italian jurists are also stressed by Autrand, 'Culture et mentalité', cited n. 24, p. 1235, and Gilmore, *Humanists and Jurists*, cited in note 71, pp. 69–73).

93. Autrand, 'Culture et mentalité', cited in note 24, p. 1236.

94. Emden, *Cambridge*, p. 421; Emden, *Oxford*, p. 786.

95. Emden, *Oxford*, pp. 1119, 1154.

96. Ibid., pp. 1990–1. He also possessed Jerome's commentary on the psalms.

97. Keen, 'Political Thought of the Fourteenth-Century Civilians', cited in note 73, especially p. 116; C. N. S. Woolf, *Bartolus of Sassoferrato. His Position in the History of Medieval Political Thought*, Cambridge, 1913, passim; M. P. Gilmore, *Argument from Roman Law in Political Thought 1200–1600*, Cambridge, Mass., 1941, ch. I.

98. F. W. Maitland, 'Wyclif on English and Roman Law', *L.Q.R.*, xii (1896), pp. 76–8; T. F. T. Plucknett, 'State Trials under Richard II', *T.R.Hist.S.*, 5th series, ii (1952), pp. 159–71. On the political concepts of civil lawyers in the employ of Henry VII, see Pronay, 'The Chancellors', cited in note 6, pp. 102–3.

99. E.g. Robert Middleton to his nephew in 1499, Emden, *Oxford*, p. 1278; Roger de Freton to Chichester cathedral in 1382, Emden, *Cambridge*, p. 244; John Purgold to the 'lyberary' of Trinity Hall, of which he was a fellow, in 1527, Emden, *Cambridge*, p. 463.

100. Emden, *Cambridge*, pp. 487, 198.

101. Ibid., pp. 421–2, 76; Emden, *Oxford*, pp. 635–6.

102. Emden, *Oxford*, pp. 717–19, 1990–1.

103. By contrast with other Cambridge institutions, about half the library stock of the King's Hall was composed of books on civil law, Cobban, *King's Hall*, cited in note 34, pp. 251–4.

104. It may be noted that Padua had had a College of Doctors, to which law graduates resident in the city came, by the early fourteenth century, J. K. Hyde, *Padua in the Age of Dante*, Manchester, 1966, pp. 124, 315–7.

105. Emden, *Oxford*, p. 1038. Curiously enough, he is not known to have been a member of that college.

106. On this institution, see Squibb, *Doctors' Commons*, cited in note 2.

107. This is clear not only from the material bequests which the civil lawyers made and the educational and religious foundations which they endowed, but from the sums of money which not a few were able to leave.

108. Alan B. Cobban, *The Medieval Universities*, London, 1975, p. 227. 'Justitia est magnum emolumentum '.

109. E. W. Ives, 'The Common Lawyer in pre-Reformation England ', *T.R.Hist.S.*, 5th series, xviii (1968), pp. 159–61.

110. On the similarity of the Burgundian situation, see Bartier, *Légistes et gens de finances*, cited in note 39, pp. 271, 273–4.

111. See above in note 18. Civil lawyers and canonists were in the majority in three Cambridge rolls for petitions for benefices sent to Rome at the end of the fourteenth century, Jacob, 'Petitions for Benefices ', cited in note 18, p. 54, n. 1.

112. Information kindly provided by Professor R. L. Storey.

113. One may note the existence of legal ' dynasties ' among the lay lawyers of the *Parlement* of Paris. In Lyon some lawyers, such as Jean Paterin, tried to encourage at least one of their children to study law by bequeathing them their legal books to facilitate study, Fédou, *Les Hommes de loi lyonnais*, cited in note 43, p. 479. For English legal ' dynasties ', see Ives, 'The Common Lawyer in pre-Reformation England ', cited in note 109, pp. 159–61.

114. 'Les boursiers constituent une sorte de descendance du fondateur ', Autrand, 'Culture et mentalité ', cited in note 24, p. 1230.

115. F. Pegues, *The Lawyers of the last Capetians*, Princeton, 1962, pp. 97, 160. For the assistance of lawyers in founding colleges at Louvain a century later, see Bartier, *Légistes et gens de finances*, cited in note 39, p. 282.

116. I wish to thank Eric Ives and Alan Cobban for their kindness in reading the text in this contribution while it was in typescript.

7

The common lawyers

E. W. IVES

'The study of English law', wrote Erasmus, 'is as far removed as can be from true learning, but in England those who succeed in it are highly thought of '.[1] This remark and others like it have set the stereotype of the common lawyer for the early sixteenth century and the two hundred and fifty years before, from the time that lay lawyers began to emerge in the latter part of the reign of Henry III. With all the confidence of Renaissance scholarship to guide us, we can see English lawyers with intellects as crabbed as the year books they cherished, with tongues uncooth with pidgin Norman-French and ambitions set firmly on the pot of gold at the end, not of a rainbow, but of a study 'naturally dreaded' by minds 'fitted for better things'. Erasmus would have found the inclusion of English common lawyers in a volume devoted to culture, scholarship, and education, incongruous to a degree.

The fact that Erasmus made his remarks in connection with the career of Thomas More ought, however, to give us pause. It is hard to believe that a man of More's character and intelligence would have remained bound to the law for so long if it had uniformly insulted his intellectual values.[2] Doubt is reinforced when other names are brought into the story. Sir Thomas Elyot, contemporary and friend of More (and like him the son of a judge), was a member of the Middle Temple and clerk of the western assize circuit; as he said himself, he had by the law 'attayned no lytle commoditie'.[3] Nevertheless he went on to be a notable humanist, in G. R. Elton's words, 'the most prolific popularizer of ideas of the day'.[4] His most famous work, *The Boke named the Gouernour* (1531) brought into wide English circulation the educational ideas of Erasmus and the cultural values of *The Courtier*, Castiglione's manual for the European nobility. As a humanist Elyot sighed at the 'barbarouse' language of English law and argued that it needed to be more 'certayne and compendiouse . . . in a more clene and elegant style', but he claimed that it was inherently the purest of all laws, and

English lawyers, if given a touch of humanist polish, the most 'noble counsaylours' in the world.[5]

Less well known than Elyot is Richard Taverner, the principal English translator of the works of Erasmus. At one time he was a member of Strand Inn and later of the Inner Temple, although his habit of quoting 'the law in Greek when he read anything thereof' could suggest that his heart was in scholarship.[6] Both Elyot and Taverner were clients of the leading Renaissance patron of early Tudor England, Thomas Wolsey, and in the same stable was another common lawyer, Thomas Cromwell. Cromwell came from a lower professional category than the others and he was never a humanist author, but he knew French and Italian (and a little German), Latin, and a smattering of Greek, and he had a humanist's interest in quality of expression. The suggestion that he had read Machiavelli's *The Prince* is well known, and he certainly owned a copy of another Machiavelli work, *The History of Florence*, as well as *The Courtier*, Petrarch's *Triumphs* and Erasmus' Latin version of his New Testament.[7] But far more important than Cromwell's own attainments were his sympathies which made him the next great patron of Renaissance scholarship after Wolsey. Certainly he saw the writer as useful to the state, but he was not merely concerned with propaganda; after all, the utility of literature to the community was an axiom of humanism. Cromwell's own interest in learning and his genuine commitment to humanist reform are seen in numerous ways, not least in his investment of £400 in the printing of the Great Bible of 1539, and most immediately for the lawyers in the plans of 1539 to graft humanist values on to the inns of court.[8]

All this is not to say that every English common lawyer was an eager advocate of humanist learning. But it is to say that intellectual life within the profession was such as to be able to appreciate Renaissance ideas and that neither the atmosphere of the inns nor the academic equipment of the lawyers was an obstacle to men who wanted to develop that appreciation further. Indeed, a profession which required a knowledge of Latin and French, however crude, was a natural place for some reception of humanist ideas.[9]

The picture of a legal profession which was aware of more than writs, rolls and pleadings is made stronger when we turn from the new fashions of Italy to more traditional interests and attitudes. Edmund Dudley, Henry VII's disgraced minister, whiled away his imprisonment in the Tower in 1509–10 by writing *The tree of commonwealth*, a work highly conventional in tone and argument but, at the least, evidence of some interest in ideas.[10] The principal native historian in the early sixteenth century was Edward Hall of Gray's Inn, the common serjeant of London.[11] John Fitzherbert, elder brother of Justice Anthony Fitzherbert, wrote the *Boke of surveying* and the *boke of husbandry* (both 1523), the earliest attempts to write in English for the layman on either subject.[12] Earlier, Richard Strangways of the Inner Temple (d.1488) had made a collection of heraldic memoranda from numerous sources which he rather grandly described as *Tractatus nobilis de lege et exposicione armorum*, and it may be that this attempt had been stimulated by some formal instruction in heraldry given at his inn.[13]

The most important lawyer and author of the fifteenth century was, without question, Sir John Fortescue. A westcountryman, trained at Lincoln's Inn and called to be serjeant-at-law in 1438, Fortescue reached the summit of the profession in 1442 when appointed chief justice of the king's bench.[14] A staunch supporter of Henry VI, he went abroad in 1461 as the nominal chancellor of the Lancastrian government in exile but he was reconciled to Edward IV in 1471, served on the Yorkist council and died in 1479 at the age of ninety. He is best known as a writer today for his panegyric on English law and legal institutions, *De Laudibus Legum Anglie*, and for his *De Dominio Regale et Politico*, sub-titled in the eighteenth century as *The Difference between an Absolute and Limited Monarchy* but now less informatively known as *The Governance of England*.[15] Fortescue also wrote some ten tracts of immediate relevance to the political struggles of the mid-century and two related genealogies, while another of his tracts, *Opusculum de Natura Legis Naturae et Eius Censura in Successione Regnorum Suprema*, contributed to the Lancaster-York dispute a lengthy discussion of the succession to kingdoms, based on first principles. He was also the author of two religious works, and a number of other moral and practical writings have been attributed to him. Fortescue's significance in any cultural assessment of the late-medieval legal profession is obvious.

As far as is known, Sir John only studied at the inns of court, yet he was clearly a man of wide scholarship. Analysis of the sources he used has revealed an easy acquaintance with the standard apparatus and ideas of the late medieval scholar—the Bible, Aristotle (quoted very frequently), Vincent of Beauvais, Boethius, St. Augustine, and St. Thomas Aquinas.[16] In some cases Fortescue had the material at first hand; more often he used one of the compendia of knowledge which were in circulation in his day. He was also substantially acquainted with both roman and canon law. Was he exceptional, or was legal education broader than is often supposed?

Christopher St. German, the principal theorist of English law in the early sixteenth century was two generations or so younger than Fortescue; he was born about 1460 and trained at the Middle Temple under the Yorkist kings.[17] Late in life he became deeply involved in the disputes of the Reformation, conducting a famous debate with Thomas More and, in all, producing seven tracts on the relation between the lay power and spiritual authority. However, his major legal work, the first part of *Doctor and Student*, was published in 1523 and was unaffected by the heightened atmosphere of religious polemic. In it he cites Aristotle, Augustine, and John Gerson on frequent occasions, relies heavily on Aquinas and makes minor references to a wide medieval bibliography of authorities. Christopher St. German also knew his canon law and the literature of conscience, to say nothing of Fortescue's own works. John Fitzherbert, as we have seen the author of the first vernacular discussions of husbandry and surveying, was much of an age with St. German but very decidedly a minor provincial lawyer *cum* farmer.[18] However, his training at grammar school and his four years at the inns gave him an acquaintance with scholarship comparable to his professional superior. In the *boke of husbandry* alone he quoted by name Ambrose, Athanasius, Augustine, Chrysostom, Jerome, and Isidore and, more recent, Gregory, Bernard, and Richard Rolle, as well as both Old and New Testaments.[19] Chaucer was alluded to, proverbs quoted in Latin, English, and French and also several verses 'lerned . . . at grammar-scole'.

Evidence of breadth of learning is more difficult to find with the majority of lawyers who never wrote for an audience. Nevertheless the ownership of books tells us something. An inventory of Serjeant Thomas Kebell, taken in 1500, shows that he possessed thirty-three titles.[20] The collection had, naturally, a wider range than citations in any particular work would have; there was no reason for Fortescue, St. German, or Fitzherbert to mention imaginative literature such as the very fine copy of the *Decameron* which Kebell owned. Yet a number of the same authors do appear, and so too several of the encyclopedias which offered collections of knowledge and quotations from the saints and authorities of the past. Kebell possessed, as far as is known, no books by canonists or civilians, although other common lawyers did, but his arguments in court show that he was by no means a stranger to these rival systems.[21] He was also familiar with the rhetoric and grammar of scholastic education. He could discuss similes, conditionals, pregnant negatives, universals, and particulars.[22] He could argue Latin syntax and point out that an ambiguity in English would have been cured in the accusative.[23] Some lawyers were even better equipped—William Crofton of Gray's Inn actually had the degree of bachelor of civil law.[24] Others were less knowledgeable; on one occasion when Kebell and Chief Justice Bryan were agreeing together on what a good sophist would say about a particular construction, Justice Townshend brought them down to earth by saying: 'I am no sophister! But I can see that . . .'.[25] Nevertheless the point is clear. As an author, Sir John Fortescue must stand out among the late-medieval legal profession but neither his learning nor his intellectual interest was a private eccentricity.

The involvement of lawyers in the world of learning was an obvious contribution to the culture of the time, but it was not the only one. The lawyers, for example, were deeply concerned with the drama. The inns of court kept the highly formal ceremonies of the medieval Christmas, with a king of misrule and his court, but it is also probable that some of the early theatrical interludes were performed for, indeed by the profession.[26] Soon after the turn of the century, John Rowe of Gray's Inn (created a serjeant in 1510) 'compiled' a 'disguisyng' which told the story of 'Lord Gouernance' who had come under the sway of 'Dissipacion' and 'Negligence' and so 'Lady Publike Wele' was 'put from gouernance'.[27] The result was the intervention of 'a greate multitude' led by 'Rumor Populi', 'Inward Grudge' and 'Disdain of Wanton Souereignetie' who drove out the evil councillors and restored 'Publike Wele' to her position. A revival of the play in 1526 seemed to Wolsey too pointed to be accidental and Rowe was thrown in the Fleet prison. The better-known activity of inns-of-court men as patrons of the drama in the later sixteenth century and as actors and playwrights had a long tradition behind it.[28]

The most remarkable lawyer in this respect was John Rastell of the Middle Temple.[29] Of course he belonged to More's circle (he was his brother-in-law) and many of his interests seem to point to the future, not the past—printing, Reformation propaganda, eugenics, a public theatre on his own land at Finsbury, an enthusiasm for (and personal involvement in) overseas exploration. Rastell, however, also had a particular talent for that late-medieval

revival of chivalry combined with allegorical pageant, which
dominated court spectacle in England until the later years of
Henry VIII. He was one of the team which decorated the famous
palace which was erected for the Field of Cloth of Gold in 1520. He
devised a mechanical pageant for the City of London to greet the
Emperor Charles V in 1522; it was concerned with the 'Elementes,
the Planettes and Starres in their places', a topic on which Rastell
also wrote an interlude. In 1527 he was substantially responsible
for the entertainment of the French ambassadors at Greenwich,
probably providing a set of the 'king's beasts' designed as candle
holders, a mechanical 'Pageant of the Father of Heaven' and a
dramatic piece, *Love and Riches*. By no means can Rastell be described as other than remarkable and highly distinctive, and the
more time he devoted to his numerous non-legal interests, the less
of a lawyer he became. But the interesting point is that the supposedly narrow, arcane world of the lawyers could produce such a
man.

Evidence that the common lawyers were also, from time to time,
patrons of art is clear, if patchy. There was certainly some market
for miniatures among the profession. This is demonstrated by the
four Whaddon folios, once part of a fifteenth-century law text and
now at the Inner Temple.[30] They consist of illuminations of the
courts at Westminster, with the folio showing the common pleas
also containing the start of the list of contents which is decorated
in gold and blue, with the running floral border typical of mid-
century book illustration. Minutely drawn and vigorously characterized, they clearly belonged to a piece of deliberately fine book-
making. And there were other examples. Thomas Kebell owned
one law book 'wele lymmed at the begynnyng with the crucifixe',
and the illuminated book of statutes which Thomas Pygot of the
Inner Temple (the future serjeant) had compiled in 1503 still survives in Oxford.[31] Additional surviving miniatures can be found,
of all places, in the pleas rolls of the court of the king's bench.[32]
Each term begins with the title *Placita coram domino rege*, the
date, and the name of the chief justice. Always written in bold
penmanship, from the middle of the fifteenth century the initial P
is, from time to time, ornamented. The first example is on the roll
for Easter 1443 where the decoration takes the form of placing an
empty shield in the curve of the letter. Five terms earlier John
Fortescue had, as we have seen, become chief justice of the king's
bench and the design clearly alludes to a legend about a Fortescue
ancestor at the Battle of Hastings. In subsequent rolls Fortescue's
name as chief justice is also embellished and there is some evi-

dence of the use of colour, but in 1460, at the height of the crisis of
Henry VI's reign, the monarch's portrait was inserted in the initial
P, between two figures, one clearly a judge. With Fortescue at that
moment firmly committed to Lancastrian rule and actively pros-
ecuting Yorkist dissidents, he had used the opportunity to express
in miniature the constitutional theory that the king's bench met
coram rege. The point is emphasized by two latin texts, 'God save
the king!', 'Oh God, let there be peace', while the king himself
says to the judge, 'Judge rightly!'. During the 1460s pictures of
Edward IV occur twice, and from 1472 almost a third of the rolls
are ornamented in some way while in Michaelmas 1478 and Trinity
1491, royal portraits again occur. That the impetus still came from
the chief justice is, however, made clear by the roll for Hilary 1487
which has a partly coloured drawing of Chief Justice William
Hussey in the capital P. Colour was increasingly applied and the
first illumination, a royal coat of arms, appears on the Hilary roll
for 1499. From 1502 most rolls are ornamented, very many in
colour.

For knowledge of the interest among lawyers in architecture and
other forms of art we must rely primarily on their wills and funeral
monuments. There was certainly substantial building at the inns
of court and chancery during the fifteenth century, and at Lincoln's
Inn the hall, rebuilt in 1489, still survives and from early in the
next century the Chancery Lane gateway, financed in part by the
septuagenarian, Thomas Lovell.[33] Together they suggest a style
and quality of construction well on a par with collegiate and
ecclesiastical building of the time. But apart from this, our information is mainly of lawyers contributing to building work at their
particular parish church. In many cases this was merely a financial matter but in others considerable interest in detail was shown.
Richard Fowler, chancellor to the Duchy of Lancaster (d.1477),
gave his executors precise instruction about the new aisle in the
parish church at Buckingham:

I woll that the forsaide ile of Saint Romwold, which ile is bigonne of newe
to be made, be fully made and parfourmed vp parfitely in all thinges att
my cost and charge. And in the same ile I wolle that ther be made of newe
a tombe or a shryne for the saide saint where the olde is nowe standyng,
and that it be made curiously with marble, in lenngh and brede as shalbe
thought by myn executours moost conuenient, consideracion hadde to the
rome. And upon the same tombe or shryne I woll that their be sett a
coffyn or a chest, curiously wrought, and altogether gilt, as it apper-
teignyth for to ley in the bones of the same saint.[34]

Several lawyers preferred to build in their lifetime. Brian Rou-cliffe, second baron of the exchequer, who died in 1494, was the son of the recorder of York and as early as 1455–8 had reconstruct-ed the church of Cowthorpe in the West Riding on a fresh site, and the brass on his tomb showed him holding the new building.[35] This was not Roucliffe's only memorial. His will shows that he had contracted with, and partly paid James Remus 'marbeler' of St. Paul's Churchyard for an epitaph in the Temple Church; 10s. was outstanding, no doubt to be paid for the filling in of the final inscription.[36]

Concern for a suitable memorial was common among lawyers, though whether more common than generally among affluent lay-folk is not yet known. Richard Fowler fitted his own into the scheme for the aisle of St. Romwold, 'a flatte stone with ymages and scochons' on the south side of the shrine.[37] Thomas Littleton prepared a tomb in Worcester Cathedral 'vnder an image of Saint Christofer', next to the altar of the saint where his parents were 'sung for' daily; he bequeathed his soul especially 'to Saint Christofer, the which our saide lorde, Jeshu Criste bere on his shuldre'.[38] William Donington of Lincoln's Inn was careful to specify:

a conuenient stone, making mencion by the sidis therof in plate of latyn whos lieth ther, with this scripture vpon the middis *Domine Jeshu, filii dei vnii pone passionem, mortem et crucem tuam inter iudicium tuum et animam meam.*[39]

He wrote his own will, providing for 10,000 masses for his parents, his brother and himself, to be said at at least nine different altars and added this codicil:

Orate pro animabus Rogeri, Elene, Willelmi et Ricardi ac eorum viuo-rum et defunctorum quibus ipsi Rogerus, Elena, Willelmus et Ricardus tenentur orare seu aliquam satisfaccionem seu beneficium facere ac pro animabus omnium fidelium defunctorum. Memorandum that billis ac-cording to this be sett at euery auter wherever masse shall be said for the seid soules.

Since the masses were to be said as soon as possible, the 'billis' were probably paper or parchment rather than anything more per-manent.

Lawyers, thus, gave substantial employment to memorial crafts-men but there were clearly problems if instead of merely verses, an effigy was also required. How was the lawyer to be presented? For

the judge or serjeant one answer was legal costume. Chief Baron
Arderne and Justice Littleton were so depicted, Arderne on his
brass and Littleton in stained glass; at Long Melford another
window shows a chief justice and two serjeants, all in costume.[40]
Other lawyers might be content with ordinary civilian dress; this
was true of John Edward of Rodmarton, Gloucestershire, described
on his 1461 brass as *Famosus apprenticius in lege peritus* although little known, or of the earlier *legus peritus* Robert Skern of
Kingston-on-Thames.[41] But law was the pathway to gentility and
the gentleman should be portrayed in armour. Sir John Portington
J.C.P. (d.1462) was therefore depicted in judicial robes with armour
underneath, a solution made more incongruous in the brass of Sir
William Yelverton, J.K.B. (c.1470) by the enormous sword he was
made to wear.[42] Other lawyers were simply shown in armour:
Robert Ingylton, *juris peritus* (1472) and at the turn of the century
Sir William Huddersfield, the former attorney-general (d.1499),
Robert Baynard, *vir egregius et legis peritus* (d.1501) and Sir John
Mordaunt, serjeant-at-law and chancellor of the Duchy of Lancaster (d.1504).[43] However we need to know a good deal more
about contemporary attitudes to gentility and knighthood and
about the self-consciousness of the legal profession before inter-
preting this material with any confidence.

The English common lawyers, thus, contributed in a number of
ways to what can be called the general culture of the later middle
ages. It was from the legal profession, too, that the principal political analysis came in fifteenth-century England, a topic which takes
us again to the writings of Sir John Fortescue. The most famous
concept associated with Sir John is that of *dominium politicum et
regale*.[44] Accepted analysis, deriving from Aquinas and Egidius
Romanus, distinguished between 'regal dominion', a state ruled
despotically, and 'political dominion' where power was exercised
politically, that is, through a constitution. Fortescue, however,
argued that there was a third variety, dominion which was mixed,
regal and political. In such a government the power of the king
was supreme except in areas where law and custom ruled; 'the
regal power', he wrote, 'is restrained by political law'.[45] Imperial
Rome and contemporary France were examples of states ruled
regally, Republican Rome of states ruled politically, but mixed
dominion was found in England and in Scotland. Where Fortescue
found the inspiration for this analysis has been hotly debated. He
claimed the support of Aquinas, but with little justification. One
source undoubtedly was his own legal and political experience

which convinced him that neither of the traditional definitions of
dominion was entirely applicable to conditions in Britain. However, it is also possible that he was reflecting the common opinion
of the legal profession of his day. Sir John shared the learning of
other lawyers; he was unlikely not to share their ideas.

The contrast of regal and political dominion was certainly familiar to fifteenth-century lawyers. One of the texts Fortescue cited
in support of the distinction was De Regimine Principum by Egidius Romanus. For most of Sir John's judicial career as chief justice of the king's bench, Sir Peter Arderne was chief baron of the
exchequer and among Arderne's books was a French translation of
Egidius.[46] No will survives for the chief justice of the third Westminster court, John Prisot of the common pleas, but it is hardly
coincidental that two of the three leaders of the profession, men
whose work took them deep into royal councils, were familiar with
the same exercise in political discussion. It would, on our present
state of knowledge, be too much to say that Fortescue's actual
formulation of dominium politicum et regale was not original. It is,
however, reasonable to speculate that he was working up a synthesis already recognised by the common lawyers and, perhaps,
originally thrashed out on the judicial bench or even at the inns of
court. The detail of Fortescue's analysis can readily be parallelled
in the reports of cases in the year books. Sir John stressed that the
political limitation on the regal power of the English king was
expressed in the institution of parliament. 'In the kingdom of
England, kings cannot legislate without the consent of the three
estates of the realm', he wrote in De Natura.[47] In 1492 Thomas
Kebell, serjeant-at-law, said of an alleged parliamentary title
claimed by King's College, Cambridge:

If it were to be an act of parliament it follows that the commons granted
and the lords etc. And the king said, 'le roy le veut', and then this would
be entered on the roll accordingly and then it is a good act, but otherwise
it is not an act at all. For if they [the plaintiffs] say that the king 'by
authority of parliament granted by his letters patent', this is no more
than a royal grant; for the commons must grant and the lords as well as
the king, for this is the whole body together. And if any part of that body
makes a grant, but not the others, it is not an act [of parliament].[48]

Fortescue said, further, that in England dominium was also limited
by the law, that the royal judges could not give judgements which
contradicted the law of the land.[49] In practice this was little more
than an insistence on due process, it did not impede the royal will,

but the judges took very seriously their obligation to see that the
rules were kept. In *Humphrey Stafford's Case* (1486) Henry VII
tried to sound out judicial opinion in advance of the trial, but the
chief justice of the king's bench persuaded the king to drop the
request as undesirable and then risked royal wrath by giving Stafford more time to prepare his defence; but legality satisfied, when
the trial came the judges gave Henry all that he had wanted and
more.[50] The strong possibility is, therefore, that many of the ideas
which Sir John committed to paper were the common stock of his
profession.

The intellectual vigour which, on this suggestion, characterized
not only Fortescue but the legal profession generally, left traces
elsewhere. Discussion in court between judges and counsel was
lively, imaginative and above all required intellectual agility. Precedent which was later to deaden the law was as yet only one guide
among several. Lawyers relied just as much on memory of cases
they had observed or taken part in, and on what other lawyers had
told them.[51] In an argument in exchequer chamber in 1466 reference was made to the abatement of a writ ' *en le Common Bank
par grand advise*' in the time of 'Master Prisot *que Dieu assoile*'
only to have Needham J. reply, 'I know and remember that a writ
of error was sued on this and it was reversed in king's bench by
the advice of Master Fortescue'.[52] In this instance memory was
probably going back a decade but an elderly lawyer's memory
might extend to forty years.[53] Counsel also argued from statute
and analogy from statute; thus in a case of error heard in king's
bench and dated 1493, Thomas Kebell tried to draw an analogy
with procedure under two statutes 'which was utterly denied by
the court'.[54] Lawyers also recognized a corpus of ideas, principles,
and accepted practice. Fortescue wrote of the common law having
rules which were known to lawyers as 'maxims'; in the year
books these first principles are termed '*eruditions*'.[55] St. German
printed two or three dozen of these but there was never a formal
list; as Fortescue said, maxims were acquired 'through the senses
and the memory'.[56]

Another element in fifteenth-century English law was 'reason'.
In its simplest meaning, reason, in the year books, is rational
argument.[57] It can also mean commonsense as, for example, the
description by Thomas Kebell of the conduct of jurymen who fled
in face of torrential rain as 'reasonable'.[58] The word could also
extend to consistency; Kebell said that it was 'contrary to reason'
for a recently promoted abbot to use his new rank to avoid paying

an obligation he had entered into when a prior.[59] In a more theoretical sense also, reason was seen as underlying the accepted
maxims and assumptions of the common law; the law was not a
hotch-potch of ambiguities, or so the lawyers wished to believe.
Grasping this rational basis and structure was, said Thomas
Littleton to his son, the key to learning the law:

by the arguments and the reasons in the lawe a man may more sooner
come to the certeinte and to the knowledge of the law. *Lex plus laudatur
quando rationi probatur.* [The Law is more praised when its reasons are
approved].[60]

St. German wrote that 'the fyrste grounde of the lawe of Englande
is the lawe of reason', and Fortescue had evidently been of the
same opinion.[61]

By 'the law of reason' English lawyers meant what European
commentators called the law of nature.[62] Justice William Yelverton
expounded the point at length in a case dated 1468:

We must act in this case as the canonists and civilians do when faced
with a new case for which they have no existing law. Then they resort to
the law of nature which is the ground of all laws and according to
whatever is decided to be the most beneficial to the common weal, so they
act, and so must we. If we were to make a positive law on this point, we
must see what is the most necessary for the common weal and accordingly make our law.[63]

Reason ordered all laws and every part of the common law. Where
precedent gave no guide, said the judges in exchequer chamber,
'we must give judgement as it seems to us by reason'.[64] Where
precedents conflicted, reason again had to be called in.[65] Even
when precedent was clear, if this was 'against reason the court
would amend it ... for perhaps it had only been tolerated in the
past and never challenged or argued out'.[66] Statute law, too, was,
in theory, subject to natural law and although this did not result in
any overt limitation on parliament it did mean that enactments
would in practice be construed in the light of reason. Early in Mary
Tudor's reign Chief Justice Bromley spelled out what was by then
a well-established tradition of interpretation:

It is most reasonable to expound the words which seem contrary to
reason according to good reason and equity. And so the judges who were
our predecessors have sometimes expounded words quite contrary to the
text, and have sometimes taken things by equity of a text contrary to the
text, in order to make them agree with reason and equity.[67]

As Serjeant John Mowbray had said a century earlier, 'law must accord with reason'.[68] English lawyers were well aware of the distinctiveness of the common law, but by insisting in theory and practice that it was grounded on the law of reason or nature they placed it firmly alongside roman law which 'is thought to be sufficient for the government of the whole world'.[69] It was an intellectual system the equal of the jurisprudence of anywhere else in Europe.

The intellectual vitality of the common lawyers which is seen in their contribution to general culture, to political ideas and in their active concern with the philosophy of the law is also seen in a lively interest in and an active production of legal literature. Because what they wrote was never of interest outside England and their own profession, because it was less concerned with substantive issues and theory than the work of the roman law glossators and because its complexity frightens historians today, it is easy to overlook the significance of what was achieved. The common lawyers, however, comprised a group with a level of literary production which equalled and perhaps outstripped both universities and was far more immediately important to the nation at large.

Pride of place must be given to the year books, collections which are made up of law reports, notes, and memoranda, organized term-by-term and year-by-year. Whatever had been true of the fourteenth century and earlier, in the fifteenth these compilations were the work of individuals who noted items as each thought fit.[70] It is impossible to say that every lawyer made a collection of this kind but it is evident that many did; thus the printed version of the year book for 1 and 2 Edward IV is based on a manuscript collected by Robert Townshend of Lincoln's Inn, later justice of the common pleas.[71] Constant reference in year book reports to *nos livres* show how numerous and varied examples were.[72] Thomas Kebell had at least two among his five law books; Sir Peter Arderne had three and possibly six.[73] It is probable that some year books such as Townshend's were deliberate exercises in reporting. This would account for his comments, such as the smile when Moyle J. asked Serjeant Littleton a question, or those of later reporters that they could not hear, or their noting of which counsel to ask for fuller details.[74] Other books may have been collections of memorabilia jotted down from time-to-time as convenient. One of Arderne's is described as 'my owne grete compiled booke of law, covered with reed ledder and a horn ypon it', which suggests that the book had attached to it some sort of ink holder.[75]

Once written, the contents of a year book might be copied and re-copied (in whole or in part), augmented, précised, conflated, weeded, or glossed as required. The evidence for this in the fifteenth-century texts is overwhelming.[76] Doublets abound. The reports for a given year may turn out to have no integrity whatever; for example, even a year like 1485–6 which soon reached the finality of print was nevertheless made up from at least three separate sources. In texts which circulated longer in manuscript there is small wonder that the connection with the alleged term or year may be partly or even wholly artificial. Material was ordered and reordered. Thus, the second item in the famous Long Quint (5 Edward IV) is concerned with royal protections at nisi prius: the following five items are dated 1425, 1435, 1442, and 1402–3 but they all refer to the same subject.[77] Since the genuine Edward IV item ends 'see similar matter after, from other books', this section of the Long Quint was obviously originally a single report, reinforced with a substantial collection of earlier precedents. Later in the century the process can be followed in more detail. For example, John Caryll, the future serjeant, carefully recorded the dates in 1485 and 1487 when he completed copies of the texts of 1439–40 and 1423–4; Caryll's own reports can in turn be partly identified in several collections, though some have been conflated with those of his son.[78] In the case of his contemporary, John Spelman J., the notes taken or collected by him were at one time arranged topically and later rearranged chronologically as far as was possible, and filled out with material from at least two other sources.[79]

Since year book material was so diverse, there was an obvious need for books which would impose some sort of order and also serve as a means of reference. These we know today as abridgments, a form which was characterized less by the shortening of material than an alphabetical arrangement by subject. Anticipations of this method can be found as early as the first quarter of the fourteenth century but the great days of the abridgment dawned in the middle of the fifteenth.[80] Textual analysis of late-medieval law books is in its infancy, but copies of ten or more abridgments from the fifteenth century have so far been identified.[81] The best known because it had the fortune to be put into print, perhaps as early as the 1480's, is Statham's Abridgment.[82] The association with Nicholas Statham of Lincoln's Inn (d.1472) has been made since the reign of Elizabeth I, but at best he was reworking and expanding existing texts and at least one other abridgment derived, in part, from the materials he used.[83] Abridgments were, of course, as likely to be copied or cannibalized as year books. The second to be published (c.1500) was *The abridgment of the booke of Assises* and this reproduced large sections of *Statham* with important additions of material especially from the *Liber Assisarum*, a year book collection of Edward III's reign. Whether this was specially prepared for the press or whether a lawyer with access to a text of the *Liber* produced a manuscript for his own use which later came into the hands of the printer Richard Pynson, is not known.[84] There were also other abridgments which have been lost, including two mentioned in the will of William Callow J. (d.1487) which have never been identified, 'oon of myne owen labour and thothir of Lincolnesin labour'.[85]

It was probably soon after Callow's death that work began on the most important abridgment of all, the *Graunde Abridgement* of Anthony Fitzherbert.[86] Published between 1514 and 1516, its three large volumes and 800 folios were the work of half a lifetime. In the words of John Rastell the printer of the *Prima Pars*:

the only prayse of the making of the seyd grete abbrigement ought to be giuyn to Antony Fitzherberd, seriant at the law, which by his grete and longe study by many yeres contynuyng hath compylyd and gederyd the same.[87]

Although it made use of *Statham*, the *Graunde Abridgement* contained four times as many citations and was rapidly accepted as the authoritative digest of existing case law. It was also a work of much greater research. In a number of places Fitzherbert included rare material which no longer survives and his assiduity in opening up the remoter evidence of the common law was one factor in encouraging the interest of the profession in the very early year books. The value of the work was much enhanced by the *Tabula libri magni abbreuiamenti librorum legum anglorum* which Rastell brought out in 1518 but which had, from the start, been projected as a guide to the main work. Fitzherbert was largely responsible, with Rastell handling the more mechanical editing in a characteristically over-ambitious manner. The outcome was an adequate guide to the *Abridgement* and through it to the major sources of the common law.[88]

Year books and the abridgement of year books were not the only literary interests of English common lawyers in the later middle ages. Other varieties of text had a long tradition and the impetus and utility of the literature of the great age of Edward I did not disappear overnight. The *Registrum Brevium* remained indispensable; Arderne had at least two copies and so did Nicholas Statham.[89] Other collections of writs were also made, sometimes of a specialized kind; for example, one text concerned with justice in Worcestershire and Warwickshire and dated *c*.1422 has been plausibly associated with a future serjeant who at that time was recorder of Coventry and J.P. for Worcestershire.[90] Treatises which opened the way to an understanding of writs also remained in use, such as the *Novae Narrationes*, while the '*Old*' *Natura Brevium* also continued current; Statham had a copy.[91]

But as well as maintaining past learning, fifteenth-century common lawyers added fresh texts. The ever-increasing bulk of statute law, demonstrated by the advent of the *Nova Statuta* to stand alongside the *Vetera Statuta*, led to the production of tables and indexes.[92] Abridgments of the statutes soon followed. The first of these was put into print at the end of Edward IV's reign from a lost text completed before 1471 but based on four earlier abridgments dating from 1455 or later.[93] Another new type of text which circulated was the 'book of entries' which listed the pleadings appropriate to particular writs. The first printed version is dated 1510, but there were earlier manuscripts; Chief Justice Frowyk (d.1506) had a 'greate boke' of entries while John Jenour's (*c*.1510) still exists.[94] The advent of printing also put into wider circulation a number of smaller, specialized books, on court-keeping and the like. Some of these had a very long and diverse history. For example, the text of *The boke of Justyces of peas* clearly existed in manuscript before the 1506 printed edition, and elements in it had antecedents as far back as the reign of Henry IV.[95] Several comparable treatments of the subject were circulating by the middle of the century while another (associated with Robert Drury of Lincoln's Inn) is very little older than the printed version, though quite distinct from it.[96]

The most important new venture in legal literature in the fifteenth century was, however, not an abridgment nor a book of practice but the first English legal text-book, Littleton's *Tenures*, a work which shaped the common law and common-law teaching for many generations.[97] In Edward Coke's famous hyperbole, 'This book is an ornament of the Common Law and the most perfect and absolute work that ever was written in any human science'.[98] Thomas Littleton J.C.P. (d.1481) wrote for his second son, Richard, a student at the Inner Temple, and with the deliberate intention of making the principles, not just the procedures of the law intelligible to the novice. His starting point was a fourteenth-century pamphlet, the *Olde Teners* which was, apparently, the only book to recommend as a student primer, and an inadequate one at that. The first two of the three parts of the '*Newe*' *Tenures* were avowedly a commentary on this existing text—'these two smal bookes haue I made for thee for to vnderstand better certain chapiters of the auncient booke of tenures'; Littleton was only concerned with land law and he ended with the remark:

And knowe thou my sonne that I will not that thou beleue that al that that I haue sayde in the saide bookes is law, for that will I not take vppon mee nor presume. But of those thinges that be not law, enquire & learne of my wise masters learned in the law.[99]

But modesty in aim and achievement concealed what was a novel, authoritative and seminal undertaking, the first 'scientific account' of any branch of the common law. It is indicative that when the next great common-law author set out to write a commentary, the first volume was *Coke upon Littleton*.

Nobody can doubt that the common law of late medieval England was enormously complex, but it is evident that the lawyers devoted a great deal of intellectual effort to making sense of the complexity. That the law worked at all was thanks to them. Where and how did they get the necessary education and background for that task and for the whole of their contribution to English life which we have been examining? The obvious answer is 'the inns of court' and with that answer we arrive at what was the last and greatest contribution of the common lawyers to the culture of late-medieval England.

It has often been noted that when Chaucer described the serjeant-at-law among the Canterbury Pilgrims, he did not mention that the lawyer had once been a member of an inn of court. Inns for lawyers had existed in the London suburbs from at least 1329 and Chaucer observed so acutely that it is surprising that he should have omitted something as obvious as the corporate life of the profession—and the more so since another pilgrim was a manciple of the Temple who looked after 'thyres ten that were of lawe expert and curious'.[100] But any surprise is of our own making; it stems from our assumption that an inn was necessarily an educational and professional institution and membership a matter of importance. Some eighty years after the Canterbury Tales, Fortescue's *De Laudibus Legum Anglie* gave the first description of the inns but once again much that we expect is missing. Virtually nothing is said of the 'school of law' in each inn and there is a clear implication that the important teaching was done by the courts 'to which students of the law flock every day in term-time'.[101] When he wrote, Fortescue had long been gone from Lincoln's Inn but the 'omissions' we notice have more to do with what we assume an inn to have been than any lapses of age. The educational activity of the inns, with all that meant in terms of professional organization— the bench, the bar, call to the bar and so on—all this was new and developing. Together Chaucer and Fortescue draw attention by silence to the creation by the common lawyers as the fifteenth century progressed of a whole educational system which from, at the latest, the reign of Edward IV, challenged comparison with the universities of Oxford and Cambridge.[102]

The earliest inns were, in all probability, little more than group arrangements among lawyers from the provinces who needed accommodation in London during the law terms, and they lasted no longer than it suited those concerned. As for training, this had been, as Fortescue indicated, a traditional responsibility of the courts. Students had places reserved for them, 'the crib', and a good deal of helpful comment from the bench seems to have been aimed at them.[103] Certain established lawyers of the fourteenth century may have taken pupils as was occasionally done in the fifteenth, but probably only by private arrangement where a practitioner was willing to take on a promising youngster or, perhaps, needed a lively office-boy.[104] The inns seem to have provided no education at all. The only formal instruction of any use to the law-student was found among the clerks of chancery.[105] These civil servants had long been housed together when in London, first in the chancellor's own household and later in hostels or 'inns of chancery' run by senior clerks. By the middle of the fourteenth century, training was being given in at least one of these hostels in the writing of documents, clerical procedures, and the handling of writs, and by the time of the Peasants' Revolt, law students were intruding on this teaching in sufficient numbers to bring a prohibition from the chancellor.[106]

Precisely what happened in the next thirty years we do not know—there is, in the words of T. F. Tout, a 'chasm of silence'— but by the first quarter of the fifteenth century the situation had changed significantly.[107] Inns of chancery are now societies, not private hostels run by individual clerks; indeed, the clerks seem to have gone and the lawyers have taken over. Even more important, inn-of-chancery education now concentrates on law for the law-

student and other inns which had previously been residential-only
are offering teaching also. Very soon it is possible to talk of the
inns of court as the greater houses recruiting from the inns of
chancery.[108] If we do not know what happened in any detail, we
certainly do not know why. Part of the explanation must lie in the
decline of the corporate life of the chancery clerks. Another factor
may have been an increased interest in education in line with that
found at this time elsewhere in England and abroad. Economic
pressures may also have played a part with the inns forced to
attract members. But speculation as to cause is outside the scope
of this essay.[109] What is important is that formal common-law
education began in England for the first time and in the distinctive
English fashion where the leading practitioners of the law also
taught it.

To see English common-law education as the creation of the
fifteenth-century legal profession is to challenge a long tradition of
scholarship.[110] Demonstration of the point best begins with the
known situation in the early sixteenth century, say the 1530s. An
entrant to the profession who aspired to be more than an attorney
would then join one of the four inns of court in his late 'teens,
possibly after a year's study of the rudiments of law at an inn of
chancery. The new arrival had two immediate goals. First he had to
become a fellow of his inn. This required attendance at three specified vacations each year for three years (or fewer if he could buy an
exemption); these were the 'learning vacations' at the start of Lent
and in August, and the revels held over Christmas and New Year.
His second object was to learn the law, and to make this possible
the novice found awaiting him a sophisticated and comprehensive
educational machine which involved every member of the inn.

The details of training varied from house to house, but the basic
pattern was uniform. The heart of the system was the learning
vacation. There a 'reading' was given, a combined lecture and
seminar course taken by a senior member of the inn, lasting for
three and a half weeks, perhaps four mornings a week. The reader
expounded a statute, clause by clause, and discussed the problems
and possibilities so raised with other senior members in the audience, even, perhaps, a visiting judge or serjeant-at-law. Further
discussion took place each day after dinner at the reader's own
table and also at the lower tables where students and practising
lawyers sat together, normally in 'messes' of four people.

As well as post-prandial debates during the time of the readings,
the student found himself engaged in regular exercises after meals

at other times in the year. The most elaborate of these was the moot. This, in effect, was a mock-trial where the senior men of the inn sat on a bench and heard their juniors plead a case, in imitation of the judges in the royal courts. Discussion then ensued, with the 'judges' and others offering their criticisms and comments in reverse order of seniority. Other exercises probably included 'bolts', less elaborate than moots, and also 'keeping a case' where a junior at each mess would expound a point and be followed by the rest of the table in order of seniority.[111]

Participation in this system of collective learning was reflected in the different categories of membership found in most of the inns. The seniors who presided at moots sat on a bench and so were 'benchers'. Those who appeared before them stood at a bar, in exact imitation of a public court. Hence non-benchers were 'barristers'. The most junior of these were grouped behind the bar, from the bencher's point of view within the sight-lines of the end of the bar; they were, therefore, 'inner barristers'. Men who were more advanced and expected to contribute to the discussion sat on either side of the 'court'; they were outside the bar and so 'outer-barristers'. The transition from one grade to the other was the 'call to the bar', wholly a domestic concern of the inn and quite separate from the right to be heard in the law courts.

We are able to be precise about the educational system at the inns in the 1530's because, as part of the debate following the dissolution of the monasteries, proposals were put forward for a new, superior 'King's Grace's House of [Law] Students' where some attention would be given to Renaissance values in education.[112] Accompanying this plan were accounts of current practice at the existing inns, based largely on the Middle Temple but applicable generally (though not in detail) to the other three. Yet the authority of the 1539 report has misled historians. In fact it disguised a system which had evolved over a century and a half and was still evolving. Evidence is, admittedly, thin and patchy. The principal source, the register or 'Black Books' of Lincoln's Inn only starts in 1422 and nowhere does it set out the constitution and education of the house. A minimum of information survives for three inns of chancery—fragmentary extracts from the lost records of Furnival's Inn and orders for Clement's Inn and Clifford's Inn which may contain fifteenth century elements.[113] This is all. Nevertheless the case for believing in an educational revolution at the inns of court in the fifteenth century is a strong one.

The most obvious indication of this is the reading.[114] The Furnival's Inn extracts mention an Autumn Reader there in 1408, and although the Black Books do not mention readings at Lincoln's Inn until the 1460s it is clear that they had been held for some years.[115] On the other hand, early readings appear to have been very primitive devices.[116] Manuscripts have been identified as early as the third decade of the fifteenth century, but not earlier. This would not necessarily be significant were it not for the nature of the early texts which do exist. These are short, elementary, and cover a great deal in a small compass; they were also repeated from occasion to occasion, almost verbatim. It is easy to see why so few survive and why earlier examples have disappeared. Readings were evidently a very basic sort of instruction. Surviving manuscripts do not carry the names of readers and Sir John Fortescue who entered Lincoln's Inn before 1420 did not remember the exercise as important enough to mention when he wrote his famous description of the inns about 1470.

In the 1470s, by contrast, readings were much more significant. Statutes were being covered in much more detail and readings took longer; in particular the Lent reading was now nearly four weeks instead of a fortnight and had overtaken the autumn series in prestige. It is even likely that the timing of the readings was changing; the earliest evidence suggests the last two weeks before Easter and the fortnight before and the week after Michaelmas, but by the sixteenth century the Lent reading clearly began on the first Monday of Lent and the Autumn reading immediately after Lammas (1 August).[117] Readings were better organized and in 1464 a regular procedure was agreed for allowing the reader six months' notice.[118] As for the manuscripts, many more have survived, often with the name of the reader, and so too collections of the cases which were discussed. The subject matter changed as well. The earlier readings were on a narrow syllabus of statutes issued before 1327, taken in an order, but later readers began to digress from the ostensible subject, so making a reading more distinctively their own. By the start of the next century the syllabus was being abandoned and it became possible to lecture on recent legislation and at the reader's individual preference. It is hard to avoid the conclusion that we are witnessing a new educational method in the process of evolution.

The position with regard to the other major learning exercise in 1539, the moot, is more difficult. The Black Books mention in 1428 an expulsion for, in part, failure to moot but nothing more is heard of the practice until late in the century, although moots are men-

tioned at Furnival's Inn in the 1450s and 1460s.[119] It may be that
Lincoln's Inn moots were recorded in a book which has since
disappeared or that attendance was impeccable so that nobody
needed to be fined for absence between 1428 and 1489-90, in
which case the occasional fines imposed after that date are evidence of impending decline.[120] It is far more likely that for much of
the fifteenth century mooting was an unsystematic business and
that the organizational details which begin to obtrude in Henry
VII's reign are evidence of the need to put the method on a more
formal basis.

The possibility that both the readings and the moots at the inns
of court were at an early stage of development in the first half of
the fifteenth century is reinforced by an examination of the system
for keeping vacations. When the Black Books opened in 1422, new
entrants to the inn were already subject to certain residence requirements, and although the presence of senior men is not specifically indicated, since novices were required to attend they must
have had something to attend and someone to supervise them.
Hence we can infer that the system by which seniors were responsible for their puisnes—the distinctive element in English
common-law organization and training—antedates the earliest inn
of court record. Nevertheless, we cannot assume that because
vacation-keeping was clearly educational in purpose in the later
fifteenth century this had been its principal significance from the
start. Indeed, all the evidence is that it was only attendance at the
Christmas festivity which mattered.

The first evidence of this is the regular listing of men bound to
'continue' at Christmas.[121] In order to qualify as a fellow in 1422,
three such vacations had to be kept but nothing else. No record
was made of anyone required to be at any other vacation and, in
marked contrast to Christmas, there were no fines for absence. The
earliest requirement for becoming a fellow had, therefore, nothing
to do with the law readings in Lent and in the autumn; learning
was voluntary—involvement in the corporate life at the Christmas
revels was what counted.[122] This emphasis on the communal
entity of the inn is also found in another and frequent entry in the
first Black Books, the taking of 'mainprize'.[123] This was a registration of all fellows, each with the names first of one and later
of two others of the inn who stood surety for him. The basic
obligation which this covered was the payment of dues to the inn
and the next was 'continuation', that is the completion of residence requirements. Only in third place is there a general cat-

egory, *omnimodis aliis oneribus*, which might cover performance of learning exercises.[124] Priority clearly went to continuation, supporting the corporate life of the society. Concern for this reached a climax in the mainprize of June 1440. Under the order for this, every existing fellow had now to find two new sureties, and *vnus erit continuator pro maior parte*; every recruit had, in future, to provide the same guarantee and also swear a newly-introduced oath of obedience to the governors of the society.[125]

The opening pages of the Lincoln's Inn records thus suggest a society where the corporate entity mattered more than educational exercises, and this is confirmed by the earliest evidence of learning vacations there. This is an order dated 1428 which laid down that fellows who lived in London and Middlesex and who wished to use the inn throughout the year had to attend at Christmas and pay commons for at least two weeks of Lent and the three weeks around Michaelmas, unless, that is, they attended in person for equivalent periods at other times.[126] Since the dates specified are those which we know were later the learning vacations at Lincoln's Inn, and since a similar learning calendar had been in operation at Furnival's Inn from before the end of Henry IV's reign, it is reasonable to conclude that Lincoln's Inn learning vacations date from before 1428 and to assume that part of the order's purpose was to encourage seniors to be present for the educational exercises.[127] This, however, was not the only or even the main purpose of the order. The overall emphasis was once again on the life of the society. If the inn was to be used in vacation, the community life was to be kept up. The one time when all vacation users were to be present was at the Christmas celebrations, not the spring and summer learning periods, and attendance at the latter could be avoided either by residence at another time or, simply, by accepting the bill for obligatory commons as a fine. As for the attendance of students, the order makes no mention of this at all.

The first determined effort to organize the learning vacations at Lincoln's Inn did not come until almost a decade after the lukewarm encouragement of the 1428 order. On 5 November 1436 there was enrolled in the Black Book a series of covenants binding nineteen fellows of the inn to be present, under threat of 20s. fine each time, at a specified number of vacations, varying from two to twelve over the next four years.[128] This had nothing to do with the keeping of vacations by new entrants. Ten of those concerned had been fellows for a decade or more, and the two who were still keeping their initial vacations contracted to attend over and beyond this. Nor was the enterprise confined to Londoners or those wanting to use the inn during vacations; for example, William Jenney from Suffolk promised to attend three Christmas, four Lent and four autumn vacations in succession. As his offer shows, Christmas still retained importance, but what is significant as against the order of 1428 was the clear definition of and the priority given in 1436 to the learning vacations. Attendance at these was described as a 'month in Lent' and 'a month in harvest', the nominal period of the reading as we know it later, and no attendance at other times was allowed in lieu. Most of the senior men, indeed, did not offer Christmas at all: John Fortescue, soon to become a serjeant, agreed for three autumn vacations; William Boeff, another future serjeant, offered to be present at Lent and the autumn for three years but 'yn Christismasse he wulle not be bound to contynwe'. Although we must, as we have seen, infer that some seniors were attending Christmas vacations as early as 1420, the agreement of 1436 was an attempt to bring in to the learning vacations on a regular basis men who were evidently not obliged nor expected to attend, and leading members of the profession at that. Education was beginning to be an important part of the activities of the inn.

That the 1436 contracts were a novel attempt to improve the educational provision at Lincoln's Inn is made even clearer by what happened afterwards. In the first place an order of April 1442 made attendance at learning vacations compulsory for new entrants.[129] Of course students had attended in the past, but, as the order admitted, this had only been a matter of 'custom'. Henceforward all newcomers were to continue for three Lent and autumn vacations as well as Christmas and all existing fellows who had not followed this curriculum were to do so. From the date of the order, the Black Books record the names of those required to attend learning vacations as well as the revels at Christmas, and also the automatic pursuit of defaulters.[130] Another administrative development consequent on the 1442 rule was the practice of listing in the Black Books the names of those admitted to the inn. Prior to this, new entrants seem simply to have been added to the current mainprize although the introduction late in 1439 of the 'sacramentum sociorum de Lyncollysyn' had probably brought into use what is now the second volume of the register as, initially, a list of oath-takers.[131] But with the new rule about vacation attendance, the recording of admission begins, and with it the whole question of exemptions from vacations which had not been necessary when the Christmas revel was the only obligation on entrants.[132]

Another development which can be associated with the 1436 arrangements is the rise of the benchers of Lincoln's Inn.[133] Management of the society was firmly in the hands of elected governors, but in 1441 we hear for the first time of 'fellows of the bench' who are given privileged rates for the accommodation of their clerks.[134] Men who played the part of judges at a moot would always have sat on 'the bench' but what seems to have happened is that once seniors accepted attendance at learning vacations as an obligation, they became recognized as a special grade of member, the benchers. That these were the same as those promising vacation attendances is evident by a later order of 1466 which talked of 'fellows of the bench' who had 'completed their vacations'.[135] The 1436 order, by establishing a liability on a particular group to occupy the bench set in train a process which ultimately made the benchers the dominant group within the society.

The importance of the 1436 agreement in the educational development of Lincoln's Inn is, thus, clear. It was not, however, without its problems and it was not the end of the road. The attempt was wildly extravagant. If all the seniors contracted to attend had turned up for the Lent vacation of 1437, there would have been fourteen or sixteen of them facing a maximum of perhaps nineteen students.[136] It was also unrealistic. At the end of the century the norm for the then obligatory attendances by seniors was only three or four per vacation and some of these defaulted, so it is not surprising that by February 1439 a number of those who had promised were being fined by the inn for non-attendance.[137] The inn, however, clearly had doubts about the scheme for the draconian 20s. was reduced in most cases to 13s. 4d. What is more, absence of both promises and fines after 1439 suggest that there was no attempt to extend the scheme beyond the expiry of the original contracts. It seems probable that some system of individual responsibility was kept up but the numbers coming forward to work the learning vacations were clearly inadequate and in the Easter term of 1466 the job had to be done again.[138] A second appeal to the public spirit of the senior fellows produced sixteen who 'of their own spontaneous desire' gave promises to attend various totals of learning vacations (not, be it noted, Christmasses), ranging from one in three to six vacations in four years.

This time, however, the promises were tied to a general order that, in future, fellows who were called to the bench should attend both readings in each of the three years immediately following their call. From this time the Black Books begin to list regularly the names of benchers due to keep vacations and the fines they incurred for default.[139] But all was not settled even yet. In 1475 an additional ruling was required to cover temporary calls to the bench in the absence of sufficient regular benchers and some time later the possibility of vacation calls was ruled out.[140] Not until the end of the fifteenth century can the learning vacations at Lincoln's Inn be said to be fully and finally organised.

The evolution of legal education at Lincoln's Inn can also be followed in the growing relationship between the call to read and the call to the bench. The 1539 report to Henry VIII stated that benchers were synonymous with readers but this was certainly not so in the early fifteenth century as we have seen, and it was still not the case at Lincoln's Inn in 1475 when a rule was made that the six vacations required of the bencher under the order of 1466 was only to count from the vacation in which he gave his reading.[141] In the 1466 order itself the fellows of the bench are described as having completed their vacations but only 'many' had 'done readings'.[142] The call to the bench was clearly separate from and came earlier than the call to read. Nevertheless the 1475 order implied that, by then, all benchers were expected to read in order of seniority, unless they had good excuse. In other words, once the call to the bench had become an established stage in promotion at Lincoln's Inn it was used to select those who would eventually act as readers and the effective identification of the two grades in 1539 was the result. This development also explains the rigid pattern of 'anciency' which governed the readings and other duties of the late fifteenth-century inn; the true selection was selection for the bench.[143]

Development of the readings in organization and content, an emphasis on vacations which changed from Christmas revels to learning, the arrangement of a teaching rota, the emergence of the benchers and their relation to the task of reading, all this marks the educational progress of Lincoln's Inn in the fifteenth century. Inevitably, too, this had repercussions on the society in general. The need to relate the call to the bench and the call to read, was clearly connected with the formalising of the election procedure for the readings, which, as we have seen, took place in 1464.[144] As the hierarchy in the inn became more defined, so a regular *cursus honorum* developed into which existing offices were fitted and new ones as these emerged.[145] The annually elected governors retained their authority throughout the century although by the reign of Henry VII the benchers were showing signs of unrest.[146] The only other early officer was the pensioner, the collector of dues from the fellows who could either be an ex-governor or an ordinary member of the house, although after 1444–5 governors were no longer selected. The earliest evidence for the readership suggests that this was already linked with the post of governor; the autumn reader was usually elected as the fourth governor for the year following his reading and the Lent reader as the third governor in the previous Michaelmas term. Once governors were no longer called on to be pensioners, that post fell into line, being held three or four years before the first reading and the subsequent fourth governorship. In the 1450s the post of Christmas marshal appears and was slotted in between the pensionership and the first reading. In the case of the treasurership the process of evolution can be followed in some detail from increasing financial burdens on the governors which were met by various experiments culminating in a governor who was first given the duties, then the title of treasurer and finally continued in office in 1455 without the duties of governor.[147] At first the post was held for several years at a time by an ex-governor, later it was taken by a more junior fellow in the years before, or overlapping with his first reading, but by the end of the century it was often held for a single year shortly after the first reading.

The result of all this rationalization is easy to see. Where William Boeff, serjeant in 1453, was registered for his first Christmas in 1428, was autumn reader in 1434, fourth governor and pensioner in 1434–5, fourth governor for a second time in 1439–40 and yet again in 1440–1 when he was also Lent reader and pensioner but was never treasurer since the post had yet to be isolated, John Newdigate, serjeant in 1510, was admitted on Palm Sunday 1483, chosen pensioner for 1495–6, marshal in 1497–8, autumn reader in 1499, fourth governor in 1499–1500 and treasurer in 1500–1.[148] Order had been established.[149]

The detailed picture of a society in the course of evolution which can be seen at Lincoln's Inn cannot be paralleled at the other inns. There is, however, considerable evidence of variety between the various houses at the end of the fifteenth century, once records begin to be available, and uniformity in detail had not been achieved in 1539, whatever the report to Henry VIII implied; uni-

formity, indeed, was probably achieved as one house imitated another. The precise constitutional practice differed from inn to
inn—who elected whom—and so too the nomenclature. What is
more, as late as the reign of Elizabeth, Gray's Inn had no insti-
tutionalised group of benchers; instead it had a category of
reader.[150] Gray's Inn did not have governors either, but from 1531
a treasurer was elected from the readers to preside over the ruling
body.[151] The Middle Temple had no governors when its records
start in 1501; it appears to have been ruled by readers although the
most important officer was clearly the treasurer who may or may
not have been a reader.[152] By the middle of the century, however,
the readers had been absorbed into a wider group of masters of the
bench.[153] As for the Inner Temple, it had a system of attendants on
the reader which was imitated by the Middle Temple in 1507 and
its treasurership too was more developed, held by a man who had
given or was about to give his second reading.[154] Readers, however, had no special standing at the Inner Temple and although
governors were elected, these were much less important than at
Lincoln's Inn.[155] It was the benchers who were the key group and
the council of the Inner Temple, its parliament, met under the
leadership of whichever senior men happened to be available.[156]

At Gray's Inn there was a further peculiarity, a separate category of membership known as 'the ancients' or 'the grand
company'.[157] This ranked below the readers but above the barristers; it was formally appointed to and charged with educational
duties, notably the keeping of learning vacations. The similarity to
the Lincoln's Inn benchers of the early fifteenth century is close,
but the formal category of bencher at Gray's Inn did not appear
until the seventeenth century when it grew from a quite separate
origin, the custom of occasionally selecting a prominent non-reader
to enjoy the status and some of the privileges of those who had
read.[158]

The conclusion seems unavoidable; at the earliest time for
which there is any information, the Temples and Gray's Inn are
found to be, no less than Lincoln's Inn, societies in the process of
evolving. The making of common law education by the fifteenth-
century common lawyers is beyond question.

The archetypal anti-lawyer joke of medieval England has the
son of the lawyer replying to the question 'what craft is your
father of' with the quip, 'Marry, he is a crafty man of law!'[159] The
evidence, however, is of a professional group which was a sizeable
part of and made a sizeable contribution to the intellectual and

cultural life of the day. Its educational construction was, perhaps, the most significant cultural development in fifteenth-century England. The importance for the lawyers themselves is evident and the system was to last for a century after 1539, though under increasing strain from 1600 as both the law and the profession changed significantly. But inns of court education was also important for the community at large as men began, in increasing numbers, to attend the inns not in order to qualify for a legal career but simply for the education and experience found there. The explosion in English higher education after 1540 could not have happened without the instructional developments at Lincoln's Inn and the other houses in the fifteenth century.[160] That Erasmus saw no virtue in them reflects his new scheme of values, although some of his disciples did approve of what they saw as the rhetorical tradition maintained at inns of court moots.[161] We, in contrast, have to give credit for what was a significant educational advance and evidence of a live intellectual community in action. Beside this we put the contributions of common lawyers to general literature, to the arts, in political analysis, and the more professional concerns of jurisprudence and specialized literature. An England bereft of the writings of Fortescue, Fitzherbert, Littleton, and the rest, and without the drama, miniatures, church building, and monumental craftsmanship paid for by the lawyers would have been poor indeed.

NOTES

1. Quoted in R. W. Chamber, *Thomas More*, London, 1938, p. 85.

2. Cf. R. J. Schoek, 'Sir Thomas More, humanist and lawyer', *University of Toronto Quarterly*, xxxiv (1964), pp. 1–14.

3. Thomas Elyot, *The Boke named the Gouernour*, H. H. S. Croft, (ed.), London, 1883, i, p. 145.

4. G. R. Elton, *Reform and Renewal*, Cambridge, 1973, p. 14.

5. Elyot, *The Gouernour*, cited in note 2, i, pp. 134, 137, 142–4.

6. Quoted in J. K. McConica, *English Humanists and Reformation Politics under Henry VIII and Edward VI*, Oxford, 1968, p. 117.

7. Elton, *Reform and Renewal*, cited in note 3, p. 10; B. W. Beckingsale, *Thomas Cromwell, Tudor Minister*, London, 1978, p. 7. On the following see, generally, Elton, *Reform and Renewal*, chapter 2.

8. J. F. Mozley, *Coverdale and his Bibles*, London, 1953, pp. 201–20; for the reform of the inns of court see this essay, p. 200.

9. For an important discussion of the intellectual life of the legal profession which has appeared since this essay was written, see John Spelman, *Reports*, J. H. Baker, (ed.), 2 vols., Selden Society, xciii–iv, 1977–8, ii, pp. 28–51, 123–35.

10. Edmund Dudley, *The tree of commonwealth*, D. M. Brodie, (ed.), Cambridge, 1948.

11. Edward Hall, *The union of the two noble and illustre famelies of York and Lancaster*, London, Richard Grafton, 1548, H. Ellis, (ed.), London, 1809.

12. Mayster Fitzherbarde, *The boke of husbandry* and *Boke of surveying*, Thomas Berthelet, London, 1523. Tradition has identified the author as the judge Antony Fitzherbert. Given the involvement of lawyers in farming this is by no means improbable and although the author makes frequent use of phrases such as 'I remytte all those poyntes to men of lawe' it is clear that he did have substantial legal knowledge; *Surveying* is planned as a commentary on the 'statute' *Extenta Manerii*. However, the author claimed to have been 'an householder this xl yeres and more', i.e. by 1483, and the will of Elizabeth Fitzherbert, widow, shows that by 1490 Antony had received no inheritance, only his 'bare finding' and provides five marks a year 'towards his exhibition at Court' [i.e. Gray's Inn]. John Fitzherbert, by contrast, inherited farming stock and the estate of Norbury from his father, precisely in 1483. The question is settled in John's favour by Antony's star chamber deposition (*post* 1527) that John had been 'send to London to the Innes of the court to lerne the lawes of the realme' and was away for four years. An active farmer with a legal education, who owned some law books (his will refers to books in Latin, French and English) and had retained some involvement in public legal affairs (he became J.P. in 1497), John Fitzherbert is exactly right as the missing author. Antony Fitzherbert, *The boke of husbandry*, W. W. Skeat, (ed.), English Dialect Society, xiii, 1881; R. H. C. Fitzherbert, 'the authorship of the "Book of Husbandry" and the "Book of Surveying"', *E.H.R.*, xii (1897), pp. 225–36; E. F. Gay, 'The authorship of the *Book of Husbandry* and the *Book of Surveying*', *Quarterly Journal of Economics*, xviii (1904), pp. 588–93. I am indebted to Dr. S. M. Wright for information about the Fitzherberts of Norbury and the references to the following wills: Ralph (1483), Staffs. R.O.:D1734/T(S)14(1); Elizabeth (1490), ibid., D641/5/T(S)14(2); John (1517–18, codicil 1521), Lichfield Joint R.O.:B/A/1/141, ff.106v.–111v.

13. B.L., MS. Harl. 2259; H. S. London, 'Some medieval treatises on English heraldry', *Antiquaries Journal*, xxxiii (1953), pp. 174–83.

14. For the following see John Fortescue, *De Laudibus Legum Anglie*, S. B. Chrimes, (ed.), Cambridge, 1949, pp. lix–lxxvii [hereafter cited as Fortescue, *De Laudibus*]. For the correction of the date of Fortescue's appointment as serjeant see S. E. Thorne, *Readings and Moots at the Inns of Court in the Fifteenth Century*, vol. I, Selden Society, lxxi (1954), 1954, p. lix.

15. John Fortescue, *The Governance of England*, C. Plummer, (ed.), Oxford, 1885.

16. Fortescue, *De Laudibus*, pp. lxxxix–xcv; he was also (and surprisingly) acquainted with works by Poggio Bracciolini and Leonardo Bruni.

17. For the following see Christopher St. German, *Doctor and Student*, T. F. T. Plucknett and J. L. Barton, (eds.), Selden Society, xcl, 1974.

18. See above note 12.

19. Fitzherbert, *Husbandry*, Skeat, (ed.), cited in note 12, passim. Most of the Latin quotations used by Fitzherbert are from J. Watton, *Speculum Christiani*, London, William de Machlinia, c.1486, R. H. C. Fitzherbert, 'Authorship', cited in note 12, p. 235 n. 17.

20. For the following see E. W. Ives, 'A lawyer's library in 1500', *Law Quarterly Review*, lxxxv (1969), pp. 104–16; cf. R. J. Schoek, 'The libraries of common lawyers in Renaissance England', *Manuscripta*, vi (1962), pp. 155–67.

21. Thomas Stotevile (d.1467) owned a set of decretals, P.R.O. PROB11/5 f.167v.; Thomas Littleton (d.1481) owned a copy of Lyndwood's *Provinciale*, ibid.,

11/7 f.25; *Les Reports des Cases*, J. Maynard, (ed.), London, 2 parts, 1678–80, Hil. 10 Henry VII, pl. 17 f.18 [hereafter cited as *Year Books*].

22. Ibid., Trin. 4 Henry VII, pl. 8 f.12; Mich.5 Henry VII, pl. 3 f.2; Mich. 9 Henry VII, pl. 8, f.13; Mich.10 Henry VII, pl. 16 f.8; Hil.10 Henry VII, pl. 17 f.18; Pas. 16 Henry VII, pl. 10 f.7; Trin.16 Henry VII, pl. 3 f.11.

23. Ibid., Mich.10 Henry VII, pl. 16 f.8.

24. W. D. Belcher, *Kentish Brasses*, London, 2 vols., 1888–1905, ii, p. 138, no. 451.

25. *Year Books*, Trin.11 Henry VII, pl. 1 f.23.

26. Players regularly performed at Lincoln's Inn from at least Christmas 1444, Lincoln's Inn, Black Book 1 ff.62v., 64v., 68, 78, 80 etc, see *The Records of the Honourable Society of Lincoln's Inn: the Black Books*, W. P. Baildon, (ed.), London, 1897–1902, I, pp. 16, 18, 20, 21 etc. [hereafter cited as Black Book and *Black Books* respectively]. Cf. A. C. Baugh, 'A fifteenth-century dramatic performance at the inns of court', *Tennessee Studies in Literature*, xi (1966), pp. 71–4; D. S. Bland, 'Interludes in fifteenth-century revels at Furnival's Inn', *Review of English Studies*, (n.s.), iii (1952), pp. 263–8 and *Early Records of Furnival's Inn*, Newcastle-upon-Tyne, 1957, pp. 24, 51–2; Spelman, *Reports*, cited in note 9, i, pp. 233–4; J. H. Baker, 'The old songs of the inns of court', *Law Quarterly Review*, xc (1974), pp. 187–90.

27. Edward Hall, *The union*, Ellis, (ed.), cited in note 11, p. 719; S.Anglo, *Spectacle, Pageantry and Early Tudor Policy*, Oxford, 1969, pp. 238–9.

28. D. S. Bland, *Bibliography of the Inns of Court and Chancery*, Selden Soc., Supplementary Series, 1965, section J.

29. For the following see Anglo, *Spectacle*, cited in note 27, pp. 165–6, 188–9, 196–7, 219–24, 262–4; A. W. Reed, 'John Rastell, printer, lawyer, venturer, dramatist, and controversialist', *Transactions of the Bibliographical Society*, xv (1917–19), pp. 59–82, and his *Early Tudor Drama*, London, 1926, passim.

30. Inner Temple, Whaddon Hall Folios; G. R. Corner, 'Observations on four illuminations representing the courts', *Archaeologia*, xxxix (1863), pp. 357–72.

31. Wiltshire Record Office 88:5/17a; Bodleian Library, Oxford, MS. Hatton 10. Thomas Jakes (d.1514) owned a 'Boke of newe statutes wryten and lymed' P.R.O., PROB11/18 f.12v.

32. For the following see E. Auerbach, *Tudor Artists*, London, 1954, pp. 17–25, 195–7, plates 1a,b,c, 2a,b,c,d, 3a, 52a.

33. *Black Books*, I, iii, pp. 187, 191, 196, 199, 200, 209.

34. P.R.O., PROB11/6 f.249v.

35. *Calendar of Inquisitions post Mortem, Henry VII* (1898–1955), ii, no. 168; *Testamenta Eboracensia*, iv, J. Raine, (ed.), Surtees Society, liii, 1968, pp. 102–4; Mill Stephenson, 'Monumental brasses in the West Riding', *Yorkshire Archaeological Journal*, xv (1900), p. 10.

36. *Testamenta Eboracensia*, iv, cited in note 35, p. 104.

37. P.R.O., PROB11/6 f.249.

38. Ibid., 11/7 f.23v.

39. Ibid., 11/7 ff.126, 126v.

40. R. Gough, *Sepulchral Monuments*, London, 1786–96, ii, 2 vols., plate 85, p. 216; W. N. Hargreaves-Mawdsley, *History of Legal Dress in Europe*, Oxford, 1963, plate 10B.

41. Gough, *Monuments*, cited in note 40, ii. plate 75, p. 305 f.1; Monumental Brass Society, *Portfolio*, ii, London, 1900–5, plate 9.

42. A. Gardner, *Alabaster Tombs of the Pre-Reformation Period in England*,

Cambridge, 1940, p. 102; H. W. Macklin, *The Brasses of England*, London, 1907, p. 177.

43. R. H. Russell, 'The monuments at Thornton, Buckinghamshire', *Records of Buckinghamshire*, vii (1897), p. 56; W. H. H. Rogers, *Ancient Sepulchral Effigies ... of Devonshire*, Exeter, 1877, p. 98 and plate 33, nos. 32, 33; Gardner, *Alabaster Tombs*, cited in note 42, p. 88.

44. For the following see S. B. Chrimes, *English Constitutional Ideas in the Fifteenth Century*, Cambridge, 1936, pp. 314–8; Fortescue, *De Laudibus*, p. xciv.

45. Fortescue, *De Laudibus*, p. 27.

46. P.R.O., PROB11/5 f.150.

47. Quoted in Fortescue, *De Laudibus*, p. 151.

48. *Year Books*, Trin.7 Henry VII, pl. 1, f.14.

49. Chrimes, *Constitutional Ideas*, cited in note 44, p. 323.

50. *Year Books*, Pas. 1 Henry VII, pl. 15 ff.22–4; Trin.1 Henry VII, pl. 1 ff.25–6.

51. E. W. Ives, 'The origins of the later year books', *Legal Studies 1972*, Dafydd Jenkins, (ed.), Cardiff, 1975, pp. 138–40.

52. *Year Books*, 5 Edward IV, Long Quinto ff.141–2.

53. Ives, 'Later year books', cited in note 51, p. 138.

54. *Year Books*, Mich.9 Henry VII, pl. 4, f.7.

55. Fortescue, *De Laudibus*, pp. 21, 115; Ives, 'Later year books', cited in note 51, pp. 137–8; *Doctor and Student*, cited in note 17, pp. 57–71. The identity of *maxima* and *erudition* (and the meaning of the latter) is established by the concurrence of St. German's maxim about writs of *capias* [ibid., p. 63] with the *erudition* discussed in *Year Books*, Hil. 11 Henry, pl. 11 f.15. Cf. A. W. B. Simpson, 'The source and function of the later year books', *Law Quarterly Review*, lxxxvii (1971), pp. 96–8. At Lincoln's Inn in 1483 *eruditiones* formed part of the curriculum, Black Book 2(1) f.53 (*Black Books*, I, p. 77).

56. Fortescue, *De Laudibus*, p. 21.

57. 'le construction par reason issera a ceo point ...' *Year Books*, Hil. 4 Henry VII, pl. 7, f.4.

58. Ibid., Hil.15 Henry VII, pl. 2, f.1.

59. Ibid., Pas.5 Henry VII, pl. 7 f.25.

60. Thomas Littleton, *Tenures*, London, Richard Tottell, 1583, f.142(2r.).

61. *Doctor and Student*, cited in note 17, p. 31; Chrimes, *Constitutional Ideas*, cited in note 44, p. 200; cf. Elyot, 'It may nat be denyed but that al lawes be founded on the depest parte of raison, and I suppose, no one lawe so moche as our owne', *The Gouernour*, cited in note 2, i, pp. 133–4.

62. *Doctor and Student*, cited in note 17, pp. 31, 33.

63. *Year Books*, Mich.9 Edward IV, pl. 9, ff.12–13.

64. Ibid., 5 Edward IV, Long Quinto f.137.

65. Ibid., 5 Edward IV, Long Quinto f.36.

66. Ibid., 5 Edward IV, Long Quinto f.110.

67. *Fulmerston v. Stewarde* (1554), Edmund Plowden, *Les Comentaries*, London, Richard Tottell, 1571, f.109v.

68. Quoted in Chrimes, *Constitutional Ideas*, cited in note 44, p. 350.

69. Fortescue, *De Laudibus*, p. 37. Some lawyers claimed that the common law was based on the civil law. John Spelman, *Reports*, cited in note 9, ii, p. 33.

70. Ives, 'Later year books', cited in note 51, pp. 143–6.

71. Ibid., p. 144.

72. Ibid., p. 138.

73. Ives, 'A lawyer's library', cited in note 20, p. 109; P.R.O., PROB11/5 ff.150, 150v. Arderne's included year books for Edward II and (apparently) 32 and 39 Edward III.

74. *Year Books*, Trin.2 Edward IV, pl. 3 f,11; Mich.8 Henry VII, pl.4, f.8.

75. P.R.O., PROB11/5 f.150.

76. Ives, 'Later year books', cited in note 51, pp. 140–3.

77. *Year Books*, 5 Edward IV, Long Quinto ff.1–5.

78. A. W. B. Simpson, 'Keilwey's reports, temp. Henry VII and Henry VIII', *Law Quarterly Review*, lxxiii (1957), pp. 89–105; 'The circulation of year books in the fifteenth century', ibid., lxxiii (1957), pp. 496–7.

79. Spelman, *Reports*, cited in note 9, i, pp. xxiii–xxxii.

80. P. H. Winfield, *The Chief Sources of English Legal History*, Cambridge, Mass., 1925, pp. 203–5.

81. (1) *Statham* [see this essay, note 82]; (2) Harvard Law School MS.41 [R. V. Rogers, 'The reports of year book 10 Henry V', *Law Library Journal*, xxxiv (1941), pp. 321–31]; (3) Cambridge University Library MS. Kk.v.1. [Winfield, *Chief Sources*, cited in note 80, pp. 212–3]; (4) B.L. Add.MS.35936 [claimed as an abridgment in *Year Books 4 Edward II*, G. J. Turner, (ed.), Selden Society, xxvi (1911), pp. xxxv–xxxvi]; (5) B.L. Add.MS.16168 [B. L. Putnam, *Early Treatises on the Practice of the Justices of the Peace in the Fifteenth and Sixteenth Centuries*, Oxford, 1924, pp. 176–7, n. 9(2)]; (6) Inner Temple, Whaddon folios [this essay, p. 186]; (7 and 8) B.L. Harl.MS.2051, Royal MS. 17EVI [Spelman, *Reports*, cited in note 9, ii, p. 173]; (9) Guildhall Library MS.208 [ibid., ii, p. 172 n. 9 where nine other 'early' examples are listed]; (10) Lincoln's Inn, Hale MS.181 [ibid., ii. 173, although cf. J. H. Baker, *English Legal Manuscripts*, London, 1978, ii, p. 49].

82. J. D. Cowley, *Bibliography of Abridgments ... of English Law to the Year 1800*, London, 1932, pp. xxxix–xli.

83. Winfield, *Chief Sources*, cited in note 80, p. 214; Cambridge University Library MS. Kk.v.1, see above at note 81; the name 'Statham' is much older, e.g. Spelman, *Reports*, cited in note 9, i, p. 74.

84. Winfield, *Chief Sources*, cited in note 80, pp. 220–4; Cowley, *Bibliography*, cited in note 82, p. xliii.

85. P.R.O., PROB11/8 f.57v. [cf. Turner, *Year Books*, cited in note 81, pp. xxxiv–xxxv]. Also unidentified to date are sources of Abridgment I in Harvard Law School MS.41 [Rogers, *Reports*, cited in note 81, pp. 323–6], of *The abridgement of the books of Assises*, London, Richard Pynson, c.1500, [see note 84 above] and of the abridgment of Edward III cases incorporated in the *Graunde Abridgement* [S. E. Thorne, 'Fitzherbert's *Abridgement*', *Law Library Journal*, xxix (1936), p. 62].

86. Antony Fitzherbert, *La Graunde Abridgement*, London, John Rastell and W. de Worde, 1514–16; Cowley, *Bibliography*, cited in note 82, pp. xliii–xlviii; Winfield, *Chief Sources*, cited in note 80, pp. 224–32; for the printers see H. J. Graham and J. W. Heckel, 'The book that "made" the common law', *Law Library Journal*, li (1958), pp. 100–16.

87. *Le Liver des Assises*, London, John Rastell, 1513–14, *Prologus*.

88. For the limitations of the *Tabula*, see Graham and Heckel, *Law Library Journal*, cited in note 86, pp. 113–16.

89. P.R.O., PROB11/5 f.150; 11/6 f.53.

90. Putnam, *Early Treatises*, cited in note 81, pp. 60–80.

91. Winfield, *Chief Sources*, cited in note 80, p. 280; P.R.O., PROB11/6 f.53.

92. Putnam, *Early Treatises*, cited in note 81, pp. 51–2.

93. Cowley, *Bibliography*, cited in note 82, pp. xviii–xix; Putnam, *Early Treatises*, cited in note 81, pp. 44–53.

94. Winfield, *Chief Sources*, cited in note 80, pp. 303–7; P.R.O., PROB11/18 ff.12v.–13, bequest of Frowyk's book to the Inner Temple Library by the second husband of his widow; Jenour's book is Library of Congress MS. Ac. 1093–4. Early sixteenth-century books of entries were also made by William Mordaunt and Edward Stubbe, Spelman, *Reports*, cited in note 9, ii, pp. 103, 175–6.

95. Putnam, *Early Treatises*, cited in note 81, pp. 43–59, 94–107.

96. Ibid., pp. 52–3, 104–6.

97. Thomas Littleton, *Tenures*, London, John Lettou and William de Machlinia c.1482; first English translation c.1532.

98. Winfield, *Chief Sources*, cited in note 80, p. 309.

99. Thomas Littleton, *Tenures*, cited in note 60, f.142(1v.).

100. J. P. Dawson, *The Oracles of the Law*, Ann Arbor, 1968, p. 36 n. 4; Geoffrey Chaucer, *Complete Works*, W. W. Skeat, (ed.), Oxford, 1894, p. 426.

101. Fortescue, *De Laudibus*, pp. 119, 117.

102. Ibid., pp. 117, 121.

103. Dawson, *Oracles*, cited in note 100, p. 9 n. 8.

104. Ibid., p. 38; *Paston Letters and Papers of the Fifteenth Century*, N. Davis, (ed.), Oxford, 1971–6, i, pp. 41–2.

105. For what follows see T. F. Tout, *Collected Papers*, Manchester, 1934, II, pp. 143–72; *Pension Book of Clement's Inn*, C. Carr, (ed.), Selden Society, lxxviii, 1960, pp. xvi–xxi.

106. Tout, *Papers*, cited in note 105, pp. 154–9, 162–5. The orders were repeated between 1410 and 1426.

107. Ibid., p. 167.

108. Fortescue, *De Laudibus*, p. 117.

109. The principal problem is to explain the eclipse of the inns of chancery; in 1396 (not 1409 as often stated) it was possible for a fellow of Clifford's Inn to become a serjeant-at-law, H. Cohen, *A History of the English Bar ...*, London, 1929, p. 449; *Select Cases in the Court of King's Bench*, VII, G. O. Sayles, (ed.), Selden Society, lxxxviii, 1971, pp. xl, lxiii. The following hypothesis may be offered: given that inns of chancery became self-governing under an elected principal, there would then be less incentive for lawyers, when established, to move out to 'residence-only' inns of court; this would produce economic pressure on the latter and encourage them to compete for student members by providing education not offered by the inns of chancery, i.e. readings on statute law; unless inns of chancery could win back seniors to give instruction in statutes, the automatic consequence would be their identification with primary and the inns of court with advanced training. The readings which did take place at inns of chancery were clearly different from those the inns of court offered, Simpson, 'Later year books', cited in note 55, pp. 104–107.

110. The challenge was first made in S. E. Thorne, 'The early history of the inns of court, with special reference to Gray's Inn', *Graya*, l (1959), pp. 79–96 and supported by Dawson, *Oracles*, cited in note 100, pp. 36–45. The remainder of this paper develops and modifies this hypothesis on the basis of a study of the manuscript Black Books of Lincoln's Inn and in the light of other recent work. I am indebted to the Benchers of Lincoln's Inn for permission to consult their manuscript.

111. The earliest use of the terms 'putting' or 'keeping the case' and 'bolt' is in 1552 and 1556 respectively. D. S. Bland, *The Vocabulary of the Inns of Court*, Liverpool, privately printed, 1964, pp. 15–16, 7–10.

112. D. S. Bland, 'Henry VIII's royal commission on the inns of court', *Journal of the Society of Public Teachers of Law*, x (1969), pp. 183–94; R. M. Fisher, 'Thomas Cromwell, dissolution of the monasteries and the inns of court, 1534–40', ibid., xiv (1976–7), pp. 111–17; R. M. Fisher, 'Thomas Cromwell, humanism and educational reform, 1530–40', *Bulletin of the Institute of Historical Research*, l (1977), pp. 151–63.

113. Bland, *Early Records*, cited in note 26; *Pension Book*, cited in note 105, pp. li–liv.

114. For what follows see S. E. Thorne, *Readings and Moots*, cited in note 14.

115. Bland, *Early Readings*, cited in note 26, p. 23; Thorne, *Readings and Moots*, cited in note 14, i, pp. xv–xviii.

116. Ibid., i, pp. l–lviii.

117. Black Book 1 f.12; 2(1) f.3 (*Black Books*, I, pp. 2, 12); Bland, 'Royal commission', cited in note 112, p. 185.

118. Black Book 1 f.134 (*Black Books*, I, p. 38).

119. Ibid., 1 f.17v. (*Black Books*, I, p. 3); Bland, *Early Readings*, cited in note 26, p. 29.

120. Ibid., 2(2) f.11 (*Black Books*, I, p. 91). The reference in the calendar to a moot in 1483 is to an *eruditio*, see this essay, p. 191. Some Lincoln's Inn books have been lost, see this essay, note 149.

121. Ibid., 1 ff.8, 9, 10, 11v., 12, *etc.*

122. That Christmas attendance was, in 1422, a recent requirement is suggested by the form of the lists which show a defective alphabetical order in 1422, some grouping by seniority in 1423 and 1424, and from 1425 regular grouping by seniority.

123. Ibid., 1 ff.1–7v., 13–16v., 24–27v., 40, 51–54v., 163v–70v., 171v–174 (*Black Books*, I, pp. 1, 2, 5, 9, 14, 52).

124. Ibid., 1 f.13 (*Black Books*, I, p. 2); the form of the first recorded mainprize [ibid., 1 f.1] is not given.

125. Ibid., 1 f.40 (*Black Books*, I, p. 9).

126. Ibid., 1 f.17 (*Black Books*, I, pp. 2–3).

127. Ibid., 2(1) f.3 (*Black Books*, I, p. 12); Bland, *Early Records*, cited in note 26, pp. 23–4. See also this essay note 129.

128. Black Book 1, ff.31–2 (*Black Books*, I, pp. 6–7).

129. Ibid., 2(1) f.3 (*Black Books*, I, p. 12). The period of the Lent vacation is now described as the week before and the two weeks after Easter.

130. The first list of discontinuers is for Michaelmas 1442, ibid., 1 f.44. The form of the record varies—the list for Easter 1445 is of those required to attend, ibid., 1 f.60v. Fines due on Christmas defaults were already certified to the pensioner or a governor, ibid., 1 ff.28, 43v.

131. Black Book 2(1) was described as 'the Great Book of Ordinances', ibid., 1 f.40, but it opens with the forms of the oaths and a list of those swearing. That names were earlier added to the mainprize is clear, e.g. Euerard, ibid., 1 f.2v., 2(1) f.14.

132. The first list is ibid., 1 f.43v., printed in *Records of the Honourable Society of Lincoln's Inn: Admissions*, W. B. Baildon, (ed.), London, 1896, I, p. 9 at ff.43, 43 and 56, [omit John Poynys]. All previous entries ibid., I, pp. 1–9 are not admissions but assignments to keep Christmas or provide mainprize.

133. Older interpretations of the constitutional development of the inns of court have been superseded by A. W. B. Simpson, 'The early constitution of the inns of court', *Cambridge Law Journal*, xxviii (1970), pp. 241–56, and 'The early constitution of Gray's Inn', ibid., xxxiv (1975), pp. 131–50; cf. J. H. Baker, 'The old constitution of Gray's Inn', *Graya*, lxxxi (1978), pp. 15–19.

134. Black Book 1, f.45 (*Black Books* I, p. 11).

135. Ibid., 1 f.145v. (*Black Books*, I, p. 42).

136. Carrying forward the total of students assigned to keep Christmas 1436; the figure for Christmas 1437 was 22, ibid., 1 ff.34, 35.

137. Ibid., 1 f.36v., also ff.33v., 35v, 36, 39v., Cf. 3 to keep *vacaciones ad bancum* Easter 1483, 3–Autumn; 3–Easter 1484, 3–Autumn (all kept); 4–Autumn 1492 (1 default), 4–Easter 1493 (3 defaults), 5–Autumn (3 defaults); 3–Easter 1494 (1 default), ibid., 2(1) ff.53, 53v., 56, 59; 2(2)ff. 18v., 22, 23, 26.

138. Ibid., 1 ff.144v.–147 (*Black Books*, I.41–3). The suggestion that some system of vacation attendance was continued after 1436 is supported by the phrase in the 1466 order describing the fellows of the bench as 'having completed their vacations'. This is unlikely to refer to vacations kept on admission since the most junior, William Huddersfield, had entered in 1455 and ten others had more than twenty years in the house; there can be no reference to the 1436 order since only one name overlaps, Henry Etwall.

139. Black Book 1, ff.149v., 152v., 155, 156.

140. Ibid., 2(1) f.30v.; 2(2) f.27 (*Black Books*, I, pp. 59, 100). The 1466 system appears to have got into difficulties about the time of Henry VI's Readeption.

141. Ibid., 2(1) f.30v. (*Black Books*, I. p. 59).

142. Ibid., 1 f.145v. (*Black Books*, I, p. 42).

143. On 'ancienty' see E. W. Ives, 'Promotion in the legal profession of Yorkist and early-Tudor England', *Law Quarterly Review*, lxxv (1959), pp. 349–54; its conclusions re benchers and readers need to be revised in the light of this essay page 206.

144. See this essay, p. 201.

145. The following is based on an analysis of appointments in the Black Books.

146. Black Book 2(2) f.48. (*Black Books*, I, p. 117).

147. Thomas Umfrey was elected treasurer in 1455 and so the governors were discharged from accounting but he was referred to as treasurer in the previous year when he was fourth governor. Prior to this the following had been tried: separate accounts by individual governors, a virtual monopoly of accounting by one governor and an extra governor, ibid., 1 ff.61–62v., 77–8, 84v.

148. Boeff: ibid., 1 ff.11v., 24, 27v., 40, 40v.; 2(1) f.1v.; Thorne, *Readings and Moots*, cited in note 14, pp. xii, xxvii; he was also second governor in 1446–7, Black Book 1 f.67. Newdigate: ibid., 2(1) f.53; 2(2) ff.34, 42, 47v., 51, 54; he was also master of the revels, 1484–5, butler at Christmas 1491–2, lent reader 1504 and second governor 1507–8, ibid., 2(1) f.58;2(2), ff.13, 17; 3 f.12. The lent readership is inferred. (*Black Books*, I, 5, 9, 10, 17, 81, 92, 94, 105, 112, 116, 120, 121, 131, 146; *Admissions*, cited in note 132, pp. 6, 22).

149. Other evidence of increasing organization at Lincoln's Inn includes: the rationalizing of the revels in 1431; the organization of the records—Black Book 1 was called 'the Black Book of manucaptors', Black Book 2(1) 'the great book of Orders' and there was 'the little black book', now lost; the regularizing of the form of accounts, ibid., 1 ff.20, 40, 61–62v.; 2(1) f.3 (*Black Books* I, pp. 4, 9, 12, 15).

150. Simpson, 'Gray's Inn', cited in note 133, pp. 138–41.

151. Ibid., pp. 133, 148.

152. Ibid., p. 142. It is improbable that either of the treasurers for 1517–22 had read and no readings are known for those in office 1504–9 *Middle Temple Records: Minutes of Parliament*, C. T. Martin (ed.), London, 1904–5, i, passim.

153. Simpson, 'Gray's Inn', cited in note 133, p. 142.

154. Cf. *Minutes of Parliament*, cited in note 152, i, pp. 20–2 and *Calendar of Inner Temple Records*, F. A. Inderwick, (ed.), London, 1896–1937, i, pp. 1, 5, 6, 7 etc. However, it was not until 1507 that the Inner Temple established a muniment chest and established master rolls for pensions and for fines and amercements, ibid., pp. 9–10.

155. Simpson, 'Gray's Inn', cited in note 133, pp. 142–3, and 'Early Constitution', cited in note 133, pp. 254–5.

156. The 'parliament' of 12 Feb. 1506 was held 'in the presence of Master Recorder [Robert Sheffield], [Robert] Fulwoode, [Edward] Halis, [John] Skote, and others' but none of those named were governors. *Inner Temple Records*, cited in note 154, p. 4.

157. Simpson, 'Gray's Inn', cited in note 133, pp. 134–5, 143–4; Baker, 'Gray's Inn', cited in note 133, pp. 18–19.

158. Simpson, 'Gray's Inn', cited in note 133, pp. 140–2.

159. *A Hundred Merry Tales* (*c.*1525) *Shakespeare Jest Books*, W. C. Hazlitt, (ed.), London, 1864, i, p. 84.

160. Cf. the view of K. Charlton that the educational system of the inns was in decline from the end of the fifteenth century, *Education in Renaissance England*, London, 1965, pp. 177–8.

161. R. J. Schoek, 'Rhetoric and law in sixteenth-century England', *Studies in Philology*, l (1953), pp. 110–27; D. S. Bland, 'Rhetoric and the law student in sixteenth-century England', ibid., liv (1957), pp. 498–508; Schoek, 'Thomas More', cited in note 2, p. 7.

8

Schoolmasters, 1307-1509

NICHOLAS ORME

It is now a well established fact that schooling was available all over England during the fourteenth and fifteenth centuries. Many institutions existed from which it could be obtained, and a wide variety of people spent their time providing it. There were three or four principal categories of school in later medieval England, and as many kinds of teachers.[1] First, there were the schools of the cities and larger towns: self-contained institutions, open to the public, and enjoying a measure of organization, continuity, and public recognition. Each was ruled by a single professional school-master (occasionally more than one), who gave most of his time to his teaching and who was a layman in status or a member of the secular clergy. Next to these came private schools with a smaller, more restricted entry. Some were maintained by great magnates for the children and wards in their households, others by the greater monasteries for their almonry boys and choristers, and yet others by schoolmasters themselves as a private venture. The masters of these schools resembled those of the public ones, and it was not uncommon for men to move from one kind to the other. A third source of schooling, of a more informal character, was provided by some of the parish clergy. Rectors, vicars, and parish chaplains sometimes taught the odd pupil in their spare time and, in the fifteenth and sixteenth centuries, some organists and parish clerks did so to the boys of parochial choirs. Finally, there were the cloister schools of the religious houses, taught by monks or friars and giving tuition at an advanced level to the novices who were under religious vows. Our concern is going to be with the first and second of these groups—the masters of the public and private schools—since they were the most professional and the best docu-mented. Monks, friars, and members of the parish clergy also made an educational contribution of value, but few of those who taught are known by name and their activities as teachers tended to be subsumed in their other, more important identity as clerics. They were primarily thought of, treated, and recorded as monks, friars, and parish clergy, rather than as schoolmasters in their own right.

The confidence with which medieval schoolmasters can be categorized fades at once when the question is raised of their numbers. We do not know with certainty how many schools there were, and we are dealing with a period of 200 years during which the total must have undergone variations. About 105 places in England are known to have possessed a public school at some-time in the fourteenth century, and about 114 during the fifteenth.[2] By the middle of the latter century, on the other hand, it was being asserted that an educational recession had taken place, and William Bingham, the founder of Godshouse (Cambridge), claimed in 1439 that over seventy schools were empty in the eastern half of England through lack of masters.[3] It seems likely, however, that the average English county contained between five and ten public schools at any moment during the later middle ages. Multiplied nationally, this produces a figure of 200 to 400 schools and masters. If this is extended by another 100 to 200 masters to cover the monasteries and the private households, a total emerges of 300 to 600. So rough an estimate is not intended to approach statistical accuracy, which is still beyond our reach, but to suggest how small schoolmasters were as a group of the population, even of its literate and clerical sections. Taken together, they were vastly inferior to the 4,500 monks and regular canons, the 2,200 friars, the 1,500 nuns, and the several thousands of parish clergy, who made up the clerical estate at its lowest ebb in the second half of the fourteenth century.[4] Individually, the single masters of the average English towns were even tinier as a numerical unit of the local community.

How did you become a medieval schoolmaster? As with most occupations there were two requirements to be met: you had to possess certain basic qualifications and to secure appointment to an actual school in a particular place. The qualifications were simple ones. Walter Bradewylle, clerk, who became schoolmaster of Ottery St. Mary in about 1380, was chosen for his 'ability and knowledge in teaching young men in grammar' and for 'the merit of his other virtues'.[5] John Bredel, chaplain, appointed to Worcester school in 1429, had 'knowledge of letters, honesty of morals, and a [satisfactory] manner of life'.[6] A third master, William Breter, who started to teach at Gloucester in the following year and was not described as any kind of cleric, survives as 'a fit and honest man, competently learned in the art of grammar'.[7] These attainments were typical of the majority. A good schoolmaster needed to be a man of good character and he had to be able to teach grammar, so that he must himself have studied the grammar course to at least the level of his highest pupils. But the average English grammar school of the later middle ages required no other qualifications than these. It was not absolutely necessary to be a celibate cleric or a university graduate. A clerk, such as Walter Bradewylle, might be a young man in his early twenties who intended becoming a priest, or a marriageable man whose way of life was largely that of a layman. Only in a few places during our period was anything more demanded. Some of the cathedral chapters confined their schools to graduates in the thirteenth and fourteenth centuries.[8] But when, after the 1350s, it became difficult to get such men to teach, non-graduates were appointed at Lincoln and Salisbury, Canterbury, and Worcester, and probably at most other similar places.[9] Towards the end of our period, when endowed schools were being founded with salaried masters, standards began to rise again, and a few such foundations reintroduced the graduation requirement. These, however, were still only a handful in number by 1509, and even among the endowed schools they were a small minority.[10]

Clerical status could also vary widely. The largest group of medieval schools—the fee-paying institutions of the towns—allowed their masters to be priests, clerks, or married laymen, without discrimination. Monasteries, too, appointed men of each category to teach their novices and almonry boys, and so did the principal endowed schools to be founded in the fifteenth and early sixteenth centuries: Eton, Magdalen (Oxford), St. Paul's, and Winchester. Certain minster and cathedral foundations—Beverley, Ripon, Wells, and York—drew back a little by requiring their schoolmasters to wear a clerical habit and to join the rest of the clergy at their daily office in the choir.[11] Yet this did not involve a vow of celibacy, and the masters remained free to marry later if not then. Only one area of teaching was absolutely restricted to priests, and that was in the small endowed schools. Most of these were also chantries between the 1380s and 1520s and expected their masters to say a daily mass for the soul of the founder; none-the-less they too were only a minority among the English schools, even at their most numerous in the early sixteenth century. All things considered, priests and graduates had the widest range of opportunities, but they never managed to establish a monopoly against non-graduates or laymen. This can be shown from a single region of England: the six counties of the South-

West. Eighty-nine masters are known to have taught in this area between 1307 and 1509.[12] Forty-six were priests, most of them (thirty) teaching in the endowed chantry schools; the rest were not so described and were probably either laymen or clerks in minor orders. Eleven were definitely graduates and another twenty-three, who were entitled 'master', possibly came into this category, but the vast majority (fifty-five) seem to have had little or no university training. Figures like these confirm that many openings existed for the mere product of the local grammar school, and equally so for the clerk who was barred from entering the priesthood by marriage, deformity, or merely by love of the way of the world.

Getting yourself a school, once you were qualified, usually meant being formally appointed to one. Most of the larger English towns, where the schools were best organized and most continuous, had educational patrons like the patrons of parish churches, who claimed the sole right to appoint the local master.[13] Bishops, archdeacons, cathedral chancellors, monasteries, collegiate churches, and a few members of the lay aristocracy all exercised this kind of patronage in the later middle ages. The endowed schools, which began to appear at the end of the fourteenth century, also had their patrons, some of whom belonged to the groups already mentioned while others were newcomers to the field: borough corporations, city companies, guilds of burgesses, and groups of country gentlemen and yeomen. Masters who were waiting for an established school to fall vacant could take employment as hired assistants—submasters or ushers as they were called—or could try to support themselves in a smaller and less desirable school or town in the neighbourhood, until they got what they wanted. We find William Buntyng teaching at Blofield (Norfolk) in 1350 before moving to Norwich school in 1369,[14] Richard Darcy formerly submaster of Gloucester in 1410 becoming headmaster of Winchester in 1418,[15] and John Hamundson being appointed to Howden in 1456 en route for York, where he died in 1472.[16] While most schoolmasters probably kept to their native regions, some used their qualifications to travel widely in search of employment. William Pocklington, for example, originated in the diocese of York, tried unsuccessfully for the school of St. Mary le Bow (London) in 1383, and ended in charge of Maidstone school a few years later.[17] His contemporary John Sampson, schoolmaster of St. Martin le Grand (London) in 1394, was an Irishman.[18] If there were no vacancy at an established school, it was sometimes possible to function in a private capacity where the control of education was not effective or did not exist. London, apart from its authorized schools, supported several private teachers in the later middle ages.[19] Bristol had free-lance masters too, apparently without authority,[20] and there were many lesser towns lacking schools or patrons where a visiting master could probably set himself up on his own initiative, provided he could find enough pupils to keep him.

Our next task is to consider how attractive a job schoolmastering was. Three factors are involved: the system of tenure, the remuneration, and the status of teachers in the community. Tenure in the English schools is a difficult subject to penetrate before the fourteenth century. Most of the early masters appear in records only once, which makes it impossible to determine how long they held their posts and whether they left them of their own free will. By 1300, however, two kinds of tenant are becoming visible. We encounter masters, especially in the smaller towns, whose appearances in records over several years or whose ownership of wives and property suggest that they were professionals who had settled down to teach for long periods.[21] In other places, particularly the cathedral cities, there were frequent successions of masters, some of them traceable to other careers, for whom teaching only represented a limited part of their lives.[22] Evidently schoolmastering had different attractions for different people. Some found it sufficiently rewarding to remain with it, or else failed to obtain anything better. Others taught merely on a temporary basis with some other end in view. Teaching a school was a useful way of filling up a few spare years. It could support you until you were old enough to be ordained, or found a benefice, or had saved enough money to go to university. The desirability of a post, however, lies not only in the ability to leave it but in the right to keep it. During the fourteenth century, in particular, many masters must have ceased to teach after a few years, not by choice but through necessity. Urban decline, plague, and parental indifference all threatened the town schoolmaster, depending as he did for his survival on the fees of his pupils. Even when his clientèle sufficed, he was not always free to teach as long as he wished. The university of Oxford, until about the middle of the fourteenth century, prohibited its graduate masters from teaching grammar for more than three years.[23] A similar custom was widespread in the schools of the north of England. Beverley, Hedon, Hexham, Howden, Lincoln, Northallerton, and York all limited their masters to terms of three or five years for at least part of the fourteenth century, and in some cases even later.[24] The tendency, however, was for tenurial conditions to improve as time went on. The Beverley master appointed for three years in 1320 managed to survive for fifteen.[25] At York the dean and chapter were obliged to suspend the three-year rule in 1368 because of the unwillingness of graduates to teach there since the previous plague. The rule continued to operate in theory, but was frequently disregarded in practice.[26] By the fifteenth century most school appointments appear to have lasted during good behaviour, while the foundation of the endowed schools and the growth of masterships in the monasteries provided an increasing number of secure paid posts. By 1509 the tenurial situation, though varying widely, was probably a good deal more favourable to more schoolmasters than it had been in 1307.

Next to security—but even more important—was remuneration. It is not clear, unfortunately, how much the masters earned in the fee-paying schools, where most of them taught until the sixteenth century. School fees can be ascertained but numbers of pupils cannot, and fees were open to augmentation from other sources, notably by the taking of boarders to live in the master's house. A safer guide to the material prosperity of the fee-earning group is to be found in their wills, of which a few survive. A good example from the fourteenth century is that of John Burdon, schoolmaster of Carlisle in 1371.[27] We do not know his age, beyond the fact that he had kept the school for nine years,[28] but the impression is that of an older rather than a younger man, who had been married but whose wife was dead. His monetary wealth enabled him to bequeath £14.13s. 4d. in separate legacies. He had about him for his use and comfort six silver spoons, a maple-wood bowl, his books (presumably of grammar), a furred coat with a hood, and a strong box containing jewellery. He was able to pay a priest to celebrate for his soul and that of his wife Christiana, and he had a circle of at least seven friends to mourn him, including a canon of the cathedral priory. Much the same characteristics appear, over sixty years later, in the will of John Seward of London, who died in 1435.[29] Seward was the master of a successful private school which he operated for many years, and lived to be seventy-one. Like Burdon he was married, but his wife survived him and they had one child. Four other relations and two friends received bequests in his will. His clothes included a green gown with belts of black and red, he had cauldrons in his kitchen, and bowls, a cup, and silver spoons to lay upon his table. He owned enough beds and chests to be able to give one of each to a friend, besides the residue of his goods which he left to his wife. He also resembled Burdon in being an owner of books—some of which, as we shall see, were probably written by himself. Both wills convey an impression of modest comfort: not ostentatious luxury but not grinding poverty either. It is likely that they represent with some accuracy the wealth of the average fee-earning masters in the larger English towns.[30]

The best evidence about schoolmasters' earnings accompanies the foundation of the endowed schools with their regular salaries. The earliest to be recorded, that of the headmaster of Winchester College in 1400, was set at £10 a year with board and lodging.[31] It probably aimed to match and perhaps to exceed the net income of the fee-paying schools, and certainly attracted applicants from such places: Chichester in 1394 and Gloucester in 1418 and 1424.[32] Later endowed schools, of which the majority were founded after 1440, adopted the sum of £10 a year purely and simply, and this became the usual rate for the job until well into the sixteenth century. Not many founders cared to set it higher, though Henry VI offered £16 at Eton in 1443 and John Colet provided the very generous sum of £34 at St. Paul's (London) in 1518. Elsewhere a few of the salaried masters who were clerics managed to hold a parochial benefice as well,[33] but there were not many such instances and in general the rate of £10 predominated. A sum of this kind raised its recipient above the lowest ranks of society, but not unduly high. The easiest comparison to make is with the incomes of the clergy which survive in taxation records. Take, for example, the clerical subsidy list for Oxfordshire in 1526.[34] The best-paid teachers in the county at that time were the master of Banbury school with £14 and his colleague at Magdalen College school whose £10 together with board and lodging probably gave him about the same. Their salaries—which were unusually high for that period—raised them with the upper half of the beneficed clergy (rectors and vicars), of whom about seventy received more than £10 a year and thirty or so more than £14. Below them the master of Ewelme school had the normal salary of £10, which put him above the lower half of the beneficed clergy, another seventy men or so, who got less. Finally came the master of Chipping Norton school, with only £6, which grouped him with the poorest of the beneficed clergy and with the crowd of 200 or so assistant curates and chantry priests. A clerical schoolmaster with £10 could therefore take comfort that he was better off than the majority of the parish clergy, but equally there were rectors and vicars above him whom he could envy, who were getting £5 or £10 a year more than he did, with less apparent effort.

If teaching paid so modestly, could greater gains be made elsewhere? Many masters, as we have already noted, did leave their schools for other work, but those of them whose careers are easiest to trace—the clerics—appear to have done only slightly better as a result. This can be illustrated by two representative biographies, one from the fourteenth and one from the fifteenth century. The first is that of William Wheatley, who was born in about the 1280s, somewhere in the region of the upper Thames valley.[35] He seems to have studied at Paris, and he got his first known benefice, Sulham (Berks.), in 1305. It was not very wealthy, having only been rated at £4 in 1291, but it probably gave him enough money to continue his studies at Oxford, for which he was given three years' leave of absence in 1306. Three years later he resigned Sulham to become master of Stamford school, which ought to have paid him better, and from there he went to Lincoln—one of the major English schools—where he appears as master in 1316. He must have been a good candidate for appointment since he was also a scholar and author whose writings we shall encounter later. Yet when he returned to parochial life as rector of Yatesbury (Wilts.) in 1317, he got a benefice that was only rated at £10, and as far as we know he held it until his death, perhaps in 1331. It was a modest achievement for so talented and travelled a man, yet it was a typical one, and it was not capable of much improvement even 150 years later. This can be seen from our second example, Edward Janyns, who was born in the 1430s or thereabouts.[36] A probable native of the Monmouth area, his first post after his ordination in 1459 was as chantry priest and grammar master of Newland (Gloucs.), four miles from Monmouth and worth about £10. He left it after four years for a succession of livings, each of which lifted his income a little until he emerged as vicar of Newland in 1476, with a stipend of about £18. He also took the opportunity, when he was well enough established, to go to university, probably in 1468, where he got a bachelor's degree in canon law. He ended his life as a respected member of the local clergy, taking his turn as rural dean and dying in about the 1490s. Like Wheatley he did not rise very high, but he seems to have done as well as an ordinary ex-schoolmaster could. Few others achieved anything better. Of the forty-six west-of-England masters who were priests, at least eighteen are known to have gone on to hold parochial benefices. Yet hardly one of them gained anything really lucrative. Their benefices paid them a few more pounds than their schools had done, but that was all. They stopped well short of the grades that counted: cathedral dignities, canonries and prebends, and wealthy parochial pluralities.

The careers of the late-medieval schoolmasters, both the professionals and the birds of passage, were thus only moderately successful. This tells us something about teaching in the period, and probably gives us a clue to the social origins of those who taught. Hardly anyone who had been a schoolmaster reached a high position between 1307 and 1509, either in Church or State. It may have been, of course, that most of them were men of mediocre talent, but this cannot have been true in every instance. There must have been a proportion of the able and ambitious who were potentially qualified to succeed. They failed to do so, nevertheless. Teaching evidently did little to forward their ambitions and may even have done them harm. It had not always been so, nor was it to be in the future. In the twelfth century an occasional schoolmaster had risen to greatness. Alexander Neckham became abbot of Cirencester and John of Salisbury ended his life as bishop of Chartres. Their successes began to be copied again at the close of our period by Thomas Wolsey, who reached the woolsack as an indirect result of teaching in Magdalen school.[37] Several other ex-masters were to sit on the privy council and the episcopal bench under Edward VI and Elizabeth. In the fourteenth and fifteenth centuries, however, the only teachers who attained this level were a small group under Henry VI: John Chedworth (tutor of Robert Lord Hungerford, and later bishop of Lincoln), John Somerset (master of Bury St. Edmunds and tutor to the king, later chancellor of the exchequer), and William Wainfleet (headmaster of Winchester, later bishop of Winchester).[38] They were the first beneficiaries of a more favourable attitude to school education which might have transformed the English scene in the middle of the fifteenth century, had not Henry's reign collapsed in civil strife. As it was, the opportunities for schoolmasters only began to widen after 1500. Until then, their work remained almost uniformly meagre in its rewards, and for this reason it had nothing to attract the well born or the well connected. They could and did make better progress elsewhere. The masters of the later middle ages must have come from modest burgess families, from the yeomanry of the countryside, or from their inferiors. Only at these levels did teaching offer its recruits an equal standard of living, or a better one.

It is not surprising, after reviewing these modest rewards and achievements, to find that the reputation of schoolmasters in society was also a modest one. Teaching failed to make an impact on the public imagination, and the public at all its levels thought little of teachers. They were not so much despised as overlooked, forgotten, and unnoticed. The Crown, for its part, did not involve itself with schoolmasters in general until the beginning of the Reformation in 1535.[39] Education was primarily an ecclesiastical matter in the middle ages, but even the Church paid it little attention compared with later centuries.[40] The ecclesiastical authorities—bishops, archdeacons, and cathedral chancellors— were concerned that a network of schools should operate over the country. They were anxious that masters should only be appointed by the lawful patrons and that once appointed they should not be threatened in their rights by outsiders trying to set up rival, unauthorized schools. The authorities intervened from time to time to appoint a local master, to decide a disputed appointment, or to deal with an unlicensed school. But they did this only at irregular intervals, in times of emergency. It was almost unknown for any ecclesiastical power to interest itself with teachers as a group on any regular basis. Masters were not presented to their bishops for institution, they were not usually expected to appear at visitations, and they hardly ever received directives about their teaching or demeanour. If the Church's leaders were aware of schoolmasters in general, they certainly took them for granted and felt it unnecessary to have any regular relations with them.

The laity appears to have taken the same view. It knew, of course, what a schoolmaster was. The English word is first recorded in the 1220s and occurs frequently thereafter.[41] People had dealings with their local pedagogue. They gave him their children to teach and they encountered him, like anyone else, in the petty disputes and transactions of everyday life. But they too seem to have been unconscious of schoolmasters as a group or the schoolmaster as a type. Only once do we hear of a confrontation between the laity and schoolmasters in general. This took place in the Peasants' Revolt of 1381 when the rebels, hot in pursuit of literates and literature—tax-collectors, lawyers, and manorial records, are said to have warned schoolmasters not to teach children grammar. The incident, however, is only recorded by one writer (Thomas Walsingham) and must, if it did take place, have been a rather minor feature of the rising.[42] The famous accusation of Jack Cade in Shakespeare's Henry VI Part II, 'thou hast most traitorously corrupted the youth of the realm in erecting a grammar school', is in the same tradition as Walsingham's anecdote from which (through Holinshed) it may have been derived.[43] But contemporary support for it is equally lacking and the man accused, James Lord Saye and Sele, never indeed founded a grammar school. Medieval English writers ignored the schoolmaster, too. Chaucer was fully aware of scholars, several of whom he portrayed in the *Canterbury Tales*, from the pupil of a petty song school to a well-educated squire and four university clerks. The only teacher to be included in the *Tales*, however, was Nero's tutor Seneca; Chaucer had no interest in contemporary schoolmasters.[44] Langland too, despite the immense range of his references in *Piers Plowman*, mentioned schoolmasters only once, and then merely as an example of men receiving lawful payment for their work.[45] Their whole appearance in medieval English writing is in fact confined to a few school lyrics and school exercises from the fifteenth century.[46] It is a very different story from the age of Elizabeth, when the quarrelsome pedant became a frequent and familiar character of literature, and Shakespeare (to take only one example) was inspired to paint his memorable portraits of Holofernes and Sir Hugh Evans.

There is little comment about schoolmasters even from the groups with which they were most concerned: their pupils and their pupils' parents. We know that a few of the masters who tutored the great and famous were rewarded for their services. John Paynel, the instructor of Edward III, was raised to be chamberlain of Chester.[47] John Chedworth was given a rectory in Dorset for teaching the grandson of Walter Lord Hungerford.[48] John Rede was made a canon of Newark College, Leicester, after tutoring Prince Arthur.[49] Largesse of this kind implies a gratitude that has not survived in words. Contrariwise we hear of a few dissatisfied customers. Robert Buck claimed to have left school at Clitheroe in 1283 because he was so badly beaten.[50] Robert Eliot of Harnhill (Kent) sued his master in 1390 for beating him, alleging damages of £20,[51] and William Skidmor, a London goldsmith, actually had the teacher of his son imprisoned in the 1460s on a similar charge.[52] These, however, were exceptional cases. What is lacking from the later middle ages is almost any assertion by any ex-pupil of what he owed (or did not owe) to his schoolmaster. Even the twelfth century has more to offer in this respect. Alexander Neckham, Gerald of Wales, and Jocelin of Brakelond are only some of its writers who put on record their affection for their masters or the affection of those they knew.[53] But such acknowledgements disappear during the thirteenth century, and they are quite absent by the fourteenth. Not until the end of the fifteenth do men again recall their schooling. The first major example is that of Thomas Rotherham, archbishop of York, in the foundation charter of the college he founded at Rotherham in 1483. Here he was moved to tell how he passed his early years in the town without a knowledge of letters, until there came 'by God's grace' a wandering teacher of grammar from whom he received his first instruction.[54] This starts the modern series of educational reminiscences, which multiply in the sixteenth century and descend in growing numbers to the present day. But they appear too late to cast any light on the relationships of masters and pupils in the period with which we are dealing.

It remains to be asked whether the schoolmasters of the later middle ages deserved the comparative neglect which they received. In some respects, perhaps, they did. Their impact upon many aspects of national life was indisputably weak. Numerically, as we have seen, they were insignificant. Their economic importance was a restricted one. A master's pupils paid him fees and (if they came from a distance) they also spent money locally on board and lodging. But school-fees barely supported the master and his usher; no school can have generated any significant capital, and the money brought into a town by visiting school-boys must have remained a very small part of the town's whole trade. The role of schoolmasters in public life was also modest. We find them being admitted as burgesses or as members of religious guilds, and very occasionally they held municipal offices. Robert Simon was elected town clerk of Henley-on-Thames in 1419,[55] William Hardynge became one of the twelve governors of Beverley in 1446,[56] and John Squire was chosen to be treasurer of Ipswich in 1483.[57] Clerical schoolmasters, too, are sometimes found discharging minor administrative duties. One acts as a papal judge-delegate,[58] another proves a will in the absence of executors,[59] while a third inquires into the vacancy of a parochial benefice.[60] But these were all peripheral activities. The principal concern of schoolmasters was with the world of learning. Their major activity lay in reading, writing, and teaching, not in trade or public administration. It was their literary and educational achievements that mattered, and to which we must turn before a proper judgment can be made of their importance.

The first and most basic function of schoolmasters, and their greatest contribution to medieval civilization, was their teaching.

They taught a wide curriculum, from the alphabet through plain-song to the various branches of Latin: its grammar, its composition, its oratory, and its elementary literature.[61] At their best they introduced their pupils to topics such as literary criticism, logic, and speculative grammar which were also part of the university arts course. They catered for thousands of pupils every year, many times more than studied at Cambridge or Oxford. Their pupils ranged from those who wished merely to read and spell, in order to understand literature in French or English, to those who sought the fluency in Latin that was necessary to enter university. It was these schoolmasters, so unobtrusive otherwise, who taught the scholars and poets of medieval England, the clergy of the parishes and the religious orders, many of the male aristocracy, the common lawyers, some of the merchant elite, certain of the yeomanry, and even a few from the classes below. Alike in the lives of Henry V and Henry VII, Bradwardine and Wycliffe, Chaucer and Langland, the Stonors and the Pastons, there lurks a schoolmaster—a forgotten contributor to the achievements in government and scholarship, literature and administration, of his more famous pupils.

Let us take care then, lest we magnify the pupil at the expense of the master. Medieval teachers were men of obscurity, as we have seen too well, but obscurity does not establish mediocrity. If some masters were unlearned, dishonest and lazy—and we know of such men—others were equally learned and diligent. They were, in the first place, collectors and owners of books: not only of the texts they used in school but of a wide variety of titles and subjects. Already in the middle of the fourteenth century they were able to draw a compliment from the greatest bibliophile of the age. When Richard de Bury completed the *Philobiblon* in 1345, he did not omit from his survey of books and their owners 'the masters of country schools and the instructors of rude boys'. He had even perused their libraries, with profitable results. 'When we had an opportunity, we entered their little plots and gardens, and gathered sweet-smelling flowers from the surface and dug up their roots, obsolete indeed, but still useful to the student'.[62] We do not know what books of theirs he found, but a number of titles survive which belonged to their successors in the fifteenth century. A fine volume of Latin chronicles owned by John Pyke of St. Martin le Grand (London) is still preserved in the British Library, with what appear to be his own grammatical notes.[63] William Fellows of Evesham bequeathed St. Gregory's *Pastoral Care*, the *Sermons* of

St. Bernard, and Hugh of St. Victor on *Ecclesiastes* to various Oxford libraries.[64] John Hamundson of York had a book of chronicles in English for his relaxation.[65] Candidates for the degree of master of grammar at Cambridge, most of whom were previous or future schoolmasters, deposited nine books as cautions between 1480 and 1501. They included a breviary, a Latin dictionary, the *Pupilla Oculi*, two books of philosophy, the Bible, an exposition of the Holy Fathers, and the *De Veritate* of Thomas Aquinas.[66] At least one master of the fifteenth century deserves to be noted as a major book-collector. When John Bracebrigge, M.A. of Oxford and master of Lincoln school, entered Syon Abbey as a chaplain after 1420, he gave it a library that included five volumes of grammar, five of philosophy, ten of medicine, and forty-six of theology, canon law, and the liturgy.[67] We cannot regard him as typical, but he certainly enlarges our concept of what a schoolmaster could acquire, given the right conditions.

Next to their reading we have a good deal of writing by schoolmasters. It falls into two categories: textbooks on grammar related to their teaching, and contributions to literature of a more general kind. The latter, which are not numerous, can be dealt with fairly quickly. The relative isolation of most teachers from the main centres of learning and patronage, to say nothing of the demands of their schools, seems to have prevented them making important contributions to scholarship or to imaginative literature, so far as we know. The extent of their activity in these fields is represented, probably accurately, by two of the masters whom we have already met: William Wheatley and John Seward. Wheatley's Latin works, which were written around 1309–16, survive in three manuscripts.[68] They include a commentary on the *De Consolatione Philosophiae* of Boethius, another on his apocryphal *De Disciplina Scholasticorum*, a handful of letters, and two hymns on the life of St. Hugh of Lincoln. Seward's effusions, which also reached three manuscripts, include *Arpyilogus*—a commentary on the story of the Harpies in Virgil's *Aeneid*, *Antelopologia*—a poem on the properties of the antelope addressed to Henry V, some Latin verse *Epigrams*, and other such works.[69] His writings, like those of Wheatley, are interesting to the student of medieval scholarship and minor Latin verse. But they are not, to be truthful, of major importance, and they certainly had no great impact on their authors' own contemporaries.

The one schoolmaster who made his mark on literature did so as a publisher rather than a writer. He was that enigmatical and anonymous figure, the schoolmaster-printer of St. Albans. Nothing remains of his life beyond the information that he operated a print-ing and publishing business in the town from about 1479 to 1486 and that he was dead by 1497, when his fellow-printer Wynkyn de Worde described him as a schoolmaster and asked God's mercy on his soul.[70] Eight of the books he published have survived. The first six, which appeared between 1479 and 1483, were university text-books in Latin on various aspects of the arts course, aimed no doubt at the university of Cambridge where no press had yet been established. They do not seem to have been very profitable, and this caused the master to change his tactics. He next attempted to penetrate the wide potential market for books in English of a popular kind. Two such volumes ultimately appeared from his press, both of which he edited personally from earlier writings: *The Chronicles of England* in 1483 and the famous *Book of St. Albans* on hunting, hawking, and heraldry, in 1486. They were, however, his last productions. Whether he ceased through failure or through death we do not know, but he certainly died too early to reap the rewards he had forseen. These went instead to others. In 1497 Wynkyn de Worde republished the *Chronicles* with greater resources and wider connections. It had a great success; it was reprinted every few years until 1528; and with a shortage of rival volumes, it must have been the major work on English history read by the literate public in England during that period.[71] *The Book of St. Albans* fared still better. Also reissued by de Worde in 1496, it outlived even the *Chronicles* to pass through more than twenty new editions, well into the seventeenth century.[72] It is a curious yet memorable fact that the numerous students of heraldry and field sports during the Tudor period owed one of their major sources of information to the enterprise of a late medieval school-master.

The main literary activity of schoolmasters, however, lay in the sphere of their work: the writing of tracts and textbooks on the various branches of Latin grammar. Some of these were advanced discussions of grammatical theory directed at other masters and scholars, but the majority were elementary in their purpose and consisted of simple expositions of Latin accidence and syntax for the use of children. The principal centre of grammatical study in medieval England was Oxford, several of whose schoolmasters produced textbooks during the fourteenth- and fifteenth-centuries, notably John Cornwall, who operated in the 1340s, and John Leland, 'the flower of grammarians', who flourished from about

1400 until his death in 1425.[73] By the middle of the fifteenth century grammar masters in other parts of England were compiling
textbooks for their pupils, including a Bristol master (probably
Robert Londe) in the late 1420s,[74] and John Drury of Beccles in
1432.[75] Local writing of this kind apparently went on throughout
the century. Later still in the 1480s, a revival of activity took place
at Oxford, centred upon Magdalen College school, inspired by the
renewal of interest in the pagan classical authors, and diffused
more widely than before by means of the printing press. The chief
textbook writers of this period included John Anwykyll, the first
known master of the school (c.1481–7), his successor John Stanbridge (1488–94), John Holt (usher in the school in 1494–6), and
Robert Whittington, one of their pupils.[76] These men were the
vanguard of a wide and active company of grammatical writers in
the first half of the sixteenth century, which also included such
names as John Colet, William Lily, and Thomas Wolsey.

Most of the school textbooks, from those of Cornwall to those of
Lily, had major features in common. Their form was based on the
Donet, the medieval version of the *Ars Minor* of Donatus, who lived
in the fourth century. They were often written in English, which
made its first appearance in Cornwall's *Speculum Grammaticale* of
1346 and was well established as the language of elementary
teaching by the middle of the fifteenth century. They combined the
practical teaching of Latin with a strong emphasis on the theory of
grammar and grammatical terminology. Finally, they presented
their material by means of a series of questions and answers
which the master could reproduce in class with his pupils:

What shalt thou do whan thou hast an Englysshe [text] to make in
Latyn? I shal reherse myn Englysshe ones, twyes or thryes, and loke out
my pryncypal [verb] and aske the questyon 'who?' or 'what?'. And the
worde that answereth the questyon shall be the nominatyf case to the
verbe, excepte it be a verb impersonall, as in this example. 'The mayster
techeth scolers'. 'Techeth' is the verbe. Who techeth? The mayster techeth. This worde 'mayster' answereth to the questyon here, and therefore it shall be the nominatyf case.

This is a passage from the *Long Parvula*, a tract on the translation
of English into Latin which exists in several versions, of which this
was printed in 1509.[77] Its clarity, simplicity, and orderliness are
immediately apparent, and can be appreciated even by a modern
audience of hopeless linguists. The method of teaching by
questions and answers was supplemented by two other devices.

One was the interpolation of mnemonic Latin verses, composed by the author himself or drawn from earlier grammarians. These summarized the rules of grammar or linked together common Latin words in a way that could easily be memorised. The other was the invention of '*vulgaria*'—English sentences which illustrated the rules of grammar in operation and which the pupils were made to translate into Latin as a means of practising their composition. The first known English *vulgaria* date from the early fifteenth century, and they went on being produced well into the sixteenth. They were an educational instrument of much importance and many applications, some of which we shall consider presently.

Textbooks of this kind obviously had an educational impact, helping as they did to instil the rudiments of Latin into generation after generation of pupils. But this was not their only value. They had significant effects on the history of English as well as of Latin, both on the study of language and on the development of literature. It can indeed be said that through their textbooks the medieval schoolmasters made a literary contribution of an indirect kind equal to the writing of many primary works of English prose or poetry. It was they, after all, who first began the study of English grammar. The school textbooks of the fifteenth century, as we have seen, set out to teach Latin through the medium of English. And as Professor S. B. Meech pointed out over forty years ago, this was important for English as well as for Latin.[78] The nature of the effect can be seen in many of the early grammars, like this example, also from the fifteenth century, in a manuscript now at St. John's College, Cambridge:

Qwerby knowyst an adverbe? For he is cast to a verbe and fulfyllyth the significacyon of the verbe. How many degre of comparison hath adverbe? Thre: the posityf, the comparatyf, and the superlatyf. How knowest the posityf degree of adverbe? For he endyth in Englysch most comunly in 'ly', as 'fayrly', 'goodly', 'swetely', and soche othyr. How knowyst the comparatyf degree? For he endyth in Englysch in 'er' or in 'ir', as 'swetter', 'betyr'. How knowyst the superlatyf degre? For he endyth in Englysch in 'est', as 'fayrest', 'fowlest', and soch othyr.[79]

Grammatical writing of this kind had a three-fold influence upon English. In the first place it necessitated the translation of grammatical terms from the original Latin: 'verbe', 'adverbe', 'comparatyf', 'superlatyf', and so on. Almost all the terms for the parts of speech, the genders and cases of nouns, and the moods and tenses of verbs were probably brought into English by schoolmasters, and certainly established their currency through use in school. Second, by using examples of English words to explain the workings of Latin, the masters were unconsciously dealing with English grammar and reducing it to a series of rules, a century and a half before the first appearance of an English grammar as such by William Bullokar in 1586.[80] Third, their approach to English grammar, like that of Bullokar and his successors, was based on their knowledge of Latin. They supposed the English language to operate on Latin principles, with the same systems of verbs and nouns, and the same kinds of constructions. It was thus the medieval schoolmasters who set the fashion, which endured so long, for treating English as a Latin analogue.

But the textbooks did not only handle words individually. They also set out to teach Latin prose style through the construction of clauses and sentences, and this in turn led them to produce passages of English prose, either as explanations of the Latin or as *vulgaria* for translation. And just as the analysis of individual English words had an effect on the study of English grammar, so the invention of English prose passages influenced the development of English prose. Here too, many years before English prose style was formally studied in its own right, it was being taught unconsciously in schools as part of the process of learning to write Latin. The study and translation of *vulgaria* by fifteenth- and early sixteenth-century schoolboys must have been a major influence upon the way they wrote their native language. It is hard to say, of course, whether the school grammars took a lead in the development of English prose style, or whether they merely followed its dominant features at the time. Some of the *vulgaria* passages were over-contrived, in order to deal with complex problems of Latin grammar, and others fall a little flat today. But at its best the English of the school textbooks set a high standard, in which elegance and terseness of manner join together with sincerity of feeling:

I was very sorry when I herde say that thy brother was dede in this pestilence, for I have lost a gentle frende and a trusty. From our first acquentance, the which was sens we were children, we were companyde togedre in on house and undre onn maister, and lightly we hade onn mynde in every mater. I cannot tell in goode faithe what losse may be comparede with this; the philosopher thought ther was nothynge more to be praisede than a goode frende.[81]

As for Robert Whittington's encomium on his friend Thomas More, a series of sentences in his *Vulgaria* of 1520, it well deserves the fame which it has acquired in modern times:

Moore is a man of an aungels wyt and syngler lernyng. He is a man of many excellent vertues; yf I shold say as it is, I knowe not his felawe. For where is the man in whome is so many goodly vertues, of that gentylnes, lowlynes, and affabylyte? And, as tyme requyreth, a man of merveylous myrth and pastymes, and somtyme of as sad gravity: as who say, 'a man for all seasons'.[82]

Finally, the writers of the school textbooks can be said to have discovered a major topic of interest in modern English literature: the evocation of childhood. Here too what began as an educational device ended as a literary influence. The schoolmasters of the later middle ages had the same general objective as their modern successors. Their task was to prepare their pupils for adult life, and this they did by introducing into their teaching as many precepts as possible about the ethics and standards required of adults at that time: religious observance, self discipline, obedience, courtesy, and so on. But like their successors today, they found that their teaching was more effective if it made concessions to their pupils and dwelt to some extent on childish things: the everyday life of children, their humour, pleasures, problems, and emotions. Matters of this kind not only held the attention of the class but actively assisted its progress to adulthood. The child who took pleasure in turning a joke into Latin was brought a step nearer to the mastery of the language he would need as an adult cleric or lawyer. The medieval school textbooks therefore included a great many references to childhood in their exercises and examples, and the masters who wrote them descended in doing so from the high study of grammar to view the world through the eyes of their pupils. They thus made the same mental transitions as modern writers for children and those who reminisce about their youth.

The best of these early evocations of childhood is undoubtedly the one in the anonymous collection of *vulgaria* written at Magdalen College in about 1500, and also the best of the whole genre:

The worlde waxeth worse every day, and all is turnede upside down, contrary to th'olde guyse, for all that was to me a pleasure when I was a childe, from iij yere olde to x (for now I go upon the xij yere), while I was undre my father and mothers kepyng, be tornyde now to tormentes and payne. For than I was wont to lye styll abedde tyll it was forth dais, delitynge myselfe in slepe and ease. The sone sent in his beamys at the wyndowes that gave me lyght instede of a candle. O, what a sporte it was every mornynge when the son was upe to take my lusty pleasur betwixte the shetes, to beholde the rofe, the beamys, and the rafters of my chambre, and loke on the clothes that the chambre was hangede with. Ther durste no mann but he were made awake me oute of my slepe upon his owne hede while me list to slepe. At my wyll I arose with intreatese, and whan th'appetite of rest went his way by his owne accorde, than I awoke and callede whom me list to lay my gere redy to me. My brekefaste was brought to my beddys side as ofte as me liste to call therfor, and so many tymes I was first fedde or I were cledde. So I hade many pleasurs mo besides thes, wherof sum be forgoten, sum I do remembre wel, but I have no leysure to reherce them nowe.

But nowe the worlde rennyth upon another whele. For nowe at fyve of the clocke by the monelyght I most go to my booke and lete slepe and slouthe alon, and yff oure maister hape to awake us, he bryngeth a rode stede of a candle. Now I leve pleasurs that I hade sumtyme; here is nought els preferryde but monyshynge and strypys. Brekfastes that were sumtyme brought at my biddynge is dryven oute of contrey and never shall cum agayne. I wolde tell more of my mysfortunes, but thoughe I have leysure to say, yet I have no pleasure, for the reherse of them makyth my mynde more hevy. I sech all the ways I can to lyve ons at myn ease, that I myght rise and go to bede when me liste oute of the fere of betynge.[83]

The author of this passage may have had in his mind (and would certainly have known) the ancient and well-worn comparison between the holy innocence of childhood and the sins and labours of adult life—the theme that is so familiar to us in its expositions by Vaughan and Wordsworth. He may also have drawn upon memories of his own childhood. To this extent he can be said to have anticipated the many modern writers who have recalled the anguish of their transition from home to school. His chief purpose, however, as many other passages in his *vulgaria* make clear, was not to sympathize with the child he portrayed but to censure and instruct him. In the eyes of the master, the change he described was a necessary and desirable progression from childish sloth, greed, and self indulgence to Christian adulthood with its sustaining virtues of hard work, obedience, and self discipline. The apparent splendour of unfettered childhood, like the apparent splendour of Falstaff's disorders in *Henry IV*, must in the end be rejected, for the sake of both society and the individual, of both the body and the soul. Shakespeare and the *vulgaria* author shared a common point of view, and both enclosed their pleasant pictures in a regular dark frame of traditional morality.

Our task is now complete. We have tried to rescue the medieval schoolmasters from their obscurity, with (it is hoped) a little success. We know how it arose. Their lack of numbers, their geographical isolation, and their modest economic importance were all against them. They never managed to develop a national organization, and they cannot be regarded as a profession. They stayed secluded in their classrooms while others no better than themselves—clerics, physicians and lawyers—traversed the world for all to see. The cleric's censures, the physician's poisons, and the lawyer's writs all made their impact upon adults, with memorable results. Schoolmasters, on the other hand, ruled only the powerless and the inarticulate, and suffered accordingly. Yet their obscurity was not their fault. If they had been given more, they might have done better. Like the schoolmasters of any age they taught what their society required with the resources which it provided. As it was, they had some solid achievements. They helped to supply the Church with clerics, the universities with scholars, and the courts with officers and lawyers. The notable increase of literacy among the laity was in part the result of their efforts. They were inventive as educationists and they exercised an unseen influence on the development of the English language. The public which ignored them was wrong, as public opinion often is. The schoolmaster's birch touched a lower and less regarded end of the body politic than did the priest, the lawyer, or the physician. Yet he too touched the body, and he made its circulation run the faster.

NOTES

1. For further discussion of the typology of medieval schools see N. Orme, *English Schools in the Middle Ages*, London, 1973, pp. 59–60, and *Education in the West of England, 1066–1548*, Exeter, 1976, pp. 1–2.

2. Orme, *English Schools*, cited in note 1, pp. 293–325.

3. A. F. Leach, *Educational Charters & Documents, 598–1909*, Cambridge, 1911, pp. 402–3; A. H. Lloyd, *The Early History of Christ's College Cambridge*, Cambridge, 1934, pp. 356–7 et passim.

4. David Knowles and R. N. Hadcock, *Medieval Religious Houses: England & Wales*, London, 2nd ed., 1971, pp. 488–95.

5. B.L., MS. Harley 3300 f.274v.

6. A. F. Leach, *Documents Illustrating Early Education in Worcester*, Worcs. Historical Society, xxxi, 1913, pp. 76–7.

7. P.R.O., Chancery Masters Exhibits, C 115/A 3 f.210.

8. Orme, *English Schools*, cited in note 1, p. 151.

9. *V.C.H. Lincs.*, II, p. 423; Orme, *Education*, cited in note 1, p. 76; C. E. Woodruff and H. J. Cape, *Schola Regia Cantuariensis*, London, 1908, pp. 34–5; Leach, *Early Education in Worcester*, cited in note 6, pp. 76–7, 90.

10. To the list in Orme, *English Schools*, cited in note 1, p. 154, n. 1, add Week St. Mary (Cornwall) (Orme, *Education*, cited in note 1, pp. 176–7).

11. A. F. Leach, *Early Yorkshire Schools*, I, Yorks. Archaeological Society, xxvii, 1898, pp. 18, 21, 82–6; *V.C.H. Yorks.*, I, p. 431; Orme, *Education*, cited in note 1, pp. 82, 86.

12. Orme, *Education*, cited in note 1, passim, with one or two additions and corrections.

13. On patronage see also Orme, *English Schools*, cited in note 1, pp. 143–50.

14. Norfolk and Norwich Record Office, Reg./2 Book 4, f.118v.; H. W. Saunders, *A History of the Norwich Grammar School*, Norwich, 1932, p. 91.

15. Orme, *Education*, cited in note 1, pp. 62–3.

16. Leach, *Early Yorkshire Schools*, II, Yorks. Archaeological Society, xxxiii, 1903, p. 87; I, cited in note 11, p. 28.

17. Lambeth Palace Library, Reg. William Courtenay, f.37; Reg. John Morton, f.182 recto and verso.

18. *C.P.R.*, *1391–6*, p. 459.

19. Orme, *English Schools*, cited in note 1, pp. 190, 210–12, 309.

20. Orme, *Education*, cited in note 1, pp. 37–41.

21. E.g. Battle (*V.C.H. Sussex*, II, p. 397) and Wakefield, (J. W. Walker, *Wakefield, its History and People*, Wakefield, 2nd ed., 1939, II, pp. 363–4).

22. Woodruff and Cape, *Schola Regia Cantuariensis*, cited in note 9, pp. 22–33; Saunders, *Norwich Grammar School*, cited in note 14, pp. 85–102; Leach, *Early Yorkshire Schools*, I, cited in note 11, pp. 21–4.

23. *Statuta Antiqua Universitatis Oxon*, Strickland Gibson, (ed.), Oxford, 1931, pp. 20–3.

24. Leach, *Early Yorkshire Schools*, I, cited in note 11, pp. 23–4, 27, 30, 90; II, cited in note 16, pp. 60–2, 84–6; *C.P.R.*, *1340–3*, p. 59; J. Raine, *The Priory of Hexham*, I, Surtees Society, xliv, 1864, p. lxxix; *V.C.H. Lincs.*, II, p. 423.

25. Leach, *Early Yorkshire Schools*, I, cited in note 11, pp. 97–100.

26. Ibid., pp. 23–4, 27–30.

27. *Testamenta Karleolensia*, R. S. Ferguson, (ed.), Cumberland and Westmorland Antiquarian and Architectural Society, ix, 1893, p. 101.

28. He was licensed to be schoolmaster of Carlisle on 23 October 1362 (Carlisle, Cumbria Record Office, Reg. Gilbert Welton, f.103).

29. V. H. Galbraith, 'John Seward and his Circle', *Medieval & Renaissance Studies*, I, 1941–3, pp. 98–9. For Seward's career see Emden, *Oxford*, pp. 1674–5.

30. See also the inventory of the goods of Richard Penyngton, late schoolmaster of Ipswich, in 1412–13 (I. E. Gray and W. E. Potter, *Ipswich School, 1400–1950*, Ipswich, 1950, pp. 3–4), and the will of John Hamundson, schoolmaster of York, in 1472 (York, Borthwick Institute of Historical Research, Probate Reg. 4 f.85).

31. T. F. Kirby, *Annals of Winchester College*, London, 1892, pp. 486, 497, 499, 510.

32. Emden, *Oxford*, p. 1588; *V.C.H. Hants.*, II, p. 284.

33. Orme, *Education*, cited in note 1, pp. 164, 183; *V.C.H. Notts.*, II, pp. 221–2; Emden, *Oxford*, pp. 1754–5, sub John Stanbridge.

34. *A Subsidy Collected in the Diocese of Lincoln in 1526*, H. E. Salter, (ed.), Oxford Historical Society, lxiii, 1909, pp. 249–78.

35. For his biography see Emden, *Oxford*, pp. 2030–1.

36. For his career see Orme, *Education*, cited in note 1, p. 162.

37. George Cavendish, *The Life and Death of Cardinal Wolsey*, R. S. Sylvester, (ed.), Early English Text Society, ccxliii, 1959, p. 5.

38. For Chedworth see Emden, *Oxford*, pp. 401–2, and Orme, *Education*, cited in note 1, pp. 128, 142; for Somerset see *Oxford*, pp. 1727–8; for Wainfleet see ibid, pp. 2001–3.

39. The first occasion seems to have been a proclamation of June 1535 (P. L. Hughes and J. F. Larkin, *Tudor Royal Proclamations*, I, New Haven and London, 1964, p. 231).

40. I am not able to add to the few examples noted in Orme, *English Schools*, cited in note 1, pp. 142–3.

41. *The O.E.D.*, Oxford, 1933, IX, pp. 217–18.

42. *Chronicon Angliae*, E. M. Thompson, (ed.), R. S., 1874, p. 308.

43. William Shakespeare, *The Second Part of King Henry VI*, A. S. Cairncross, (ed.), Arden, London, 3rd ed., 1957, p. 124 and note.

44. *The Works of Geoffrey Chaucer*, F. N. Robinson, (ed.), London, 2nd ed., 1957, p. 195.

45. William Langland, *Piers Plowman*, W. W. Skeat, (ed.), London, 2 vols, 1886, I, B Text III, line 221.

46. Orme, *English Schools*, cited in note 1, pp. 139–41.

47. *C.C.R.*, *1327–30*, p. 573.

48. Emden, *Oxford*, pp. 401, 985.

49. Ibid., pp. 1555–6.

50. *Calendar of Inquisitions Post Mortem*, IV, 1913, pp. 171–2.

51. Edith Rickert, *Chaucer's World*, London, 1948, p. 118.

52. P.R.O., Early Chancery Proceedings, C 1/46/162.

53. Orme, *English Schools*, cited in note 1, p. 135.

54. Leach, *Early Yorkshire Schools*, II, cited in note 16, p. 110; *Educational Charters and Documents*, cited in note 3, pp. 424–5.

55. *Henley Borough Records*, P. M. Briers, (ed.), Oxfordshire Record Society, xli, 1960, p. 28.

56. Leach, *Early Yorkshire Schools*, I, cited in note 11, p. 104.

57. Gray and Potter, *Ipswich School*, cited in note 30, p. 12; *V.C.H. Suffolk*, II, p. 327.

58. Several schoolmasters were appointed as judges-delegate in the thirteenth century (Jane E. Sayers, *Papal Judges Delegate in the Province of Canterbury, 1198–1254*, London, 1971, pp. 132–3).

59. Orme, *Education*, cited in note 1, p. 196 n. 5.

60. Ibid., p. 163.

61. For a fuller account of the grammar course see Orme, *English Schools*, cited in note 1, pp. 87–115.

62. Richard de Bury, *Philobiblon*, M. Maclagan, (ed.), Oxford, 1960, pp. 94–5.

63. B.L., Royal MS. 13.C.XI f.254v.; Sir G. F. Warner and J. P. Gilson, *Catalogue of Western MSS. in the Old Royal and King's Collections*, British Museum, London, 1921, II, pp. 106–7.

64. Emden, *Oxford*, p. 675.

65. Borthwick Institute, cited in note 30, Probate Reg. 4 f.85.

66. *Grace Book A ... of the University of Cambridge*, S. M. Leathes, (ed.), Cambridge, 1897, pp. 151, 165–6, 168, 191, 203; *Grace Book B, Part I*, Mary Bateson, (ed.), Cambridge, 1903, pp. 24, 143.

67. Emden, *Oxford*, pp. 239–40; C. Garton, 'A fifteenth-century Headmaster's Library', *Lincolnshire History and Archaeology*, xv, 1980, pp. 29–38.

68. Emden, *Oxford*, pp. 2030–1.

69. V. H. Galbraith, 'John Seward and his Circle, cited in note 29, pp. 85–104.

70. *The Boke of St. Albans*, W. Blades, (ed.), London, 1905, pp. 7–23; Rachel Hands, *English Hunting and Hawking in 'The Boke of St. Albans'*, London, 1975, pp. xv–xvii.

71. A. W. Pollard and G. R. Redgrave, *A Short Title Catalogue of Books Printed in England*, London, 1946, nos. 9,995–10,002.

72. *The Boke of St. Albans*, Blades, (ed.), cited in note 70, pp. 22–3; Pollard and Redgrave, *Short Title Catalogue*, cited in note 71, no. 3,308–14.

73. R. W. Hunt, 'Oxford Grammar Masters in the Middle Ages', *Oxford Studies Presented to Daniel Callus*, Oxford Historical Society, new series, xvi, 1964, pp. 163–93.

74. Oxford, Lincoln College, MS. lat. 129.

75. S. B. Meech, 'John Drury and his English Writings', *Speculum*, ix (1934), pp. 70–83.

76. On these masters see R. S. Stanier, *A History of Magdalen College School*, Oxford, 2nd. ed., Oxford, 1958, and Orme, *English Schools*, cited in note 1, pp. 107–12.

77. *Longe Parvula*, London, Wynkyn de Worde, 1509, (STC.23164), f.Aiv. The punctuation and the use of capitals in this and all passages that follow has been modernized.

78. S. B. Meech, 'Early Application of Latin Grammar to English', *Proceedings of the Modern Language Association of America*, l (1935), pp. 1012–32.

79. Ibid., p. 1025.

80. On Bullokar see the article in *D.N.B.*

81. *A Fifteenth-Century School Book*, W. Nelson, (ed.), Oxford, 1956, p. 45.

82. *The Vulgaria of John Stanbridge and Robert Whittinton*, Beatrice White, (ed.), Early English Text Society, clxxxvii, 1932, pp. 64–5.

83. *A Fifteenth-Century School Book*, Nelson, (ed.), cited in note 81, pp. 1–2.

9

A tribute to A. R. Myers
and a bibliography of
his historical writings

CECIL H. CLOUGH

Alexander Reginald Myers, known to his many friends as Alec, died as a consequence of cancer on 2 July 1980, aged sixty-seven, on the eve of his retirement from the Chair of Medieval History at the University of Liverpool. He was born on 3 November 1912 in Wharfedale, and was taught for a career in the sciences at Hudders-field College. However his interest in history proved so strong that he virtually prepared himself for the Higher School Certificate History as a Main Subject in a year. In 1931 he won the Hulme Hall Scholarship to Manchester University to read History, and in the course of holding this award for four years he gained a First Class Degree in History in 1934, the year in which he received the Mark Hovell Book Prize as the best student of thirty-five candidates in the Final Examinations. Within fifteen months of registration for the M.A. Degree at Manchester University he presented early in 1935 his thesis entitled: 'The Commons in the Parliaments of Henry V and the Minority of Henry VI'. That dogged determi-nation that was one of his characteristics had been strengthened by a childhood and early career moulded by adversity. A sniper's bullet blinded his father in the trenches of the First World War, thereby truncating his family's prosperity. Alec had dearly wished to go to Oxford to read History, and gained common entrance to Jesus College, but his parents could not afford to send him.

In October 1935 began Alec's service to the University of Liver-pool, when he was appointed an Assistant Lecturer in its Depart-ment of Medieval History. The Department then consisted of himself as assistant to G. W. Coopland, who was Head but not a professor. Apart from war service in the Royal Navy, when he served as an intelligence officer in a destroyer, Alec Myers re-mained at Liverpool University until his death. He had become a Lecturer in 1936, a Senior Lecturer in 1956, and a Reader three years later. In 1967 he succeeded Christopher Brooke to the Chair. In 1956 he supplicated for his Ph.D. Degree at the University of London with a thesis: 'The Black Book of the Household of Edward IV and the Ordinance of 1478', which was published in 1959 by Manchester University Press. Twenty years later he reached the pinnacle of his university career when he became an Officer of the University as Dean of the Faculty of Arts.

Despite dedicated teaching and heavy administrative responsibilities, undertaken with thoroughness, Alec published widely, principally in the field of English history of the later middle ages. Indeed he made his reputation with his *History of England in the late middle ages*, the fourth volume of 'the Pelican History of England'. It first appeared in January 1952 and reached its eighth revised edition in 1976. His *English Historical Documents*, which is volume IV in the series edited by D. C. Douglas, was published in 1969. It is a monumental work that occupied him for some twenty years, and one that a scholar of the period ignores at his peril. It is particularly important for the wealth of material and insight that it provides on constitutional and administrative affairs, which remained the focus of Alec's attention from the days of his M.A. thesis. His *Parliaments and estates in Europe to 1789*, published in 1975, was his last major study. This work demonstrates the extension of his specialism to the Continent and beyond the limits of the medieval period. A foretaste of this appeared in an important paper that he had given to the International Commission for the History of Representative and Parliamentary Institutions. This study entitled: 'The English Parliament and the French Estates-General in the Middle Ages' was published in *Album Helen Cam* in 1961. The bulk of his scholarly articles appeared in *English Historical Review*, *Bulletin of the John Rylands Library*, *University of Toronto Law Journal*, and *Bulletin of the Institute of Historical Research*, as the accompanying bibliography of his writings indicates. His scholarship brought him recognition, though generally it has been undervalued, perhaps because he himself was modest of his achievements and in no way trendy. He was elected a Fellow of the Royal Historical Society in 1939, and ten years later elected a Fellow of the Society of Antiquaries. He was a member of the Council of the Royal Historical Society, 1970–4, and held the office of President of the Historical Association of Great Britain from 1973 to 1976. He was President of the Record Society of Lancashire and Cheshire from 1967 until his death.

Alec Myers was most expansive at home, and fortunate in a very happy family life, which meant so much to him. A convert from non-conformity to the Anglican Church, he became a pillar of the Anglican community at Birkenhead, where he first resided on his appointment to Liverpool University, and for the past twenty years or so at West Kirby. His *The story of the churches of West Kirby Parish* was written in order to raise funds for the restoration of St. Bridget's Church, which was to mark the centenary of that Church's restoration in 1870. Such was the demand that in 1973 a second edition appeared and it is still in print. Apart from being a distinguished medievalist and teacher closely associated with Lancashire and Cheshire, Alec Myers will be remembered particularly on the Wirral as exemplifying Christian ideals.

Bibliography of the
publications of A. R. Myers
excluding reviews

'Parliamentary petitions in the fifteenth century', *English Historical Review*, lii (1937), Part I, 'Petitions from individuals or groups', pp. 385–404; Part II, 'Petitions of the Commons and Common Petitions', pp. 590–613.

'A parliamentary debate of the mid-fifteenth century', *Bulletin of the John Rylands Library*, xxii (1938), pp. 388–404.

'Some observations on the procedure of the Commons in dealing with bills in the Lancastrian period', *University of Toronto Law Journal*, iii (1939), pp. 51–73.

'The captivity of a royal witch: the household accounts of Queen Joan of Navarre, 1419–21', *Bulletin of the John Rylands Library*, xxiv (1940), pp. 262–84; xxvi (1941), pp. 82–100.

'John of Lancaster, Duke of Bedford', 'Jack Cade', 'Edward IV', 'Sir John Fastolf', 'Humphrey of Lancaster, Duke of Gloucester', 'Henry IV', 'Henry V', 'Henry VI', 'Sir John Oldcastle', 'Richard III', 'Richard Neville, Earl of Warwick', 'Sir Richard Whittington', in *Chambers's Encyclopaedia*, M. D. Law, (ed.), London, George Newnes Ltd., new ed., 15 vols., 1950, respectively at: II, p. 188; II, p. 755; V, pp. 2–3; V, p. 599; VI, p. 395; VII, pp. 17–8; VII, p. 18; VII, p. 18; X, p. 192; XI, pp. 683–4; XIV, p. 440; XIV, pp. 573–5. Reprinted in ibid., rev. ed., 1962, with the same pagination. Reprinted in ibid., M. D. Law and M. V. Dixon, (eds.), London, Pergamon Press Ltd., new rev. ed., 15 vols., 1967, respectively at: II, p. 189; II, p. 740; IV, p. 826; V, p. 571; VI, p. 393; VII, p. 20; VII, p. 20; VII, p. 21; X, p. 212; XI, pp. 670–1; XIV, p. 413; XIV, p. 550.

'The Later Middle Ages, 1200–c.1530' [a report of the year's work], *Annual Bulletin of Historical Literature: dealing with publications of the year 1950*, G. R. Potter, (ed.), xxxvi (1951), pp. 22–33.

'Neuerscheinungen zur Geschichte Englands im Mittelalter. Forschungsbericht für die Jahre 1939–1948' (translated in collaboration with H. Liebeschütz), *Historisches Jahrbuch*, J. Spörl, (ed.), lxx (1951), pp. 364–87.

A history of England in the late middle ages. The Pelican history of England, vol. IV, Harmondsworth, Penguin Books, Ltd. 1952, xvi + 264 pp.; 1956, 2nd ed., xvi + 264 pp.; 1959, 3rd ed., xvi + 264 pp.; 1961, 4th ed., xvi + 264 pp.; 1963, 5th ed., xvi + + 269 pp.; 1966, 6th ed., 283 pp.; 1969, 7th ed. (incorporating 31 illustrations), 285 pp.; 1971, 8th ed., 285 pp.; 1976, 8th ed. with revisions, 285 pp.

'The Later Middle Ages, 1200–c.1530' [a report of the year's work], *Annual Bulletin of Historical Literature: dealing with publications of the year 1951*, G. R. Potter, (ed.), xxxvii (1952), pp. 15–20.

Ibid., *Annual Bulletin of Historical Literature: dealing with publications of the year 1952*, G. R. Potter, (ed.), xxxviii (1953), pp. 15–24.

'Some household ordinances of Henry VI', *Bulletin of the John Rylands Library*, xxxvi (1954), pp. 449–67; xxxvii (1954), pp. 11–13.

'The character of Richard III', *History Today*, iv (1954), pp. 511–21; [a letter in reply to correspondence] pp. 709–10.

'Parliaments in Europe: The representative tradition', *History Today*, v (1958), Part I, pp. 383–90; Part II, pp. 446–54. Reprinted in *Parliamentary Affairs*, ix (1956), pp. 48–56, 173–87. Extracts printed as 'Representation as a European tradition', in *Early English Parliaments*, G. P. Bodet, (ed.), Boston, Mass., D. C. Heath and Co., 1967 (Problems in European Civilization series), R. W. Greenlaw, and D. E. Lee, (eds.), pp. 91–100.

'The household of Queen Margaret of Anjou, 1452–53', *Bulletin of the John Rylands Library*, lx (1957–8), pp. 79–113, 391–431.

The household of Edward IV, Manchester, Manchester University Press, 1959, xii + 315 pp.

'The jewels of Queen Margaret of Anjou', *Bulletin of the John Rylands Library*, xlii (1959), pp. 113–31.

'The outbreak of war between England and Burgundy in February, 1471', *Bulletin of the Institute of Historical Research*, xxxiii (1960), pp. 114–5.

'A vous entier: John of Lancaster, Duke of Bedford, 1389–1435', *History Today*, x (1960), pp. 460–8.

'Edward III', 'Humphrey, Duke of Gloucester', 'House of Lancaster', 'Sir Henry Percy', in *Collier's Encyclopedia*, L. Shores, (ed.), [New York], Crowell-Collier Publishing Co., 24 vols., 1962, respectively at: VIII, pp. 628–9; XII, p. 357; XIV, pp. 282–3; XVIII, p. 576.

'The English Parliament and the French Estates-General in the Middle Ages', in *Album Helen Cam*, Louvain-Paris, 2 vols., 1960–1 (Studies presented to the International Commission for the History of Representative and Parliamentary Institutions, xxiii–xxiv), ii, pp. 139–53.

'Europa im 14. Jahrhundert', in *Propyläen Weltgeschichte*, Berlin-Frankfurt-Vienna, Verlag Ullstein, 12 vols., 1960–5, V, G. Mann and A. Nitschke, (ed.), (1963), pp. 563–618. Italian trans., 'L'Europa nel xiv secolo', in *I Propilei*, Milan-Verona, A. Mondadori, 11 vols., 1966–70, V (1968), pp. 657–714. Dutch trans., 'Europa in de viertiende eeuw', in *Universele wereldgeschiedenis*, The Hague-Hasselt, Uitgeverij Scheltens & Giltay N.V., Uitgeverij Heideland-Orbis N.V., 12 vols., 1974–78, V (1975), pp. 601–59.

'Margaret Beaufort', 'Thomas Bourchier', 'Edward IV', 'Edward V',

'Elizabeth (Woodville)', in *The Encyclopaedia Britannica*, H. S. Ashmore, (ed.), London, Encyclopaedia Britannica Co., 14th ed. rev., 24 vols., 1963, respectively at: III, p. 339; IV, p. 22; VIII, pp. 6–8; VIII, p. 8; VIII, p. 293. The pagination in some cases is different in the subsequent annual printings of this edition.

'An official progress through Lancashire and Cheshire in 1476', *Transactions of the Historic Society of Lancashire and Cheshire*, cxv (1964), pp. 1–29.

'Walter Hungerford, Baron Hungerford', 'Richard III', in *The Encyclopaedia Britannica*, J. V. Dodge, (ed.), London, Encyclopaedia Britannica Co., 14th ed. rev., 24 vols., 1964, respectively at: XI, p. 876; XIX, pp. 287–8. The pagination in some cases is different in the subsequent annual printings of this edition.

'The rise and fall of Jacques Coeur', *History Today*, xvi (1966), Part I, pp. 445–51; Part II, pp. 547–54.

'Francis Lovell, Viscount Lovell', 'Margaret of Anjou', 'John de Vere, 13th Earl of Oxford', 'Richard Woodville, Earl Rivers', 'Wars of the Roses', 'Jane Shore', 'Richard, Duke of York', in *The Encyclopaedia Britannica*, W. E. Preece, (ed.), Chicago, Encyclopaedia Britannica Inc., 14th ed. rev., 24 vols., 1967, respectively at: XIV, p. 367; XIV, pp. 862–3; XVI, p. 1178; XIX, p. 364; XIX, pp. 627–9; XX, pp. 445–6; XXIII, pp. 899–900. The pagination in some cases is different in the subsequent annual printings of this edition.

'Royal Household', in *Chamber's Encyclopedia*, M. D. Law and M. V. Dixon, (eds.), London, Pergamon Press Ltd, new rev. ed., 15 vols., 1967, at XII, pp. 22–4.

'The household of Queen Elizabeth Woodville, 1466–7', *Bulletin of the John Rylands Library*, l (1967–8), pp. 207–35, 443–81.

English Historical Documents, 1307–1485, London, Eyre and Spottiswoode, 1969 (vol. IV of a series in 12 vols., D. C. Douglas, ed.), 1,315 pp.

The study of Medieval History [Inaugural lecture delivered at the University of Liverpool, 7 November 1968], Liverpool, Liverpool University Press, 1969, 35 pp.

'The wealth of Richard Lyons', in *Essays in medieval history presented to Bertie Wilkinson*, T. A. Sandquist and M. R. Powicke, (eds.), Toronto, University of Toronto Press, 1969, pp. 301–29.

'Henry VII', 'Sir James Tyrrell', in *The Encyclopaedia Britannica*, Sir William Haley, (ed.), (Chicago, Encyclopaedia Britannica Inc.), 14th ed. rev., 24 vols., 1969, respectively at: XI, pp. 365–7; XXII, p. 453. The pagination in some cases is different in the subsequent annual printings of this edition.

London in the Age of Chaucer, Norman, Oklahoma, University of Oklahoma Press, 1972 (Centres of Civilization series, vol. 31), xii + 236 pp.

'Introduction' to George Buck, *The History of the Life and Reign of Richard III* (first published, London, 1646), London, E. P. Publishing, 1973, pp. v–ix.

Parliaments and Estates in Europe to 1789, (London, Thames and Hudson, 1975 (Library of European Civilization, G. Barraclough, ed.), 180 pp. Extracts printed as 'The Parliaments of Europe and the age of the Estates' [Presidential lecture to the Annual Conference of the Historical Association at Cardiff, 17 April 1974], in *History*, lx (1975), pp. 11–27.

'George William Coopland: A biographical appreciation', in *War, Literature and Politics in the Late Middle Ages*, C. T. Allmand, (ed.), Liverpool, Liverpool University Press, 1976, pp. 1–11.

'A parliamentary debate of 1449', *Bulletin of the Institute of Historical Research*, li (1978), pp. 78–83.

'History books for schools: 42', *History*, lxiii (1978), pp. 229–37.

'Tudor Chester', *Journal of the Chester Archaeological Society*, lxiii (1980), pp. 43–57.

'Parliament, 1422–1509', chapter six of *The English Parliament in the Middle Ages* [A tribute to professor J. S. Roskell], Richard G. Davis and J. H. Denton (eds.), Manchester, Manchester University Press, 1981, pp. 141–84.

'The Book of Disguisings for the Coming of the Ambassadors of Flanders, December 1508', *Bulletin of the Institute of Historical Research*, liv (1981), pp. 120–9.

INDEX

ANNE CLOUGH

Where a woman's maiden and married names are known she is listed
under her married name. A woman who has married more than once
is listed under her last-known married name.
Italic figures refer to folding genealogical tables.